THE KESTREL

For Elizabeth

THE KESTREL

by Andrew Village

Illustrated by

KEITH BROCKIE

T & A D POYSER

London

ISBN 0 85661 054 2

First published in 1990 by T & A D Poyser Ltd
24–28 Oval Road, London NW1

Text set in Monophoto Baskerville
Printed and bound by Butler & Tanner Ltd, Frome and London

British Library Cataloguing in Publication Data
Village, Andrew
  The kestrel.
  1. Kestrels
  I. Title   II. Brockie, Keith 1955–
  598.91

ISBN 0–85661–054–2

Contents

List of photographs

List of Figures

8   List of Figures

List of Tables

12 List of Tables

Preface

I wish I could start this monograph with some childhood reminiscence of my first encounter with Kestrels. In fact, I knew rather little about them before they became the subject of my PhD thesis. Although I grew up on farms, and developed an early passion for all things wild, Kestrels were birds I saw only occasionally. My family lived in east Essex during the early 1960s and, although I was unaware of it at the time, Kestrels had become almost extinct in that part of Britain as a result of pesticide poisoning. In 1965 we moved to Dorset, where Kestrels were more plentiful, but the demands of school exams in spring meant that I had little chance to study them at close quarters.

All that changed abruptly when I finished my zoology degree, at Durham University in 1975, and was lucky enough to get a studentship to study Kestrels and Short-eared Owls under the supervision of Ian Newton. I had met Ian the previous year, when I spent the summer term helping with his Sparrow-hawk project in Scotland. This should have prepared me for work on raptors, but my interest in birds was my undoing: I was assigned to counting song-birds at 4 am, while my ornithologically-ignorant fellow students got the prized job of watching Sparrowhawks at the nest. So when I arrived in Edinburgh to start my research career, I was excited, full of ideas and appallingly ignorant about birds of prey.

Fortunately, Ian's expertise more than made up for my lack of experience, and he was able to channel my ill-placed enthusiasm to better effect. My study area was in a large area of young conifer plantations at Eskdalemuir, about 100 kilometres south of Edinburgh. There was deluxe accommodation provided in the shape of a battered caravan that had clearly been sent there to live out its few remaining years in peace and quiet. I decided to start fieldwork straight away, and went down in mid October during a spell of bright sunshine and clear blue skies: weather, I was later to learn, that was all too rare at Eskdalemuir. Mick Marquiss, who was working with Ian on the Sparrowhawk project, had kindly agreed to come over from Dumfries and show me the ropes. He duly arrived on the second day, and my education commenced. As we drove around the forest tracks, he pointed out the likely Kestrel roosting sites, showed me where they would sit during the day and taught me the art of trapping raptors.

We caught several Kestrels during the week, and I had my first experience of seeing them at close quarters. Mick made handling raptors seem so easy that I seriously underestimated the difficulties of getting rings and wing-tags onto a bird that has an extremely sharp beak, matching talons and no hesitation in using either on human flesh. My first effort ended after half-an-hour with the Kestrel and I glaring at each other wildly, while I dripped blood from dozens of talon-pricks and bites! Needless to say, such inducement soon taught me to handle my subjects in such a way that neither I, nor they, came to grief.

Such were the beginnings of my association with Kestrels. The reason for choosing Eskdalemuir as a study area was because the young conifer plantations were ideal habitat for voles, and thus for vole predators such as Kestrels and owls. Although I did some work on owls, I soon concentrated my attention on Kestrels and, influenced by Ian's Sparrowhawk study, became especially interested in what regulated Kestrel numbers. A three-year studentship is hardly long enough to come to grips with such questions, but I was lucky enough to have the chance to continue studying Kestrels elsewhere. When Ian transferred to Monks Wood (in Cambridgeshire, England) in 1979, I was hired to complete the fieldwork for the tenth year of the Sparrowhawk study in Scotland and then moved to England to look at Kestrels in farmland. The Pesticide Monitoring Scheme at Monks Wood had been analysing pollutant levels in Kestrel carcasses since the early 1960s, but there was little detailed knowledge of wild populations with which to assess the significance of the levels that were being found. So, after a further year in Scotland, in which I finished my thesis and finally got to work on Sparrowhawks, my wife and I moved to England where I started a second study of Kestrels.

The change in location had advantages and disadvantages. Moving to such a radically different environment as eastern England enabled me to view the species from a new perspective, and the contrasts between the two studies form an important aspect of this book. The disadvantage of moving was that I had to start again with an unmarked population, so my results are based on two studies lasting five and seven years, rather than one lasting twelve years. This is not a serious flaw, but it does mean that I have incomplete information on such important, and currently vogue, topics as the lifetime reproductive output of individuals or the effects of age on reproduction and survival.

Although this book is based largely on my own work, I have referred to the fairly extensive literature on Kestrels to fill any gaps in my own studies. Recent work by the Raptor Group at Groningen University in Holland has greatly expanded our knowledge of the hunting behaviour and energetics of Kestrels, and I have quoted their work extensively in several chapters. The need to make each chapter fairly self-contained has inevitably led to some repetition but I have tried to minimise this as far as possible. The frequent comparisons made between Kestrels and Sparrowhawks throughout the book are no accident, and obviously reflect my association with Ian Newton's studies and the strong influence of his ideas. Added to which, it is interesting to compare the two species because they are raptors of a similar size that have different diets and nesting habits.

Acknowledgments

I have already alluded to Ian Newton's major influence on my studies. Anyone who is interested in raptors, or indeed any aspect of avian population ecology, will be well aware of his leading contributions to the subject. He originated or refined many of the ideas in this book, and I thank him for his unstinting advice and encouragement, as tutor, colleague and friend. As if all this wasn't enough, he also read the manuscript and suggested many useful improvements.

Several other colleagues have helped with the Kestrel studies in various ways. Mick Marquiss was a fount of good advice, and he and Anne made me welcome in their home on many an evening when the caravan at Eskdalemuir was too bleak to face. Nigel Charles was trapping voles at Eskdalemuir while I was working there, and he kindly made all his data available for my use, as well as passing on his vole traps when he had finished with them. In England, David Myhill did much of the vole trapping and gave valuable assistance from time to time. Nigel Westwood analysed most of the farmland pellets, and provided several of the photographs used for plates and illustrations. Others who have helped at various times in England include Ian Wyllie, Christer Wiklund and Jonathan Thompson. The staff of the British Museum at Tring generously allowed me access to the extensive collection of falcon skins, and the British Trust for Ornithology kindly supplied me with a computer tape of all the National Ringing Scheme recovery data for Kestrels up to 1984.

Neither of my studies would have been possible without the co-operation of farmers and landowners. In Scotland, the Economic Forestry Group allowed me free access to Eskdalemuir Forest, and provided materials for nestboxes. Ronnie Rose was particularly helpful, and his unique approach to wildlife management, and wealth of good stories, brightened many days when the hill-fog and rain brought a halt to fieldwork. The English study areas cover so many farms that it would be impossible to mention all the owners by name, and unfair to single out a few. All of them deserve thanks for their tolerance, and many for their encouragement and enthusiasm for the study.

Several people helped by translating papers, the most diligent being Leena Hazelkorn and my mother, Marianne. Scientists are not the best of writers, and the translators' heroic efforts with conjugated German nouns and convoluted jargon were much appreciated. My sister Nicola also spent several days deciphering my handwriting when she typed earlier drafts of various chapters. Paul Joyce skillfully drew some of the maps and figures, and Keith Brockie has provided excellent illustrations.

I am not sure why those who are owed the most always get left until last. This book has been a joint effort with my family: I did the writing and they did the suffering. My wife Elizabeth endured my absences and absent-mindedness without complaint, and read the whole manuscript in draft.

CHAPTER 1

Introduction

There can be few people in Britain who do not know what a Kestrel looks like. Kestrels are instantly recognisable when they hover, and their habit of hunting over motorway verges has made them familiar to nearly everyone. This familiarity breeds a certain contempt, and the sight of a Kestrel is unlikely to quicken the pulse of an experienced birdwatcher to the same extent as a Peregrine or Merlin. Falconers also regard Kestrels as subjects for beginners, and the title of a book by Barry Hines, which was later made into the film 'Kes', came from an old doggerel that alludes to the Kestrel's lowly status:

> *... a Merlin for a Lady, a Goshawk for a Yeoman,*
> *a Sparrowhawk for a Priest, a Musket for a Holy Water Clerk,*
> *a Kestrel for a Knave.*

For the scientist, the very abundance of Kestrels makes them an attractive subject for study. They occur in densities sufficient to give reasonable sample sizes, can be fairly easily caught and marked, and some live in areas where other raptors are scarce. The need to understand the ecology of birds of prey became apparent in the 1960s, when it was realised that their position at the top of the food chain made them vulnerable to the effects of pollutants. The widespread declines of the Peregrine and Sparrowhawk caught ornithologists by surprise, and highlighted how little was known about the factors that normally control their numbers. Kestrels were less seriously affected by pesticides, but they nonetheless declined alarmingly in some eastern districts of the country, and will always be potential victims of man's pollutants. Understanding their ecology is important, therefore, both for conservation purposes and for the wider understanding of how animal populations are regulated. This book is based largely on my own research on Kestrels over the past 13 years, first in Scotland and then in England. I have tried to compare the ecology of Kestrels in contrasting habitats, to discover how they adapt to different environments, and what determines their numbers.

A BRIEF INTRODUCTION TO THE KESTREL

Kestrels are smaller than many people imagine. Perhaps their relatively long wings and tail make hovering Kestrels appear larger than they really are. Female Kestrels are slightly bigger than males, but even they are rarely more than 35 cm long, with a wingspan of about 80 cm and a maximum non-breeding weight of about 250 g. Kestrels are thus similar in size to Hobbies, larger than Merlins, and fall roughly between the size of male and female Sparrowhawks. People not familiar with birds of prey often mistake Kestrels for Sparrowhawks, and the confusion is deepened because 'Sparrowhawk' seems to have been an old country name for the Kestrel. This may explain why American Kestrels have, until recently, been called 'Sparrowhawks', even in the scientific literature. However, the confusion is mainly one of semantics, and Kestrels can easily be distinguished from Sparrowhawks by their longer, more pointed wings, brown colouration and habit of hovering.

In Northern Europe, Kestrels feed mainly on small rodents, which they hunt from perches or by hovering flight. They are adaptable hunters, however, and will take a wide variety of other prey, including small birds, lizards, large insects and earthworms. This flexibility in diet enables them to live in many kinds of environment, and Kestrels are found throughout Britain in habitats that range from busy cities to desolate moorland. However, they are predominately open-country birds, and are absent from dense woodland unless there are clearings where they can hunt.

In common with other falcons, Kestrels do not build a nest, but merely scrape a shallow depression in substrate into which they lay up to six or seven eggs. Many sites are utilised, but the more frequent are ledges on buildings or cliffs, holes in trees or the disused stick-nests of other bird species. Breeding in Britain is from March to July, the first eggs appear in April, and most young fledge in June or July. Kestrels are almost always monogamous, and are highly territorial around the nest. Breeding pairs are usually spaced some distance apart, but the separation can vary considerably and pairs occasionally breed in small groups or colonies.

In winter, Kestrels normally occupy individual or pair territories. Those breeding in areas that have permanent snow cover in winter migrate to warmer parts, but populations elsewhere may be partially migrant or almost totally sedentary.

The Scottish grassland study area at Eskdalemuir. Most of the area was covered in young conifer plantations, but the trees were still small and the predominant habitat was ungrazed grassland. Mature trees were scarce on the open hill-sides, and most were in small shelterbelts in the valleys. Photos: A. Village.

THE STUDY AREAS

My studies of Kestrels have encompassed three different habitats. From 1975 to 1979, I worked in a large area of grassland at Eskdalemuir in south Scotland. Most of the area was covered with young conifer plantations, but the trees were still small, and the dominant vegetation was dense, ungrazed grass. In 1980, I moved to England and have since worked in two farmland areas, one fairly typical of lowland farms in England, the other an area of intensive arable fenland. The features of the three study areas are central to much of what follows, so I shall describe each in some detail before outlining the study methods used.

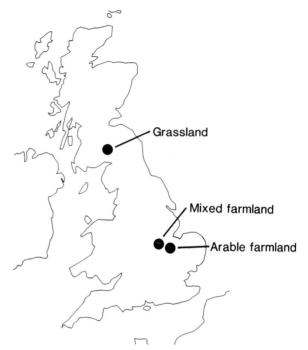

Fig. 1. Location of the Kestrel study areas.

The Scottish grassland area

This was about 10 × 10 km of hillground to the north of Eskdalemuir village in the Southern Uplands of Scotland. The topography was typical of the region: the hills were rounded, with little exposed rock, and the valleys were drained by fast-flowing streams and rivers. The study area straddled the watershed between the River Esk to the south, and the River Tweed to the north. Until the mid 1960s the region was almost entirely given over to sheep farming, with a few cattle in the more sheltered valleys. The arrival of commercial forestry in 1965 rapidly transformed the landscape as the grazed grassland (called sheepwalk) was fenced and planted with conifers such as larch and spruce. The planting of Eskdalemuir Forest was spread over a decade or more, but the majority was done during 1969–74, so that by 1975 over 60% of the area was under trees less than eight years old.

The exclusion of sheep resulted in a vigorous growth of grass in the first few years after planting, and this provided ideal habitat for small mammals, especially the Short-tailed Voles* favoured by Kestrels. This ungrazed grassland was the dominant habitat during my Scottish study, so I have referred to Eskdalemuir as the 'grassland' study area. The other main habitat was unfenced grassland, grazed at varying intensities by sheep and cattle. This sheepwalk covered about 30% of the area, and was somewhat similar to the

---

* Scientific names not given in the text can be found in Appendix III.

permanent pastures of the English mixed farmland area (see below), though the latter were better drained and more heavily grazed.

There were few mature trees at Eskdalemuir, and nearly all of these were conifers such as spruce, larch or Scot's pine, mostly in small shelterbelts planted in the valleys and along small streams. On the hillsides there were a few small woods, or single trees, growing by abandoned farmsteads and sheepfolds. Disused Carrion Crow nests in these mature trees provided the main nesting sites for Kestrels, which therefore tended to breed mainly in the valleys, with fewer pairs nesting on the hillsides.

Weather had an important influence on Kestrels in the area, and I was fortunate that the staff of Eskdalemuir Observatory made their detailed weather records available for my use. Rainfall was high, averaging over 1500 mm a year, and snow cover was frequent, but not permanent, in winter (Table 1). Lying snow almost certainly made hunting more difficult for Kestrels, so their winter food supply varied unpredictably.

The mixed farmland area

The two English study areas were about 25 km apart and some 350 km south of the Scottish grassland area (Fig. 1). Being at a lower altitude, and in the east of England, the annual rainfall was only a third of that at Eskdalemuir, and there was less likelihood of prolonged snow cover (Table 1). The mixed farmland area covered about 120 km^2 to the south of Rutland Water, on the boundary between Leicestershire and Northamptonshire. It included the valleys of the River Welland and its tributary the Chater, and was traditionally pasture for sheep and beef cattle. There was a marked change to arable farming during the 1970s, and this continued during my study, so that permanent pasture was largely confined to water meadows beside the rivers. The main crops were winter wheat and barley, with smaller amounts of oilseed rape, tic-beans and sugarbeet. The intensification of arable farming also caused the demise of much of the rough, ungrazed grassland, and all that remained were small patches or strips along hedgerows, road verges and disused railways.

The southern boundary of the study area comprised two large woods, with mixtures of conifers and hardwoods in 20–30 ha blocks, some of which were mainly rough grass with small trees. There were several other smaller woods in the area, but a good proportion of the trees grew along the hedgerows that surrounded most fields. Ash trees were especially common in hedges, and many had hollow trunks or branches that provided suitable nesting sites for Kestrels. Kestrels also nested on old buildings or strawstacks, so potential breeding places were abundant and distributed fairly evenly across the area.

The arable farmland area

The countryside changes dramatically a few kilometres to the east of the mixed farmland area as the undulating hills give way to the flat fenlands that surround The Wash. Much of this low-lying terrain is below sea level and was originally marshland. It has been progressively drained, and today it is almost entirely arable farmland. The black fen soil is extremely fertile, and grows good crops of wheat, and roots such as sugarbeet, potatoes and carrots. There are few trees and virtually no hedges, fields being separated by numerous small

The mixed farmland study area in Leicestershire, England. The main crops were wheat and barley, but some permanent pasture remained in the valleys. Hedgerow trees were widely scattered through the area and these provided hole nesting sites for Kestrels. Rough, ungrazed grass was confined mainly to hedgerows and road verges. Photos: A. Village.

ditches that drain into larger dykes and rivers. There is almost no pasture, and only a little rough grass along the sides of drains and roads.

With two such contrasting farmland habitats only a few kilometres apart, it seemed worthwhile to study Kestrels in both areas concurrently. I chose an area of fen between Ramsey and Chatteris as this was near to Monks Wood, where I was based. Most of the fen was only just above sea level, but the towns were built on higher ground which had a clay soil and more trees. The local farmers call these raised areas 'hills' and (having just come from Scotland) I had some difficulty in adjusting to the fact that this term referred to any land more than a few metres above its surroundings!

Finding nests in the mixed farmland area required a great deal of time-consuming searching, so I was unable to include more than about 80 km² of the arable area in the first few years. In 1984 I increased this to over 250 km², which ensured a larger sample of pairs each year thereafter.

Resources for Kestrels in the three areas

The most important resources for raptors are supplies of food and nesting sites (Newton 1979). The three areas just described allowed me to study Kestrels with different levels and distributions of these two resources. The food supply for Kestrels in the Scottish grassland area was potentially very good, but also variable. Voles can change in abundance from year to year, and their densities in Northern Europe fluctuate in cycles lasting four to six years. The densities in peak years may be ten times that in poor ones, and populations can increase or decline very suddenly, over the course of a few months. In addition to these annual cycles, voles vary in abundance during the year, and densities are generally lowest in spring and highest in autumn. Numbers therefore decline during winter, and I have already mentioned the effects of snow in further reducing the availability of voles to Kestrels.

The two farmland areas did not experience regular vole cycles, and the scarcity of vole habitats reduced the opportunity for a really high Kestrel food supply. On the other hand, the mammal fauna was more diverse and other sources of food, such as small birds and invertebrates, were more abundant than in the Scottish grassland area. This diversity of prey, together with the milder winters, meant that Kestrel food supply was likely to be less variable

The arable farmland study area in Cambridgeshire, England. This flat, drained fenland was intensively farmed for wheat and root crops. There were no pastures or hedges and few trees. Rough grass was found along road verges and on the banks of the numerous drainage ditches. Photo: N. J. Westwood.

than in the grassland area, both between and within years.

The study areas also differed in the abundance and distribution of potential nesting sites for Kestrels. The grassland area had many old crow-nests, but they were unevenly distributed because most of the suitable trees were concentrated in the valleys. Kestrel nesting sites in the mixed farmland area were also fairly abundant, but more evenly spaced in trees along hedgerows. In the arable farmland area, there was a scarcity of trees and the few suitable nesting sites were scattered widely over the whole area.

METHODS

The methods used to study raptors are not particularly sophisticated and rely more on hard work and field-craft than on technical wizardry. I have described the important techniques in the relevant chapters, or in the appendices if a more detailed description seemed necessary. A major part of both studies was to catch and mark full-grown Kestrels so that they could be individually identified. Kestrels are fairly easy to see, and wing-tagging proved to be a useful way of telling them apart. I used soft nylon cloth to make tags, which were fastened to the patagium (a loose flap of skin at the leading edge of the wing). The process was quick and painless, and Kestrels soon adjusted to the tags, preening them into place alongside the wing coverts. Each Kestrel was given a unique colour combination and, by using ten colours, I could distinctively mark about 100 birds of each sex.

Being able to distinguish individual Kestrels in this way was an enormous asset. In winter, I could estimate their territory size and be fairly confident of finding all the Kestrels in a given area. In summer, I could also register new occupants at nesting sites without having to retrap individuals still present from the previous year. When a good proportion of the population had been marked, incomers could be quickly spotted, and this helped in locating closely adjacent pairs which might otherwise have been assumed to be the same pair. All wing-tagged Kestrels were also identified with a numbered leg-ring, as were nestlings – though they were not wing-tagged because this would soon have exhausted the possible colour combinations. Wing-tag combinations were reused if I knew a bird had died, or if it had not been seen for more than 18 months, so over the years I was able to tag more than 300 Kestrels in Scotland and 500 in England.

Wing-tagging was useful in showing which individuals were present at a given time, and in helping to enumerate the population. It also gave some information on home-range size, but I found it necessary to check the results by radio-tracking. This enabled me to locate Kestrels even when they were out of sight, and was particularly useful where the visibility was reduced by trees. In Scotland, where the visibility was good, I fitted ten Kestrels with transmitters, which was sufficient to enable me to correct the range size of birds carrying only wing-tags. In England, the visibility was poorer, especially in mixed farmland, so I put transmitters on over 50 Kestrels between 1982 and 1986. More details of marking Kestrels are given in Appendix II.

During the breeding season I tried to find all the nests in the study areas and mark as many of the breeding and non-breeding birds as possible. Pairs

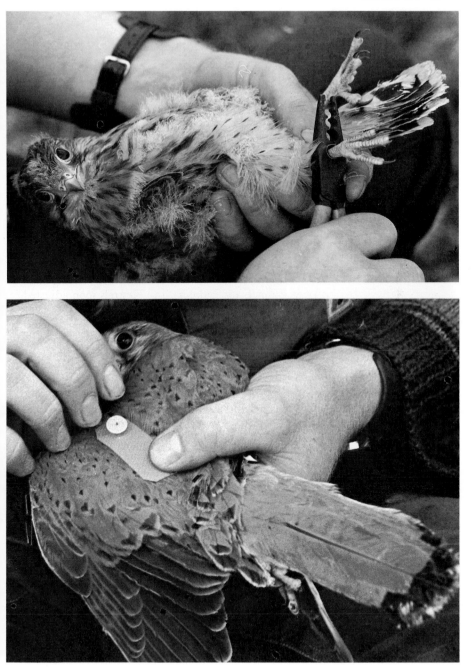

Marking Kestrels was an important aspect of the studies. Uniquely numbered leg-rings were put on nestlings and full-grown birds, and the latter were also marked with coloured wing-tags. This allowed birds to be identified without recapture, thereby reducing the trapping effort in later years. Photos: N. J. Westwood.

Finding Kestrel nests can be difficult, but gaining access to some can be even harder. A ladder helps, but sometimes professional help is needed: the third photograph shows a fireman climbing to a Kestrel nesting site on a house in West Germany. Photos: N. J. Westwood & A. Kostrzewa.

were found by seaching all the likely nesting area for signs such as droppings and prey remains, or by watching in early spring. Searching was done from March onwards in order to find pairs that did not lay eggs or failed early in the breeding cycle. Kestrels were caught with decoy traps in hunting areas or with noose traps on the nest, and in most seasons I was able to mark about 80–90% of the breeding birds of each sex. The coverage in winter was more variable, and depended on what particular observations or experiments I was involved with at the time. The population in Scotland was fairly low in winter, so I could cover most of the area if the weather was mild and the hill tracks were not blocked by snow. In England, I usually worked only one farmland area at a time, and trapped Kestrels in sections of the main study area. Within these sections I tried to catch all the Kestrels present, so the proportion of birds marked was as high as that during the breeding season, but over a smaller area.

Small-mammal trapping

Estimating the abundance of Kestrel prey was as important as counting the Kestrels themselves. It was not possible to get accurate estimates of the density of all the possible prey species, but the abundance of small mammals was a useful index of food supply because they were the most important food for Kestrels. In the Scottish area, the dominant small mammals were Short-tailed

Voles and Common Shrews, whereas in the English farmland areas there was a wider variety of species, and Bank Voles, Woodmice and House Mice were also present.

Vole numbers in the grassland area were monitored every year by Nigel Charles as part of a wider study of small mammals in the Southern Uplands, and he kindly let me use his results. Traps were operated at the same 20 trapping sites twice a year, in April and October, when voles were near their annual low and high respectively. Seventeen sites were within planted areas, the remainder were in grazed sheepwalk.

At each site, pairs of unbaited snap-traps were set across vole runs at 24 randomly chosen locations. I used the number of Short-tailed Voles (or Common Shrews) caught per trap site as an index of their abundance in the grassland area. The index was not a true density, but had been shown to be correlated with actual densities by trapping-out fenced areas until no more voles were caught (N. Charles, unpublished).

I used the same type of traps in England, but set them in grids or lines, rather than at random. This was partly for convenience, and partly because I was forced to trap in small patches or strips of rough grass, where there was little alternative to trap lines. In each farmland area, 30 traps were set at each of six sites in January, April, July and October, and the mean number of voles, mice or shrews per site was used as an index of small-mammal abundance. This index was not directly comparable with that from the grassland area, but it indicated changes in the small-mammal populations over time or differences between the two farmland areas.

At Eskdalemuir, vole numbers in the young plantations were high in 1975, declined during 1976 and reached very low levels in spring 1977 (Fig. 2).

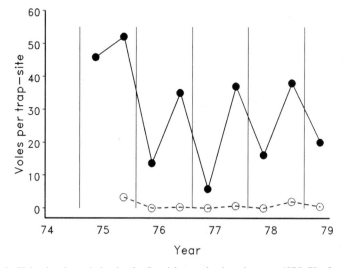

Fig. 2. Vole abundance index in the Scottish grassland study area, 1975–79, for young plantation (●) and sheepwalk (○). Voles were most abundant in young plantation, but reached low numbers in spring 1977. Note that abundance was assessed twice per year.

During the summer of that year they began increasing, and spring densities were moderately high in 1978 and 1979. Vole densities in the grazed sheepwalk showed less marked changes because, even in good years, there were far fewer voles than in the young plantations. In the farmland studies, voles were abundant in both areas in spring 1981, but declined thereafter (Fig. 3). Although there was considerable seasonal variation, spring vole densities were consistently low after 1981. The two farmland areas differed in the abundance of mammal species, with fewer voles, and more Woodmice, in the arable area than in mixed farmland. Woodmice showed stronger seasonal variations than voles, but numbers in any one season were fairly consistent from year to year.

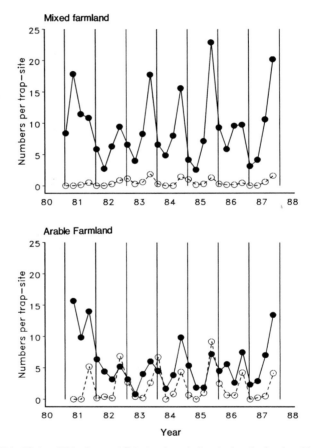

Fig. 3. Vole (●) and Woodmouse (○) abundance indices in the mixed and arable farmland study areas, 1981–87. Spring vole densities were high when the study began, but declined thereafter. Woodmice were more plentiful, and voles scarcer, in arable than in mixed farmland. Abundance was assessed four times per year.

CHAPTER 2

Kestrels around the world

Kestrels occupy a wide geographic range and can live in most environments, apart from extreme deserts, dense forests and areas of permanent snow cover. European Kestrels *Falco tinnunculus* breed thoughout much of Europe, Africa and Asia, while kestrels of similar appearance and habits are found in the East Indies, Australia and the New World. The kestrel group is thus truly cosmopolitan, and there are few places where you cannot see the familiar hovering profile. Despite their widespread distribution, nearly everything we know about kestrels comes from studies done either in Europe or in North America, and this book is mainly about European Kestrels in the more northerly parts of their range. This chapter is an attempt to redress the imbalance by describing the distribution of kestrel species around the world, and their possible inter-relatedness. Kestrel species are easiest to describe relative to the nominate race of the European Kestrel, so I shall describe it first and then compare the species in the kestrel group with each other, and with other small falcons.

DESCRIPTION OF EUROPEAN KESTRELS

Kestrels are structurally similar to other members of the genus *Falco* such as Merlins, Hobbies and Peregrines. They have relatively long, pointed wings,

Head of an adult male European Kestrel. Notice the notch in the beak (the 'tomial tooth'), which is typical of falcons. Photo: N. J. Westwood.

short necks, powerful beaks and strong talons. Falcons kill by biting, and for this their beaks have a characteristic notch called the 'tomial tooth'. As in most birds of prey, the female is larger than the male, though in European Kestrels the difference amounts to only about 4% of the male wing chord (Fig. 4).

The most striking dimorphism between the sexes is in the adult plumage colours, and this is unusual in raptors. Males are grey on the head, rump, upper tail-coverts and tail, and pinkish red on the back and scapulars. These latter feathers are usually spotted black, the markings varying from tiny flecks

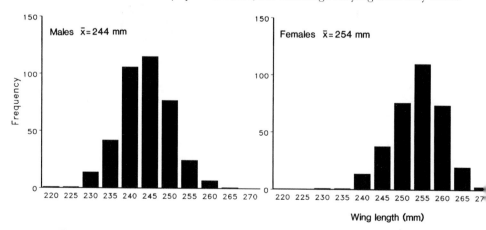

Fig. 4. Histograms of wing chord for 389 male and 337 female Kestrels trapped in Scotland and England. The mean length for males (244 mm SD = 6.4) was about 4% less than that for females (254 mm SD = 6.3).

to broad bars. The tail often has some bars, but these rarely go right across the feather, apart from a broad terminal band. Females, on the other hand, are predominately brown, especially on the head and back. The rump and tail feathers are brown, tinged with varying degrees of grey in adult females, and have black bars that vary in intensity and width. The back feathers are barred, rather than spotted, and the head is normally streaked with black. Both sexes have pale underparts, males being slightly paler than females and having black spots, rather than the streaks of females. In some adult males the cere, legs and feet tend to be a brighter, more orange-yellow than in females.

Kestrels in their first year look like adult females, and they are hard to sex at this age (Village, Marquiss & Cook 1980). Juveniles are most reliably distinguished from adult females by the buff fringe on the main flight feathers. Fledglings of both sexes have a broad fringe to these feathers and, although this eventually abrades on the outer primaries, it persists on the inner ones. Female-like individuals with buff fringes wider than 2 mm can thus be classed

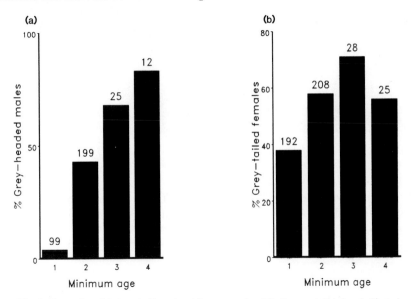

Fig. 5. Proportion of (a) male Kestrels with pure grey head feathers and (b) female Kestrels with grey (but barred) tail feathers, among birds trapped in Scotland and England. Sample sizes are given above the bars. Year classes were from 1 August to 31 July.

as juveniles and those with smaller fringes are almost invariably adults. A second diagnostic feature of juvenile plumage is the shape of the black streak on the flank feathers under the wing. The streak is broad and continuous in first-year birds, but hour-glass shaped in adults (Village, Marquiss & Cook 1980), a difference that also occurs in some other kestrel species.

It is difficult to sex juveniles on the basis of their original plumage. About 50% of juvenile males have a grey or grey-brown rump, upper tail-coverts or tail, but the rest are like females in having solid brown upper plumage, with thick bars or streaks. The only reliable way to sex such juveniles is to identify

Male (left) and female (right) European Kestrels. The male has a spotted back and uniform tail, whereas the female is barred in all the upper plumage. Photo: R. Rose.

the adult body feathers that gradually appear during the first year of life. The start and speed of this moult varies between individuals, but about 40% of juveniles have some adult feathers by September and nearly all do so by January (see Chapter 6). The adult plumage is not fully acquired until the end of the first year, when wing and tail feathers are moulted. Males are then distinct from females, but about 60% retain a strong brown cast to the head feathers, and may have large spots or bars on the back. In subsequent years the head usually becomes pure grey, though this is not a reliable way of ageing adult males because about 10% retain a brown tinge to the head even after several years (Fig. 5a). From the second year onwards, most females show some grey in the rump or tail, in contrast to juveniles (Fig. 5b), but this again is variable and not wholly diagnostic of age.

In European Kestrels, certain characters seem typically male and others typically female. Male features are greyness (versus browness in females) on the head, rump and tail, spotting or lack of marking (versus barring or streaks) on the body feathers, and smaller size. To compare the subspecies of *tinnunculus*, or *tinnunculus*-like species, I scored various parts of the plumage, as well as overall size, according to how closely they conformed to the typical male or female pattern just described (Table 2). The plumage scores were made mainly on skins from the British Museum, supplemented, if necessary, by descriptions given in the literature. This gave an approximate measure of how similar races or species were to one another, and allowed sexual dimorphism to be quantified on the basis both of plumage and size.

Species in the kestrel group

There are no clear rules for defining exactly what makes a kestrel different from any other small falcon. This explains why the number of kestrel species varies from 13 to 16, depending on which book you read. Most authorities give 13 species the common name of kestrel, though a few species are rather different from the bird we are familiar with in Britain. The main divisions are between New and Old World species and, within the latter group, between rufous- and grey-plumaged kestrels. The single species in the New World, the American Kestrel *F. sparverius*, occurs thoughout most of North and South America in a number of geographic races (Table 2). It has distinctly different plumage from Old World kestrels, especially around the head, which has a chestnut spot in the centre of a grey crown, and two striking black bars on the cheeks.

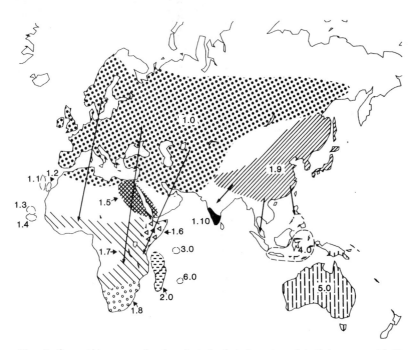

Fig. 6. Geographic range of rufous kestrels that do not overlap their range with F. tinnunculus. *Subspecies are shown only for* F. tinnunculus. *The numbers refer to the species or subspecies numbers given in Table 2, arrows to migrations of northern* tinnunculus *races.*

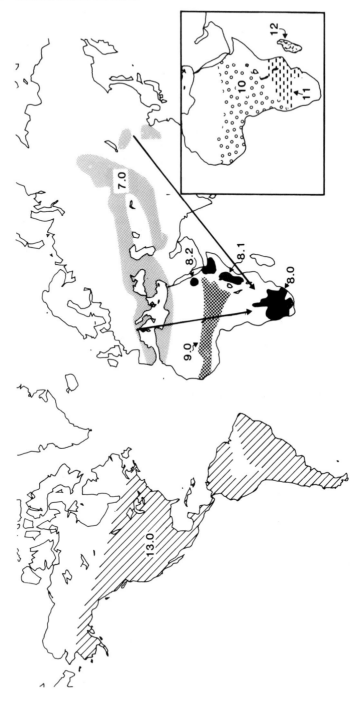

Fig. 7. Geographic range of other kestrel species. Arrows show the migration of Lesser Kestrels, which winter in southern Africa. Numbers refer to species numbers in Table 2. (pages 296–7). Inset shows the distributions of the African grey kestrel species.

The grey kestrels are all from Africa, and have been put in a subgenus, *Dissodectes*, to distinguish them from the other Old World forms that are mainly rufous in colour (Snow 1978). There are three grey species, the Grey Kestrel *F. ardioacius*, Dickinson's Kestrel *F. dickinsoni* and the Madagascan Banded Kestrel *F. zoniventris*. The first two species have non-overlapping (allopatric) ranges in mainland Africa and may be fairly closely related (Fig. 7). The Banded Kestrel has adapted to hunting in forests, and has plumage that is more reminiscent of accipiters than of kestrels.

The remaining species are the Old World rufous kestrels, sometimes grouped into the subgenus *Cerchensis*. This is mainly to distinguish them from the grey kestrels, and not because the nine rufous forms strongly resemble each other. In addition to European Kestrels, the species in this subgenus include the Moluccan Kestrel *Falco moluccensis* from the the East Indies, and the Australian or Nankeen Kestrel *F. cenchroides*. These three species do not overlap in their geographic range (Fig. 6) and have been considered, along with American Kestrels, to be isolated forms of the same *tinnunculus* 'super-species' (Cade 1982). Also included in this super-species were the three species from the Indian Ocean islands of Madagascar (*F. newtoni*), Seychelles (*F. araea*) and Mauritius (*F. punctatus*). Cade considered that these six species were derived from a single species that became isolated on large land masses or small oceanic islands. The implication is that they would merge if their ranges overlapped, and only geographical separation prevents them interbreeding. This may be true of the first three species, but the others are highly specialised in both appearance and habits, and are clearly separate species.

This leaves the three rufous species that overlap their ranges with *tinnunculus*, namely the Fox Kestrel *F. alopex* and the Greater Kestrel *F. rupicoloides*, which are both African, and the Lesser Kestrel *F. naumanni*, a colonial-nesting species that breeds in Europe and north Asia but winters in Africa (Fig. 7). Despite the overlap of their geographical ranges, Lesser Kestrels are similar to European Kestrels, particularly the females, and they would seem, on morphological evidence at least, to be more closely related than most other rufous species. Fox and Greater Kestrels are both large, show little sexual dimorphism and occupy separate regions of Africa. However, they are quite different in many other respects, and may not be closely related.

Other species that are sometimes referred to as kestrels are the Red-footed Falcons *F. vesperinus* and *F. amurensis*, and the Red-headed Falcon *F. chicquera*, though their relationship to kestrels is uncertain.

Diagnostic features of kestrels

Kestrels vary considerably in their appearance, so is there any reason for considering them a separate group, with the implicit assumption that they have evolved from a recent common ancestor not shared with the other falcons? A major problem in answering this question is the lack of detailed knowledge about many species, especially those in Africa and southern Asia. I have tried to glean information on plumage colour, size and behaviour from a variety of sources, though a thorough analysis will have to wait until we know more about the little-studied species. There are several criteria that might be used to classify kestrels:

1. Hovering. Hovering is often thought of as the chief characteristic of kestrels that sets them apart from other falcons. This is difficult to quantify, not least because even typical kestrels hover only occasionally at some times of year (Chapter 4). The grey kestrels are said to hover infrequently, Fox and Mauritius Kestrels not at all (Brown *et al* 1982), though so little is known of these species that this may be untrue. It is not clear if hovering requires particular morphological adaptations, or whether it is simply a behavioural feature. Non-hovering kestrels are not obviously different in structure from hoverers, apart from Fox Kestrels, which have unusually long tails and rarely hover. Prolonged hovering is primarily used when hunting small mammals, and its frequency in a given species may simply reflect the main prey being taken. Although hovering falcons are kestrels, not all kestrels hover, so hovering is not entirely diagnostic.

2. Wing-to-tail ratio. A second way of separating kestrels from other falcons is by their size and shape. Kestrels are sometimes described as relatively short-winged falcons, so I compared the wing and tail lengths of all species of falcon for which data were available (Fig. 8a). I used tail length rather than the preferred body length, because the latter measure was available for only a few species. Kestrels vary in size from the Seychelles Kestrel, the smallest falcon, with a mean wing length of only 148 mm in males and 158 mm in females (Watson 1981), to the Fox Kestrel, with a wing length in both sexes of about 280 mm. This size range overlaps with several other falcons, but kestrels have tails that are 60–70% of wing length, shorter than most bird-eating falcons. The falcon which is closest in size and shape to the kestrels is the Red-headed Falcon, which occurs in India and Africa. This species appears to have no close relatives (Snow 1978), but, as mentioned above, it has sometimes been referred to as a kestrel. The outliers in the kestrel group are the Fox Kestrel (large and long-tailed) and the Seychelles Kestrel (small but kestrel-shaped). On this measure at least, the 'aberrant' grey kestrels are surprisingly similar in shape to the *tinnunculus*-like species.

3. Relative toe length. As well as being long-tailed (or short-winged), kestrels also differ from other falcons in having relatively short toes (Fig. 8b). Foot structure tends to reflect the diet in raptors, and those mainly eating birds have longer toes and claws, relative to their tarsus length, than those that feed on mammals or reptiles. Kestrels have middle toes that are about 60–70% of the tarsus length, compared with 80–100% in most bird-eating falcons, but the separation is not as clear as with the wing-to-tail ratio. On toe length, Red-headed Falcons are quite different from kestrels, and their long toes and marked sexual dimorphism points to a more avian diet.

4. Plumage colour. As I have pointed out, plumage colour is very variable in kestrels, even among species that are apparently closely related, so it is probably a poor way of distinguishing the group from other falcons. If rufous or chestnut plumage is used to classify kestrels it excludes the grey forms, which, admittedly, some authors have described as behaving unlike typical kestrels (Brown & Amadon 1968, Brown *et al* 1982). However, these species are not closely related

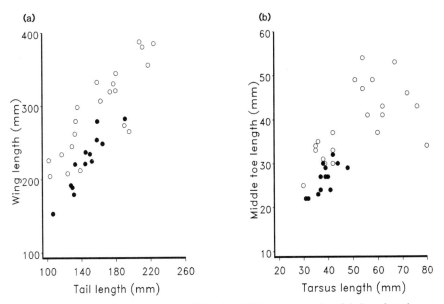

Fig. 8. Relationship of (a) wing-to-tail length and (b) toe-to-tarsus length in kestrel species (●) compared with other falcons (○). Values were averages for the sexes (see Table 2). Kestrels are generally longer-tailed and shorter-toed than other falcons of the same wing or tarsus length.

to any other small falcons, and their shape is nearer to that of kestrels than to Hobbies, Merlins or Red-footed Falcons.

5. *Plumage dimorphism.* Sexual dimorphism in plumage is more frequent in kestrels (seven of 13 species) than in other falcons (two of 21 species) or other raptors. This makes it, to some extent, a characteristic of kestrels, but not one that is diagnostic. Among rufous kestrels, some species are sexually dimorphic (*tinnunculus, naumanni* and *cenchroides*), whereas in others both sexes have plumage that is typical either of males (*araea* and *newtoni*) or females (*moluccensis, rupicoloides, alopex* and *punctatus*) (Fig. 9). In six of the seven dimorphic species, juveniles resemble females and are more brown and barred than adult males. The exception is the American Kestrel, which is unusual in having a distinct juvenile plumage for each sex. Among the non-dimorphic species, juveniles usually resemble the adults, so juveniles have similar plumage to adult females in all but one kestrel species. Dimorphism is therefore associated with a distinct adult male plumage.

Plumage dimorphism may owe more to the geographical location of the species than to any ancestral lineage. Rufous kestrel species from high latitudes are more sexually dimorphic than those from the tropics (Fig. 10a). There is no obvious reason for this, and the correlation exists largely because of the marked dimorphism of three high-latitude species (*tinnunculus* and *naumanni* in the northern hemisphere, *cenchroides* in the south). It may, therefore, be a chance effect, but the trend also occurs within the subspecies of *F. tinnunculus*,

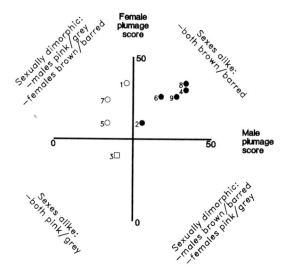

Fig. 9. *Plumage/size index of male versus female rufous kestrels. A low score represents 'male' characters (pink and grey colour, spots or no marking and small size) while a high score repesents 'female' characters (brown, barred feathers and large size). Numbers are species numbers given in Table 2. For further details, see text page 32.*

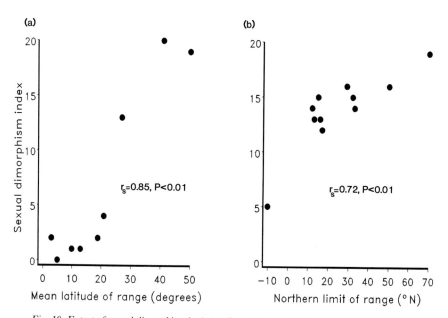

Fig. 10. *Extent of sexual dimorphism in (a) rufous kestrels and (b) tinnunculus subspecies in relation to the latitude of the geographic range. Dimorphism was measured as the absolute difference between the sexes in the plumage/size index, so a high value indicates strong dimorphism (see Table 2).*

though here the most southerly subspecies is the least dimorphic (Fig. 10b). If these trends are real, they could have arisen for several reasons. Plumage colour might be important for breeding or territorial display in males, but for camouflage in females and immatures. A number of other falcons and raptors that show plumage dimorphism, such as Merlins and harriers, are ground-nesting, which suggests that dimorphic plumage is related to protecting the incubating female and young from predators. However, this does not explain why tropical kestrels should be less dimorphic than those at higher latitudes, nor why some non-dimorphic species have male-type plumage and others female-type.

In summary, there is no clear-cut way of defining the kestrel group. In terms of size and shape they do seem to be distinct from most other falcons, though hovering behaviour and plumage are too variable to add to this discrimination. Until we have more information, our definition of kestrels must remain broad enough to include the 13 species in Table 2, even if it remains easier to say what a kestrel isn't than what it is! One technique that may give a better idea of the relationships among small falcons is the analysis of enzyme poly-morphisms. This measures the degree of similarity between species by com-paring variations in the molecular structure of enzymes. This, and the more recent technique of DNA 'finger-printing', may be the only way of unravelling the position of kestrels among the falcons.

BIOGEOGRAPHY OF KESTRELS

Before discussing the ancestry and evolution of kestrels, I shall digress slightly to examine the distributions of the various species and subspecies. It is important to understand how kestrel populations become isolated from one another because this is thought to be the main way in which new species evolve. Isolated groups may diverge from the parent stock, either because local conditions impose different selective pressures, or because the population is small and has only a part of the total species gene-pool. The degree of dis-similarity between isolated and parent populations depends on a number of factors, such as the amount of genetic exchange between them, the length of time they have been separated, the size of the isolated population, and differ-ences in selection pressures. In theory, small populations that have been completely isolated from the parent stock for a long time should be more dissimilar than populations only recently separated, or those between which there is still some interbreeding.

Distribution and isolation of the tinnunculus subspecies

The ways in which kestrel populations have become separated are complex, and far from understood. The problem is perhaps best illustrated by the distribution of *tinnunculus* subspecies. Over fifteen races have been described, but most authorities recognise only eleven, and some of these are doubtfully distinct. The nominate race breeds throughout Europe, the Middle East and Northern Siberia, up to about 70° N (Fig. 6). Over much of its northern range it is migratory, or partially so, and some individuals from Europe and central

Greater Kestrel nesting in a disused crow nest. This large, African kestrel shows little dimorphism between the sexes, and is unusual in having a white iris. Photo: M. Filmer.

USSR winter in Africa as far south as Angola and Zimbabwe, whereas birds from Siberia probably winter in India and Indo-China. The subspecies *interstinctus* replaces the nominate from east of the Himalayas to Northern Manchuria, and from south of the Gobi desert to southern China. Some individuals of this population winter in India and Indo-China, though they apparently do not breed there, apart from *F. t. objugatus*, which is resident in southern India and Sri Lanka. In Africa there are four mainland subspecies and four on the Atlantic islands off the north west coast, the latter comprising two subspecies on the Canary Islands and two on the Cape Verde Islands. The various *tinnunculus* subspecies differ in colouration and size, most being smaller, more rufous, darker or less sexually dimorphic than the nominate race.

It seems reasonable to suppose that these subspecies represent populations of *tinnunculus* that are partly or completely isolated, so that individuals from one population rarely breed with those from elsewhere. This isolation arises for several reasons:

1. Geographical separation. Some isolation of populations is inevitable in a species that occurs over such a wide range, even if there are no physical obstacles for birds to cross. Most northern Kestrels migrate in a northeast-southwest direction, and there is little east-west movement, so some divergence of *interstinctus* from the nominate form is likely just because of the distances involved.

2. Physical barriers. Isolation resulting from geographical separation may be intensified by physical barriers, which can break a gradual cline change into a series of discrete 'steps'. The four mainland African *tinnunculus* subspecies are partly separated from the nominate race by the Sahara and Arabian deserts where there are very few breeding Kestrels. Although these deserts can be crossed by Kestrels, they must, nonetheless, reduce the exchange of genes between populations in the north and south. Similarly, the high mountains of the Ethiopian plateau may increase the separation of the Somalian subspecies *archeri* from *rupicolaeformis* in Eygpt and *rufescens* in the west, though there is both morphological and geographical overlap of these races (Brown *et al* 1982).

Water seems to be a more effective barrier to movements than land. Kestrels make fairly long sea crossings on migration, so the presence of water is not a sufficient explanation for the existence of some island races of *tinnunculus*. The Canary Islands, for example, have two Kestrel subspecies that are separated by less than 50 km of water, and the same is true in the Cape Verde Islands. The small size of oceanic islands, and their distance from the mainland, makes immigration unlikely. Selection should favour birds that stay once they arrive, so isolation of these populations could arise largely because most individuals are highly sedentary, and rarely move between islands.

Some *tinnunculus* subspecies are not separated by any obvious physical barrier. This is the case between *rufescens*, the central African race, and the South African Rock Kestrel *F. t. rupicolus*, which is found as far north as central Angola and southern Tanzania. Although there is an obvious physical barrier, the large area of rain forest in Zaire where there are few Kestrels, the two races apparently intergrade south of this, in Angola and Namibia (Snow 1978).

The presence of *rufescens* south of the forest suggests that this physical barrier is not the sole reason for the existence of the two subspecies.

3. Physiological barriers. Another way in which populations might become genetically isolated is by separation of their breeding seasons. European Kestrels that migrate to Africa may find themselves wintering while the local population is breeding. Some migrants might breed with the local race, causing gene-flow between these populations, but this is unlikely because the northern birds would not be in breeding condition, having just bred in Europe. Within Africa, the Somalian subspecies *acherii* may be isolated because it seems to breed at a different time of year to neighbouring populations (Chapter 14). To some extent, then, the separation of *tinnunculus* into subspecies results from a mixture of geographical, behavioural and physiological barriers.

Geographical isolation of kestrel species

The same sort of factors which have led to the isolation of European Kestrel races may also have led, over longer periods or under more intense selection, to the kestrel species we see today. For example, the *tinnunculus*-like species *F. moluccensis* and *F. cenchroides* are separated by long distance and water from European Kestrels, and the resulting isolation is presumably complete and has acted for some time. The Moluccan Kestrel is kept apart from *tinnunculus* by a large swath of land and sea that includes Northern India, Indochina and the Philippines, where the latter species winters but does not breed. Such gaps in the distributions of species-groups are called disjunctions, and may occur for

The Seychelles Kestrel is the smallest falcon, and the plumage of both sexes resembles that of male European Kestrels. Photo: J. Watson.

Adult male Red-footed Falcon. These kestrel-like falcons breed from Eastern Europe to Siberia and winter in southern Africa. They share features with kestrels and with bird-eating falcons such as Hobbies. Photo: M. Goetz.

many reasons. In this case it is not clear why Kestrels that are obviously mobile enough to reach these areas do not stay and breed. The apparent absence of Moluccan Kestrels from Sumatra and Borneo (Smythies 1960), when they occur in adjacent islands, is also puzzling and requires more detailed study.

There is a similar disjunction between the range of Molluccan and Australian Kestrels, the latter occurring thoughout the mainland and as far north as New Guinea, where it is mainly a winter vistor. It is also said to winter within the range of the Moluccan species in Java and the Moluccas (Pizzey 1980), which makes the disjunction of their breeding ranges even more surprising. If these gaps are real, and not just due to poor information, they may be related to similar disjunctions in many small-mammal species in this area, which is the

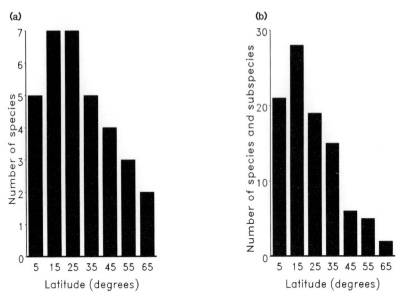

Fig. 11. Number of kestrel (a) species and (b) species plus subspecies in relation to latitude. Species or subspecies were counted more than once if their range spanned more than one 10° latitudinal band. As in many other species groups, kestrels show greater speciation in the tropics than at higher latitudes.

transition zone between the Oriental and Australasian biogeographic regions (Darlington 1957).

The divergence of adjacent kestrel populations is most noticeable near the equator, and the number of species and subspecies decreases at higher latitudes (Fig. 11). This is consistent with the widely observed trend for greater speciation in the tropics, and in kestrels it is probably because populations near the equator are largely sedentary, whereas those from high latitudes are migratory and interbreed over a wider area. The separation of some of the island races of Molluccan and American Kestrels is less than 100 km, but their racial status, if correct, must owe as much to their sedentary nature as to the physical barrier of the sea. If European Kestrels in Britain were as sedentary, we should expect at least three subspecies on our various offshore islands!

Where island groups are small, and more than about 1000 km from the mainland, the isolation is complete and has resulted in separate species, such as those on Mauritius and the Seychelles. Both these species have become specialised for the local terrain, which was originally thick forest. The Mauritius Kestrel has rounded, almost hawk-like, wings which are more reminiscent of forest-dwelling accipiters than of kestrels (Jones & Owadally 1985). Mauritius Kestrels have failed to adapt to the massive deforestation of the island since man arrived, and they have declined almost to extinction.

Geographical isolation probably explains how some kestrel populations could have diverged into separate species or subspecies. It is more difficult to see how overlapping (sympatric) populations could have become genetically isolated and so formed new species. This applies to the rufous and grey species in Africa, which overlap with *tinnunculus* over most of their ranges. Kestrel species that are currently sympatric may have diverged because of isolation acting in the past, but whether this was due to geographical or behavioural barriers is unknown.

Where kestrel species do overlap, they either segregate into different habitats, or specialise on different prey. An example of the first kind of segregation is seen on the mainland of Africa, where there are five breeding species- two rufous, two grey and various races of *tinnunculus*. In South Africa, Greater Kestrels seem to behave rather like European Kestrels, and are found mainly in farmland and grassy areas. The local race of *tinnunculus*, the Rock Kestrel, is usually found near rock outcrops and may be restricted in its niche by competition with Greater Kestrels and with the Black-shouldered Kite *Elanus caeruleus*. The latter is similar in size to *tinnunculus*, but feeds almost exclusively on small mammals and hunts mainly by hovering.

Segregation by specialisation on different prey seems likely in European and Lesser Kestrels, which breed sympatrically in southern Europe and Asia, and winter together in Africa. They are similar in size and, although Lesser Kestrels are slightly narrower-winged, the females of the two species are almost indistinguishable. However, Lesser Kestrels are largely insectivorous, and probably because of this they often feed in flocks and sometimes breed in large colonies. They have moved into a more specialised niche than *tinnunculus*, but the divergence is as much behavioural as physical.

THE EVOLUTION OF THE KESTREL GROUP

Within the kestrel group, it is apparent that some species are more alike than others; does this tell us anything about the course of evolution among these species? The underlying assumption is that strong similarities between two species reflect a recent common origin, an idea that dates back to Darwin. Interpreting the degree of similarity is not always simple, however, because convergent evolution of non-related species can make them look alike, and rapid divergence can do the opposite for isolated populations of the same species. It is not yet certain if all kestrels evolved from a single ancestral species or if they represent the convergence of several lines of small falcons.

The species most resembling *tinnunculus* are the Lesser, Australian and Moluccan Kestrels. The latter two species may have diverged from a common *tinnunculus* ancestor because of their geographical isolation, but Lesser Kestrels must either have been isolated in the past, or arisen from a different ancestral line. In the Indian Ocean species, the Seychelles and Madagascan Kestrels are more similar to each other than to Mauritius Kestrels, and there may have been two separate colonisations of these island groups. The former two species are unusual among rufous kestrels in having females with 'male-type' plumage, and it may be no coincidence that this also occurs in the Southern African race of *tinnunculus*. The other rufous species, the Fox and Greater Kestrels are geographically isolated on mainland Africa, so they might be divergent forms of the same original species. However, they are quite different both in appearance and habits, and it seems unlikely that they are closely related.

The remaining species are the American Kestrel and the three Old World grey species. *F. sparverius* is quite different from most Old World kestrels in size and plumage, and Boyce & White (1987) thought it might be the most recent form. They suggest it arose through colonisation by an Old World species, but it might equally have evolved from a separate group of falcons that came to resemble other kestrels by convergence. The two mainland species of grey kestrels in Africa do not overlap in their distribution, and seem to be closely related. The grey kestrels may have had the same ancestry as Red-footed Falcons: although the latter are long-winged, hobby-like falcons, they travel to wintering grounds in Africa from as far away as eastern Siberia, and could have evolved there at the same time as the grey kestrel species (Boyce & White 1987). The Madagascan Banded Kestrel is perhaps the least understood species. It shares some features with the mainland grey kestrels, but it appears to have specialised for forest-dwelling, and may have diverged from grey kestrels in a similar manner to Mauritius Kestrels in the rufous group.

With such a paucity of information, it is not surprising that a number of evolutionary trees have been proposed for the kestrel group (see Boyce & White 1987). The ancestral lines within these trees depend on whether features such as hovering and plumage dimorphism are assumed to be primitive or more recent traits, and whether they arose once, or several times in the kestrel group. The most likely branches would be between Old and New World species, between rufous and grey species, and between *tinnunculus*-like species and other rufous kestrels. Where Mauritius, Banded and Lesser Kestrels fit in is largely a matter of speculation, and perhaps the only firm conclusion is that we currently lack the data to infer the course of kestrel evolution.

SUMMARY

Kestrels are relatively long-tailed, short-toed falcons that are somewhat different from most other falcons of a similar size. Other characters, such as plumage colour, hovering and sexual dimorphism are less consistent, and not wholly diagnostic of the group. The Old World kestrels can be divided into grey and rufous species, the latter including the *tinnunculus*-like species that are found across Europe, Africa, Asia and Australia. Kestrel species may diverge into different races over fairly short distances, especially in the tropics. This is probably due to reduced genetic exchange in sedentary populations near the equator, compared with migratory populations at high latitudes. Apart from some obvious divergences and similarities, the evolutionary relationships among the kestrel group are poorly understood, and await more sophisticated diagnostic techniques.

CHAPTER 3

Diet and prey selection

The type of food that an animal eats has profound effects on its lifestyle.
Breeding is usually timed in relation to periods when food is most abundant;
animals often migrate to avoid seasonal shortages of food; and many aspects
of behaviour and morphology are adapted to capturing food. Studies over the
last decade or so have shown that some birds have complex foraging behaviours
that are finely adjusted to optimise their energy intake. The adjustments are
made by varying the choice both of prey and foraging technique. Kestrels feed
on animals that vary in size and agility, and they hunt in several different
ways. Hunting techniques are described in the next chapter; here I examine
the food of Kestrels and how their diet varies in relation to the availability of
prey.

Prey selection, and the factors that affect it, are important aspects of Kestrel
ecology. Fortunately, Kestrels produce pellets of undigested prey remains that
are fairly easy to find at roosts and nests, and we probably know more about
their diet than that of most diurnal raptors. Kestrels are highly adaptable

feeders and will take almost anything they are able to kill. However, the majority of food studies in temperate regions have found that the most important prey are small mammals, especially diurnal voles of the genus *Microtus*. When Kestrels rely heavily on other prey it is usually because voles are scarce or absent. Switching to alternative prey allows Kestrels to persist in areas they would otherwise abandon, but they are rarely as abundant, or as successful in breeding, as under good vole conditions. The list of alternative prey is remarkably long, and includes most mammals up to the size of young Rabbits, birds as large as Woodpigeons, and lizards, snakes, frogs, insects, earthworms, fish and even crabs! Kestrels clearly have a wide choice of possible prey, but they normally take only a limited selection of the species present in the local area.

In order to make meaningful comparisons between areas, or over time in the same area, it is necessary to quantify the importance of each prey type in the diet. Unfortunately, this is not as easy as it at first appears. Several different methods have been used, each of which has its problems (Appendix I). An unbiased estimate of the diet should be based on the frequency with which each prey type is taken. This is almost impossible to measure in practice, and the best estimate is usually some sort of index of relative frequencies. Such indices may show how the diet varies over time, or between areas, but they do not necessarily reflect the precise frequencies with which different prey are eaten, because some are digested more thoroughly than others. This is not a serious drawback if the same methods are used throughout, but problems do arise when trying to compare studies. For example, analyses of partly-digested stomach contents give greater emphasis to soft-bodied prey than do those using pellets, which are the end-product of digestion. Futhermore, the results of pellet analysis will differ according to whether or not individual items were counted and, if so, how carefully. Such variation makes it difficult to compare the many estimates of Kestrel diet in the literature, therefore much of this chapter is based on my own work in Scotland and England, where the methods of analysis were similar. Those interested in a more detailed discussion of the problems in measuring diet should first read Appendix I.

RANGE OF PREY IN THE DIET

In any one area, a fairly small number of species usually forms the bulk of the items taken. Such species are reported from most studies and, within those studies, turn up in most samples analysed. Prey of secondary importance are sometimes taken in large numbers, either because they are unusually abundant and easy to catch, or because the main prey are scarce. Infrequent items represent chance meetings of Kestrel and scarce prey that are probably of little significance to the ecology of the predator. The prey taken by Kestrels fall roughly into four main groups:

Small mammals
More than 22 species of mammal from 12 families or sub-families have been recorded as Kestrel prey in Europe. Most frequent are microtine voles, the Short-tailed Vole in Britain, or its Continental counterpart, the Common Vole. Both species inhabit rough grassland, but Short-tailed Voles make runs

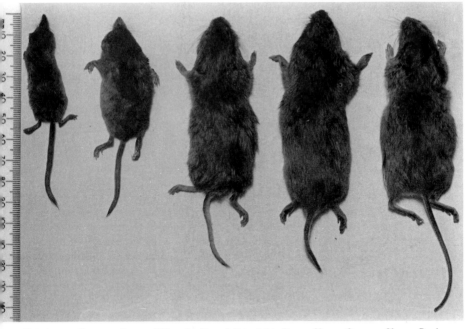

Frequent small-mammal prey of Kestrels. From left to right: Pygmy Shrew, Common Shrew, Bank Vole, Short-tailed Vole and Woodmouse. Photo: N. J. Westwood.

on the surface in thick vegetation, while Common Voles tend to live in burrows. Adult voles normally weigh about 20 g, but male Short-tailed Voles may reach three times this weight in peak vole years. One or other vole species dominate the diet of Kestrels in large areas of rough grassland. At Eskdalemuir, voles were present in at least 80% of all samples of pellets throughout the study, and all the teeth found suggested Short-tailed Voles rather than Bank Voles (Village 1982a). This coincided with the importance of Short-tailed Voles in snap-trap samples, where they formed 79% of the small mammals and almost all of the rodents. In reclaimed polders in Holland, which consisted largely of rough grass and reeds, Common Voles were the only vole species taken by Kestrels, and made up 87% of the mammal prey (Cavé 1968). Pastural habitats, with more arable land, hedgerows or woodland, are preferred habitats for Bank Voles and Woodmice, which are correspondingly more frequent in Kestrel diets in such areas. In my farmland areas, for example, 15% of all pellets contained remains of Woodmice.

All three species of shrew that occur in Britain are taken by Kestrels, though the rare Water Shrew much less so than either the Common or Pygmy. Any distaste shrews may have to mammals does not, it seems, affect Kestrels which, like most birds, have a poor sense of smell. Common Shrews are normally the most abundant shrew species in pellets, though Kestrels will feed on Pygmy Shrews if the latter are locally abundant (Simms 1961). On the Continent, species such as White-toothed Shrews are also taken by Kestrels (Thiollay 1963).

Mammals that are rarely eaten include the young of large species such as hares, Rabbits, squirrels and rats, as well as those that are difficult to catch or normally unavailable, such as bats, Moles and Weasels. The largest mammal I have seen being killed was a 120 g leveret. It was initially attacked by a male Kestrel that was able to hold it but not to kill it. After a few minutes the male's mate flew down from a nearby perch and dispatched the leveret with several bites to the base of the skull. The female Kestrel could barely carry her victim, and I was able to chase her off and weigh it.

I have found Moles on Kestrel nests several times; on each occasion the weather had been wet for some days, so perhaps the Moles had been forced to the surface by water-logging. The records of Kestrels taking Weasels suggest an interesting confrontation, which may not always go the Kestrel's way. I once watched a juvenile male Kestrel stoop at a Weasel that was running across a ploughed field. The Weasel turned and sprang up at the Kestrel, hissing loudly, whereupon the latter, having hovered overhead for several seconds, decided to leave well alone and flew off!

Birds
Identification of bird species from pellets is normally impossible, as most feathers are ground to a fine powder in the gizzard. Skeletal remains are not

diagnostic of species, unless there is a distinct beak or foot present. Feather remains can be grouped according to the major order (eg passerines, game birds, pigeons etc) if some barbules remain sufficiently intact to show the shape of the microscopic nodes (Day 1966). The most useful data on the bird species taken by Kestrels come from direct observation of kills, or from the identification of plucked feathers found at nests. The latter method requires some practice because, to the untrained eye, most feathers appear to be an identical uniform brown! However, with patience, it is possible to learn the tell-tale features that distinguish the feathers of one species from those of another.

As with mammal prey, the range of species taken is wide, but a few dominate in most circumstances. These are often open-country species such as Skylarks, Meadow Pipits and Starlings. At Eskdalemuir, nearly all the bird remains at nests were Meadow Pipits or Skylarks, the most abundant species in the area. In Holland, over 70% of bird remains on young polders were Starlings (Cave' 1968), which were also commonly taken by Kestrels in my farmland study areas. In the mixed farmland area, Kestrels took a wide variety of small birds, ranging from Great Tits to Collared Doves, which reflected the greater species diversity in that environment. Most remains I identified were of Starlings, House Sparrows and, in spring, young Song Thrushes or Blackbirds.

The largest adult birds taken by Kestrels are about the size of Woodpigeons. I have seen Kestrels eating Woodpigeons, but never actually killing them, and it is likely that they usually take only dead or dying adults, and immatures. A radio-tagged female Kestrel I was following ate steadily at a pigeon carcass for over 45 minutes, by which time she had some difficulty in flying and spent the rest of the day sitting on a nearby post. The largest bird I have seen carried by a Kestrel was an adult Turtle Dove, caught by a male in July. The dove would have weighed around 130 g, and the Kestrel could move it only with a series of short glides, low over the ground. Kestrels also take the young of much larger species, such as ducks, gulls, waders and game birds.

In spring and early summer, Kestrels prey on recently hatched or fledged birds, rather than adults. The remains of fledgling birds plucked by Kestrels can be distinguished from adults by the half-grown state of the feathers, and these are commonly found at the nest. Fledglings are slower and less wary than adults, and therefore vulnerable to predation by Kestrels and other raptors such as Sparrowhawks (Newton & Marquiss 1982a). Predation on broods of precocial species may be heavy in the first few days after hatch, when they are most at risk. I have had several reports from farmers who have seen ducklings being taken by Kestrels and, in some cases, this apparently resulted in the loss of the whole brood. I found remains of young game birds at Kestrel nests only rarely, but in several cases there were a number of similar-sized carcasses, suggesting that Kestrels were making repeated raids on the same brood. Kestrels nesting in coastal areas of Holland made themselves unpopular with birdwatchers by taking many chicks of rare wader species (J. Buker), and at Minsmere in England they occasionally take Avocet chicks (Hill 1988).

Invertebrates

Apart from a few cases, invertebrate remains in Kestrel pellets are difficult to identify to the species level, and most workers have been content to group them under headings such as beetles, earthworms or grasshoppers. The species taken are those that Kestrels can both detect and catch, and these tend to be the large, slower-moving species that live on the surface. Thus, the most frequent beetles are ground beetles (*carabidae*) and dor beetles (*geotrupidae*). Fast-flying prey is unusual, though dragonflies and flying ants have been recorded. Termites are often taken in Africa, where European Kestrels can be seen feeding on emerging swarms in the company of Lesser Kestrels and Red-footed Falcons.

It is likely that only larger invertebrates, with sizeable chitinous parts, leave any remains in pellets, so some smaller species may be missed altogether. Spiders are rarely recorded in pellets, but were present in several Kestrel stomachs examined through the Monks Wood carcass scheme (N. Westwood). My experience of watching Kestrels feeding on invertebrates in pasture fields, was that they often took items that were less than 5 mm long. Kestrels sometimes stayed on the ground after a strike, picking up these tiny prey after short runs along the ground. Even large items may leave no remains in pellets, as was probably the case for a Kestrel that was seen eating slugs- so many, in fact, that its foot became covered in a large ball of slime! Earthworms usually leave some remnant chaetae, though several workers failed to search for these and thus underestimated the importance of earthworms in the diet.

Reptiles and amphibians

Lizards are the main prey in this group, and are taken almost throughout the Kestrel's geographic range, though only in summer in northern latitudes. Slow Worms and snakes have also been recorded, but only rarely (I. Newton, Hagen 1952). Amphibians seem to be much less frequent than lizards, and are probably vulnerable only during the brief spawning periods. The only Common Toad I have recorded as Kestrel prey was a road casualty in Eskdalemuir; this was also one of the few cases of carrion feeding I have seen. Toads have a poisonous skin, and the demise of this particular individual may have allowed the Kestrel to get at the harmless flesh.

The above four groups include most of the prey taken by Kestrels, though they by no means exhaust the list of potential food, which includes fish (Batten 1959), crabs (Richards 1947) and carrion. Besides the toad carrion mentioned above, I have also seen a Kestrel eating the remains of a dead lamb that had been skinned by a shepherd. Lamb remains would not have shown up in pellets because only the flesh was eaten, and this would apply to any large carcass. Even so, I doubt if carrion feeding has been seriously underestimated, and it is probably not common in Kestrels. I have several times found parts of large prey on nests, in each case following prolonged wet weather during the nestling stage. The remains included the haunch of an adult hare, the leg of a fox cub and parts of an adult Pheasant, all of which must have been taken as carrion.

VARIATIONS IN KESTREL DIET

At Eskdalemuir, I analysed 1,400 pellets collected from April 1976 to July 1979, excluding August and September each year (Table 3). Diet in the two farmland study areas was assessed from over 3,000 pellets collected from October 1980 to July 1985 and grouped into two-monthly periods (Table 4). In all three study areas, Short-tailed Voles were the most frequent items, occurring in the majority of pellets in each two-monthly period. The frequency of some other prey species fluctuated considerably, however, and this was mainly due to changes in their abundance relative to voles.

Seasonal variations in diet
Voles and shrews showed little seasonal variation in the diet, but this was

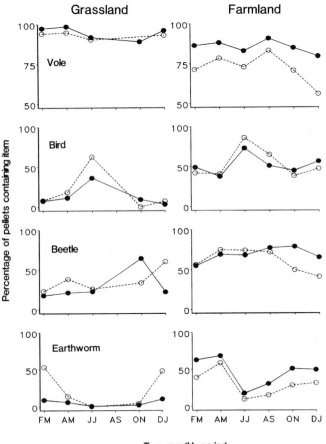

Fig. 12. Seasonal variation in the diet of Kestrels in Eskdalemuir grassland 1975–79 (● = young plantation, ○ = sheepwalk) and farmland 1980–85 (● = mixed farmland, ○ = arable farmland). Each point is the proportion of pellets from a two-month period that contained the particular item. For sample sizes, see Tables 3 and 4.

not so for some other prey which had regular peaks at certain times of year (Fig. 12). Small birds, for example, were eaten mainly in June and July, when their fledged young were most abundant. Birds were rarely taken during winter in the Scottish grassland area because most species had left the hill ground to avoid the harsh weather. Earthworms showed a peak occurrence in pellets during early spring, when the ground was unfrozen but waterlogged. These conditions were likely to bring worms to the surface, where they were vulnerable to Kestrels hunting over short vegetation. In summer, earthworms were mostly absent from pellets, probably because they would have been aestivating well below the surface.

Similar seasonal peaks in birds and earthworms have been noticed in other studies (Yalden & Warburton 1979), along with peaks in prey such as lizards (spring and summer), frogs (spring) and grasshoppers (autumn). Seasonal fluctuations in vertebrate prey seem to reflect variations in the availability of each species, and Kestrels probably take whatever they most often encounter and can easily catch. Insects, however, may be more abundant in summer than in winter, but this increase is not reflected in their frequency in Kestrel pellets. Invertebrate prey alone may be sufficient to maintain a Kestrel for short periods but, in Britain, breeding Kestrels require more food than invertebrates can normally supply. It is not profitable for Kestrels to transport small items to the nest, so any decline in invertebrate prey in the summer diet may reflect a change in their suitability, rather than their availability. Nonetheless, invertebrates such as beetles are eaten by Kestrels throughout the breeding season (Fig. 12, Itämies & Korpimäki 1987), and seasonal peaks were not very marked. Some beetles may be eaten by adults away from the nest, or get into pellets from the guts of small birds and shrews brought to the nest as food for the young.

Habitat variation in diet

As well as seasonal fluctuations, Kestrel diets also varied between my study areas, and even between different habitats within the same area. At Eskdalemuir, Kestrels living in sheepwalk ate more birds and earthworms than those living in young plantations (Fig. 12). A useful way of quantifying the variability of the diet was to record what proportion of pellets contained solely vole remains. When most pellets consisted of nothing but vole, other items were clearly less important, and there was little diversity to the diet. Pellets from young plantations were more likely to contain nothing but vole remains than were those from sheepwalk, pointing to at greater diversity of Kestrel diet in the latter habitat (Fig. 13a). The difference may have been partly due to the low vole numbers in sheepwalk, and partly because the shorter vegetation there made invertebrates easier to detect.

The main difference in diet between the Scottish grassland and English farmland areas was the greater diversity of prey in the farmland areas, especially among small mammals. A greater variety of mammals lived in the farmland areas, and a number of species in addition to *Microtus* were identified in pellets. The most common were Woodmice, Bank Voles and Common Shrews, but less frequent items included House Mice, Brown Rats, Harvest Mice and Water Voles. I have seen Kestrels taking rats in farmland more

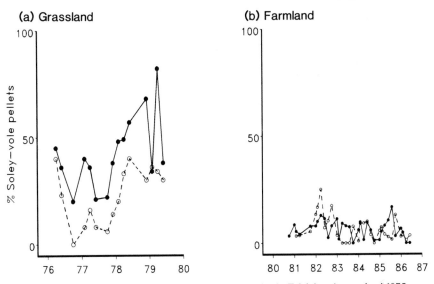

(a) Grassland

(b) Farmland

Fig. 13. *Proportion of pellets containing solely vole remains in Eskdalemuir grassland 1975–79 and farmland 1980–86 (legend as in Fig. 12). Kestrels were most heavily dependent on voles in grassland, especially in young plantations and in the good vole years of 1978 and 1979.*

frequently than was revealed in pellets, and I suspect that rat remains were scarce in pellets because Kestrels picked the flesh off the skull and large bones. This has also been noticed in captive Kestrels that were fed laboratory rats (Yalden & Yalden 1985).

Woodmice were never recorded as prey at Eskdalemuir, but they were fairly frequent in the farmland pellets, especially in autumn and winter. Woodmice are normally nocturnal rodents, but I have seen Kestrels catch them during the day. The mice move into crops during the summer, and become available to Kestrels during and after harvest. Kestrels take some rats and mice by following beet or potato harvesters, and the numerous stories I hear from fenland farmers confirms this as common behaviour in that area.

Other prey items were also more frequent in the two farmland areas compared to the Scottish grassland. Birds were more important prey throughout the year, but especially in winter, when 40–60% of pellets contained bird remains, compared with less than 10% at Eskdalemuir at that season (Fig. 12). This doubtless reflected the greater abundance of wintering birds in the English study areas, where winters were less severe, and food for small birds more abundant than in the Scottish hills. Similarly, the greater frequency of earthworms was in line with the larger area of grazed pasture and tilled land in the farmland habitats. Farming operations that disturb the soil bring some worms to the surface and Kestrels take advantage of this by following ploughs and cultivators. This may make earthworms available to Kestrels throughout the winter in arable land, even when they are unavailable on pastures.

Because of the relative abundance of non-vole prey in the two farmland areas, few pellets contained solely vole remains (Fig. 13b). Even in a poor vole year, at least 20% of pellets from young plantations at Eskdalemuir had no prey other than voles, and this rose to over 80% in a good vole year. Although the majority of pellets in the English farmland areas contained voles, fewer than 10% contained no other items, so Kestrels there were clearly less dependent on voles than in the Scottish grassland area.

Comparison of diet between the two English farmland areas

The main differences in diet between the two farmland areas were the higher frequency of earthworms, and lower frequencies of Woodmice and grasshoppers, in the mixed than in the arable farmland (Figs 12 & 14). There was more pasture in mixed farmland than in the arable fenlands, and this probably caused the difference in the frequency of earthworms in the diet, because worms were more numerous in pastures than in arable fields.

Over the whole year, 23% of arable pellets contained mice, compared with only 8% of mixed farmland pellets, the difference during the autumn and winter peak of mouse numbers being even greater (35% versus 10%). The contrast in voles was less obvious than in mice; 76% of arable pellets had vole remains compared to 87% of mixed farmland pellets, and there was less seasonal variation (Fig. 12). These differences were related to the frequency of voles and mice in the two farmland study areas, and this is dealt with later.

Age and sex variations in diet

The variations in Kestrel diets over time, or between habitats, make it difficult to compare prey selection in males and females or adults and first-year birds. Ideally, comparisons should be made between birds occupying the

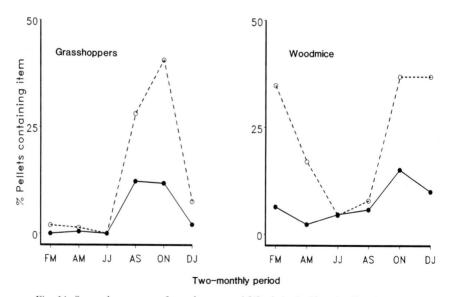

Fig. 14. Seasonal occurrence of grasshoppers and Woodmice in Kestrel pellets from mixed (●) and arable (○) farmland, 1980–86. For sample sizes, see Table 4.

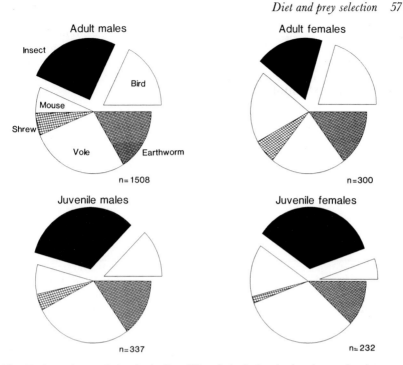

Fig. 15. Age and sex variations in the diet of Kestrels in the farmland study areas in winter. Pie slices are based on a proportion of the total prey-occurrences (n), so pellets containing several different types of item contributed more than once. Juveniles of both sexes ate more invertebrates, and fewer birds, than did adults.

same area at the same time, but this is hard to achieve. In the two farmland areas, I was able to collect pellets at the roosts of radio-tagged individuals of known age and sex, and this allowed some comparisons of diet during winter.

The most consistent trend to emerge was the higher frequency of insects, and lower frequency of birds, in juvenile than in adult pellets (Fig. 15). This doubtless reflected the ease with which insects could be caught compared to small birds, the latter evidently requiring hunting skills that had to be learned.

Differences in the diets of males and females were not as marked as those between adults and juveniles, and were not always consistent across the two farmland areas. However, in both mixed and arable farmland, males took more insects than did females, as might be expected from their smaller size. In American Kestrels, wintering males take more insects and fewer vertebrates than do males (Meyer & Balgooyen 1987), so maybe the same is true for European Kestrels. Diet is related to sexual size-dimorphism in some other raptors (Newton 1986), so it would be interesting to know if the slight size dimorphism in Kestrels is paralleled by a slight difference in diet between males and females.

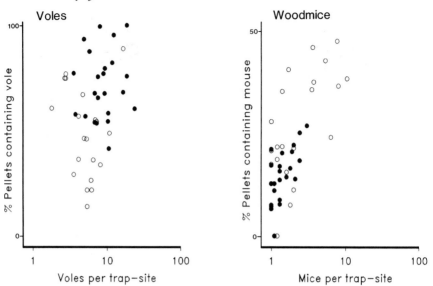

Fig. 16. *Relationship between the occurrence of mammal prey in Kestrel pellets and the snap-trap index for voles and Woodmice in mixed (●) and arable farmland (○). The y-axis is the arcsine transformation of the proportion of pellets containing vole or mouse remains for a two-monthly period, and the x-axis is log-scaled. The overall correlations were stronger for mice (r=0.712, P<0.001) than for voles (r=0.29, P<0.06).*

KESTREL DIET IN RELATION TO SMALL-MAMMAL ABUNDANCE

To measure the abundance of each type of Kestrel prey would be an impossible task, even over small areas. However, I was able to measure the relative abundance of small mammals using snap-trapping, and could then relate this to their frequencies in Kestrel pellets. Unfortunately, snap-trap indices may not reflect the actual abundance of species in the environment, because some may be more easily caught than others, and trapability may vary from season to season. However, the method gave a rough idea of temporal changes in mammal numbers, and variations in the relative abundance of species caught almost certainly reflected genuine differences between habitats.

Kestrel diet in the Scottish grassland area in relation to voles

In the Scottish grassland area, the number of voles was the main factor determining the compostion of Kestrel diet. Shrew numbers were fairly constant from year to year, and Kestrels took shrews most frequently in 1977, when voles were scarce. Vole abundance also affected the diversity of Kestrel diets over and above the seasonal fluctuations in availability of other items. I have already mentioned the greater frequency of non-vole items in the diet of Kestrels in the vole-poor sheepwalk habitat than in the young plantations, where voles were more plentiful. This also applied in both habitats between good and poor vole years, and the proportion of vole-only pellets was positively correlated with the spring vole index (Village 1982a).

Kestrel diets in the farmland areas relation to voles and mice

In the two English farmland areas, the main sources of variation in small-mammal densities were area-related (more voles and fewer mice in mixed than in arable farmland), and seasonal (highest numbers in autumn, especially for mice which had a more pronounced seasonal peak than voles). Year to year fluctuations in vole abundance were less than in the Scottish grassland area, at least for most of my study. Combining data for both farmland areas, there was a significant correlation between the proportion of pellets containing either voles or mice and the relevant snap-trap index (Fig. 16). These correlations held even after allowing for area or seasonal differences and for fluctuations in the density of the other mammal prey. In other words, Kestrels took mice because mice were more abundant, and not simply because voles were scarce.

The slopes of the two regressions suggested that voles may have been preferred to mice. Even when virtually no voles were caught in snap-traps, at least 50% of Kestrel pellets contained voles. Woodmice, however, were usually absent from pellets if few were caught in traps, and were present in only 50% of pellets even at peak mouse densities. This seems plausible in view of what is known of Kestrel diets from elsewhere, and because the nocturnal habits of mice make them less available to Kestrels than diurnal voles. However, the same result would have arisen if mice were more easily caught than voles in snap-traps, and it is not sufficient proof that Kestrels selectively took voles above their relative abundance to Woodmice.

Non-mammal prey in relation to vole abundance

The frequency with which Kestrels took non-mammal prey in the English farmland areas was not strongly affected by vole or mouse numbers, and there was no negative correlation between the occurrence of non-rodent prey and rodent (voles plus mice) snap-trap scores. Kestrels, it seemed, were selecting each prey species according to its abundance, irrespective of the current vole density. This made sense in a farmland environment, where non-vole prey constituted an important part of the overall food supply. At Eskdalemuir, where the habitat was mostly ungrazed grass, any change in vole numbers had a major effect on the total food available to Kestrels. In good vole years, Kestrels ate little else but voles, and took alternative prey only if it was easily caught or seasonally abundant.

Diet in the grassland study area was thus largely determined by the density of the most abundant prey, and this has also been shown in a similarly vole-rich habitat in Finland, where Kestrels altered their diet only in response to changes in the numbers of the most abundant vole species (Korpimäki 1985a). In my farmland areas, however, vole habitats comprised only a fraction of the landscape, and even large changes in the number of voles in these small patches would not have greatly altered the total vole density in the area. The variations in vole numbers I recorded in the farmland areas were not sufficient to make voles the only prey worth taking, and mice, birds and invertebrates were all important alternatives.

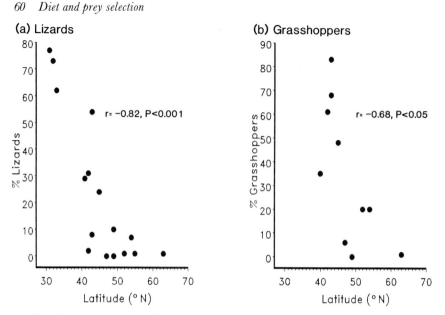

Fig. 17. *Proportion of (a) lizards among vertebrate items and (b) grasshoppers among invertebrate items in the summer diet of kestrels at various latitudes in Europe and the Middle East. Further details are in Table 5. In southern latitudes, lizards largely replace voles in the diet, and grasshoppers and crickets replace beetles.*

REGIONAL VARIATION IN KESTREL DIETS

This section compares the diets of Kestrels in various parts of their geographic range. Differences between studies, in the methods used and the accuracy of recording, mean that such comparisons are fraught with problems. Even studies using the same methods may have collected pellets over only a short period, so it is hard to tell if differences between areas are real, or merely reflect seasonal or annual effects. To reduce some of these sources of error, I selected only those studies that had measured diet in summer (March-September) by enumerating items. It was necessary to exclude results (including my own) based on the percentage of pellets containing prey items, not because these were inaccurate, but because too few workers had used this method. As in other aspects of their ecology, there is a serious dearth of Kestrel food studies outside Europe, and I could find little published information of any substance from Africa or Asia.

Diet in relation to latitude

The data in Table 5 range from Finland in the north to Corsica and Israel in the south. Surprisingly, no correlation emerged between latitude and the proportion of invertebrates in the diet. If Kestrels in southern Europe do eat more insects than those in the north, the trend may not show up in summer because breeding birds rely mainly on large prey to feed their young. Insects are frequently eaten in late summer and autumn, so variations in the time when samples were collected could have further obscured any trend. An additional problem is that estimating the proportion of invertebrates in pellet samples requires meticulous counting and a certain amount of judgment. Some of the variation between studies could be due to observer bias, so comparison of samples analysed by the same person may be a better way of exploring this relationship. Three of the estimates in Table 5 were by Jean-Marc Thiollay (1968a), who found higher proportions of insects in Kestrel diets in southern France and Corsica compared with those in northern France.

Although the ratio of vertebrates to invertebrates in Kestrel diets may not change much with latitude, there are some marked differences in the ratio of some items within these two groups. The proportion of lizards among vertebrate prey increases further south in Europe, as does the proportion of grasshoppers among invertebrate remains (Fig. 17). These correlations are presumably due to the greater abundance of both these prey items in the warm, dry climates of southern Europe than in the north, where grasslands are richer and voles more abundant. The trend in grasshoppers could have been influenced by the strong seasonal changes in their abundance, so a more detailed study comparing autumn samples is needed.

In general, Kestrel diets in the northern temperate areas seem largely to comprise small mammals, birds and beetles, whereas those in warmer areas are based more on lizards, birds and grasshoppers. This generalisation needs to be tested further with data from tropical and sub-tropical parts of the Kestrel's range, but it seems reasonable in view of the relative changes in abundance of these prey groups with latitude.

Local variations

The above regional patterns again show that Kestrel diets reflect the available prey. At any latitude, the diet may also be influenced by local anomalies in prey abundance. In Ireland, for example, field voles are absent, and Kestrels there rely mainly on Woodmice and birds (Fairley and Mclean 1965, Fairley 1973). Similarly, several studies of urban Kestrels have shown a greater dependence on small bird prey than is the case in rural areas (Crichton 1977, Yalden 1980, Pikula *et al* 1984), which undoubtably reflects the abundance of House Sparrows and Starlings, and scarcity of voles, in most cities.

SUMMARY

Kestrels are predominantly small-mammal predators in northern Europe, but they feed on a wide variety of other small prey, including birds, lizards, insects and earthworms. Where voles are plentiful, they tend to be the most important items in the diet, though other prey, such as fledgling birds or earthworms, are taken when seasonally abundant. During poor vole years, or in poor vole habitats, Kestrels take a wider variety of prey. In the Scottish grassland area, changes in vole density had little effect on the proportion of Kestrel pellets containing vole remains, which was always high. However, vole density had a marked effect on the occurrence of other prey in the diet, suggesting that the latter were taken according to their abundance relative to voles. In the English farmland areas, where there was less vole habitat, the frequency of voles or mice in pellets was correlated with their abundance, but vole density had little effect on the occurrence of other items. The regional differences in the diets of Kestrel confirm that they select prey that is most abundant or most easily caught, and that they can partially adjust to what is locally available.

CHAPTER 4

Hunting and eating

The Kestrel's hovering hunting technique is, perhaps, its most familiar feature, and the one that most easily distinguishes it from other European raptors. But Kestrels also hunt from perches, and are therefore able to alter their method of hunting to suit the type of prey, the prevailing weather and their energy requirements. Kestrels can also vary their meal times regardless of when the prey is caught, by storing it for later consumption. This flexibility in hunting and feeding allows Kestrels to adjust their energy expenditure and intake to meet periods of high food demand or uneven availability.

Kestrels are well adapted to catching small, agile prey on the ground, and make full use of their keen eyesight, sharp talons and strong beaks. Vertebrate prey is pounced on from a rapid dive, grabbed with the talons and killed by biting, usually at the base of the skull. Attacks on less agile prey, such as beetles or earthworms, tend to follow slow, shallow glides, and the Kestrel lands close to the prey then takes it directly in the beak.

We know little about the visual perception of Kestrels, though apparently they can discern some colours (Kulgawczuk 1962), and the forward position of the eyes gives a degree of binocular vision which helps in judging distances.

It is evident from watching their behaviour, however, that they are able to locate prey at remarkable distances. Perched Kestrels may make strikes at beetles over 50 m away, or at small birds at distances of 300 m or more. Because of this, Kestrels are often thought to have magnified vision compared with humans, but they may simply have greater discrimination or enhanced sensitivity to prey movements. Small mammals and birds that 'freeze' will often go unnoticed by Kestrels- an annoying ruse that is frequently used by trap decoys!

HUNTING TECHNIQUES

Kestrels usually hunt either from a perch or from the air. They occasionally take invertebrates by making short runs along the ground between pounces, but this usually occurs during bouts of hunting from perches and is not really a separate technique. Flight-hunting mostly entails searching from a fixed position in the air, a behaviour that makes Kestrels instantly recognisable and has led to their country name of *windhover*. Flying Kestrels sometimes make a rapid search of large areas by soaring, often to great heights. This seems to be a distinct method of hunting, but it is rarely used unless there are suitable thermals. Whatever the method, periods of searching are interspersed with attacks at prey, called *strikes*. These usually end with the Kestrel on the ground (full-strikes), though sometimes dives are abandoned in mid air (half-strikes).

Perched-hunting

Kestrels hunt from any structure that provides a perch from which they can scan the ground. The most frequently used perches are electricity or telephone poles, which are of a suitable height and usually run along road verges or other hunting habitat. However, Kestrels will also use trees, buildings, bridges, fence posts and even stationary vehicles. I once watched a Kestrel hunting a stubble field by moving from bale to bale as each was made.

A perched-hunting Kestrel typically changes perch about every 5–10 minutes (Shrubb 1982, Pettifor 1983a), though it may spend longer on high perches than on low ones because high perches offer a bigger scanning area. When prey is seen, the Kestrel may either glide down and strike at it directly, or fly out and hover over the spot for a closer look. The maximum distance that Kestrels travel during a strike depends partly on the prey type and partly on the surrounding vegetation. Strikes at small mammals and invertebrates tend to be closer to the perch than do those directed at small birds. Prey on the ground is probably seen at greater distances where there is little effective cover, and I have noticed that strikes at small mammals tend to be closer to the perch when the vegetation is tall.

It is often difficult to decide if a perched Kestrel is hunting or just resting. It is fairly obvious when a Kestrels is actively hunting because it has an upright posture, continually scans the ground and frequently changes perch. It also bobs its head several times before it strikes, which may enable a better judgement of the distance to the prey. All these behaviours are fairly distinct from those of non-hunting Kestrels which sit hunched up with feathers fluffed out,

Kestrels often hunt from perches, especially in winter. Photo: R. Rose.

or preen. However, even such apparently inactive birds will strike at prey if they happen to see it, and this raises a problem in measuring the hunting performance of perched Kestrels. Perched-hunting will appear less efficient than it is if it includes all time spent perched, but deciding whether or not a perched Kestrel is hunting can involve a certain amount of guesswork. I consider a Kestrel is perched-hunting only if it is obviously alert and scanning the ground, though other workers have used different criteria and this has to be remembered when comparing the hunting performance recorded in different studies.

Hover-hunting
In a strict aerodynamic sense, hovering means flying above a fixed ground

postion in still air. Kestrels need some wind if they are to stay in a fixed position because what they actually do is to fly into the wind so that the forces of weight and drag are exactly matched by the lift from the airstream and the thrust of their wings. This requires them either to beat their wings continuously (which is equivalent to normal flapping flight), to hold them outstretched but motionless (equivalent to gliding) or a mixture of the two. John Videler and his colleagues in Holland made a detailed study of flight-hunting in Kestrels, and suggested the term *windhovering* to cover both flapping and gliding flight during the stationary bouts of flight-hunting (Videler *et al* 1983). This was a compromise to appease the technically-minded students of flight mechanics, while preserving a term that is immediately understood by all. I shall use the term 'flight-hunting' to cover both windhovering and the movements between windhovering bouts.

Anyone who has watched a Kestrel hovering on a blustery day cannot fail to marvel at the incredible co-ordination required to maintain position in a constantly changing airstream. While the Kestrel's wings and body are buffeted about like a flapping rag, its head stays fixed, as if pinned by invisible clamps. One Kestrel, analysed by high-speed film, moved its head by less than 6 mm in any direction while hovering in a wind gusting from 4.8 to 7.5 m per second (17–27 kmph) (Videler *et al* 1983). This required almost instantaneous adjustments to the angle of the wings and tail to allow for the rapid changes in wind strength and direction.

The degree to which hovering Kestrels flap, as opposed to glide, depends on the speed of the wind and the slope of the ground. On calm days, hovering Kestrels must almost always flap, whereas in windy conditions they may glide continually or intermittently (Fig. 18). Gliding also requires a strong upward component to the wind, so Kestrels flight-hunt only on the windward sides of slopes (Village 1983a), and they often ride the updrafts of buildings or other obstacles. Intermittent flapping and gliding is particularly noticeable in strong

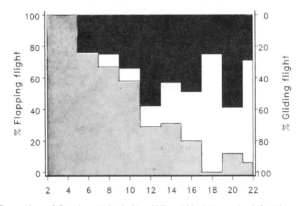

Fig. 18. Proportion of flapping (stippled), gliding (black) or mixed flapping and gliding (white) during flight-hunting at various wind speeds. Based on spot observations of Kestrels in the Eskdalemuir grassland study area (from Village 1983a). In strong winds, hovering Kestrels spent more time gliding and less time flapping.

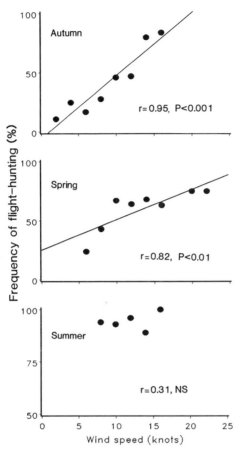

Fig. 19. Frequency of flight-hunting by Kestrels in Eskdalemuir grassland in relation to the wind speed. Based on spot-observations of hunting birds (from Village 1983a). Kestrels hunted on the wing mainly on windy days in autumn and spring, but at all wind speeds during the breeding season.

winds, when Kestrels have to beat their wings to prevent themselves being blown backwards, rather than to create lift. Videler *et al* (1983) found that during intermittent flapping and gliding Kestrels allow themselves to be blown backwards a few millimetres during the glide, but keep their heads still by stretching their necks. The neck extendes to about 4 mm before the wings start to flap, bringing the body forward again so that another glide is possible. The whole cycle takes less than a second, and requires almost unbelievable co-ordination. The advantage of using gliding whenever possible, even for such short periods is that it is energetically much cheaper than continuous flapping. The Kestrel that John Videler filmed, glided for 7–21% of each windhovering bout, and saved an estimated 25–44% of the energy that would have been required for continuous flapping flight at that wind speed.

Kestrels that are able to hang in the air by continuous gliding probably save a great deal of energy compared to those that have constantly to flap their wings. This makes hovering on calm days relatively energy-expensive, and Kestrels usually resort to hunting from perches when there is no wind. At Eskdalemuir, this was most evident in the autumn or winter because, in summer, Kestrels hovered even when there was little wind (Fig. 19). I had no evidence for a decline in flight-hunting in strong winds, though this seems likely if Kestrels have continuously to beat their wings to remain in the same place. Videler *et al* (1983) found that the average length of hovering bouts was about 25 seconds at intermediate windspeeds, but less than 15 seconds in winds of less than 6 m per second (22 kmph) or more than 12 m per second (44 kmph). Aerodynamic theories of bird-flight predict that the energy costs of flight-hunting are lowest at intermediate windspeeds, so Kestrels seemed unwilling, or unable, to hover for long if unfavourable wind conditions increased the energy costs. Clearly, wind plays an important role in determining when and where Kestrels hunt, how they hunt and how efficiently they do it.

Soaring

This method is used less often than hovering, partly because it requires air thermals, and partly because it is not a very effective way of searching for small mammals. During soaring bouts, Kestrels are almost continuously on the move, stopping only briefly to hover if they spot prey. They may reach a considerable height and can cover several kilometres in a few minutes.

Moving at such speeds and height, it is unlikely that Kestrels can readily spot invertebrates or most small mammals, and they are probably searching for more visible prey such as small birds. I rarely, if ever, recorded soaring at Eskdalemuir, where voles were the most important prey and Kestrels could nearly always get some uplift from the many steep slopes. Soaring was more frequent in the farmland areas, especially on sunny days between April and August. Soaring can be under-estimated from sightings alone, because soaring Kestrels are difficult to see and cannot be followed for long. It may be an important hunting method where the ground is fairly flat, when birds are important prey and when the weather is hot enough for suitable thermals.

Kestrels that see prey while soaring may dive at it gradually, stopping to hover on the way down, or may make a spectacular strike from several hundred feet. Kestrels rely heavily on surprise to catch small birds, which can usually reach the safety of cover if they notice the predator in time. A Kestrel soaring at height may be unseen by even the most wary sparrow or starling. I have several times seen Kestrels soar for many minutes over a field, waiting until a flock of small birds below had moved sufficiently far from the protection of the hedge. The Kestrels then dived suddenly, between the flock and hedge, hoping to catch stragglers before they reached safety.

Other hunting methods

Although the above methods are the most commonly used ways of getting food, Kestrels are very adaptable feeders, and will, if necessary, scavenge carrion or steal prey from other birds (*kleptoparasitism*). Short-eared Owls seem to be popular vicitims to rob, probably because they are the only vole predators of a similar size that hunt during the day. At Eskdalemuir, Kestrels usually attacked owls from a perch, taking off as soon as they saw an owl make a pounce. If the owl was successful and stayed down with the kill, the Kestrel would dive at the owl, until it either dropped the vole or left it on the ground. I suspect that piracy of Short-eared Owls may be fairly common where the two species concentrate in good vole areas, and it has been reported elsewhere (Korpimäki 1984). Attacks at owls may easily pass unnoticed because a Kestrel will break off quickly if it sees the owl coming up with empty talons. When I had learnt to recognise the characteristic attack (which is similar to that used against small birds), I made a point of scanning where the Kestrel was heading and, often as not, I saw an owl rising from the grass.

In two years at Eskdalemuir I recorded the outcome of 13 attacks at owls, and 30% of these resulted in the Kestrel stealing the food (Village 1987a). During the winter of 1977–78, one particular Kestrel spent much of the day watching Short-eared Owls hunting in its territory, and seemed to rely almost entirely on their efforts for obtaining its own food. Why Short-eared Owls allow themselves to be robbed is not clear- they are slightly larger than Kestrels, but may not be as manouverable, especially when they are just taking off. Kestrels will also take food from one another, as well as from some other predators such as Barn Owls or Sparrowhawks (Shrubb 1982, Newton 1986).

HUNTING PERFORMANCE

Kestrels are one of the few raptors that can be kept in sight long enough to give a reasonable estimate of hunting performance. This is by no means easy, even if the individuals are radio-tagged, but it is more feasible than trying to follow secretive species like Sparrowhawks, or larger raptors such as Peregrines or Eagles. Several people have studied the hunting behaviour of Kestrels, or ecologically similar raptors such as Black-shouldered Kites. Most have used three main measures of performance: the proportion of strikes that is successful (*strike success*), the frequency of strikes (*strike rate*), and the frequency of kills (*capture rate* or *yield*). The latter is probably the most relevant, though the other two variables can give some insight to factors that are affecting hunting yield. The results of these studies differ in detail, but are consistent in showing that hunting yield depends on prey type, the hunting method and the time of year.

Hunting success and prey type
Not surprisingly, Kestrels capture beetles and other invertebrates more quickly than they do voles or small birds, whatever hunting method is used (Table 6). In the Scottish grassland study area, capture rates of invertebrates were three times higher than of mammals during flight-hunting, and six times higher during perched-hunting. There were similar differences in farmland for perched-hunting, but flight-hunting Kestrels rarely took invertebrates, so a meaningful comparison between prey types was not possible. The differences in capture rates were due both to higher strike rates and greater strike success for invertebrate prey. This probably reflects the greater abundance of invert-

ebrates (leading to more strike opportunities) and their lesser ability to escape attacks, compared to birds or mammals.

Vertebrates also differ in vulnerability, Kestrels usually being better at catching mammals than birds, particularly when flight-hunting (Table 6). In Holland, the poor yield for birds was due both to low strike rates and low strike success (Masman *et al* 1988b). In my farmland study, perched-hunting Kestrels in winter made frequent strikes at birds, but only 5% of these were successful. Most of the attacks at birds ended with the Kestrel swerving away as the prey flew off, and I counted these as strikes, even if the Kestrel had not actually landed. The low success rate of strikes at birds undoubtedly reflects the difficulty Kestrels have in taking small birds by surprise. In winter, success was most likely at dawn or dusk, when poor light enhanced the chance of a surprise attack. In summer the majority of birds taken are those that have recently fledged and are therefore more vulnerable than their wilier parents.

Hunting success in relation to hunting method

For any type of prey, flight-hunting usually yields more prey per hour than does perched-hunting. This is difficult to test for invertebrates, which are rarely taken by flight-hunting Kestrels, though I was fortunate to get reasonable samples from young Kestrels flight-hunting for beetles in the autumn of 1979 at Eskdalemuir (Table 6). In that instance, their strike success was similar to that of Kestrels perched-hunting for invertebrates, but flight-hunting gave twice as many strike opportunities, and hence double the capture rate. For mammals there was a three-fold difference between the methods at Eskda-lemuir, which compares with a difference of between five and ten-fold in mixed farmland.

These differences between flight- and perched-hunting are similar to those found by Richard Pettifor (1983a) in arable fenland, and for Black-shouldered Kites in South Africa (Tarboton 1978), but were much smaller than those in the Dutch study, where perched-hunting yield was only 0.13 mammals per hour compared with 3.92 per hour for flight-hunting (Masman *et al* 1988b). The difference between these studies may depend more on how perched-hunting was defined than on any genuine difference in hunting success. The Dutch workers also had some estimates of the hunting success rate of soaring, which was less than that of perched-hunting in the case of mammal prey, but about the same for small birds. These are figures for the whole year, and may underestimate the effectiveness of soaring for taking fledglings in summer.

Whatever the prey, flight-hunting seems to offer more strike opportunities than hunting from a perch. This may be because flying Kestrels are higher, and can move rapidly from one patch to another, thereby scanning more ground in a given time. By searching from directly overhead, they may also increase their chances of seeing prey, particulary if the grass is tall. Flying also enables Kestrels to hunt areas that are beyond the scanning range of perches, which would otherwise be unexploited. Prey density may be higher in open areas than around frequently used perches, where there may be local depletion of prey.

The actual process of pouncing on prey seems fairly similar, whether it is from the air or from a perch, and this may explain why strikes are equally likely to succeed by either method. The decision whether or not to dive at prey must presumably depend on the likelihood of a successful outcome. Such judgements may require a skill that has to be learnt, in which case juvenile Kestrels should fail in more strike attempts than adults. Kestrels in their first few months of independence certainly seem to make many unsuccessful strikes, some at wildly inappropriate objects. Mike Shrubb (1980) reports one young Kestrel attacking the twitching ears of a full-grown hare crouching in a stubble field!

SEASONAL CHANGES IN HUNTING SUCCESS

The amount of prey caught by Kestrels is higher during the breeding season than at other times of year. This is not only because breeding Kestrels spend more time hunting, but also because prey becomes easier to catch. Two studies have examined seasonal changes in the hunting performance of Kestrels taking mainly small mammals. Pettifor (1983a) found that flight-hunting yielded only slightly more prey per unit time in summer than in winter, because an increase in strike rate was almost matched by a decrease in strike success (Table 6). Perched-hunting, however, showed little increase in strike frequency, but a decline in success led to an overall decrease in yield.

The Raptor Group in Holland, in contrast, found a marked increase in capture rates for flight-hunting in summmer (Fig. 20), due largely to an increase in strike success. This was also apparent for strikes from perches, though these were less frequent in summer than in winter, causing a lower perched-hunting yield. They interpreted these results to mean that prey was

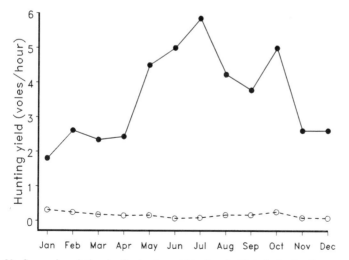

Fig. 20. *Seasonal variation in the hunting yield of male Kestrels in the Lauwersmeer, Holland. (Re-drawn from Masman et al 1988b). Yield is expressed as the number of voles caught per hour of perching (○) or flight-hunting (●).*

more vulnerable in summer, either because there were more juvenile or active voles in summer, or because other behavioural changes made voles less able to escape a strike.

Changes in prey behaviour could explain why strikes from either method were more successful in summer. Strike rate, however, should also have been faster in summer because the increasing vole numbers should have resulted in more strike opportunities. However, the strike rate during flight-hunting remained constant- probably, they suggested, because the growth of vegetation offset any increase in vole density. The summer decline in strike rate from perches might have been because taller vegetation hampered perched-hunting more than flight-hunting. These interpretations, if true, suggest that Kestrel breeding seasons are not timed directly to changes in vole abundance, but to changes in the vulnerability of voles to Kestrel predation. The slight decline in yield during August and September coincided with the moult in adults, so the loss of flight feathers may have adversely affected strike success.

To summarise, Kestrels have two main hunting methods: flight-hunting, which is primarily a mammal hunting technique, requiring considerable energy but having high capture rates; and perched-hunting, which is used for a variety of prey and is less energy demanding but has lower capture rates.

CHOICE OF HUNTING METHOD

In general, Kestrels flight-hunt if they are looking for small mammals and if the wind speed is appropriate. However, there is a marked change in method, from mainly perched-hunting in winter to mainly flight-hunting in summer, that is independent of seasonal changes in wind speed or prey type. I first noticed this in Eskdalemuir (Fig. 21); it was also apparent in the English study areas and has been found independently by several other people working on Kestrels (Shrubb 1982, Pettifor 1983a, Masman *et al* 1986). The summer increase in flight-hunting is more obvious in males than females, and reaches a peak when they are feeding young in June and July. The frequency declines after the young become independent, and the time spent flight-hunting in winter is only one third of that in summer (Masman *et al* 1986).

The increase in flight-hunting leads to a corresponding decline in the frequency of perched-hunting, which probably reflects to the relative costs and capture rates of the two methods. Kestrels need catch only enough food for their own maintenance in winter, and can therefore afford relatively low capture rates. Hunting from perches is a good way to meet the daily food requirements in winter because it entails little effort. Some flight-hunting is necessary if the yield from perched-hunting is too low, but this is usually done when the wind conditions make hovering most efficient. In summer, males are under quite different constraints because they have to catch not only enough food for themselves, but also for their partners and offspring. Flight-hunting is then necessary because it alone can provide food quickly enough to meet the daily requirements of the whole Kestrel family.

These ideas have been confirmed recently by the more detailed investigations

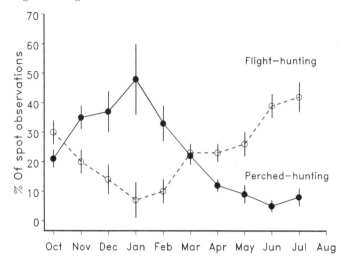

Fig. 21. Seasonal changes in the hunting method of Kestrels in the Eskdalemuir grassland study area (from Village 1983a). Vertical bars are ±2 SE. The main method of hunting changed from perching in winter to flying in summer.

of the Groningen Raptor Group, who have also concluded that the behaviour of Kestrels is consistent with the notion that they try to minimise energy expenditure in winter, but maximise energy gain, within certain limits, in summer. The situation is probably more complicated than this, and I return to it in a more detailed look at energy budgets in the next chapter.

CHOOSING WHEN AND WHERE TO HUNT

To some exent, the choice of where to hunt is linked with the hunting method. Perched-hunting Kestrels are limited to places where there are suitable perches, while flight-hunting Kestrels prefer updrafts on the windward sides of slopes and obstacles. The search for suitable updrafts sometimes takes Kestrels outside their normal home range if the wind is blowing from an unusual direction and their are no windward slopes within the usual range (Village 1980). Work in Holland has also suggested that the choice of where to hunt is strongly influenced by previous experience. One Kestrel used the same hunting locations, at about the same time of day, over several successive days, even catching prey at about the same time and place each day (Rijnsdorp *et al* 1981). I found similar results when radio-tracking Kestrels in farmland, where some birds moved around their range in somewhat stereotyped patterns, using a fairly fixed circuit several times during the day. The behaviour is particularly noticeable in winter, when a Kestrel will rely heavily on a series of selected perches and rotate from one to another.

Once Kestrels learn that food can be caught more readily at a particular time of day, they may quickly alter their behaviour to take advantage of temporary situation. Rijnsdorp *et al* (1981) found that a wild Kestrel, which they fed at the same time and place each day, soon began flying to the feeding site at about the right time. Obviously this was a slightly artificial experiment, but it does indicate the way in which Kestrels can adjust their hunting patterns to increase their efficiency.

Even more remarkable behaviour was noted by the same group in an area where Kestrels fed mainly on Common Voles. The voles lived in burrows, but came to the surface to feed in distinct two-hourly cycles at certain times of year. Kestrels, and other vole-eating raptors, were found to flight-hunt mainly during such periods, when most of the voles were on the surface and vulnerable to predation (Fig. 22). Whether this was a direct response to the increased hunting yield, or a learnt rhythm that allowed Kestrels to anticipate vole availability, was not clear. The Kestrels probably adjusted their behaviour by trial and error initially, but the ability to learn quickly would soon train them to hunt at the appropriate times. Adjustment of the daily behaviour pattern is vital for Kestrels, because the time and place at which prey are available varies from season to season. Common Voles, for example, show stronger daily cycles of activity in winter than in summer (Daan & Slopsema 1978), and the changes in diet over the year suggest that Kestrels must monitor the availability of different prey items.

EATING PREY

Having caught prey, a Kestrel may eat it immediately or store it for consumption over the next day or so. Small items, such as invertebrates, are

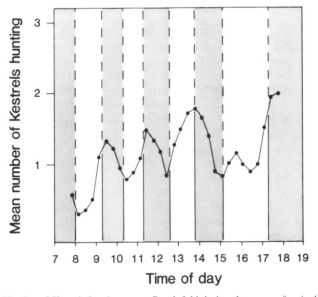

Fig. 22. Number of Kestrels hunting over a Dutch field during the course of a single day in February 1982, in relation to the surface activity of voles. Shaded areas show the times when voles were active on the surface; the line is based on a three-point running mean of the number of Kestrels counted in 20 minute periods. Re-drawn from Raptor Group RUG/RIJP (1982).

usually eaten at once while the bird is on the ground, though Kestrels will sometimes fly up with prey in one foot and nibble at it by bringing the foot forward and bending the head downwards. Mammals and birds require more work, and may be carried to a small hillock, fence-post or horizontal branch before being eaten. Voles are held with the feet and plucked at with the beak, tearing them into bite-sized pieces. Small birds are treated in a similar fashion, though they are usually plucked of their feathers first.

Kestrels eat most parts of voles, except for the grass-filled stomachs and some fur. My impression is that well-fed Kestrels waste more of the kill than do hungry ones. In grassland, where vole numbers were high, I often found piles of fur and gut remains at vole kills around nests. One female that was particularly well supplied by her mate ate only the bodies of voles and left the skulls intact. In farmland, where voles were less abundant, Kestrels sometimes ate the whole carcass, and I rarely found any vole remains, even when I checked places where Kestrels were seen eating.

Not surprisingly, the time taken to eat a kill depends on its size. It takes a Kestrel about 2 minutes to eat a 10 g shrew, but nearly 10 minutes to eat large voles of 30–40 g (Masman *et al* 1986). It takes longer to eat birds than mammals of the same size because of the time spent plucking feathers and this, combined with the larger sizes of many bird kills, means that the handling time can often be half an hour or more. I once watched a female Kestrel feed at a Woodpigeon carcass for 45 minutes with hardly a pause, and she still hadn't finished it.

CHOOSING WHEN TO EAT: CACHEING BEHAVIOUR

It might seem reasonable to suppose that Kestrels are motivated to hunt by hunger, that they eat the prey they catch to relieve that hunger, and then wait until they are hungry before hunting again. While this may be true to some extent, research over the last few years has shown that feeding behaviour is much more complicated, because Kestrels choose not only where and when to hunt, but also when to eat the food they catch. Although the need to obtain food must ultimately influence the foraging behaviour of Kestrels, the decisions of when to hunt and when to eat are to some extent independent.

Many raptors will return to large kills that they are unable to move or to eat in one attempt. Cacheing, however, is the deliberate hiding or storing of prey, which is eaten later, and seems to be frequent among falcons. It has been known for some time that European Kestrels cache food (Clegg 1971), but few quantative data were available until the study by the Raptor Group at Groningen. I rarely recorded cacheing in the grassland study area, but this was because I spent little time watching Kestrels continuously. In farmland, where I radio-tracked individuals for hours at a time, it soon became clear that Kestrels cached food on most days.

Kestrels usually store larger items, such as voles or birds, the smallest cached items being about 15 g (Rudolf 1982, Masman *et al* 1986). Kestrels that are about to cache a kill often spend several minutes looking for a suitable site, bobbing their heads up and down or making short flights over the ground. Cache sites are normally some feature on the ground that stands out from the background: a tussock of grass, clod of earth or the base of a fence post are favourite places, though sites off the ground are sometimes used (Table 7). Caches are rarely buried or covered, but are either tucked into a crevice or simply laid on top of a clod or tussock. Although this may leave them vulnerable to theft by scavengers, surprisingly few seem to be stolen, and most are successfully retrieved. This usually takes place later on the same day or during the following day. Kestrels retrieving caches may fly go directly to the site, or alight nearby and start looking around, much as they do when hiding food. This search can take several minutes and is not always successful, so leaving caches in a visible spot may help Kestrels with poor memories!

The function of cacheing

Kestrels probably cache for several reasons, all of which separate food capture from ingestion. One obvious function of cacheing is to store prey that has been caught more frequently than is needed to satisfy hunger. I have seen Kestrels cache several times under these circumstances, usually when they are hunting in fields that have just been disturbed by ploughing or harvesting. For example, in October 1984 I watched a juvenile female take a young rat from a field of sugarbeet that had been harvested the previous day. Harvesting had evidently exposed a litter of barely-weaned rats that were now wandering about on the surface. The Kestrel cached the first rat and returned to the same hunting perch; she took another young rat from the same spot four minutes later, which she cached some 50 m from the first. This process was repeated until she had taken six rats in less than ten minutes and had cached them all at different sites within 300 m of the hunting perch.

Such rapid killing is not always in response to human activity: I saw another female Kestrel take and cache five young rats from the edge of a field, apparently as her naive victims explored their surroundings for the first time. In this instance, and others, the first kill made was cached and a later one eaten, so the use of caches was not simply because the Kestrels were satiated. I do not know if all these multiple caches were retrieved successfully. Five young rats is several day's supply of food for a Kestrel in winter, and it is unlikely that they would all remain undetected by scavengers for that long, even if the Kestrel could remember so many different cache sites.

Cacheing may also allow Kestrels to continue hunting during other, less dramatic, times of increased food availability. These may be periods of good weather, or temporary peaks of prey activity such as those mentioned earlier for Common Voles. Disposing of a prey item quickly might be important if it would take a long time to eat and if the periods of increased prey availability were relatively short. As most prey can be eaten within a few minutes, it seems unlikely that Kestrels often cache solely in order to resume hunting without delay.

Another reason for cacheing prey is to ensure that food is available for an evening meal. This is most obvious in winter, when prey is usually cached in the morning or early afternoon and retrieved just before dusk (Collopy 1977, Rijnsdorp *et al* 1981). This creates a peak in food intake at the end of the day which is not reliant on any increase in hunting success at that time. Rijnsdorp *et al* (1981) suggested that saving food until evening may reduce the energy

Kestrels expend during flight-hunting because there is less body weight to carry during the day. They calculated a saving of some 7% of the daily energy expenditure if Kestrels postponed a 22 g vole meal until evening. More recent data have shown that neither sex has a evening feeding peak in summer (Masman *et al* 1986), and this argues against the foregoing idea, which suggests that males should still show the evening peak because they flight-hunt even more in summer than in winter. Another possible reason for the evening feeding peak in winter is that it enables Kestrels to start the long winter nights with a full stomach. This has been shown to be vital in small birds, and may be important even for those as large as Kestrels.

As well as concentrating feeding at particular times, cacheing is also used to spread meals more evenly, either over a single day, or from one day to the next. Female Kestrels that are being fed by their mates still cache some prey, which is then used to even out any fluctuations in prey delivery by the male (Rijnsdorp *et al* 1981). In a similar way, some caches left overnight in winter can be an important sources of food if weather, or other conditions, make hunting less successful on following days (Masman *et al* 1986).

Cacheing, then, is an important behaviour that allows Kestrels some choice in when they will eat the prey they catch. This may even-out feeding when hunting success is erratic, or concentrate feeding at times when extra food is needed. For predators such as Kestrels, where hunting success is often governed by chance, some method of bridging sudden hard times or profiting from a glut will clearly enhance their chance of survival.

SUMMARY

Kestrels hunt from perches or on the wing by hovering and soaring. Perched-hunting is used to catch most sorts of prey, but hovering is used mainly to catch small mammals. Perched-hunting requires little energy expenditure by Kestrels, but has a low yield, whereas hovering has a high yield but is energy-expensive, particularly at low wind speeds. Kestrels hunt mainly from perches in winter, when they have low food demands, but by flight-hunting in summer, when breeding males have to capture large amounts of food for their young. The hunting behaviour of Kestrels is tuned to the availability of their prey, and individuals can time hunting bouts to cycles of vole availability during the day. Kestrels often delay eating vertebrate prey items, which are instead stored for later retrieval. This is sometimes in response to a sudden flush of food that cannot be eaten in one meal, but it is mainly used to buffer Kestrels against temporary food shortages. Food intake can thus be evened out, despite irregular hunting success caused by bad weather or low prey availability.

CHAPTER 5

Food intake, energetics and body weight

As well as a knowledge of what Kestrels eat, it is also of interest to know how much they eat, and how the energy obtained from food is used. Any effect of food supply on breeding performance must be caused by variations in the daily food intake of individuals. Accomplished hunters that catch more prey ought to breed earlier, and rear more young, than poorer hunters. This sounds obvious enough, but it is not easily demonstrated in wild birds and, until recently, most of what was known about daily food consumption in Kestrels came from observations at a few nests (Tinbergen 1940, Cavé 1968), or from falconers. Thanks to recent work in Holland, however, we now have a much clearer idea of how much prey wild Kestrels require, and how the energy it yields is partitioned between various activities. A first step in drawing up such 'energy budgets' is to find out how much food is eaten and how much energy this gives to the Kestrel.

FOOD AND ENERGY CONSUMPTION

Kestrels that are kept in captivity at room temperature, and which spend most of the time perching, eat either about 36 g of day-old chick or about

19 g of laboratory mouse per day (Kirkwood 1981a). The difference in the quantity of chicks and mice required reflects variations in their fat content and roughage, and each amount is equivalent to an energy intake of about 150–170 KJ/day (1 KJ = 0.24 Kilocalories). These values are averages of several Kestrels, obtained by precise weighing of total food intake and then deducting energy left over in pellets and excreta. The energy content of the different foods was found by burning samples in a bomb calorimeter and measuring the heat given off. The actual food requirement of any particular bird will vary around these figures, depending largely on size, because large birds eat more than small ones.

The above estimates do not tell us much about wild Kestrels, which expend more energy in flying and hunting than captive ones, and will therefore require more food. James Kirkwood partly overcame this problem by using tame Kestrels that were fed by hand but allowed to roam free during the day (Kirkwood 1980a). The birds had never hunted for themselves, and it was apparent from their pellets that they ate little but the controlled diet. The food consumption of these free-living Kestrels was about 60 g of chick a day, equivalent to 270 KJ, or 1.7 times the consumption of caged, inactive birds. The difference presumably reflected the greater activity of the free-ranging birds, though this activity was probably less than most wild Kestrels because the tame birds were not hunting.

The Raptor Group at Groningen in Holland have obtained more direct estimates of the energy intake of wild Kestrels during the year. Their estimates of daily food consumption are the most accurate yet available for any wild raptor. They followed birds for whole days and recorded their activity and all the kills they made (Masman *et al* 1986). To measure daily energy intake, they recorded how long it took Kestrels to eat each kill. This meal duration was then compared with that for eating prey of known weight, obtained by watching Kestrels retrieve and eat caches that the observers had previously found, weighed and replaced. The energy content of voles was found by bomb calorimetery of samples collected throughout the year.

Using such techniques, they found that in winter the mean energy intake was about 270 KJ/day for either sex (Fig. 23), equivalent to roughly four voles each. In summer, this rose to over 400 KJ/day in males and 317 KJ/day in females, equivalent to eight and six voles respectively. Females ate most food during egg-laying and incubation, when they assimilated about 35% more energy per day than in winter. Their intake declined suddenly when the young hatched, because they gave most of the food delivered by the male to the young, and they made good the loss by using their own body reserves accumulated during the preceding weeks.

The high food consumption of males in summer was while they were intensively flight-hunting (ie in the first 10 days after hatch), and reflects the high energy costs of flight. Under most circumstances, energy consumption increased linearly with the amount of flight-hunting during the day. However, this was only true of up to about 4–5 hours of flight-hunting a day. Above this level, there was no further increase in food consumption, presumably because males were unable to assimilate energy fast enough to support higher rates of activity. Males flight-hunting for five hours a day had to eat about eight voles,

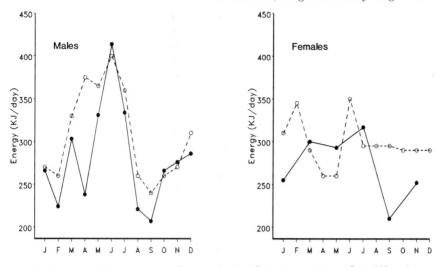

Fig. 23. Seasonal changes in the daily energy intake (●) and expenditure (○) of Kestrels in the Lauwersmeer, Holland. Re-drawn from data in Masman et al (1988a).

equivalent to almost half their body weight. It is unlikely that Kestrels could absorb more food than that in a day, so they must have used energy reserves if they flight-hunted for more than 4–5 hours, which may explain the decline in male body weight during the nestling stage (see below).

ENERGY EXPENDITURE

The second step in building up an energy budget is to estimate energy expenditure. This could be done simply by using the figures for energy intake already given, and assuming there was always an equilibrium between intake and expenditure. However, this is not always so, especially if individuals are changing weight, and a better way of calculating energy expenditure is to sum the energy costs of each of the day's activities. This latter method is also useful because it shows how the available energy is used by the birds. By matching independent measures of energy intake and expenditure, it should be possible to predict when weight is likely to be gained or lost and to compare this with seasonal changes in weight observed in wild birds. One drawback of the method is that it requires a detailed knowledge of both the time spent on various activities (often called a 'time budget') and their energy costs.

I used time budgets in Scotland to obtain approximate figures for the daily energy expenditure of Kestrels through the year (Village 1980). The time budgets were calculated from spot observations (that is recording the activity of Kestrels when they were first seen), and the energy costs of each activity were taken from published estimates based on laboratory studies of other non-passerine birds. This was a very rough-and-ready approach because spot observations tended to overestimate flying time, and the published estimates of the energy costs of flying varied widely between species. Nonetheless, my results suggested an approximate doubling of energy expenditure from winter to summer, at least in males, but I had no way of knowing how accurate the published energy estimates were.

The Dutch Raptor Group has also used time budgets to calculate energy expenditure, but with a much more detailed analysis of the duration of activities and their energy costs. One major hurdle was an accurate assessment of the cost of flight. Their rather novel approach was to use captive Kestrels that were trained to fly from one person to another along the corridors of the university zoology department (Masman & Klaassen 1987). By rewarding the birds each time they made the trip, they were able to induce them to fly up to 20 km a day. The Kestrels were given just enough food to keep their body weight constant, so it was possible to calculate from how much they ate the energy consumed by birds at different frequencies of daily flying. The costs of other behaviours, and metabolic activity, were also measured in the laboratory, and a detailed picture of seasonal variations in energy expenditure was produced by applying these estimates to the activity budgets of wild Kestrels.

To check these results, the Dutch Group also estimated energy consumption using the doubly-labelled water technique. Wild birds were trapped, injected with trace amounts of heavy water and then released. Heavy water $(D_2^{18}O)$ has the same chemical properties as ordinary water, but the atoms of hydrogen and oxygen are unusual isotopes that can be recognised by the minute traces of radiation that they emit. The injected isotopes soon mix evenly with the body fluids, and a small sample of blood taken prior to release will give the initial concentration of isotopes. A few days later the same bird is recaptured and the concentrations of isotopes are measured in a second blood sample. The change in concentration of isotopes between the first and second captures is proportional to the metabolic activity, and hence total energy consumption, during the intervening period. This accurate technique could only be applied to a few individuals, but comparison with the results from time budgets showed that the latter gave good estimates of overall energy expenditure (Masman *et al* 1988a).

The energy expenditure of Kestrels as estimated from time budgets was also in fairly good agreement with that for energy intake estimated from prey capture rates (Fig. 23). The main disparities were during egg-laying and incubation, when males were difficult to see when they were eating, and in September, when insect prey (which was not quantified) may have added significantly to the overall energy intake. Unfortunately, the estimates of energy intake and expenditure were not sufficiently accurate to permit useful investigation of any disparities between the two in given individuals. Even so, the two values are probably very similar in most individuals, and gross disparities could only last for a short time; birds would soon die if they had insufficient food, or would cut their intake if they became overweight. Some idea of the balance of intake and expenditure is possible, however, by examining seasonal changes in body weight.

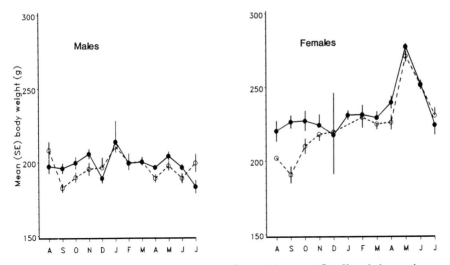

Fig. 24. Mean (SE) body weight of adult (●) and first-year (○) Kestrels by month. Combined data for Eskdalemuir grassland (1976–79) and farmland in England (1981– 87). First-year birds were generally lighter than adults, especially in early autumn. Females were heavier than males, especially during the breeding season.

SEASONAL CHANGES IN BODY WEIGHT

Individual Kestrels can fluctuate in weight considerably over a few weeks or months. These changes result from the accumulation or loss of body reserves (mainly fat and some protein), and reflect the overall energy balance. In general, birds will gain weight when intake exceeds expenditure and lose weight when the reverse is true. In what follows I have used changes in the mean weight of Kestrels trapped in my study areas to chart the seasonal trends, assuming that these reflect the variation seen within any particular individual. Although this is not always true, the patterns held good in most ringed birds that were caught more than once in the same year. Part of the variation in weight is due to size, so the sexes had to be treated separately. Within the sexes, the variation in weight due to size was relatively small, and correcting weight for wing length made little difference to the results.

Variation in mean weights during the year

In both sexes, the mean weight of trapped birds increased during autumn and early winter, the average gain from September to January being about 20–25 g (Fig. 24). The increase in mean weight was most marked in juveniles, partly because many of the light-weight individuals present in early autumn probably died, so only the heavier ones would survive to be caught later in the winter. This was not the only explanation, however, because juveniles that were caught twice in their first winter were invariably heavier on the second occassion than on the first. Small-mammal numbers reach their peak in late autumn, and the good food supply seemed to enable Kestrels to build up body reserves with which to face the harsher conditions of late winter. Adults that had bred successfully the previous summer apparently had few reserves left by early autumn, and juveniles seemed to lose reserves rapidly during their first few weeks of independent life. Maintaining large reserves would be an unnecessary burden in autumn, when days are still long and the weather good, but may be important in winter, when rain or snow might prevent hunting for days at a time.

Changes in weight after January differed between the sexes. The weight of males peaked in January, and gradually declined until July. The decrease seemed to be in two stages: one during late winter, which was most evident in yearling males, the other in breeding males during the nestling stage in June and July. In females, by contrast, there was little or no late-winter decline in weight, but a sharp increase in May. This increase was associated with egg-laying (see below), and started earlier in adult than yearling females.

The disparity between the weights of adults and first-year birds was less in spring than in autumn. Most juveniles died before the end of December (Chapter 19), and only the more proficient hunters were likely to outlive the winter. Even so, on average, first-year birds remained lighter than adults in most months from January to July, suggesting that many were still inferior hunters. The age-related difference in weight was less marked in females because many of the yearlings were mated with adult males, and their food intake was related more to their partner's hunting ability than to their own.

Body weights during the breeding cycle

In breeding birds, the normal equilibrium between energy intake and expenditure is disrupted by the differing roles of the sexes. Males expend energy capturing food they do not eat, and females eat food that they do not catch. As a result, females increase in weight during courtship, maintain most of the increase through egg laying and incubation, and only decline in weight when the young have hatched (Table 8). Males, on the other hand, show no increase during courtship and incubation, but a slight decrease during the nestling stage.

A more detailed description of these weight changes is given in the relevant chapters on the breeding cycle; and the relationship of female body weight to breeding performance is dealt with in Chapter 15. Here, it is sufficient to note that the changes in weight during breeding arise from changes in the energy budgets of the sexes, and that successful breeding requires females to increase their energy intake at the expense of males, who must increase their energy expenditure. This is true of most raptors, where there is a division of labour during the breeding season, and similar patterns of weight change have been reported in several other species, including Sparrowhawks (Newton *et al* 1983b).

SEASONAL VARIATIONS IN THE ENERGY BUDGET

The seasonal changes in energy budgets and body weights could have been

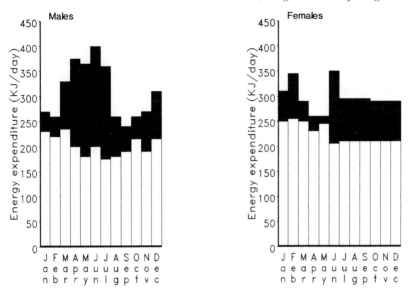

Fig. 25. Allocation of energy expenditure in male and female Kestrels during the year in Holland. Bars show the proportion of energy used in flight activity (shaded) versus tissue growth and metabolism (unshaded). Both sexes had a similar annual energy expenditure, but males used a higher proportion for flight-hunting, especially during the breeding season. Re-drawn from Masman et al (1988a).

predicted from the way in which Kestrels alter their hunting behaviour from winter to summer and from the differing roles of the sexes during breeding. The low energy expenditure in winter arose because both sexes hunted mainly from perches, rather than on the wing. Females in winter had a slightly higher energy expenditure than males because they were larger, but both sexes expended about 25% of their energy on daylight activities such as flying or perched-hunting (Fig. 25). In autumn, reduced activity, coupled with reasonably high hunting yields, allowed birds to increase energy intake above expenditure and thus to gain weight.

The high energy expenditure of males during summer was entirely due to the increase in flight-hunting during the breeding season, which required almost half the daily energy intake (Fig. 25). Females, on the other hand, had a peak of energy requirements during the start of the breeding cycle, when they were accumulating reserves prior to egg-laying, but a much lower expenditure than males during the incubation and early nestling stages, when they were relatively inactive. One surprising result of this was that breeding females had a similar annual energy expenditure to their mates, despite their larger size. During the year, females used a higher proportion of their energy on metabolism and tissue growth, and less on activity, than did males.

The constraints on food intake which operate at different times of year may well determine which birds survive in winter, and which pairs breed successfully in summer. In summer, the amount of food that males supply to their female or young is determined both by the hunting yield (ie the amount of prey caught per unit time), and the time spent hunting. An increase in hunting time can make up for low hunting yield, but only up to a point. Kestrels seem unable to assimilate more than about 400–500 KJ per day, probably because of the sheer bulk of food this represents, but the maximum intake will only enable about 4–5 hours to be spent flying. Beyond this, the energy needs must be met from stored reserves, which cannot make up the deficit for more than a few days. The high energy costs of flight thus seem to explain why Kestrels do not spend all day hunting, even if prey is scarce and they breed unsuccessfully due to lack of food (Masman *et al* 1986). If males are restricted to 4–5 hours of flight-hunting per day, the number of captures per hour of hunting becomes crucial, and hunting ability vital in achieving breeding success. This is another case where putting in long hours of overtime will not make up for inefficient use of working hours!

In winter, less time is spent flight-hunting than in summer and overall energy consumption is low. Although energy considerations still seem to influence hunting behaviour, it is not obvious why Kestrels spend so little time flight-hunting in winter. Hunting on the wing would supply a winter day's food in 1–2 hours, allowing the rest of the time to be spent at roost, sheltered from inclement weather and hidden from predators. However, Kestrels in winter spend most of their time in the open, hunting from perches, which is a much slower way of catching food than flight-hunting. Clearly, factors other than getting food as quickly as possible must influence behaviour in winter. One of these may be the need to stay in the open to advertise territory-ownership and to watch for intruders. These can easily be combined with perched-hunting, making it unnecessary to flight-hunt unless food is really scarce.

The choice of hunting method in winter may also be related to the risks inherent in each method. The consequences of failing to catch food when flight-hunting may be more serious than when perched-hunting, particularly for juvenile birds whose reserves are already low. A study of the hunting behaviour of juveniles in their first winter may be of relevance here, because they are poor hunters and will experience daily food-shortages more often than adults. Juveniles flight-hunt more than do adults, at least in autumn, probably because their success rate is too low for them to rely entirely on perched-hunting. The high mortality of juveniles from starvation at this time suggests that even using flight-hunting does not guarantee sufficient food for survival.

SUMMARY

The daily energy expenditure of free-living Kestrels varies from just under 300 KJ in winter to nearly 400 KJ for breeding males feeding nestlings. At most times of year, energy intake matches expenditure, and rises from the equivalent of about four voles per day in winter to about eight per day in summer. Males hunting for their mates, or broods, expend large amounts of energy, and the total time they are able to flight-hunt seems to be limited to about five hours by a ceiling on the amount of food they can assimilate in a day. Changes in the energy intake/expenditure balance are reflected in seasonal changes in body weight. Normally, both sexes become heavier during winter, presumably because they then need more body reserves, and because the low energy costs of perched-hunting make it easier to gain weight. Females show a marked increase in weight that coincides with reduced energy expenditure and increased food intake during courtship-feeding by the male. Differences in weight between adults and first-year birds are consistent with the idea that the latter have greater difficulty in catching food, and therefore lower body reserves, than adults.

CHAPTER 6

Moult

As other birds, Kestrels spend a considerable part of each day caring for their feathers. They waterproof them with a secretion from the preen gland, comb them into position and generally ensure that each feather is in the best possible condition. Such time is well spent, especially in a bird whose hunting technique relies heavily on feathers for uplift and accurate steering during hovering. Despite all this attention, feathers eventually become worn and need to be replaced if they are to function efficiently. Kestrels moult all their feathers once a year, replacing those in different parts of the body in a fairly fixed sequence. They cannot afford to lose the ability to fly, so moult is spread over several months to minimise the number of feathers missing at any one time.

A Kestrel's feathers weigh about 20–25 g (Masman 1986), or about 10% of the body weight. They are composed mainly of proteins called keratins, made from amino acids extracted from the bird's food. Although the amount of new feather material to be provided seems relatively trivial, especially for a bird that has a high-protein diet, moulting birds need to produce extra blood-vessels in order to grow the new feathers. In addition, loss of the old feathers reduces insulation, and results in an increased heat loss from the body.

The net result is a considerable extra energy burden during moult, which is no doubt why it takes place at the time of year when food is most plentiful.

Moult in adult Kestrels lasts from May to October, and overlaps with the latter half of the breeding season. First-year birds undergo a gradual moult of their body feathers, which starts after they fledge and continues until the following summer. This moult does not include the primary and tail feathers, which are shed at the same time as in adults.

I measured the progress of moult in Kestrels by recording the stage of growth of each primary and tail feather in the birds I trapped. The standard way of naming feathers is to number the primary and tail feathers from the innermost (1) outwards, and the secondaries from the outermost (1) inwards. I scored primary and tail feather growth from 0 to 5, using fixed criteria that related to the stage of development, so that old feathers counted as zero and fully-grown, new feathers as five (Newton & Marquiss 1982b). The sum of the individual feathers gave a maximum score of 50 for each wing when all 10 primaries were full-grown, and 30 for each half of the tail. Moult was usually symmetrical in the wings and tail, so the total moult score was double that for each side. Other feather tracts are moulted at a fairly fixed time relative to these two groups of feathers, so the primary and tail moult scores were a reasonable estimate of the overall progress of moult. I recorded the state of the body feather moult in juvenile birds by scoring the head, back, rump and upper tail-coverts from 0 (no new feathers) to 5 (all new feathers). This was easier to judge in males than females because the new plumage was quite distinct from the old in all these parts of the body.

THE POST-FLEDGING MOULT

The progress of the body-feather moult in juveniles was highly variable, some birds changing nearly all their feathers before they were a year old,

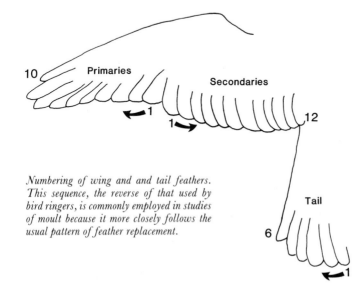

Numbering of wing and and tail feathers. This sequence, the reverse of that used by bird ringers, is commonly employed in studies of moult because it more closely follows the usual pattern of feather replacement.

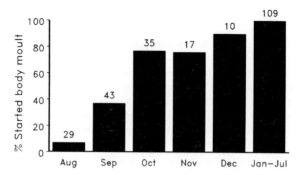

Fig. 26. Start of body-feather moult in first-year Kestrels. Bars show the proportion of trapped birds that had replaced at least one feather on the head, back, rump or upper tail-coverts. Sample sizes are shown above each bar.

whereas others replaced very few. The proportion of trapped juveniles that had started moult increased gradually during the winter, and all those examined after December had at least one new feather somewhere on the body (Fig. 26). There seemed to be no clear sequence to this moult, and new feathers were scattered across the back, rump and tail coverts. The head was often last to get new feathers, and they usually showed as a fringe at the back of the neck.

I was not sure if the new feathers produced before July were then replaced along with the remaining juvenile plumage during the main moult, or if they were retained until the following year. In males, the second feathers on the head were often tinged with brown (see Fig. 5), and these seemed to be retained until the third calender year. This suggests that at least some of the adult feathers grown in the first year may be retained, and that some could be almost two years old when finally shed.

THE SEQUENCE OF MOULT IN ADULTS

The annual moult in adults follows a more definite schedule than the partial juvenile moult, though there is still considerable variation between individuals. Although the various body-feather tracts are all in moult during the peak phase, the upper tail-coverts and rump usually start before the underside or wing coverts, which in turn precede the back and head. Similarly, the flight feathers start a week or more before the tail, though both finish at about the same time (Fig. 27).

The flight feathers are replaced in sequence, starting with the fourth primary and fifth secondary and moving inwards and outwards from these points. A typical order for the primaries would thus be 4–5–6–3–7–8–2–9–10–1, which is similar to that found in other falcons (see diagram). The order in the tail is more complicated as it starts with the innermost (1), jumps to the outermost (6), returns to the second feather and thereafter proceeds outwards, giving a typical sequence of 1–6–2–3–4–5. The inner tail feather is normally fully grown before 6 and 2 are shed almost simultaneously, and these in turn are usually well grown before the final three are replaced in rapid succession. The patterns in wings and tail can vary, particularly where moult proceeds in two directions in the same tract. In the primaries, for example, 7 may be lost before 3, 2 before 8 and 1 before 10.

Most of the birds I handled were in the early stages of moult, and few had more than two or three primaries growing at once. Individuals sometimes completed growth in one feather before starting the next, and gaps in the wing were often quite small. Later in the season, during August and September, adjacent feathers may be lost more quickly, and gaps become most evident. Gaps are particularly noticeable in the tail, where the last three feathers often grow at the same time. During the height of moult, adults spend much of the day sitting inactively (Masman *et al* 1988b). Flight-hunting is kept to a minimum, possibly because it is inefficient to hover when there are sizable gaps in the flight or tail feathers. The sequence of wing moult in Kestrels is different from Sparrowhawks, which tend to moult more conventionally from the inner primaries outwards (Newton & Marquiss 1982b). The pattern in Kestrels may reduce the size of gaps in the wing by having two moult waves

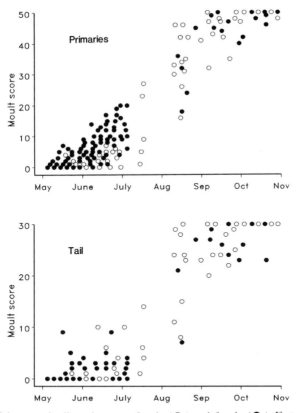

Fig. 27. Primary and tail moult scores of male (○) and female (●) Kestrels. Moult started sooner in the wings than in the tail, and sooner in females than in males.

instead of one, but its universality among falcons suggests it is not solely an adaptation of Kestrels to the demands of hovering flight.

THE DURATION OF MOULT

I could not measure the duration of moult in individual Kestrels, but an average value could be estimated from the proportion of trapped birds that were moulting in each 10-day period through the season (Fig. 28). The dates on which approximately half the sample had started growing some feathers or finished moult gave durations of 136 days for females and 122 days for males. These figures agreed with the regressions of primary moult scores on date (Fig. 27), and were similar to estimates of 130 days for the equivalent moult of four captive Kestrels in Holland (Masman 1986). The total moulting period is longer than the primary or tail moult scores suggest, because body feathers are replaced after the primaries have finished, and the captive Kestrels in Holland took 180 days for the whole moult.

My results showed that males started later than females, but finished at about the same time, so their rate of moult was faster. I could not tell if those that began early also finished early, and there may have been considerable variation in the rate of moult between individuals of the same sex. A few breeding birds seemed to stop moulting when they had young in the nest: about 20% of 74 full-grown Kestrels examined during the nestling stage had some new primary feathers (usually one), but showed no active moult in wings or tail. This phenomenon, known as *arrested moult*, is common in some other bird species, including Sparrowhawks (Newton & Marquiss 1982b), and may occur because a bird is short short of food at some time during moult. The proportion of Kestrels in arrested moult was significantly higher among males than females (Table 9), which may have been because males did most of the hunting for the brood and had fewer resources to spare for growing new feathers.

FACTORS AFFECTING THE START OF MOULT

In Sparrowhawks, the start of moult in females is related to when they lay and to their age. Moult usually begins just before the first egg is laid in first-year birds, and just after in adults (Newton & Marquiss 1982b). My Kestrel populations in Scotland and England had different mean laying dates, so I wondered if the start of moult varied accordingly, or if its timing was independent of breeding. For each population, I estimated the average start of the moulting period either from the starting dates of primary moult for individual birds, or from the date on which half the sample of trapped birds had begun to moult.

I calculated the date on which individuals began moult by using the rate of growth of primary feathers. This rate was calculated from five females that were caught twice during the growth of their first-moulted primary, and was about one moult-score point per five days, equivalent to a growth rate of 25

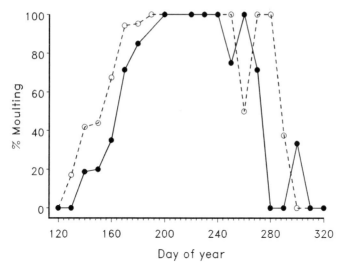

Fig. 28. Period of primary moult in male (●) and female (○) Kestrels. Each point is the proportion of birds caught during a 10-day period that were moulting.

days per feather. This technique (similar to that used in the Sparrowhawk study) could be used only for birds that had not fully replaced their first primary, because moult may have been arrested before subsequent feathers were shed. There were insufficient males to estimate their rate of feather growth, so I used the same figure for each sex. This probably made the starting dates of males slightly early because they seemed to moult faster than females, so the real differences between the sexes may have been even greater than those I had observed.

Start of moult in males and females

In both the Scottish and English study areas, females began moulting before males. This was true in first-year birds and adults, though the difference was significant only when the age groups were combined, because of the small sample of males (Table 10). In Scotland, females began moult about 20 days before males, but in England the average difference between the sexes was only 10 days. Similarly, the proportion of females caught during incubation that were in moult was almost twice as high as the proportion among males trapped over the same period (Table 11).

Later moulting by males also occurs in Sparrowhawks (Newton & Marquiss 1982b), and in both species it is presumably related to their role in providing food for the female or young during most of the breeding cycle. Males cannot afford to hamper their hunting efficiency by losing feathers when their mates are incubating. The energy expenditure of males is also at its highest during the incubation and nestling periods, and they may be unable to allocate much energy to feather synthesis until the female starts to help feed the young.

Females, on the other hand, are relatively inactive during incubation and take advantage of their good food supply by replacing some feathers before the nestling stage.

Start of moult in relation to laying date

In females, but not males, the start of moult was correlated with laying date (Fig. 29). The trend was present in adult and first-year females in both study areas, but the sample of adult females in Scotland was rather small. Moult usually began some days or even weeks after the first egg was laid, and most females replaced at least one feather during incubation. There was no way of estimating when moult began in those Kestrels that had not shed any feathers when I caught them, so any birds that laid early and moulted late were not likely to be included in Fig. 29. Allowing for these latter birds, it seemed that the correlation between the start of moult and laying date arose because few females started moulting before they laid eggs. Once laying had commenced, there was considerable variation in the interval before the first primary was shed.

Start of moult in relation to age

In both the Scottish and English study areas, first-year females began moult at about the same time of year as did adult females (Table 10). First-year birds laid later than adults, on average, so they must have started moult sooner in their breeding cycle. In both age groups, moult usually began after laying, but the lag was only 4–5 days in first-year birds, compared with 12–17 days in adults. This age-related difference could have arisen if moult was timed to

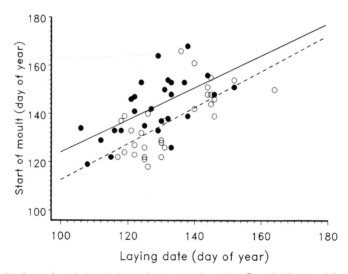

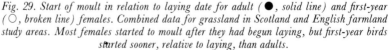

Fig. 29. Start of moult in relation to laying date for adult (●, solid line) and first-year (○, broken line) females. Combined data for grassland in Scotland and English farmland study areas. Most females started to moult after they had begun laying, but first-year birds started sooner, relative to laying, than adults.

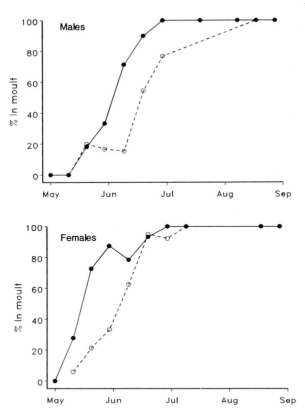

Fig. 30. Differences in the start of moult between the Eskdalemuir grassland (●) and English farmland (○) study areas. Each point is the proportion of birds trapped, during a 10-day period, that had started to replace their primary feathers.

calender date, rather than laying date, because the start of moult would then find adult females further into incubation than the late-laying juveniles. However, this was not the sole explanation, and the regressions in Fig. 29 suggest that first-year females moulted sooner than adults at any given laying date. In males, the samples were too small to draw any firm conclusions, but there was no indication that first-year birds moulted sooner than adults, either in terms of calender date or stage of the breeding cycle.

Start of moult in Scotland and England

The differences between my two study areas in the timing of moult seemed largely related to the earlier laying dates of the Scottish population. The regressions between the start of moult and laying date in females were not significantly different between the two areas, either in terms of intercept or slope. Females in Scotland started moult some 14 days sooner than those in England, but in males the difference was only 5 days and not statistically significant (Table 10). The difference was also apparent in the proportion of trapped birds that had started moult: in Scotland over 80% of females and 30% of males examined at the end of May had begun moult, compared with less than 20% of females and less than 15% of males in England (Fig. 30). The only suggestion that Scottish Kestrels moulted earlier, relative to laying date, than those in England was the higher proportion of females that had started moult when trapped in incubation (Table 11). However, the difference was slight, and statistically significant only in first-year females.

Taken together, the results suggested that, in females at least, moult is timed to start after laying. Most, but not all, females replaced several primaries while they were incubating or brooding, but some then suspended the completion of moult until after the young were fledged. Laying cannot be a necessary stimulus for moult, because non-breeding birds also moult, but it may hasten its start, and thus allow females to renew some feathers while they are relatively inactive and well fed. Males, on the other hand, are highly active during most of the breeding cycle, and may be unable to start moult until later in the season.

THE ENERGETICS OF MOULT

We now have a fairly accurate estimate of the energy requirements of moult thanks to recent work by the Groningen Raptor Group in Holland. They measured the oxygen consumption of captive Kestrels, and found a positive correlation between the Basal Metabolic Rate (BMR) and the intensity of moult (Masman 1986). From this relationship, they calculated that the energy needed to produce 1 g of feather was 103 KJ. This agreed fairly well with independent estimates based on the amount of extra food eaten by moulting Kestrels, which averaged about 125 KJ/g. The cost of producing feathers resulted in an increase in the BMR of about 30% when moult was at its most intense.

The increased energy demands apparently arose for several different reasons. Firstly, there was some increase in metabolic activity necessary to produce feather proteins, though this was only slight. Secondly, there was some tissue growth during moult, particularly around the feather follicles, and this would also have required more energy. But the most important reason for the greater energy demand during moult was the increase in the rate at which birds lost body heat. This was partly because insulation was reduced as feathers were shed, but there must have been other reasons because Kestrels began to lose more heat before moult started. The physiological changes associated with moult include increases in the number of blood vessels in the skin, the blood volume and body temperature, all of which may have added to the rate of heat loss from moulting birds.

The reduced insulation of Kestrels during moult means that they are vulnerable to changes in the ambient temperature, and cold weather will have a greater effect than usual in increasing the daily energy expenditure. It may thus be no coincidence that moult is at its height during the warmest months of the year. Kestrels in the wild seem to offset the extra energy costs during the peak moult period by reducing their flight activity to a minimum, and their overall energy expenditure is no higher than in mid winter (Masman *et al* 1988a). Kestrels may be able to reduce activity because vole numbers are approaching their annual peak, and the good supply of food means that the daily requirements can be caught without prolonged hovering. Although breeding birds that are feeding young may have already begun to moult, the main period of feather replacement is probably after the young become independent. The energy demands on breeding birds then fall suddenly, and they use the spare capacity to moult while the food supply is good, days are long and temperatures are high.

The Dutch workers used their detailed information on seasonal changes in the energy balance of free-living Kestrels to predict the consequences of shifting the period of moult to other times of year (Masman & Daan 1987). This showed clearly that moulting at any other time would increase the extra energy required for moult, and their Kestrel population moulted when it required least energy to do so.

SUMMARY

Kestrels replace all their feathers every year. Juveniles start replacing body feathers in their first winter, but the main flight and tail feathers are replaced when adults are moulting, from May to October. Primary and tail feathers are shed in a fairly fixed sequence, similar to that in other falcons. Moult is timed partly to calender date and partly to the start of laying. Breeding females usually begin to moult during incubation, when they have low energy expenditure, but they may stop producing new feathers if they help their mates to catch food for the chicks. Males moult later in the breeding cycle than females, when their energy demands are decreasing. The extra energy-costs of moult arise for several reasons, chief of which is the increased rate of heat loss from the body. By moulting at the warmest time of year, and when food is most plentiful, Kestrels are able to remain fairly inactive, and thus keep their energy expenditure to a minimum.

CHAPTER 7

Home range and territory

Many animals spend the whole of their lives within a comparatively small area. Even species that disperse widely when young often settle as they mature, and usually stay in the same restricted locality thereafter. Migratory animals are clearly an exception, but even they tend to spend the whole of one season in the same place, and often return to it in successive years. Breeding birds have restricted movements because they must remain near their nests but, even in winter, most individuals confine themselves to a particular area, rather than wandering at random over the countryside. Such an area is called a *home range*, a term first used by people studying small mammals to describe the ground covered by an animal during its day-to-day activities. An animal may exclude others (usually of the same species) from using part, or all, of its home range, and such defended areas are *territories*. The home range, then, can be larger than the territory, but not *vice versa*.

Appendix II describes in some detail the methods I used to mark Kestrels individually and measure the size of their home ranges. Information on the behaviour of individually marked birds is hard to come by, and there are few good estimates of the sizes of Kestrel ranges or territories. Consequently, most of what follows is based on my own work, either in Scotland, or in the two English study areas, though I have referred to other studies where appropriate.

FACTORS AFFECTING THE USE OF RANGES

Kestrels rarely use all parts of their home range with equal intensity. I have already mentioned the way in which they sometimes move within their winter range in a fairly fixed pattern from day to day or during a single day (Chapter 4). When radio-tracking, I found some individuals used the same places day after day, and only frequent checks would reveal them in other parts of their range. The range or territory can be seen as offering its occupant a variety of resources, such as hunting sites, roosts and, in summer, nest sites. The distribution of these resources will often determine how the range is used, though the exact location of territory boundaries may also depend on the behaviour of neighbouring Kestrels.

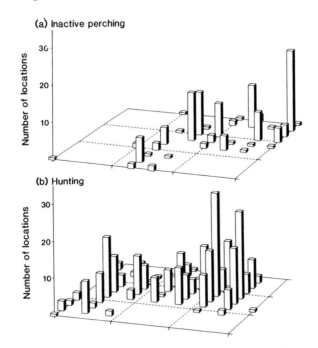

Fig. 31. *Locations of (a) inactive perching and (b) hunting, for a radio-tagged female Kestrel in mixed farmland, winter 1981/2. The height of the bars is proportional to the intensity of range use for each purpose. Some parts of the range were used for hunting but not for inactive perching.*

Kestrels spend a surprisingly large amount of time sitting, apparently doing nothing. They often have preferred perches for this, which are not necessarily where they do most of their hunting (Fig. 31). A pair I radio-tracked one winter in mixed farmland often met at a large ash tree, where they would sit together and preen. Other well-used sites are in good hunting areas, such as patches of rough grass or grazed pastures. The places where Kestrels flight-hunt may change on a daily basis, particularly when fluctuating wind conditions create updrafts in different places.

Position of the range relative to the nest

Although nest sites and roosts can be important, the home range is not necessarily centred around them. I have several times found radio-tagged birds roosting outside their usual daytime range, sometimes up to a kilometre away. Similarly, male Kestrels in the breeding season, seldom forage equally in all directions from the nest, which is sometimes at the edge of the range.

Kestrels take relatively large prey items compared to passerines, and therefore make fewer visits to the nest each day. Reducing the time taken to carry prey to the nest is probably unimportant to Kestrels, so they are not constrained to nest in the centre of their home range. The position of the nest in the range seems to depend partly on the relative locations of nest-sites and hunting areas, and partly on the location of other Kestrel pairs. This was most obvious in the Scottish grassland area, where males at isolated nests centred their range on the nest, whereas males of closely adjacent pairs reduced range overlap by hunting in opposite directions from their respective nests (Village 1980).

Territory boundaries

It is not known for certain if Kestrels use landmarks such as hedges or roads as territory or range boundaries. This is unlikely in summer, when ranges are large and overlap, but could happen in winter when territories are small and rigorously defended. One juvenile at Eskdalemuir had a small winter-territory centred along a line of electricity poles. She would move along these poles if approached, but always turned back at one particular pole at a bend in the line. Her neighbour did the same from the other direction, and it seemed they were using the pole as a boundary marker.

Particular features of the landscape might become almost permanent boundary markers if successive birds occupying the same area have similar-sized territories. However, incoming birds have to fit into the existing territorial system, so that any similarity with the boundaries of the previous occupant's range may reflect constraints imposed by neighbours, rather than the use of a prominent feature of the landscape as a marker. Kestrels can probably defend areas most effectively when they can easily detect intruders, so the edges of territories often seem to be features that limit visibility from favourite perches, such as woods or the crests of hills.

SEASONAL TRENDS IN RANGE BEHAVIOUR

Kestrel home ranges and territories are unlikely to remain static throughout the year. Changes are most obvious where migrants move in and out, but even in sedentary populations there has to be some adjustment in autumn to accommodate the year's crop of young. The seasonal variation in dispersion differed between grassland and farmland, so I shall describe the two areas separately.

Grassland territories in autumn and winter

At Eskdalemuir, there were major changes in the dispersion pattern of Kestrels in spring and autumn as the summer migrants arrived or left. After the breeding season, one or both members of the breeding pairs left the area, and new birds moved in to establish winter territories. I don't know exactly how this happened, because I did little fieldwork during the main settling period in August or September. By October, most pairs had already separated and there were few new birds arriving. Some pairs remained on their previous breeding range, but one partner (usually the female) left by December, when all territories where held by single birds. Although there was little overt territorial fighting, the absence of any significant overlap of ranges (Table 12) implied that birds held strongly defended territories.

As the winter progressed, the number of Kestrels declined, and any empty spaces were usually filled by neighbours expanding their territories. For example, two marked males, a juvenile (WP) and an adult (PP), disappeared from their territories in December 1977, and in both cases neighbouring males soon started using the vacated area (Fig. 32). I was able to document in detail seven such instances where all the birds involved were wing-tagged (Table 13). It was not always certain when the original bird left, but in several cases I was sure that the neighbours moved into the empty space within a day or

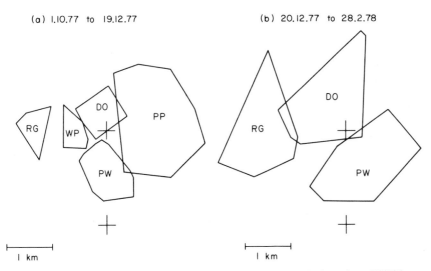

(a) 1.10.77 to 19.12.77   (b) 20.12.77 to 28.2.78

Fig. 32. Changes in Kestrel territories in part of the Esk Valley during winter 1977/78. Each range is identified by the wing-tag combination of the occupant. When PP and WP disappeared, neighbours expanded their territories to fill the vacated areas. From Village (1982b).

so. I never saw 'intruders' using the vacated territory while the owner was still present, so there was no evidence that occupants were forced out by neighbours. None of the seven birds was seen again, and two were found dead, one on its territory and the other 7 km away.

This process of declining numbers and territory expansion continued during the winter, so that territories gradually became larger as the season progressed. The mean size in autumn was 1–2 km², but this had virtually doubled by late winter (Table 12). The fact that increases in territory size coincided fairly closely with the loss of a neighbour suggested that, at this time of year, territory size was determined by the local Kestrel numbers, rather than *vice versa* (see Chapter 8).

Grassland ranges in spring

The gradual increase in territory size in winter was interrupted in March by the influx of birds from their wintering grounds. Some were returning to the area to breed again, and would often pair with their previous mate if he or she was present. Others were untagged and probably newcomers settling in the area for the first time. The new arrivals occupied places previously used by winter residents, which were reluctant to give up parts of their territory. There was an increase in territorial displays and fights in March and April (see Fig. 37), and newcomers seemed to establish themselves by sheer persistence, forcing a wedge between previously neighbouring winter residents. As more birds arrived and pairs formed, territories were gradually reduced until all the nest sites used that year were occupied. Kestrels in spring may still have had fairly large ranges, but they spent so much time near the nest that I rarely saw them in outlying, undefended areas until later in the breeding cycle.

I was able to follow the settling of pairs in part of the Esk Valley in some detail during 1977. The sequence is shown in Fig. 33, which only identifies territories by males. The boundaries were based on rather few observations in some cases, and probably show the centre of activity, rather than the whole range. The wintering birds were two solitary males, GO and PP, which were the first males to mate because their females arrived in early March. During the second and third weeks of March, two new pairs (males DG and OM) formed on territories between the original two pairs. On 25 March, another pair (male BR) forced their way between OM and DG, and the latter male and his female shifted their territory southwards to where they eventually nested. The final pair to settle (male GG) was first seen on 13 April, and established north of the BR pair. This male had an unusually large range (16 km²) and a small territory around his nest. He was frequently chased out of neighbouring territories, and may have had to go some distance to find somewhere to hunt unmolested by other Kestrels. Nonetheless, this pair reared young, unlike the BR pair which failed in late May and left the area. Their vacated territory was soon hunted in by males from neighbouring nests.

The shifts of territory boundaries in spring occurred rapidly and in a series of discrete steps, corresponding to the arrival of new birds. On a small scale it was not easy to relate the change in numbers and territory size to any obvious change in food supply. The influx of birds in March was before there was any noticeable increase in the numbers of voles, which did not start producing

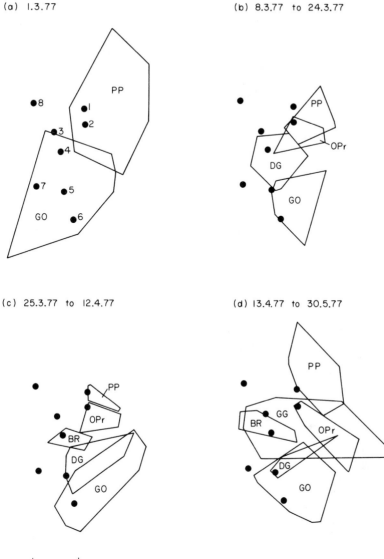

Fig. 33. Changes in Kestrel ranges in part of the Esk Valley from March to May 1977. For explanation, see page 102. Filled circles are nests used in 1977 by the following males: PP(1), OM(2), GG(3), BR(4), DG(5), OG(6) and other males not shown (7 and 8). From Village (1982b).

litters until April or May in that year. As in autumn, the most immediate influence on territory size was the number of birds in the area, the more birds the smaller their territories.

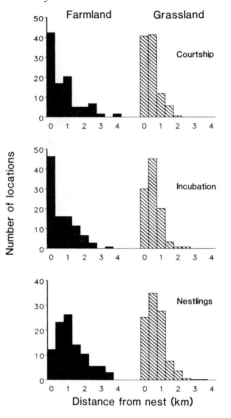

Fig. 34. *Frequency histograms of the distance from the nest at which males were radio-located during various stages of the breeding cycle in Eskdalemuir grassland (hatched) and farmland in England (shaded). In both areas, males stayed close to the nest during the pre-laying stage, but went further afield when feeding their young. Males in farmland generally spent less time near the nest than those in grassland.*

Grassland ranges in summer

During the nestling stage, the average range-size was about 3–6 km², which was slightly larger than the territories of the solitary winter residents. Unlike winter, however, ranges were occupied by pairs and only partly defended, with some pairs sharing hunting areas. This was less marked in early spring, because males mostly stayed near the nest. However, once females were incubating, males ranged further afield (Fig. 34), some hunting more than 4 km from their nest in the late nestling stage. This led to some areas being shared by several different males which were not necessarily from adjacent nests. Shared areas were usually on open hill ground, away from occupied nests, and were often used by males that bred in the valleys.

Although several birds used the same patch of hillside, they rarely did so together, and I probably would have assumed they were the same male had they not been wing-tagged. When two birds did meet, they might dive at one other briefly, but fights were less prolonged than near nests in spring and the protagonists usually separated quickly and continued hunting.

Not all the range was shared with other Kestrels in summer, and most pairs defended a territory around the nest. The size of the territory varied between pairs, depending partly on how close neighbours were. Where several pairs bred in the same wood, they usually had small territories and shared much of their range. Even so, pairs avoided each other by hunting in different directions from the nest, as mentioned above. In general, the proportion of the male's range that was shared increased with increasing distance from the nest (Fig. 35). The overlap at any given distance was also greater, on average, in 1978 when Kestrel density was high, than in 1977 when it was low.

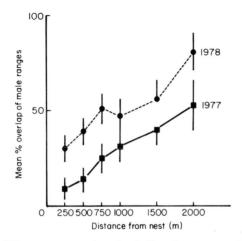

Fig. 35. Mean (SE) percentage overlap of male Kestrel ranges at various distances from the nest. Based on 20 ranges in each year in the Eskdalemuir area. There was less overlap near the nest than further away, and less at all distances in the poor vole year of 1977 than the better vole year of 1978. From Village (1983b).

In summary, Kestrels in grassland had exclusive, solitary territories outside the breeding season, which increased in size as the population density fell. The ranges occupied by pairs in summer were as large as those of individuals in winter, but the higher Kestrel density and uneven distribution of nest sites resulted in greater overlap of ranges. Summer territories were thus confined to an area around the nest, which varied in size between pairs and between years.

Farmland ranges in autumn and winter
The seasonal changes in ranges in farmland were different from those in grassland in several respects, mainly arising from the greater stability of the wintering population in England.

In mixed farmland I was able to measure territory size in autumn and

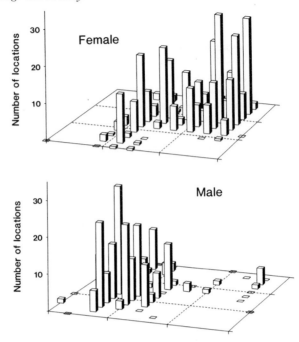

Fig. 36. Use of a shared home range by a pair of Kestrels during winter 1981/2 in mixed farmland. The height of the bars is proportional to the intensity of use by each partner. Usually, the male and female hunted separately, but would occasionally use each other's range and often met to sit together at particular perches.

winter for several years (Table 12). In each case there was little change between the two seasons, unlike the increase in territory size in each year in grassland. Average territory-size was around 2 km² outside the breeding season, but there was much less variation from year to year than at Eskdalemuir. This stability was reflected in the behaviour of breeding pairs, many of which remained together throughout the year. About a third of winter territories were occupied by pairs that had bred the previous summer, or would do so the next. The limited data I had for radio-tagged pairs in winter suggested that each member had its own preferred hunting areas, though they would frequently meet during the day, and most of their ranges overlapped (Fig. 36).

Territories in arable farmland seemed less stable than in mixed farmland, though I was unable to measure territory size accurately in all years. The change from summer was also more obvious here than in mixed farmland, because of the lower breeding density and bigger influx of winter visitors. In 1984 and 1985, I followed the change in territories from August to October in some detail. The process of settling appeared to be similar to that in spring at Eskdalemuir, with the large summer-ranges of residents being compressed gradually as incomers (in this case mainly juveniles) arrived.

In September, it was common to see several young Kestrels hunting together in the same place, often only a few metres apart. Such late-summer congregations were not family parties, and have been recorded elsewhere. For example, several county bird reports record Kestrels hunting together in groups at this time of year. The overlapping of ranges was somewhat deceptive, because it implied the absence of territorial behaviour. In fact, there was a marked increase in aggresssive encounters in autumn (Fig. 37), either between juveniles and residents, or between juveniles themselves. These apparently contradictory observations arose because juveniles seemed to be inefficient at defending territories, and rather sporadic in their aggression. I several times saw juveniles that had been hunting close together suddenly start to fight, usually because one bird dived at the other. Such fights could be very aggressive, with the combatants tumbling to the ground and grappling with their talons. The birds would eventually separate, sometimes to resume hunting in the same place as if nothing had happened.

Fights became less frequent as autumn progressed, and by October or November territory boundaries were established and relatively stable. It was hard to tell if this was because young birds had improved their ability to expel intruders, or because intrusions were less likely once birds had estabilshed territories. The net result of the influx in autumn was a decline in average territory-size, which was slightly smaller in winter than in early autumn (Table 12). There was then a period of relative stability in winter until birds began leaving the area in March and April.

Farmland ranges in spring and summer

Although there may have been some new arrivals in spring in both English study areas, most of the breeding population was already present during the previous winter, some having settled in the autumn. There was less territorial fighting in spring than in Scotland (Fig. 37), probably because fewer incomers were jostling for breeding sites. Ranges again increased in size from winter to

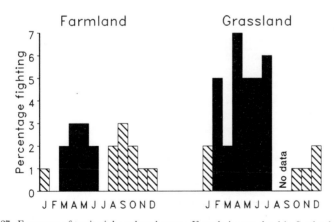

Fig. 37. *Frequency of territorial combats between Kestrels in grassland in Scotland (1976– 78) and farmland in England (1981–85). Based on the percentage of Kestrels that were fighting when first sighted. Solid-shaded bars refer to breeding males only, hatched bars to both sexes in autumn and winter.*

Radio-tracking Kestrels in the arable farmland area. This useful technique enables individuals to be located quickly and followed for long periods. Photo: N. J. Westwood.

summer, though in farmland the average summer-size was larger than in grassland, being 5–10 km² (Table 12). The extent of overlap in summer may have been underestimated, compared to grassland, because of the greater difficulty in seeing birds, but my data suggest there was usually less overlap of summer ranges than at Eskdalemuir. So, although farmland ranges were larger than in grassland, the lower breeding density resulted in less, not more, range overlap.

The large areas of exclusive range in summer could have arisen either because Kestrels defended large territories, or because the lower breeding density made overlap less likely. Recent work in the arable farmland area, using decoys to test territorial defence, has shown that males were reluctant to attack intruders more than a few hundred metres from their nest (C. G. Wiklund), so although territories were larger than in grassland, some lack of overlap was merely the result of low summer density.

CHANGES IN DISPERSION PATTERNS FROM WINTER TO SUMMER

In both studies, but especially in grassland, there was a marked seasonal difference in Kestrel dispersal. In winter, individuals or pairs occupied home ranges from which other Kestrels were excluded and which therefore corresponded to territories. In summer, pairs defended small territories around the nest, but males ranged more widely, often sharing hunting grounds with others. This pattern has been noticed in other studies (Cavé 1968) and may apply to other Kestrel species (Village 1987b). There are a number of possible explanations for this change, all of which may be true to some extent.

The overlapping of ranges in summer may be related to the relative distribution of nests and food, as suggested by Ian Newton (1979). In good food areas, capable of supporting a high density of pairs, overlap of ranges may result from the enforced clumping of nests, which prevents pairs dividing the area into neat territories, and causes ranges to overlap. The food resource can then be exploited only if birds hunt away from their nest in unoccupied adjacent areas. This seemed to be the case at Eskadalemuir, with nests at high density in the valleys, and an overlap of ranges on the adjacent hillsides. A similar situation apparently held in Holland, where Kestrels nested in boxes placed close together in grids (Cavé 1968), and may also happen at other sites where Kestrels nest semi-colonially (Fennel 1954, Peter & Zaumseil 1982). In places where food supply is poorer, or nest sites more widely dispersed, pairs may have more space around the nest and so be less likely to overlap ranges. To some extent this was true in farmland, though territories were also larger.

Nest spacing was probably not the only factor affecting range overlap, and in both my studies there seemed to be a qualitative change in male ranging behaviour from winter to summer. The change may be related to the switch from mainly perched-hunting in winter to mainly flight-hunting in summer. The greater food demands on males in the breeding season may force them to roam more widely to find hunting areas, which would be difficult to defend if they were widely separated from each other. The greater proportion of avian prey in summer could also affect hunting tactics by forcing Kestrels to keep moving from place to place in order to surprise small birds. It is interesting to compare the situation with Sparrowhawks, which are the about the same size as Kestrels but which feed almost entirely on small birds. Sparrowhawks have large overlapping ranges, even in winter (Marquiss & Newton 1982a), so the summer ranges of Kestrels may partly reflect their more Sparrowhawk-like behaviour at that time of year.

Reasons for defence in winter and summer

Perhaps a better way to look at the problem is to ask why Kestrels are territorial in winter. They could, after all, simply share ranges, as in summer, and avoid one another when they meet. Defending a territory, however, may be the best way of ensuring a food supply that will last until spring. Once sedentary prey such as voles have stopped breeding in autumn, the principal food supply is no longer being renewed and must slowly decline over winter. Excluding other Kestrels from hunting habitat may slow the rate at which the food source is depleted. It follows from this that Kestrels no longer need to defend hunting territories in summer because the food supply is increasing. The main role of summer territories thus becomes the defence of the nest site or female.

There is certainly good circumstantial evidence that defence of the nest or mate in summer is at least as important as defending a source of food. I have seen intruding males displaying to females on several occasions, and cuckoldry may be more frequent than is commonly supposed. The need for males to be near the nest to ward off intruders was illustrated by an adult bird that I radio-tracked at Eskdalemuir in 1978. He was trapped at his nest-site on 17 April, where he had been engaged in typical courtship behaviour with a female for several days. He was released the next day after being fitted with a transmitter, but by then his female was already being courted by a second male. Despite several attempts, the original male was unable to reoccupy his old territory, and eventually found a new nest and mate a few kilometres away. I located this male 14 times during the pre-lay period from 20–26 April, and on ten occasions he was hunting away from the nest. On 26 April I noticed his female was being courted by a yearling male that was displaying vigorously at the nest. After about ten minutes, the adult male arrived on the scene and started chasing the yearling; the fight lasted several hours and was apparently resumed on the next day. It was probably no coincidence that the male was at, or near, the nest on seven of my next eight visits!

There is clearly scope for more work to determine the exact role of territory defence in Kestrels. There is sufficient evidence to show that behaviour changes from winter to summer, and that this may be related to changes in food supply, nest dispersion or mate guarding. Unravelling the influence of these factors will require a more experimental approach: nest spacing can certainly be manipulated, but changing the food supply, or demand for mates, would be much more time-consuming operations.

RANGE AND TERRITORY SIZE IN RELATION TO FOOD SUPPLY

Although it is widely accepted that the area ranged over, or defended by, an animal is likely to be related to food availability, comparatively few studies on birds have been able to measure both range size and food supply. Estimating range size, even with marked birds, is never easy, and many species whose range size can be measured feed on prey whose density cannot. Fortunately, I had estimates of vole abundance for each of the study areas, which enabled me to relate the size of Kestrel ranges and territories to seasonal and annual fluctuations in food supply. The measures of vole abundance were indices, rather than absolute estimates of population density, so they could not be used to compare directly the grassland and farmland areas. However, the grassland area had much more vole habitat than did farmland, and therefore a higher overall vole density.

Grassland ranges in relation to vole numbers
There were three sources of variation in vole numbers at Eskdalemuir: *seasonal variation*, caused by the summer increase and winter decline; *annual variation*, due to the year to year changes of the vole cycle; and *spatial variation* between different parts of the study area. The latter was only important in autumn and winter 1977, when voles were more numerous in the north of the area than in the south. I combined all these sources of variation by calculating the mean range size and vole index for each season, from autumn 1975 to summer 1978, and by using separate figures for the north and south of the study area in autumn and winter 1977. This gave 11 separate estimates of average range-size, which were negatively correlated with the vole index (Fig. 38). The relationship was not linear, but was nearly so when log range size was plotted against the vole index. I don't know if the curve of this relationship had any true biological significance, because the vole index may not itself have

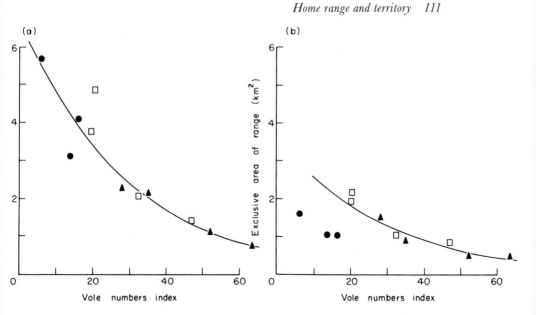

Fig. 38. *Relationships of (a) home-range and (b) territory size to vole abundance in the Eskdalemuir grassland area. Each point is the mean of at least five Kestrel ranges in autumn (▲), winter (□) or summer (●). Lines were fitted to all points in (a) and to autumn and winter only in (b). From Village (1982b).*

been linearly related to actual vole density. However, a curve made more sense than a straight line, because it implied that Kestrel ranges would not decline in size indefinitely as voles increased, but would reach a lower average size limit of around 1 km². Unfortunately, vole numbers were never high enough to show if Kestrel ranges could be further compressed, but this seems unlikely with such a mobile bird.

The relationship of territory size to vole numbers was as expected, bearing in mind that territories roughly corresponded to ranges in winter, but not in summer. Territory size was thus correlated with vole numbers outside the breeding season, but values for summer were lower than expected from the vole numbers because only part of the range was defended at that time of year. Despite this, the three values of territory size during the breeding season still seemed to be inversely related to vole numbers. This was supported by the terrtorial fights between breeding Kestrels, which were further from the nest of the territory occupant, on average, in 1977 (when voles were scarce) than in 1978 (when voles were more numerous), implying that territories were indeed smaller when food supply was better (Village 1983b).

Farmland ranges in relation to vole numbers

In the two farmland areas, I measured range sizes at various times of year from 1981 to 1985. It was difficult to measure ranges simultaneously in both

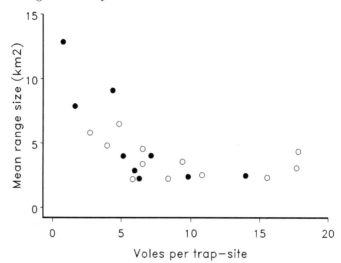

Fig. 39. Relationship of Kestrel home range size to vole abundance in the mixed (○) and arable (●) farmland areas. Each point is the mean of several ranges measured in autumn, winter or summer. For further details, see Table 12.

areas in every year, so data for some periods were missing. Plotting mean range-size against the vole index gave a negative relationship that was similar to that in grassland (Fig. 39). However, there was considerable scatter, and much of the correlation depended on the large summer-ranges in arable farmland during low vole years. When each area was analysed separately by season, there were significant correlations only for arable farmland in autumn and winter. Nonetheless, the seasonal changes in Kestrel ranges generally mirrored those in vole numbers, so there were good grounds for pooling the seasonal estimates within each study area. This showed a negative correlation between range size and vole numbers in arable but not mixed farmland.

Comparisons between the study areas

The correlations between Kestrel range-sizes and vole numbers were consistent with the changes in Kestrel densities (see Chapter 8). Kestrel numbers declined as food became scarce and those birds that remained used more space. The results did not show if Kestrel numbers were controlled by territory size or *vice versa*, and this required some experimental manipulations (see Chapter 8). The relationship of range size to vole numbers was closer in grassland than in farmland, especially outside the breeding season, and this was consistent with the higher proportion of voles in the diet in grassland. The winter diet in farmland was more diverse than elsewhere, so voles were probably a less reliable guide to the true food supply. Kestrels may have been able to offset any decline of vole numbers in winter by switching to alternative food, such as invertebrates or birds. This was not possible in spring, when voles were the only prey sufficiently abundant to allow pairs to breed. This may explain why range size in mixed farmland was related to vole numbers in summer but not in winter.

SUMMARY

Kestrels occupy home ranges that vary in size from less than 1 km^2 to over 10 km^2, and may be partially or totally defended. In the Scottish grassland area, where part of the breeding population migrated away for the winter, Kestrels held solitary territories outside the breeding season. The size of these territories increased as Kestrel population density declined, because the remaining birds took over the gaps left by those which died or moved away. In summer, pairs defended a territory around the nest, but outlying parts of the range were shared with other pairs. Ranges varied from around 5 km^2 at low vole densities, to less than 1 km^2 when voles were abundant in autumn.

Ranges in the farmland study areas were larger, on average, than in grassland, but size was also inversely correlated with vole abundance. Changes in territories in autumn and spring seemed to coincide with the arrival or loss of neighbours, so territory size may have been determined by the Kestrel population density, rather than *vice versa*.

CHAPTER 8

Winter density

At the end of the breeding season the Kestrel population consists of post-breeding adults, adults that did not breed and recently independent juveniles. The size of the total population in the coming winter will depend on how many of these birds survive, but local densities will depend mainly on how they distribute themselves over the wintering range. Post-breeding migrations result in a major redistribution of Kestrels, so that the numbers settling, or remaining, in an area in autumn may bear little relationship to those present at the end of the breeding season. The change in densities is most obvious at the extreme latitudes of the geographic range: in the north, Kestrels move out altogether, whereas in southern Europe and Africa wintering birds far outnumber the local residents (Brown *et al* 1982). In other areas, where only some Kestrels migrate, the change from summer to winter is less predictable and depends largely on the conditions prevailing at the time.

Although most movements take place between September and November, densities in winter may not remain stable for long. There will almost invariably be some deaths and, if losses are not replaced, the density will continue to decline until incomers arrive to fill the gaps. The return to breeding areas may begin as early as January or February in southern Europe and Africa, so the winter population in these areas may be constantly changing. In many areas, then, a single figure for winter density is misleading, and a full understanding of what regulates winter density requires some understanding of how numbers fluctuate, both between and within winters.

COUNTING KESTRELS IN WINTER

It is more difficult to measure the absolute population density of Kestrels in winter than to estimate breeding numbers. The basic unit in summer is the nest, which at least stays in one place and can be distinguished with certainty from other nests! In winter, the basic units are individual birds, but these move around and can be difficult to tell apart, particularly if they have large ranges. Thus, reliable estimates of Kestrel winter densities are scarce in the literature.

Fortunately, Kestrels are reasonably easy to see in winter, and they can be censused by regular counts. These may not give absolute densities, but they can show how numbers change over the course of the season, or from one year to the next. The usual technique is to count from a vehicle driven over a fixed route, and such *roadside counts* have been widely used in North America to measure both the abundance and sex ratios of wintering Kestrels (Craighead & Craighead 1956, Koplin 1973, Mills 1976). The technique has also been used to some extent in Europe (Reichholf 1977), and I found it the least time-consuming way to monitor the winter population. The rest of this chapter is based largely on roadside counts which I made over three winters in the grassland area, and seven winters in farmland.

The way of counting was different in the two studies. At Eskdalemuir, I had no fixed route, but regularly used the same forest tracks and minor roads within the study area throughout the year. I recorded all the Kestrels (and Short-eared Owls) seen each time I drove along a particular section of road, and from this produced an index of abundance by dividing the total number of Kestrels seen by the distance travelled (in km). Because of the more extensive nature of the farmland study, it was necessary to set aside specific times for the census, rather than to monitor Kestrels continually. I therefore used a fixed, 80-km route in each area and, where possible, drove it three times a month from October to April.

The visibility of Kestrels in the three study areas was quite different, so the indices did not allow any direct comparisons of densities between them. However, I spent several winters marking Kestrels and finding all the individuals in sections of all three study areas. This gave me independent estimates of actual population density, and I used these to calibrate the roadside counts. The calibration was only approximate, but sufficient to give some idea of differences in winter numbers between the three study areas. Converting the indices to actual densities made no difference to any year-to-year trends within areas, but it did permit more accurate comparisons between areas.

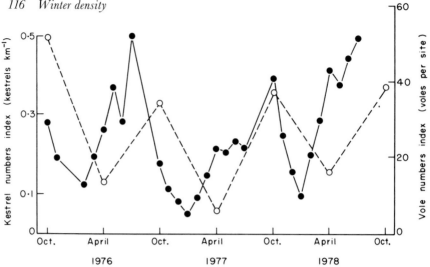

Fig. 40. Monthly variations in Kestrel abundance in the Eskdalemuir study area, as measured by roadside counts. Open circles show the vole index, which was estimated twice-yearly. In each year, Kestrel numbers declined in late autumn and increased in early spring. From Village (1982a).

SEASONAL PATTERNS OF WINTER ABUNDANCE

In each of the three study areas, the density of Kestrels changed during the course of the winter. The pattern of this change was reasonably consistent from year to year, but differed between the areas, partly because most Kestrels were summer migrants at Eskdalemuir but residents, or winter visitors, in the two English farmland areas.

Winter density in the grassland area
At Eskdalemuir, most of the breeding birds present in summer left between July and October. By October only 34% of those birds marked in the previous summer were still in the area, and only 11% of these were known to have migrated subsequently. The loss of some breeders did not necessarily lead to a decline in density, however, because other Kestrels took their place. These incomers included a few locally raised juveniles, some unmarked adults and a variable number of juveniles from elsewhere. The number of birds settling differed between years and was not related to the number of young raised locally, so density in October could be higher, lower or about the same as in the previous breeding season.

Few immigrants arrived after the middle of October, and the density of Kestrels declined sharply by 30–50% over the next 2–3 months (Fig. 40). The decline was probably due to a mixture of emigration and mortality, but I had insufficient recoveries to prove that this was so. Of 39 tagged Kestrels disappearing between October and January, three were females that returned next spring, two were juveniles found dead locally, and the rest were unaccounted for.

The first influx of breeders began in late February, and numbers increased rapidly during March and April. Although I continued the census during the breeding season, the counts were less accurate because they had to be adjusted for incubating females, which could not be counted. Nonetheless, the results suggested that the high numbers were maintained through the breeding season, and this agreed well with my estimates of breeding density. Thus, the overall pattern of winter numbers was for a variable amount of settling in August and September, a steep decline from October to January and a rapid increase from February to April. This resulted in considerable variation in winter numbers, with a maximum ten-fold difference between the lowest density (10 birds/100km² in 1977) and the highest (102 birds/100km² in 1978).

Winter density in the two farmland areas

In England, few breeding birds migrated in autumn and, although numbers declined through the winter, density in January was about twice that at Eskdalemuir (Table 14). There was also little or no influx of breeders in the farmland areas in early spring, and some Kestrels seemed to move out of the arable area at the end of winter. The usual pattern of winter numbers in farmland was, therefore, a decline from October to April, though there were important differences between the two farmland areas.

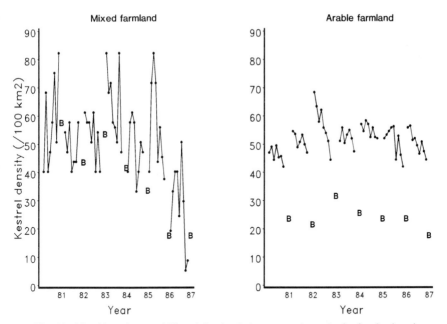

Fig. 41. Monthly estimates of Kestrel density during seven winters in the farmland study areas, from roadside counts. Each point is the mean of up to three counts per month from October to May. B = density of breeding birds, estimated by finding nests. Density usually declined from autumn to early spring in both areas. Breeding density was roughly similar to the total spring density in mixed farmland, but it was much lower than total spring density in arable farmland.

In arable farmland, where the breeding density was consistently low, winter densities always seemed higher than those in the preceding summer. I could not be completely certain of this because the summer density estimates excluded non-breeding birds, but October densities were always higher than in the preceding April, and much higher than the previous breeding density (Fig. 41b). This implied an immigration of birds after the breeding season, and I investigated this in more detail by monitoring a part of the arable area from August until October in 1984 and 1985. There were few birds present in early August, apart from some non-breeders and those that had just finished breeding. Incomers were mainly juveniles that started arriving in mid September. Numbers increased rapidly until late October or early November, and then began to decline. The decline seemed somewhat erratic, possibly due to sampling errors, but early spring densities were always lower than those in mid winter. The extent of the winter decline varied from year to year, but even the biggest change (70 to 40 birds/100km^2 in 1983) was less than at Eskdalemuir, and was probably due mainly to mortality. However, a few marked Kestrels that disappeared over the winter were found elsewhere, so some losses were due to emigration.

In mixed farmland, the seasonal changes of winter density were less consistent from year to year than in arable farmland. Autumn numbers were higher than those in the previous April in four years and lower in three. Breeding densities were more closely related to winter densities than in arable farmland, but were sometimes higher and sometimes lower than numbers the following autumn (Fig. 41a). Apart from 1986/7, winter densities again averaged about 50 Kestrels/100km^2, but the pattern differed from year to year. There was an decrease in density from winter to spring in three years and an increase in four, though the increases were modest compared to the grassland area. The lack of a consistent seasonal pattern to winter density in mixed farmland was also matched by a greater variability in density than in arable farmland. The highest autumn densities were around 80 birds/100km^2, and the lowest spring densities 10/100km^2. The latter figure was in 1987, an unusually poor year, and declines in other years were about 80 to 40 birds/100km^2.

Reasons for the different seasonal patterns of winter numbers

The change in numbers during winters in Eskdalemuir were probably typical of much of northern Europe where Kestrels are partially migratory. A 'U'-shaped curve of abundance would result from breeders migrating in autumn and returning in spring. However, this was not sufficient to explain the early-winter decline in Eskdalemuir, because migrant breeding-birds had already left, and the decline resulted mainly from the loss of birds that settled *after* the breeding season. These were mainly dispersing juveniles and, although some may well have moved to milder climates as the weather deteriorated, none was known to have returned to the area the following spring, and most of them probably died.

The arable farmland area seemed to be a wintering ground for some birds, and higher densities in winter than summer have been noticed elsewhere in the Cambridgeshire fens (Cambridgeshire County Bird Report 1969). I did not know the origin of many of the wintering birds, but some may have come from northern England or Scotland (Chapter 16). Even so, the seasonal changes in the fens were not a mirror-image of those in Scotland, because numbers in both areas declined from October to January, and it would be too simplistic to assume the higher winter density in the arable area was solely the result of the migratory patterns of more northerly birds.

The mixed farmland area seemed intermediate to the other two, with numbers declining fairly consistently from October to January, but not thereafter. Although there was some evidence of birds arriving in the area in spring, this was not a true return migration and may have resulted from passing migrants settling because they found suitable conditions. Similarly, although winter numbers were sometimes higher than subsequent breeding numbers, the difference was less marked than in arable farmland, and there was little evidence that the mixed farmland was used as a wintering ground by many birds. This contrast between the two farmland areas was interesting because they were only about 30 km apart, and had a similar climate. Presumably the arable area offered a good wintering habitat, either because the low summer-density meant more vacant territories in autumn, or because the winter food supply was better.

WINTER DENSITY AND FOOD SUPPLY

The resource most likely to limit Kestrel numbers in winter is food. Kestrels, particularly juveniles, are not tied to a breeding place, so they can move around in search of food and should, in theory, concentrate in areas where food is most plentiful. Winter densities, therefore, ought to be more closely related to food supply than breeding densities (Newton 1979). The winter food supply will depend on the density of prey in autumn, how fast the prey declines over winter and how the availability of prey is affected by weather, especially snow cover. In regions of permanent winter snow, winter food supply is predictably bad, and Kestrels leave before the weather deteriorates. In this case, proximate factors must operate in autumn to reduce numbers in advance of the decline in food levels. In places where birds settle in autumn, and some remain all winter, both the initial settling density and the subsequent losses may be more directly related to the availability of food.

Winter density and food supply in the grassland area
In Eskdalemuir, the autumn and winter densities were correlated with the vole index, but with data for only three years I could not test this separately within each season (Fig. 42). The correlation therefore arose largely because both Kestrels and voles were abundant in autumn and both declined during winter. This raises the possibility that each species responded in parallel to some seasonal effect, rather than vole numbers causing changes in Kestrel numbers. The latter alternative is the most likely explanation, but full proof requires firmer evidence.

In early spring, Kestrel and vole numbers diverged dramatically. Migrant Kestrels arrived in March and April before there was any noticeable increase

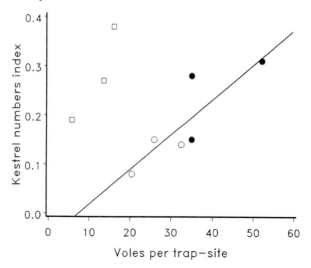

Fig. 42. Correlations of Kestrel and vole abundance in the Eskdalemuir study area during autumn (●), winter (○) or summer (□), 1976–78. The correlations were significant for autumn and winter values combined (solid line: r=0.85, df=4, P<0.05), but not for summer (r=0.98, df=1, P<0.12).

in vole numbers. Kestrel densities in spring were often as high as, or even higher, than the preceding autumn, even though vole densities were much lower. There are several explanations for this, such as the increase in daylength allowing Kestrels more time to hunt, the improving weather increasing the prey available to Kestrels, and changes in the behaviour of voles in spring making them more vulnerable to predation (Masman *et al* 1988b).

If the winter decline was largely because snow cover reduced food supply, the rising temperatures in late winter would suddenly unmask a food supply that had previously been unexploitable. This would explain why midwinter Kestrel densities in Eskdalemuir were lower than in farmland, even though vole densities must have been higher due to the greater amount of vole habitat. However, it does not explain why Kestrels in the Scottish study area declined in November and December, before the heavy snows came, nor why they declined during the mild winter of 1975/76, when there was little snow. Some decline in density would be inevitable, even without snow, because losses not connected with food shortage, such as road accidents, disease or predation, would not be replaced if there were no migrants available to fill the gaps.

Winter density and food supply in farmland

In the farmland areas, Kestrel and small-mammal numbers were again correlated, largely because both showed parallel seasonal declines. In each area, the decrease in Kestrel density followed the decline either in voles or Woodmice, whichever was the main prey. In mixed farmland, for example, voles were more abundant that Woodmice and were the main mammal prey for Kestrels (Chapter 3). Kestrel numbers during seven winters were significantly correlated with the vole index, but not the mouse index (Fig. 43a). The relationship held between years within the midwinter period (December to February), but not during autumn or early spring.

In the arable area, Woodmice were more abundant than in mixed farmland, and were more frequently eaten by Kestrels (see Fig. 14). Kestrel numbers in arable farmland were therefore more closely correlated with mouse than with vole numbers (Fig. 43b). Unfortunately, none of the correlations held within periods, so it was again difficult to tell if the relationship was a true cause and effect, or simply a corresponding seasonal decline both in Kestrels and mice. The correlations may have been weakened because Kestrels took significant quantities of other prey, such as birds and invertebrates.

Although these correlations are only circumstantial evidence, they provide the best proof yet that Kestrel numbers in winter are influenced by the density of their main prey. The lack of correlation between years within most periods was not surprising, given that seasonal variations in vole or mouse abundance

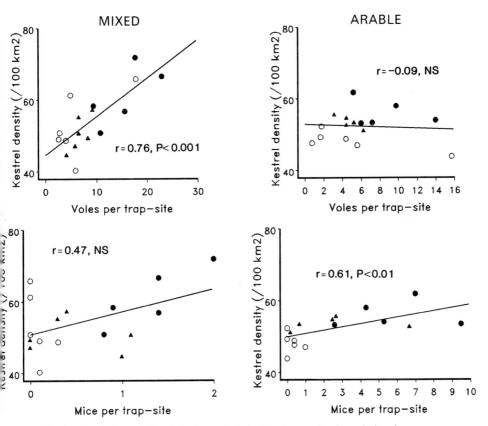

Fig. 43. Correlations of Kestrel density and vole or Woodmouse abundance during six years in mixed and arable farmland. Lines are linear regressions fitted to all points for autumn (●), winter (▲) and spring (○). Kestrel density was more closely related to vole than mouse numbers in mixed farmland, while the reverse was true in arable farmland.

were often much greater than those from year to year. In both farmland areas, vole and mouse numbers usually declined from winter to early spring, and Kestrels showed a similar decline in most years. A notable exception was the winter of 1980/81, when vole numbers in mixed farmland apparently increased from winter to spring. The seasonal pattern in Kestrels numbers was also the reverse of the usual decline (Fig. 41), suggesting the Kestrel/vole relationship was not just a seasonal effect. Unfortunately, this was the first year of the study and I did not start trapping small mammals in arable farmland until spring, so I could not tell if the same was true for that area. However, there was no increase in Kestrels that winter, and spring numbers were not especially high, despite the abundance of voles. Kestrel numbers in the arable area thus seemed to follow the sharp seasonal decline in Woodmice, irrespective of vole densities. The transient abundance of Woodmice in the arable fens made the area suitable for Kestrels in winter, but not in summer.

THE MECHANISM OF POPULATION REGULATION IN WINTER

Kestrels are strongly territorial during winter (see Chapter 7), and will attack Kestrel intruders. If such attacks prevented birds from settling in an area, territorial aggression may be responsible for limiting local Kestrel density in winter. At Eskdalemuir, when Kestrels disappeared from their winter territory, the space they left was soon used by a neighbour (see Fig. 32), and it seemed that, at that time of year, territory size was determined by Kestrel density, rather than the other way around.

The effects of declining Kestrel density and territory size could not be separated from the effects of declining food supply: shortage of food may both have increased the likelihood of birds dying or moving elsewhere and increased the aggression (and hence territory size) of the birds that remained. To separate these two effects, I removed birds from their territories in winter to see if they were replaced by new birds occupying the same area. If they were, it would imply that the number of Kestrels able to settle (and hence population density) was limited by the territorial behaviour of the birds already resident in an area. Although the original idea for the experiment came from observations in Scotland, I was not able to implement it until some years later, during the farmland study.

The experiments required a great deal of fieldwork because it was important to know which birds were occupying which territories, before and after the removal. This meant catching and marking up to ten birds in adjacent territories for each experiment, removing a bird from the centre of the group, and monitoring the use of the vacated area for at least the next two weeks. Ideally the experiments should have been done in September, when territories were being established and aggression was most likely to have prevented birds from settling. Unfortunately, it took several weeks to catch and mark enough birds, and the instability of the population in September meant that it was the middle of October before I was sufficiently certain of the territory system to remove any residents.

In autumn and winter of 1982 and 1983 I did seven removal experiments, involving ten territories and nine birds (Table 15). More than one bird was removed in two experiments, and one individual was removed, released and then removed a second time. None of the ten territories was occupied permanently by unmarked Kestrels settling in the area for the first time. However, in three cases, unmarked birds were seen in the vacated area, but none stayed longer than 12 days. In four of the seven experiments, neighbouring birds were seen to use the the vacated territories, though none used them regularly. I released seven of the ten birds after 2–8 weeks, and all but one successfully reoccupied their original territory for the rest of the winter.

The results showed that territorial behaviour was not limiting population density at that time of year, though they would have been easier to interpret if there had been no replacement at all, or if all the vacated territories were immediately occupied by strangers. Three of the vacant territories were temporally occupied by incoming Kestrels, so there seemed to be some transients looking for winter territories. That they were unable to stay for long implies that such birds were not prevented from settling on a territory solely by the aggression of other birds, and that transients may be less capable of holding a territory than residents. The vacated territories were still tenable, because most released birds reoccupied them later in the same winter. The fate of two of the three settlers was known: one adult male established a territory some 7 km away where it remained for several years. The other adult male left the removal area after ten days and was found dead 12 km away about 2 weeks later.

The expansion of neighbours into the gaps created by removing territory holders was as expected from my observations at Eskdalemuir. It suggests that territory size was at least partly dependent on the proximity of neighbours, so that the more birds there were in a given area, the smaller were their territories. This does not conflict with the idea that Kestrel density and territory size were related to the food supply because food levels may have determined how many Kestrels settled in an area. The removal experiments showed that Kestrels were not fixing the size of their territories directly to the amount of food, otherwise they would not have expanded or contracted their territories in response to the absence or re-introduction of their neighbours. The relationships of Kestrel density, territorial behaviour and food supply are discussed more fully in Chapter 20.

SUMMARY

Kestrel densities in autumn depend on how many individuals remain after breeding, and how many settle during the post-fledging dispersal stage. At Eskdalemuir, density declined sharply from October to January, and increased thereafter as migrants arrived at the start of the breeding season. In the English farmland areas, numbers usually declined from October to April, though less steeply than in the grassland area, so that the midwinter density was twice as high as at Eskdalemuir. The arable fenlands seemed to be a wintering ground for birds that bred elsewhere, and density increased sharply during September and October.

The decline in Kestrel numbers from autumn to midwinter was correlated with declines in the main prey: voles in Eskdalemuir and mixed farmland, Woodmice in arable farmland. In spring, the increase in Kestrel numbers in Eskdalemuir was not related to any increase in vole density, and may have been possible because Kestrel density was below the level that could be supported once the snow melted and voles became more accessible. In farmland, there was seldom any increase in Kestrel density in spring, so numbers may have remained below the level that the food supply could support because there were few transient birds to fill any territories that had become vacant during winter.

CHAPTER 9

Nesting sites

As with other falcons, European Kestrels do not build a nest, but simply scrape a shallow depression in the substrate of the chosen nesting site. The inability to construct a nest platform seems to restrict the variety of places where some species of falcon can nest, and their breeding distribution is limited by the availability of suitable nesting cliffs. European Kestrels have largely overcome this problem by adapting to a wide range of sites, and they are opportunistic nesters *par excellence*. The most common sites are the disused stick-nests of other bird species, ledges on cliffs or buildings and holes in trees. But virtually any structure that is moderately inaccessable to mammal predators, reasonably sheltered and can hold the eggs is a potential site. This, together with an equal versatility in diet, probably explains why Kestrels have been able to colonise such a wide variety of habitats, and it is an important factor in their success in adapting to man-made environments.

Disused crow nests in conifers were the most frequently used type of nest site for Kestrels in the Scottish study area. Photo: K. Taylor.

TYPES OF NEST SITES USED BY KESTRELS

Stick nests

These are usually the abandoned nests of other bird species that are about the same size as Kestrels, or slightly larger. The range of species is wide, but in Britain the more frequent (in approximate order of importance) are Carrion Crow, Magpie, Rook, Sparrowhawk, Pigeon and Heron. In addition, Kestrels sometimes nest on top of abandoned squirrel dreys. The nest-cup of crow nests usually collapses after a year or so, producing a flat surface of mud and leaf-mould, which Kestrels scrape into a depression. Where the wool lining remains intact, or in nests with little lining material, Kestrels seem not to bother scraping, and lay their eggs in the existing cup. Stick nests used in previous years by owls or Kestrels have a layer of pellet and prey remains, which forms the substrate. Crow nests are usually in such poor condition by the time crows and Kestrels have raised young in them that few survive to be used a second or third time.

It is rare for Kestrels to usurp occupied nests from their owners, and they normally take empty nests that are at least a year old. However, Kestrels will occupy new nests abandoned earlier in the same year, and this happened at Eskdalemuir when nests became vacant after the gamekeepers finished their annual purge of crows. In Africa, Greater Kestrels sometimes take over the nests of Black Crows *Corvus capensis* before the crows have a chance to lay (Osborne & Colebrook-Robjent 1982).

At Eskdalemuir, most Kestrels nested in old crow nests that were either in isolated trees, or in small coniferous shelterbelts. Finding crow nests in thick conifer stands is not easy, and in some cases I had to resort to crawling on all fours under the dense, low canopy. It was useless to try and spot nests from below, but I soon discovered that crows left tell-tale signs under successful nests. Such signs were usually a few sheep bones, twigs from deciduous trees, or bits of wool caught in the lower branches of the nest tree. An awkward struggle up the tree, through the clinging mat of branches, was usually rewarded by finding a nest hidden in the canopy. In this way, I was able to find most of the old crow nests in a small shelterbelt, irrespective of whether or not Kestrels used them. It was fairly easy to tell if the nest was too disintegrated for Kestrels to use, so I had a reasonable estimate of both the number of potentially usable sites and the number actually occupied by Kestrels.

Rock ledges

These encompass a wide range of sites, from small crags that are almost indistinguishable from the hillside, to towering rock faces and sea cliffs. In

Ledges on cliffs or crags are often used by Kestrels in some coastal and upland areas of Britain, but they were not important in the present studies. Photo: K. Taylor.

most cases the ledge is small, but fairly difficult to reach, with at least 2–3 metres of vertical rock below it and no easy access from above. However, Kestrels will occasionally nest on rock outcrops where the nest ledge can be reached without climbing. Kestrels may compete for cliff sites with Peregrines, and they often occupied unused eyries when Peregrines declined in the 1960s and 1970s (Ratcliffe 1980). Kestrels will sometimes nest within 200 m of Peregrines, but this can have its drawbacks, as Kestrels have been recorded among plucks at Peregrine eyries!

Tree holes

These were the most frequently used sites in my farmland study areas. Kestrels may use any hole that is large enough for the female to sit in, though they prefer large, open holes formed when the main trunk or large branches rot. They seem to avoid holes more than about 75 cm deep, which, in my experience, are more likely to be used by tree-nesting Barn Owls. The frequency with which particular tree species are used depends on what is available locally and the propensity of each tree species to form suitable holes. In my mixed farmland area, ash trees provided 62% of the holes for Kestrels, which was partly because they were the most abundant hedgerow tree, and partly because they often began rotting at an early age. Many of the holes I found were in the trunks of otherwise heathly ash trees that had either lost a large branch, or had been excavated by Green Woodpeckers some years previously. Woodpeckers may initiate the decay, or choose trunks that are already rotten. In either case, their holes seem to accelerate decay, and this eventually enlarges both the cavity and the entrance, making them suitable for Kestrels.

Other commonly utilised trees were elm (25%), oak (3%) and black poplar (3%). Beech and chestnut trees were fairly common in the mixed farmland area, but were seldom used as they had few suitable holes. Although some tree species were more likely to have holes than others, there was no evidence that holes in any one tree species were preferred to similar holes in any other.

The abundance of tree holes has changed over the last decade or so as a result of Dutch elm disease and changes in farming practice. Osborne (1982) found some evidence in the British Trust for Ornithology (BTO) nest records that there had been a decline in the number of Kestrels nesting in elms, and that this coincided with the spread of Dutch elm disease. As the elms have rotted they have been felled, as have many other hedgerow trees that interfere with modern farming practice. Over the seven years of my English study I found 154 trees with suitable nesting holes, 53% of which were used by Kestrels at least once. About 35% of all sites were lost during the seven years because the tree was either felled or blown down. Some new sites became available as holes were enlarged by decay, but there was still a net loss of natural sites. This has not yet reached a level that would affect Kestrel breeding densities (see Chapter 10), but might do so in the future if the present trend continues. The solution would be either to provide nestboxes or for landowners to leave some rotten branches on hedgerow trees.

Man-made stuctures

Although some other falcons will nest on buildings (for example, Peregrines

Tree holes were the most frequent nest site (circled in upper photo) in the farmland study areas. Most were in ash trees or dead elms. Photos: A. Village.

Kestrels have long been associated with man, and often nest in or on buildings. Typical sites in the farmland study areas were inside disused barns (above) or grain stores (below). The nest in the grain store was on a ledge inside the building, and the birds used the hole in the roof for access. Photo: N. J. Westwood.

in some areas), the Kestrel has developed the behaviour to a fine art. The German and Scandinavian names for the Kestrel, *Turmfalke* or *Torenfalke* mean 'Tower Falcon', and witness to its long-established habit of nesting in churches or other tall towers. Some of the many other structures used include gasometers, disused chimneys, straw stacks, barns, bridges, cranes, electricity pylons and even window boxes in high-rise flats! Some of these sites are open ledges, similar to those on natural rock faces, whereas others are enclosed holes, more like those in trees. Again, the main prerequisite is that the site is sheltered, protected and has a substrate that can be scraped to hold the eggs. These criteria can be met by some rather odd places. I found one pair nesting in the rainwater hopper of a disused downspout on the side of an old barn. The guttering feeding the hopper had long since collapsed and the hopper had filled with debris, making a suitable, if incongruous, nest site.

The habit of nesting on buildings has enabled Kestrels to exploit food sources in cities that could otherwise be reached only by long flights from surrounding countryside. Several urban populations of Kestrels have been studied (Pike 1979, Pikula *et al* 1984), and there are probably some breeding pairs in most towns and cities in Britain. Nesting pairs often seem oblivious of the comings and goings around them, and will sometimes tolerate any amount of disturbance. One female, nesting in a hollow steel girder on the side of a building, continued to lay her clutch even after the first two eggs were removed, the girder painted inside, and the eggs replaced (Pike 1981). In Israel, nesting in window boxes is now common place in Tel-Aviv and other towns (Leshem 1984), and some females become so tame that they can be observed from within the room at a distance of less than a metre. Male Kestrels also lose their fear of humans, which can result in home-owners having to defend themselves against aggressive territory-holders every time they open the window!

Nesting on the ground

With such versatile nesting habits it is perhaps surprising that Kestrels rarely nest on the ground. The instance often cited is the population in the Orkneys

Kestrels sometimes nest in window boxes on high-rise flats. In Israel this has become commonplace in some towns and the birds show little fear of humans. Photo: Y. Leshem (Israel Raptor Information Centre).

that nests in long tunnels in heather, or in Rabbit burrows (Balfour 1955). The unusually high frequency of ground nests is associated with a lack of other suitable sites and the absence of predators such as Foxes or Stoats. Nonetheless, other birds of prey such as Merlins and harriers nest on the ground where there are predators, so it is hard to see why Kestrels don't do the same, particularly in the large expanses of upland Britain that are devoid of other suitable nest sites.

Kestrels may, in fact, attempt to nest on the ground in open areas, but are rarely recorded because their nests are soon found by predators. I found a nest at Eskdalemuir on a steep hillside, in a cleft under a rock. The site could almost be considered a crag, but was not on a ledge and could be reached without climbing. This nest was destroyed by predators, as was a second ground nest that I found in mixed farmland in an open Dutch barn. The barn was empty, apart from one bale of hay, on top of which a pair of Kestrels had laid six eggs. I found the nest just as the young were hatching, but they disappeared within a few days, probably eaten by a cat.

Other recorded instances of ground nesting tend to be from areas where there are few other natural sites, such as the sand-dune coast of East Germany (Piechocki 1982), the Norfolk Broads (Seago 1967) or the Cambridgeshire fens (M. Webber). Most ground sites offer at least some protection from weather or predators, but, even so, the growing young must be highly vulnerable. These instances suggest that some Kestrels may attempt to nest on the ground in many areas, but the habit becomes established only where there are few, if any, mammalian predators.

Artificial nesting sites

Although these could be classed as man-made structures, I have treated them separately because, unlike the former group, they are sites specially erected for Kestrels or other raptors. Kestrels will readily occupy nestboxes, and these have been used in many areas to supplement the naturally available sites (Cavé 1968, Hamerstrom *et al* 1973, Burton 1986, Bang 1986). Suitable boxes are rectangular, and measure about 50 cm x 30 cm x 30 cm. They may be open along the side, at one end, or have a suitably-sized entrance hole. However, virtually any sort of box will do, provided it remains dry and has some material inside that the Kestrels can scrape into a depression. I mix peaty soil with sawdust, as the latter on its own tends to blow out of the box in dry weather. I have found Kestrels nesting on the bare boards of boxes that had no lining, but the eggs roll about and are easily chilled or broken.

Boxes are most likely to be used by Kestrels if they are at least 200 m from places frequently used by humans, and at least 3 m off the ground. I usually put boxes with end entrances in trees, and those with the long side open on buildings. The entrance should face south or south-west, so the box is sheltered from the prevailing winds, but warmed by the sun. Boxes on north-facing walls tend to become waterlogged in winter, and may not dry out in wet springs.

At Eskdalemuir, crow nests were the usual Kestrel nest site, so I built artificial stick nests as well as nestboxes. These consisted of a 40 cm diameter wire basket lined with a few twigs, followed by grass, moss and finally soil. I

Kestrels will readily take to artificial sites such as nestboxes. These open-fronted boxes were used on buildings in the arable farmland area. Photos: A. Village & N. J. Westwood.

tied them to conifer trees, usually near the top of the canopy, but sheltered from rain, in the same sorts of places as crow nests. Kestrels and Long-eared Owls readily took to these artifical sites, and their breeding success seemed no different from pairs in natural stick nests. The occupants seemed oblivious of the wire netting, and I soon learnt that there was no need to spend hours trying to disguise it.

I used artificial sites to ensure that the number of nesting sites available to Kestrels was fairly constant from year to year or to experimentally increase the number of sites in certain places. The ability to manipulate Kestrel nesting sites was an important asset in trying to understand the factors governing population density. It has also allowed Kestrels to breed in areas where they were previously absent, or very scarce, and there have been several studies of populations that nest almost entirely in boxes (Cavé 1968, Dijkstra *et al* 1982, Burton 1986).

REGIONAL VARIATION IN NEST SITES

Regional variation in the nest sites used by Kestrels largely reflects what is available in any given area. In upland areas, most sites are either stick nests in conifers or rock ledges; in lowlands, holes in trees are more important (Table 16). At Eskdalemuir, 90% of natural nests were in old crow nests, because there were few crag sites and only one tree hole. In the farmland areas, however, holes were the main site used, and only 7% of breeding attempts were in stick nests. A similar difference is apparent in the nest record cards of the British Trust for Ornithology, though rock ledges were recorded more frequently in northern Britain as a whole than at Eskdalemuir. This is partly because my study area had little exposed rock, but also because cliffs may be over represented in the BTO cards. Many cliffs are traditional sites used every year and are more likely to be recorded than transient sites in crow nests, that are easily overlooked.

As expected, Kestrels in towns and cities make greater use of buildings than those in rural areas. In tropical regions, kestrel species also nest in cliffs and disused stick nests. Common sites for several species are the dense crowns of palm trees, which may provide sheltered platforms or enclosed holes. Dickinson's Kestrels seem to nest almost exclusively in the crowns of Borassas palms, and their breeding distribution seems to follow that of the palm in parts of Africa (Brown *et al* 1982).

FACTORS AFFECTING THE CHOICE OF NEST SITE TYPE

In general, European Kestrels show rather little preference for one type of site over another, and use whatever is readily available. There is some anecdotal evidence that local traditions in nest-site usage may be important, and that Kestrels may prefer to nest in sites similar to the one in which they were reared. In the mixed farmland area there were many old crow nests available which were never used, even though some appeared to offer better sites than the tree holes that were occupied. This may have been because most crows nested in deciduous trees, and their nests were rather exposed in early spring, but I doubt if this fully explains why they were so rarely utilised. A similar phenomenon occurs in Peregrines (Newton 1979, Ratcliffe 1980), which use stick nests in trees in certain parts of the world but not others, even though this would greatly extend their breeding range.

This raises the question of whether there is a genetic component in nest-site selection, or whether Kestrels learn what a nesting site looks like from their experience as nestlings. The former seems unlikely, but the evidence is somewhat contradictory, and a full answer will require more detailed experimentation. Individuals can certainly breed in different types of site from the ones in which they were raised and they can also change site types between years. At Eskdalemuir, I had several Kestrels that were reared on ledges but bred in stick nests in trees, or *vice versa*, and one marked pair that used a ledge in 1976 and 1978 but a nearby tree site in 1977 and 1979. But there are some instances where birds seem to show remarkable selectivity in nest sites. In England I had two sites on old windmills, one in each farmland area, about 25 km apart. One of the few Kestrels I have recorded as moving between the two areas was reared on the windmill in the mixed area and found breeding at the other windmill site two years later.

Such cases are interesting, but do not show the general trends, and it is difficult to tell if birds have a preference without a detailed knowledge of what choices they had available before they bred. It is possible that individuals prefer a particular type of site, but will use another if nothing else is available. One way to explore nest-site selection is to experiment with captive birds. This has been done for American Kestrels that were reared either in enclosed boxes or on open ledges (Shutt & Bird 1985). They were offered a choice of the same two types of site when they first started to breed, but all used the enclosed boxes, irrespective of where they were reared. This may not be a definitive answer to the question, however, because American Kestrels in the wild nest almost exclusively in holes, so European Kestrels may be a better choice for study.

BREEDING SUCCESS AND TYPE OF NEST SITE

Another likely influence on the choice of a nest site is the chance it offers for successful breeding. This will depend on a variety of factors such as the accessibilty of the site to man or predators, protection from rain or flooding, the likelihood of collapse and the space available for the brood. None of these factors is necessarily dependent on whether the site is a stick nest, ledge or hole, though each type may be prone to different problems. Stick nests, for example, are more likely to collapse than tree holes, while the latter are more prone to flooding. It was difficult to compare the breeding success of Kestrels using different types of site in the grassland area because so many were in stick nests, but a study in Ayrshire, where there were roughly equal numbers of rock ledges and stick nests, showed no consistent differences in clutch size or fledging success between the two (Riddle 1979). Inaccessible sites were less likely to be disturbed by egg collectors, but this did not deter birds from using sites that were robbed every year. Kestrels in my farmland areas used a greater range of sites, but again there were no significant differences in laying dates or fledging success between types. Nestboxes may provide better sites than stick nests, and a recent German study found clutches in boxes were larger, possibly because those in stick nests suffered partial predation by corvids (Hasenclever *et al* 1989).

THE DISPERSION OF NESTS AND NEST SITES

The dispersion of nests refers to their distribution in the landscape relative to one another. Dispersion patterns of raptor nests may vary between or within species, from regular spacing to colonial nesting (Newton 1979). Kestrel species exhibit the full range of these dispersion patterns, with regular spacing in Greater Kestrels and colonial nesting in Lesser Kestrels (Table 17).

In European Kestrels there is considerable variation in the spacing of nests between years and from one area to another. Potential nesting places are seldom so evenly distributed, or sufficiently abundant, to allow Kestrels to space their nests regularly, as do other raptors such as Sparrowhawks (Newton 1986). The dispersion patterns of European Kestrel nests usually fall into one of three categories:

1. Irregularly spaced. This is probably the most common pattern, where the distance between neighbouring pairs varies, but is rarely less than a few hundred metres. The irregular spacing of Kestrel pairs is largely because usable sites also are unevenly spaced. This pattern was typical in the farmland study areas, where nest sites were scattered throughout the environment, and Kestrel densities were relatively low (Fig. 44 b & c). The distance between nests varied from 40 m to over 5 km, but the average was 1–1.5 km, with less than 7% of pairs nesting within 200 m of their nearest neighbour.

2. Clumped. Where nest sites are unevenly distributed, some Kestrels may be forced to nest close to one another, sometimes in groups of several pairs.

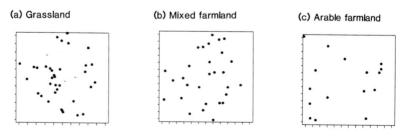

(a) Grassland   **(b) Mixed farmland**   **(c) Arable farmland**

Fig. 44. Patterns of Kestrel nest dispersion in the Eskdalemuir grassland and the farmland study areas. Each map shows the location of Kestrel pairs in one year of the study. Axes are marked at 1 km intervals. Pairs were more evenly spaced in the two farmland areas than in grassland.

Clumping of nests occurred in the grassland area, where some small shelterbelts had two or more pairs in some years (Fig. 44a). Nest spacing was more variable than in farmland, and nearly 40% of pairs were closer than 200 m to their nearest neighbours. Several instances of two or three close-nesting pairs were reported from upland areas of Aryshire (Riddle 1979), and clumping of nests seems to be frequent in Upland Britain in good vole years.

Close nesting was unusual in the farmland areas, but occasionally two pairs would nest next to one another in adjacent hedgerow trees. In one such instance, where two pairs bred only 40 m apart, the male at one site was the two-year old son of the male at the other, but I do not know if closely adjacent pairs are often related. Urban Kestrels seem to nest in small groups fairly often, and there are several published references to clumps of nests in suburban parkland (Tinbergen 1940, Parr 1969, Kurth 1970, Riddle 1979).

3. Colonial. In extreme cases, up to dozens of pairs may nest in the same small area, in what is effectively a colony. Colonies of European Kestrels have been found on large natural rock faces in Japan (Fennel 1954, Hyuga 1956), in rookeries that have many disused nests (Peichocki 1982), and on man-made structures such as gasometers and motorway bridges (Peter & Zaumseil 1982). One colony in a gasworks in Leipzig consisted of 7–9 pairs breeding in a lattice of 96 identical cavities (Piechocki 1982). Some females laid single eggs in several cavities apparently because they forgot where the original nest was. Although small groups of close-nesting Kestrels have been reported several times in Britain, colonial nesting has not, and most of the European records I can find are from Germany (Table 18). It is not clear in all cases whether the surrounding area was devoid of possible nesting sites, but this seems unlikely in many instances, so some other explanation is needed.

There is no clear distinction between these types of nest dispersion, and the patterns observed vary along a continuum. Kestrels probably try to space themselves where possible, but may be forced to nest close to other pairs if food is plentiful and there are no alternative sites. Clumping of nests does not result from reduced aggression, and adjacent pairs will still defend the nest vigorously from intruders. Even at colonies there seems to be much displaying and fighting, although pairs must obviously tolerate others nearer to their nests than is usual. The amount of ground a Kestrel can defend seems to depend partly on how many other pairs are trying to breed. This in turn is related to food supply, so nest spacing is the product of food supply and nest-site availability (Newton 1979, Village 1987b). Colonial nesting is most likely where there is plenty of food, but nest sites are limited to a small area, and more even spacing may result if sites are scattered through the feeding area.

Kestrels rarely occupy all the usable sites in an area, so pairs are usually spaced further apart than usable nest sites. Site spacing can be quantified by measuring the distance from each nest to its nearest neighbour, and comparisons made of the frequency histograms of these distances. In the grassland area, usable sites were highly clumped, because most small woods contained several old crow nests, and most were within 200 m of their nearest neighbour

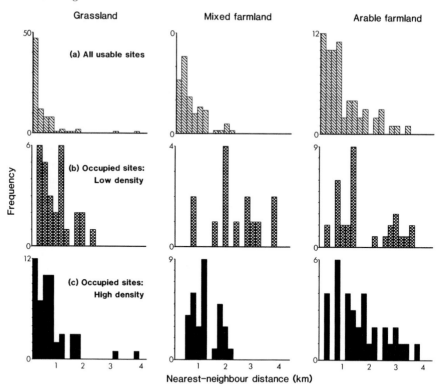

Fig. 45. Frequency histograms of the nearest-neighbour distances of (a) all usable nesting sites, (b) sites occupied by Kestrels during a low-density year and (c) occupied sites during a high-density year. In all areas, occupied sites were further apart than all usable sites, especially at low breeding densities. Kestrel pairs were spaced further apart in the English farmland than in Eskdalemuir grassland, and rarely nested closer than 200 m.

(Fig. 45). Occupied sites were further apart than this, on average, and were within 200 m of each other only in a few instances in good vole years. Kestrel nests were thus spaced further apart than usable nest sites, a situation sometimes described as *over dispersion*.

In the farmland areas, usable sites were more evenly spread than in grassland because trees with suitable holes were scarce and scattered among hedgerows. However, occupied nests were again over-dispersed relative to usable sites (Fig. 45), so in every year, in all three areas, there was a surplus of usable, but unoccupied, nest sites (Table 19). In the grassland area at least, many of these surplus sites were within the territories of existing Kestrel pairs and may not have been available to other pairs (see Chapter 20).

The distribution of usable nest sites was fairly constant from year to year in any one area. Sites became unavailable if they collapsed over winter or were occupied early in the season by other species such as Long-eared or Tawny Owls. New sites became available fairly often in Eskdalemuir because crows usually built nests every year. Fewer sites became available in farmland because tree holes took some years to decay to a suitable size, and there was a decline in natural nest sites during my study. In contrast to useable sites, the spacing of occupied Kestrel nests was much more varied from year to year, and depended on the overall breeding density. Increased breeding density was associated with greater clumping of nests because incomers had to settle in gaps between existing pairs, rather than occupy large vacant areas. In the grassland study area, Kestrel nests were more clumped in good voles years than a poor one (Fig. 45). In the mixed farmland area, breeding density declined by over 60% from 1981 to 1987, and pairs became spaced further apart as a result. In arable farmland, however, there was less variation in breeding density between years, and spacing was also more constant.

SUMMARY

Kestrels do not build a nest, but lay their eggs in a depression scraped in the substrate of the nesting site. They nest in a variety of places, including ledges on cliffs or buildings, holes in trees, or the disused stick nests of other bird species in trees or on cliffs. Kestrels will sometimes nest on the ground, but rarely where there are mammalian predators such as Foxes or Stoats. Nestboxes and artificial stick nests are readily exploited and are a useful means of manipulating the availability of nesting sites.

Breeding pairs are usually spaced further apart than are usuable sites, but regular spacing is unusual. In most areas, pairs are spaced at irregular intervals, though some pairs may nest within a few metres of one another if sites are scarce and food is plentiful. In extreme cases, Kestrels nest in colonies of ten or more pairs on the same cliff or building. Kestrels will rarely, if ever, occupy all the potential nesting sites in an area and, in my studies, there was always a surplus of unoccupied but usable sites.

CHAPTER 10

Breeding density

As in most other raptors, much of what we know about the population ecology of European Kestrels comes from studies during the breeding season. Although Kestrel nests are not always simple to find, it is easier to get an estimate of population density by counting nests than by trying to count the birds themselves. In most cases, the number of active nests is taken as a measure of population size, and many reports on the status of raptors quote figures for the total number of breeding pairs. It is important, therefore, to know the accuracy of breeding density estimates, how breeding density relates to total population density, and what factors govern the density of breeding pairs.

The spring population consists of individuals that will not mate that year (*non-breeders*), those that will mate but will fail to produce eggs (*non-laying pairs*), and pairs that will lay at least some eggs. I have mostly expressed breeding density as the density of laying pairs, which is correlated with, and usually about 10% less than, the total density of territorial pairs.

PUBLISHED ESTIMATES OF BREEDING DENSITY

The mean nearest-neighbour distance of occupied Kestrel nests could be used as an index of breeding density, but the usual practice is to give the number of pairs per unit area. Nearest-neighbour distance is useful for measuring annual variations in one area, but it can be misleading with small samples if nests are unevenly spaced. There are dozens of estimates of Kestrel breeding density in the literature, and these ought to enable some useful comparisons between habitats and over time. Unfortunately, many of these estimates are inaccurate, so before dealing with Kestrel breeding density in detail, I shall outline why such bias exists and how it can be avoided.

Sources of error in estimating Kestrel breeding density
The two main sources of error result from the irregular spacing of nests and the difficulty in finding them. Where nests are clumped, the density within a clump may be very high, but obviously cannot be extrapolated to a wider area. In such circumstances it is necessary to search enough ground to include several clumps, as well as the empty areas between them. Some published density estimates are from studies that began with several Kestrel nests in the same small area. Where searching was restricted to this small area, the density measured will be strongly influenced by the original high concentration of nests, the bias being more serious the smaller the area searched. This partly explains why most breeding densities quoted from small study areas are higher than those from large ones (Table 20).

At the other end of the scale, trying to measure density over too large an area can also cause problems. Kestrel nests can be frustratingly difficult to find, and I often have to visit some sites five or six times in one season to be certain there are no Kestrels nesting there. So the risk of missing nests must increase as more and more ground is searched, and this may cause density to be underestimated in some studies.

Typical examples are the large-scale surveys of some English counties which relied heavily on volunteers reporting sightings of Kestrels over a season. Maps were then produced showing clusters of sightings, which were assumed to represent different pairs. Although some nests were also found, the coverage was often uneven and some areas were not searched at all. The density estimates were usually calculated by assuming that clusters of sightings with no nest represented a single pair. The assumption may hold if pairs are nesting some distance apart, but this is not always true. The likely result was that some pairs were missed, and estimates from large areas tend to be uniformly low.

It could be argued that workers chose large areas *because* density was low and they wanted a good sample of pairs. This does not seem to have been so, however, as in most cases the limits of the study were fixed at the outset, often using county boundaries. Pairs may also have been missed in areas that were searched late in the nesting season, because only the successful pairs were likely to be found.

The result of these sources of error is that published estimates of Kestrel breeding density show a strong negative correlation with the size of the area surveyed (Fig. 46). I found this using about 30 estimates published prior to

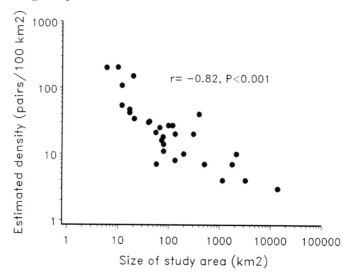

Fig. 46. Correlation of published estimates of Kestrel breeding density with the size of the area searched (re-drawn from Village 1984). Notice the logarithmic scales on both axes. Details of each estimate are given in Table 20.

1983, and it has recently been confirmed with a larger sample from West Germany (Kostrzewa 1988). The bias is most evident in very small (<50 km^2) or very large (>500 km^2) areas, and logarithmic scales were necesary to fit a linear relationship. Densities from studies covering 80–200 km^2 showed little correlation with the area searched, and this size of study area seems to be the best compromise.

My own experience is that about 100 km^2 is large enough to give a reasonable density estimate, and can be covered by one full-time worker, or several part-time ones. In recent years, I have been able to cover a total of 350 km^2, but only because I now have a thorough knowledge of where the nest sites are in each of my areas. Someone starting a new study should choose a block of about 100 km^2, preferably at random, and thoroughly search it to find every pair. The intial searches should be done before most pairs have begun laying because those pairs that fail early in the breeding cycle may vacate their site, sometimes leaving no sign that it was previously occupied (Village 1984).

BREEDING DENSITIES IN THE GRASSLAND AND FARMLAND AREAS

Because of the apparent bias, it is difficult to draw any firm conclusions from the published estimates of Kestrel breeding density. However, my records should be comparable because they were collected in the same way from areas of a similar size. The number of pairs in the three areas varied from year to year, but was generally highest in the grassland area (32 pairs/100km^2 over four years), intermediate in mixed farmland (19 pairs/100km^2 over seven years) and lowest in intensive arable farmland (12 pairs/100km^2 over seven years). The mixed farmland area showed a steady decline in breeding numbers from 1983, so recently the density has been similar to, or below, that of the arable area, where numbers remained fairly constant (Table 21). These variations amounted to a three-fold difference in annual density within areas, and a two to three-fold difference in mean density between areas. Finding the cause of these fluctuations is central to understanding population regulation in this species.

FACTORS LIMITING KESTREL BREEDING DENSITIES

Of the many possible factors that might affect breeding numbers in raptors, two stand out as being most important: food supply and the availability of nest sites (Newton 1979). Either of these may prevent further growth of the breeding population, which is limited by whichever resource is in shortest supply. The exceptions may be populations that suffer unusually high mortality, such as those persecuted by man or poisoned by his pesticides, where there are insufficient individuals to reach the density permitted by food or nest sites. This could be so during population declines, or temporally true of recovering populations, but Kestrels are fortunate, compared with some other raptors, in having escaped the worst effects of pesticides and gamekeeping, so they are more likely to be resource-limited.

In some sense, it is intuitively obvious that Kestrel breeding density must be related to the supply of food or nest sites. Kestrels cannot live where they have nothing to eat, and cannot breed without somewhere to lay their eggs. The questions of interest are whether wild populations actually reach the limits of their resources, how closely numbers are tuned to resource levels, and how any adjustment comes about.

The best way of testing whether a particular resource is limiting a wild population is to increase that resource experimentally. If this leads to a sudden increase in population density, and all other factors remain unchanged, then the level of that resource was, by definition, the *limiting factor* to population growth. The opposite experiment, of reducing a resource level, is not quite so easy to interpret, because lowering a resource may make it become limiting, even though it isn't normally so. Thus, food supply may limit a population, but removal of all the nest sites will doubtless lower breeding density, even though nest sites were not the natural limiting factor.

Complications can also arise when resources are increased if several different resources are required for breeding and all are at similar levels. Food supply, for example, might be the only factor limiting a population, but providing extra food may result in only a small increase in breeding density, because Kestrels immediately come up against a shortage of nest sites. Such small responses to experimental manipulations would be difficult to detect, and field experiments may give clear results only where populations are severely limited by a single resource.

Evidence that food supply limits Kestrel breeding density
Experimentally increasing the food of Kestrels over a wide area is extremely

difficult, and has not yet been attempted. So the evidence we have that food limits breeding numbers comes from observing natural variations in prey density, either between areas or between years in the same area. Evidence from comparisons between areas is limited because of the difficulties in comparing published density estimates, but the differences between my Scottish grassland and English farmland areas support the idea that the food level affects Kestrel breeding densities. The highest densities I recorded were in the grassland study area, which had the most vole habitat and therefore the best food supply. The lowest densities were in intensive arable farmland, where there was little vole habitat and, presumably, little food.

Annual fluctuations in prey densities in the same place are further indications of the link between Kestrel numbers and food supply. The evidence is best where Kestrels eat mainly voles, because vole abundance can be measured and is the single most important factor affecting the food available to Kestrels. Vole cycles are a great help in this respect, because they introduce yearly variations in Kestrel food supply that mimic those that researchers would like to produce experimentally. Such 'natural experiments' allow Kestrel densities to be measured in a variety of food conditions, but they do not completely obviate the need for proper experiments, because they cannot exclude the effects of other factors besides vole numbers that also change during vole cycles.

The sudden increase in the numbers of Kestrels, and other vole predators, during vole plagues has long been known. Written accounts usually amount to little more than anecdotal reports, but they are nonetheless useful records of rare events and can make interesting reading. Adair's (1891 & 1893) reports of the 1890–2 vole plague at Eskdalemuir and Roxburghshire give a vivid picture of how Kestrels and Short-eared Owls increased in response to the incredible numbers of voles in the area, and how quickly they declined when the vole numbers crashed.

As well as casual accounts, some authors have more systematically recorded Kestrel numbers over several years and related them to 'good' or 'bad' vole years. The latter may have been assessed subjectively, or by records of vole damage over a wide area. Hagen (1969) found that Kestrel nests at Dovre, Norway, varied from 14 in a peak vole year to only one during a vole minimum. Snow (1968) analysed the BTO ringing returns and found peaks in the number of Kestrel broods ringed in northern Britain that corresponded to assumed vole peaks over a 40-year period. Vole cycles seem roughly synchronous in much of the Pennines and the Southern Uplands, so increases in the number of broods ringed probably reflected a higher number of pairs breeding in the north in good vole years.

Few studies have been able to measure Kestrel and vole numbers in the same area over several years. Anton Cavé (1968) did so for a population of Kestrels in reclaimed polders in Holland, from 1960 to 1964, and this is still one of the best population studies of raptors yet published. The Kestrels nested in boxes set out in three separate blocks about 15 km apart. Each block covered 3 x 3 km and consisted of a 9 x 9 grid, so that boxes were spaced evenly at 300–400 m intervals. Kestrel breeding density was taken as the number of clutches found, which may have slightly overestimated the true value because a few females laid a second clutch in a new box after failing on the first attempt.

Voles were snap-trapped on the dyke adjacent to each block, and rainfall and temperature were recorded daily at pumping stations within each block.

Multiple regression showed that Kestrel breeding numbers were negatively correlated with rainfall, positively correlated with temperature but, surprisingly, not correlated with vole numbers. He thought this was probably because his vole index was inaccurate, but his data suggest a reasonable positive correlation apart from the last year, when Kestrels were more numerous than indicated by the vole index. The significant correlations of rainfall and temperature were assumed to have reflected the effect of weather on Kestrel hunting, and hence food supply, during late winter and early spring. Food supply may therefore have been limiting Kestrel breeding numbers, but there was no evidence of a direct link between Kestrel and vole numbers.

As far as I am aware, the best correlation between Kestrel breeding numbers and vole numbers to date comes from a long-term study in Finland (Korpimäki 1985b). Kestrel numbers in 63 km^2 of farmland varied from nearly 40 pairs in the best vole year, to less than five pairs when vole numbers crashed. This, perhaps, is not surprising in view of the more pronounced vole cycles at such high latitudes, where changes in vole density can override any other factors that might affect Kestrel numbers.

The variations in Kestrel density in my Scottish grassland area were not as extreme as those in Finland, but they nonetheless corresponded with year to year changes in vole numbers. There was a positive correlation between the density of territorial pairs and the spring vole index, but with only four years data this was not quite statistically significant ($r = 0.95$, $P < 0.06$). There was also a significant difference in nest spacing between years, nests being further apart in the poor vole year of 1977 than in better vole year of 1978 (Chapter 9). As in Finland, the grassland area was good vole habitat, where Kestrels were largely migratory. Breeding numbers were therefore determined in spring, when there was an influx of birds, and the number able to settle was closely related to the prevailing vole density.

The situation in the farmland areas was more complicated because there was less vole habitat and because breeding Kestrels were largely drawn from those that wintered in the area. There was no significant correlation between spring vole numbers and the total Kestrel density, as estimated from roadside counts, whether combining the mixed and arable areas or treating them separately. The correlation between voles and the density of laying pairs was almost statistically significant (Fig. 47a, $r = 0.51$, $P < 0.06$), but the relationship arose mainly because the highest spring vole numbers were in 1981, which was also the best Kestrel breeding year in mixed farmland. In the other years, the density of voles was low, so there was insufficient variation to show a clear relationship with Kestrel numbers.

One reason for the poor correlation between Kestrel and vole numbers in farmland was the effect of winter weather. In mixed farmland there was a sharp decline in breeding density after 1983, and this was correlated with mean temperature in the preceding winter (Fig. 47b). Low temperatures were associated with increased likelihood of snow cover, which reduced the availability of invertebrates and voles, and forced Kestrels to rely on birds, which they found difficult to catch (Chapter 4). This seems to have resulted

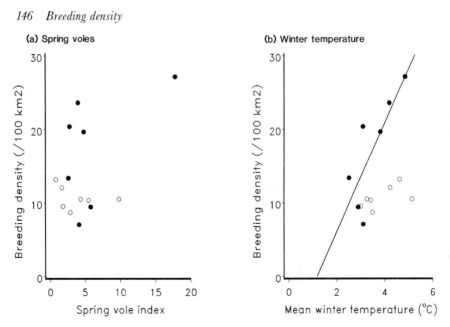

Fig. 47. *Relationship of Kestrel breeding density to (a) the abundance of voles in spring and (b) the temperature during December-January over seven years in mixed (●) and arable (○) farmland. The only significant correlation was between density and winter temperature in the mixed farmland area (solid line: r=0.51, P<0.05).*

in low Kestrel numbers in late winter, which were not replenished by any spring influx. Breeding numbers were thus lower than expected relative to spring vole numbers in years following severe winters. In arable farmland, Kestrel breeding densities were uniformly low, and seemed unaffected by annual variations in vole numbers or weather. Winter numbers were largely determined by the numbers of Woodmice, which always reached low densities by spring, so Kestrels may have been scarce in spring, even after mild winters.

Evidence that nest sites limit breeding density

Manipulating the availability of Kestrel nest sites over a wide area is much easier than doing the same for their food, so the evidence linking nest-site availability to nesting density is as much experimental as circumstantial.

There are several cases in European Kestrels, and other kestrel species, where the use of nestboxes has apparently increased breeding density (Cavé 1968, Hamerstrom *et al* 1973, Burton 1986, Bang 1986). In areas of good hunting habitat, with no natural nest sites, the effect can be dramatic: on one reclaimed polder in Holland, Kestrels increased from 20 pairs in 1959 to 109 in 1960, following the erection of 246 nestboxes in the intervening winter (Cavé 1968). Unfortunately, the winter also coincided with a rise in vole numbers, so not all the increase in Kestrels was due to the additional nestboxes. This highlights the need for careful interpretation of the results of such manipulations. Nestboxes are ideal Kestrel nest sites, and they are likely to be preferred to many, less suitable, natural sites. Erecting boxes may do no more than bring in Kestrels from their original sites, and it is difficult to be sure that a real increase in density has taken place unless it was measured in previous years and in adjacent control areas.

At Eskdalemuir, in 1976 and 1977, there were some large areas of hill ground with no usable nest sites and no breeding Kestrels. Some Kestrels hunted in these areas, but they were either birds breeding in the valleys or unpaired non-breeders. In January and February 1978, I put up 17 nestboxes and artificial stick nests in these areas, 11 in young plantation and six in sheepwalk. That year about half the boxes were used in each area, but there were no Kestrels breeding in similar areas where I had not put boxes (Village 1983b). Lack of nest sites was thus limiting Kestrel breeding density in these large open areas, and some of the boxes I put up that year have been occupied by Kestrels ever since (R. Rose).

In other habitats, the provision of nestboxes may not increase Kestrel density so dramatically. Failure of Kestrels to use boxes is hardly ever reported in the literature (but see Petty 1985), so it is difficult to tell which habitats have a surfeit of natural sites and which do not. I repeated the nestbox experiment in farmland by erecting about 25 boxes in 50 km² sections of the mixed and arable farmland areas in 1985. In this case there were no large, unoccupied areas of ground, but the new boxes effectively trebled the usable sites in the arable experimental area, and almost doubled them in mixed farmland.

However, neither area showed any corresponding increase in Kestrel breeding density over the next three years (Table 22). Thus, Kestrel numbers in both farmland areas were not limited by lack of nest sites, even though the density of natural sites in arable farmland was much less than in mixed farmland.

In some areas, Kestrel density may be limited by competition for nest sites with other species that also do not build their own nests. Long-eared Owls often use nestboxes or artificial stick nests intended for Kestrels. At Eskdalemuir, owls bred earlier than Kestrels (Village 1981), and thus had precedence for nest sites. On several occasions, Kestrels bred in nests previously used by Long-eared Owls in the same season, and this has been reported elsewhere (Cavé 1968). Kestrels may also compete with Peregrines for cliff sites, and there are reports of Kestrels taking over eyries after the original occupants had failed in their breeding attempts and moved away (Ratcliffe 1980).

Evidence that mortality limits breeding density

Mortality may well be involved in adjusting Kestrel populations to resource levels. In a population where numbers are higher than the food supply can support, the excess birds may die of starvation. In such cases the resource is said to be the *ultimate* limiting factor on the population, and starvation is a *proximate* factor. In order for mortality itself ultimately to limit Kestrel populations, it has to be high enough to keep numbers below the levels that food or nest sites are capable of supporting. When this happens, there are insufficent birds to fill any vacant breeding territories. This could happen if there was heavy mortality due to predation, pesticide poisoning or human persecution, assuming in each case that well-fed Kestrels were as vulnerable as under-fed ones.

Although Kestrels do fall prey to some larger raptors and to carnivores, there is little evidence that such predation ever holds breeding numbers below resource levels. The same is true for human persecution, though there is no quantitative data for the early years of the century, when Kestrels were more at risk from gamekeepers than they are today. The shooting of Kestrels, and robbing of nests, may certainly reduce the number of pairs that successfully fledge young but, if it is to lower the breeding density, it has to be sufficient to restrict the number of birds available to pair in early spring.

Kestrel breeding density and pesticides

Mortality caused by organochlorine pesticides may well have lowered Kestrel breeding densities in some parts of Britain during the 1960s and early 1970s. The effects were less severe than for Sparrowhawks or Peregrines, and this, together with the greater difficulties in counting Kestrel nests, means that the evidence is rather scant. Questionnaires sent out in 1964 reported declines in many south-eastern counties of England, but few in the north or west (Prestt 1965). Local county bird-reports also indicate that the decline was first noticed in the early 1960s, and that recovery started within three or four years in some areas (Table 23). It is difficult to place too much reliance on these data, however, because few records were kept before the decline was publicised, and recorders soon lost their enthusiasm for systematically sending in records when Kestrel numbers had started to recover. The initial decline in Kestrels in

eastern England coincided with the first widespread use of dieldrin, aldrin and heptachlor as seed dressings, and a similar, but more widespread, decline occurred in Sparrowhawks (Newton 1986). Unfortunately, the decrease also coincided with two very hard winters, in 1961 and 1962, and this has been suggested as the cause of the low numbers of Kestrels recorded in the Common Bird Census in the early sixties (O'Connor 1982). This seems unlikely to be the only cause, however, because the reduction in Kestrel breeding density was restricted to the areas of heavy pesticide use, and declines of such a scale have not followed other hard winters. Furthermore, the levels of pesticides in some carcasses examined in the Pesticide Monitoring Scheme at Monks Wood would almost certainly have caused death, and the recovery of Kestrel numbers coincided with restrictions in pesticide usage that started in 1962 (Cooke *et al* 1982).

Some decline in breeding density is normally associated with hard winters, so it is difficult to distinguish the effect of the hard winters in the early 1960s from pesticide poisoning. What is clear is that that Kestrels became rare breeding birds in much of Cambridgeshire, Norfolk, Suffolk, Essex and Kent in the early and mid 1960s, and that this coincided with pesticide-induced mortality. Numbers started to recover by 1965 in some counties, but not until the late 1970s, after aldrin and dieldrin were further restricted, in the worst affected parts of Cambridgeshire. When I began work in the arable farmland area in 1980, nearly all the farmers I spoke with commented on the increase in Kestrels they had noticed over the previous five years or so. There is no evidence that Kestrel breeding numbers are currently depressed by pesticides in the arable study area, or elsewhere in Britain, but the difficulties in obtaining sound evidence mean that such a possibility cannot be entirely discounted.

THE NON-BREEDING SURPLUS

It may seem strange to devote a section to non-breeding birds in a chapter on breeding density. However, to understand fully what limits breeding numbers it is necessary to know if there are non-breeding birds present during the breeding season and, if so, why they do not breed. Breeding density is the product of the total population density and the proportion of that population that breeds. If all the Kestrels present in an area breed, breeding density is probably limited by whatever controls total population density, such as winter mortality and the number of birds that settle in spring. If, on the other hand, some birds do not breed, then whatever prevents them from doing so is likely to be the ultimate limit to breeding density. This might not be so in species where immature birds are unable to breed until they reach a certain age, because mortality could reduce adult numbers below resource levels but still leave non-breeding immatures in the area. Kestrels, however, can breed when a year old, even though few do so in most circumstances.

Circumstantial evidence that non-breeders exist
In all three study areas I have had marked birds present throughout the breeding season that failed to get a mate or, if they did, failed to produce eggs. It is difficult to define when Kestrels start to breed because some form pairs only temporarily early in the season and give up before laying eggs. The number of such non-laying pairs I recorded varied from year to year and between areas. In the Scottish grassland area, about 6% of pairs failed to produce eggs, compared with 13% for the English farmland areas. It was difficult to tell how many birds remained unpaired during the summer because non-breeders were difficult to trap or count. In most years I caught some unpaired individuals, but these might have been only a fraction of those actually present. In the farmland study, I calculated that at least 30% of the tagged Kestrels known to be alive in summer were not breeding (see Chapter 18). This is similar to Sparrowhawks, where about 45% of females present during the breeding season were not paired (Newton 1985).

A second way of estimating the numbers of non-breeding birds present in spring was to compare the density of breeding pairs with the density estimates from roadside counts (Chapter 8), which included both breeders and non-breeders. This was possible in farmland because there was little, if any, influx of Kestrels in spring, so the breeding population was mainly drawn from birds already present in March and early April. Combining both farmland areas, there was a significant correlation between the total spring density and the density of laying pairs (Fig. 48). Apart from one point, the total population density estimate always exceeded the breeding density (as it should), but the

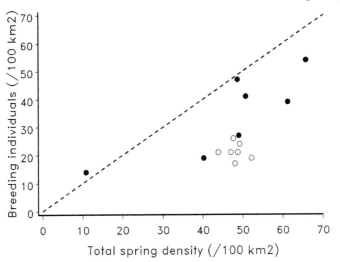

Fig. 48. Relationship of Kestrel breeding density to the total population density in early spring in mixed (●) and arable (○) farmland. The line is the expected trend if all the population bred. Total density was estimated from roadside counts during March and April, the density of breeding individuals was taken as twice the number of laying pairs. Breeding density was roughly dependent on the total density of Kestrels at the end of winter (r = 0.63, df = 12, P < 0.02).

difference between the two varied from year to year. The average density of paired birds was 32 individuals /100 km², and the average total density was 47 /100 km², suggesting that non-breeders comprised about a third of the total population, a similar figure to the estimate from tagged birds.

Obviously these results were open to some error, and the proportion of the population not breeding may vary from year to year. There was some suggestion of a high proportion of non-breeders when breeding density was low, which would arise if fluctuations in breeding density were partly due to birds not breeding, as well as to changes in total population density. However, the slope of the regression depended on a single outlying point at low density in mixed farmland, so it is not yet possible to be certain of the relationship between the levels of the paired and unpaired segments of the population.

Other evidence for the existence of non-breeders comes from cases where breeding birds are able to replace a mate that has died naturally or been shot. When this happens late in the breeding season, it suggests that the incoming bird was not breeding beforehand, and was unlikely, otherwise, to have done so. Replacement of shot or injured raptors has been reported in several species (Newton 1979), including Kestrels (Frere 1886, Village 1983b). In some instances the new bird takes over the clutch or brood of the previous occupant, whereas others start a new breeding attempt. A similar line of evidence is the occupation of abandoned Long-eared Owl nests by Kestrels late on the season, after the latter would normally have started breeding. Piechocki (1982) also cites a case where the shooting of Rooks late in the season resulted in several Kestrel pairs immediately occupying the vacant nests, again suggesting they may not otherwise have bred that year through lack of a suitable site.

Experimental evidence for the cause of non-breeding

To see if non-breeders could be induced to breed, I have used experiments that mimic the observations quoted in the previous section. The first of these were *removal experiments*, in which one or both members of breeding pairs were deliberately taken from their territories after they had started nesting. If birds were replaced by others that then bred, it indicated that some Kestrels were prevented from breeding because they lacked a suitable mate, territory or nest site, or any combination of these. The second were *late-nest experiments*, which involved erecting artificial nest sites late in the breeding season. To ensure freedom from interference by existing pairs, I put these late sites outside Kestrel territories, in gaps between breeding pairs. These second experiments tested more specifically if non-breeding was the result of insufficient nest sites, rather than a shortage of a mate or a suitable territory.

Both experiments were started only after I was sure that all the pairs that would normally breed that year had already settled on their territories. The timing was important because birds occupying nests (or coming in as replacements) early in the season might otherwise have bred elsewhere. Starting the experiments late in the season made it unlikely that breeding birds would take up the vacant nests, and wing-tagging confirmed this was so. The best time to experiment was in the first three weeks of May, as this was late enough to avoid normal breeding birds but early enough to give incomers a chance of producing eggs.

In the Scottish grassland area, over three years, I removed one partner from four pairs (three females and one male), and both members of one pair (Table 24). Three of the four single birds removed from the pairs were replaced (two females and the male), but not the removed pair. The male partners of the removed females were both wing-tagged and they were the birds that mated with the new females in each case.

In the farmland areas, 13 males and 12 females (all from different pairs) were removed, or died, late in the season between 1985 and 1987 (Table 24). Males and females were replaced, but females more often (67% versus 31% for males). New pairs formed after a female had been removed were more likely to produce eggs later that season than were pairs formed after male removals (67% versus 8%), and much more likely to fledge young (42% versus 0%).

In the late-nest experiments, I made 19 nest sites available over two years in Eskdalemuir and more than 50 over four years in each farmland area (Table 25). The results in the two studies were quite different, with 10 nest sites (53%) occupied in Eskdalemuir but none in the two farmland areas. The lack of response in farmland was consistent with the failure of even early-erected boxes to increase Kestrel breeding density, and confirmed that, in these areas, breeding was not limited by a shortage of suitable nesting sites.

The status of incomers in removal and late-nest experiments

The status of Kestrels that came in as replacements or late-nest occupants seemed to vary, but most were apparently unpaired first-year birds. A notable exception was a pair in Eskdalemuir in 1978 that was present from early March, and which was frequently seen displaying at a crow nest in the solitary spruce tree in their territory. I climbed the tree on 20 April, to see if they had started laying, but was surprised to find a Long-eared Owl incubating a clutch in the crow nest. The Kestrels continued to display in typical fashion for over two weeks, but were able to take over the nest only after the owls failed, on 8 May.

The female laid her first egg within four days of the nest becoming available, so she must have already started to form eggs in the oviduct (Meijer 1988). What the pair would have done if the owls had not failed was not certain, though the fact that they laid more than two weeks later than the mean laying date for that year suggests they had nowhere else to breed. When non-breeders were unpaired prior to the experiments, the interval from removal (or nest availability) and laying was longer (mean = 14.5 days, Table 26), and similar to that found from first pairing to egg laying in captive American Kestrels (Porter & Wiemeyer 1972: 13 days; Bird & Lague 1982: 11 days).

The majority of incomers were first-year birds, though some were adults (Table 27), and this probably reflected the composition of the non-breeding sector. Yearlings may have found it difficult to compete with adults for resources because of their inexperience. In the Scottish grassland area, adult males defended an area around their nest, and this excluded other males from using nearby unoccupied nests. In the farmland areas, unpaired males had access to nest sites, but were rarely able to breed, even when they came in as replacements on breeding territories. This seemed to be because they could not catch enough prey, irrespective of the degree of competition from adults. Females, however, may have competed with each other for suitable males, and there was some evidence for this. In four of eight removal experiments in which I released the removed females at the end of the breeding season, they ousted the incomer and re-paired with their original male later in the year. In one instance I released the original female while the incomer was still incubating. She must have immediately reclaimed her mate, because I flushed her off the eggs when I visited the nest a few days later. Unfortunately, none of the eggs hatched, probably because they were chilled during the take-over, so I do not know if the original female would have raised the incomer's brood.

SUMMARY

Although there are many estimates of Kestrel breeding densities in the literature, most are of limited use because they are affected by the size of the area searched. In my studies, breeding density varied from around 32 pairs/100 km^2 in the Scottish grassland area to 12 pairs/100 km^2 in arable farmland, with mixed farmland being intermediate between these extremes. There was also up to a three-fold variation in densities within areas from year to year.

The evidence linking Kestrel breeding density to food supply comes mainly from migratory Kestrel populations in Northern Europe, which feed largely on voles and therefore experience marked changes in food supply from year to year. In the English farmland areas, breeding density was related to the number of Kestrels present at the end of winter, which in mixed farmland was dependent partly on the severity of the winter weather and hence winter food-supply. Spring vole numbers had some effect in increasing Kestrel breeding density, but only in an exceptionally good vole year. Lack of nesting sites seemed to limit breeding density in parts of the Scottish grassland area, but not in the farmland areas.

In the grassland and both the farmland areas, there was a surplus of non-breeding birds capable of mating with breeding birds that lost their partners. These surplus birds were largely, but not entirely, yearlings. In Eskdalemuir the surplus was apparent in both sexes, and nest sites that became available late in the season outside existing territories were often occupied. In farmland there were males and females among non-breeders, but males were less likely to be replaced than females and, if they were, the new males never bred successfully. There seemed to be no surplus males in farmland that were limited in breeding solely by lack of a nest site, and most of those present that were able to feed a female were also able to find a mate and somewhere to breed.

CHAPTER 11

The breeding cycle:
pair formation and courtship

In Kestrels, as in most birds, the breeding cycle can be divided into several
stages, from pair formation to the independence of young. The main stages,
covering the incubation and nestling periods, are of fairly fixed duration, but
the start of laying may vary by several weeks between pairs in the same area.
In Britain, Kestrel breeding activity usually begins in late February or March,
when migrants move northwards and start pairing, and resident pairs initiate
courtship behaviour. Laying starts sometime between mid April and late May,
and the young fledge during June and July. Juveniles remain in their natal
territory for about a month after fledging, which means that most pairs finish
their breeding cycle by mid or late August. The timing of breeding is quite
different at lower latitudes, especially in the tropics, where seasonality is less
pronounced. Breeding seasons are dealt with in more detail later; in the
following three chapters I describe the different stages of the breeding cycle,

155

concentrating on the behaviour of the parents and the development of the young.

CALLS AND DISPLAYS DURING THE BREEDING CYCLE

A number of behaviours are either confined to the breeding season, or occur much more frequently then than at other times. Courtship and territorial displays were first described in detail by Lucas Tinbergen (1940), who recorded the behaviour of eight pairs of Kestrels over three years in Holland. The following account is based on his descriptions, though I have added my own observations where appropriate. Much of the activity of Kestrels during the early part of the breeding season is concerned with forming or maintaining the pair bond, and defending the nest site. In some cases these are not entirely distinct behaviours, because displays that advertise to a mate are also used to ward off intruders. I have described the calls and displays separately because, although some calls are closely linked to certain displays, a given call can be used in several different circumstances.

Calls

Kestrels are noisy birds, especially when breeding, and the latin name *tinnunculus* derives from their 'ringing' calls. There are two basic types of call, which I have defined according to their usual context.

1. Alarm calls. The usual alarm call has been variously described as '*vite-vite-vite*', '*kee-kee-kee*' or '*kik-kik-kik*', and is often heard when pairs are disturbed with young in the nest. It is also used during fights with other Kestrels, especially with persistent intruders near the nest, and at potential predators, such as Buzzards or corvids. Alarm calls given to intruding humans are slightly different from the more urgent calls uttered during persistent mobbing of other birds. For example, Kestrels attack crows in a twisting dive, and the syllables of the alarm call become uneven, with a different emphasis on each note. This change in the call at high intensity was noted by Tinbergen, who named it the *aggression call*, and it may be used when Kestrels mob any large predator. I heard this same call on a memorable occasion recently, when I climbed to a Kestrel nest at the very top of a tall spruce tree and flushed the male. I had just secured my safety harness, and was admiring the view, when a Goshawk flew out of the wood and started circling overhead. The male Kestrel took exception to this, and for several minutes I was treated to a grandstand view as he repeatedly dived at the hawk, his calls ringing around the valley.

2. Signal calls. As with alarm calls, signal calls are used in a variety of situations, and they vary in intensity, pitch and duration. The usual call is a series of high-pitched trills described as '*vrii-vrii-vrii*', '*heerre-heerre-heerre*' or '*quirrr-rr quirrr-rr*'. Tinbergen termed this the *lahn* or signal call because it is frequently used between partners during nest inspections, copulation or prey deliveries. Females utter this call when soliciting copulation or taking food from the male, and the young use it to beg for food. It denotes excitement or mild alarm and may be given when intruders are first seen in the vicinity of the nest, prior to attack.

Males, and to a lesser extent females, also use a second signal call during displays near the nest. Sequences of signal trills are interrupted by sharp, clipped notes which have been translated as '*tsick*', '*kit*' or '*clip*'. These are heard early in the breeding cycle, when either sex visits the nest during courtship displays, and seem to be associated with sexual excitement. Later, the male uses this call to signal his arrival with food, and the female when she feeds small chicks. Males also have a different expression of excitement during copulation, which is more like the alarm call, but with a faster, less distinct, repetition of each syllable.

Displays

1. Rocking flight. Members of breeding pairs are often seen soaring together in early spring. Sometimes they rise to great height and begin a rapid, level flight with distinct, flicking wing beats, interspersed with short glides. During this flight, the bird may rock from side to side, tilting the underside. This rocking display is often at considerable height, so it is easily missed (Tinbergen, for example, does not mention it in his account), and difficult to judge its context or purpose. In most cases where I have seen this behaviour, I have soon spotted an intruder, or a displaying neighbour, so it is probably used mainly in territory defence. It also occurs between members of a pair or even in unpaired birds. One male Kestrel at Eskdalemuir that lost his partner just before egg laying used the rocking display a great deal for several days afterwards, apparently trying to attract a mate.

The rocking display is sometimes accompanied by the '*tsick*' call, and this, coupled with the flickering wing movements and flashing of the pale underside, must make the performer noticeable for some distance. Kestrels probably use rocking flights to advertise their presence, either to intruders, or to potential mates. They can travel some distance during these displays, and I saw one male finish near the nest site of a neighbouring pair some 2 km away.

2. V-flight. The rocking display often ends with a spectacular dive onto the nest from several hundred feet. The wings are held in a backward 'V' and the bird drops at great speed, only slowing at the very last moment. I once arrived at a Kestrel nestbox just as the male executed a V-flight. The box was on the side of a deer stool, and I was about to lean over from inside to check it, when I caught sight of the male plummeting towards me. He landed with a thump on the top of the box, giving the excited *tsick* call, and only then noticed me a few feet away. It was hard to say who was the more surprised.

The V-flight is largely, but not exclusively, a male display and it also occurs during low-level courtship flights near the nest. I have found that watching displaying males is a useful method for locating nests in thick conifer stands, where old crow nests may be completely hidden. There are drawbacks, however, because excited males will 'V'-flight into any handy tree, which has led me to several fruitless climbs!

3. Winnowing-flight. During courtship flights near the nest, both sexes often have a characteristic, slow flight, called *zitterflug* by Tinbergen. The wing beats are very rapid but shallow, so that sometimes only the wing tips seem to move. Kestrels fly this way before and after copulation, during pre-lay visits to the nest, and when chasing intruders. The '*lahn*' and '*tsick*' calls are common during these winnowing flights, which again seem to express general excitement.

FREQUENCY OF DISPLAYS AND FIGHTS

Where Kestrels are largely migratory, the arrival of summer visitors heralds the start of breeding. If most of the breeding population arrives in spring, there is a great deal of territorial and courtship behaviour prior to egg-laying. At Eskdalemuir, summer visitors began arriving in late February, and either formed pairs among themselves or with the previously unpaired winter residents. In areas where most pairs remain together in winter, there is less upheaval among the resident population, and courtship behaviour gradually increases from late winter onwards. In my farmland areas in east England, many pairs stayed together after breeding, and new pairs formed mainly in autumn or early spring. Some spring pairings were between new arrivals, but most were between birds that had been neighbours in the previous winter. I saw some paired males take an occasional prey item to their mates in February, nearly three months before egg laying, though this was rare so early in the season.

The difference in the frequency of displays between the Scottish and English study areas is apparent in Fig. 49, which is based on the behaviour of Kestrels when first seen. Such 'spot observations' may not give the true frequency of a

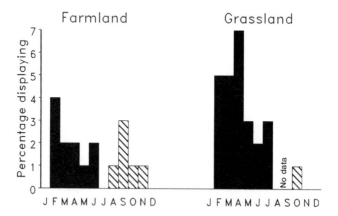

Fig. 49. Percentage frequency of sexual displays among Kestrels in the Eskdalemuir grassland and the farmland study areas. Based on the percentage of spot observations of activity when birds were first sighted. Shaded bars refer to breeding males, hatched bars to both sexes in autumn and winter. During early spring, displays were more frequent in the partially migrant grassland population than in the sedentary farmland population. Compare this figure with Fig. 37, which shows the same result for territorial fights.

behaviour, but they are useful in making comparisons between areas or over time. The greater frequency of courtship displays in Eskdalemuir may have been due to the relatively short time from pairing to egg laying, and the fact that all birds had to establish pair bonds at the start of the cycle. Resident pairs in England engaged in some courtship behaviour, such as mutual preening or display flights, throughout the winter and may have required less overt display to maintain the pair bond than did newly-formed pairs.

The high frequency of territorial displays at Eskdalemuir (see Fig. 37, Chapter 7) reflected the upheaval in the home range system at the end of winter. Such changes were less marked in England, as there seemed to be fewer birds trying to force their way into the existing territorial framework. In addition, nest sites at Eskdalemuir were more unevenly dispersed than those in the farmland area, and neighbours were often only a few hundred metres apart. This must have increased the chances of territory violations, compared to isolated nests. Experiments with Kestrel decoys showed that farmland pairs were still aggressive during the early part of the breeding season (C. G. Wiklund), so the more frequent fighting at Eskdalemuir was probably related to the high number of intrusions as pairs established territory boundaries.

THE ARRIVAL OF MIGRANTS IN SPRING

At Eskdalemuir, I spent a great deal of time in the study area from February onwards, and so I had a fairly good idea of when most birds arrived. The date when I first saw a bird on its territory was not necessarily the day it arrived, but it could be used to compare the times of arrival in different years, either between the sexes or between adults and first-year birds. I also used the first date on which I saw the partner in the territory as the last possible pairing date, which allowed comparison of the mating period (arrival to pairing) and courtship period (mating to egg laying).

Individual migrants arrived in Eskdalemuir between 17 February and 5 May, the mean arrival date being slightly earlier in 1976 than in the other three years (Fig. 50), possibly due to the unusually mild weather in the first two months of that year. Migrant males and females arrived over the same period, with no difference in their mean arrival dates. However, within pairs, males were more likely to pair with later arriving partners than *vice versa*. The first migrants consisted of roughly equal numbers of males and females, but the sex ratio among the winter residents was biased towards males (Chapter 18). The incoming females usually paired with the resident males, leaving a surplus of migrant males to wait for more females to arrive. This resulted in a surplus of unpaired males during the settling period, which diminished only as the latest females arrived.

The date on which a bird was first seen also depended on its age and whether it had bred in the area before. In 1978 and 1979, when enough records were obtained, adults tended to arrive before first-year birds and, in 1978, returning migrants began arriving before new birds (Fig. 51). The difference between adults and first-years may have arisen for several reasons. Firstly, adults may have been able to leave their wintering grounds before first-year birds because

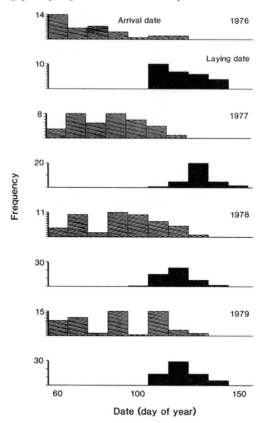

Fig. 50. Histograms of pairing (hatched) and laying (shaded) dates for Kestrels in the Eskdalemuir area, 1976–79 (after Village 1985a). Dates expessed as day of the year (1 = 1 January).

they were in better condition to face the journey and any food-shortage when they arrived. Secondly, adults may have wintered nearer to the breeding grounds and, therefore, took less time to reach them in spring. Juveniles do seem to migrate further than older birds (Chapter 16), but the speed at which some birds are known to migrate makes it unlikely that distance to the wintering ground could fully explain the observed differences in arrival time. A final possibility is that first-year birds were, in fact, present early in the settling period, but not on territories. Defending a territory may have been too difficult for yearling males until the food supply improved later in the season, or they may not have attempted to establish a territory early in the season if they were inferior birds and likely to be evicted by late-arriving adults. These possibilities cannot be ruled out altogether, but it is unlikely that I would have overlooked significant numbers of first-year birds early in the season.

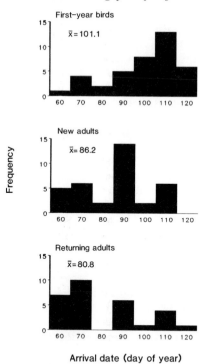

Fig. 51. Histograms of arrival dates in the Eskdalemuir grassland area, 1978–79, in relation to age, sex and previous breeding in the area (after Village 1985a). On average, adults arrived before first-years and returning migrants before new migrants.

The difference in arrival dates between returning and new migrants was less marked than that between adults and first-years, and may have been a chance effect. If it was a real trend, it could have been for the reasons just mentioned, or because returning migrants had a definite destination, whereas other adults might simply have moved until they found a suitable territory or partner. Several of the 'new' migrants that arrived early in 1979 turned out to be two-year old adults returning to their natal area, so they were also migrating to a particular destination, though probably breeding for the first time.

THE SELECTION OF MATES

It is difficult to follow the process of pair formation in most wild birds, so we have to infer what happens when birds select a mate from the final choices they make, that is, from the matings observed in the breeding population. There are two separate questions that can be asked: firstly, is there any evidence that pairs mate selectively and, secondly, how does this selection, if any, come about? To answer the first question, it is necessary to compare the number of pairings among birds with a particular trait, with that expected if mating was entirely random with respect to that trait. If the two frequecies differ significantly, it is reasonable to suppose that some sort of selective mating occurs.

One obvious feature is age. This is related to breeding performance, so there is good reason for Kestrels to choose partners of the most productive age. Kestrels have a distinctive plumage in their first year, but I was unable to age adults exactly unless they had previously been caught in their first year of life or were ringed as nestlings. It was therefore several years before I had accumulated large samples of known-aged adults, and neither of my studies was sufficiently long to allow investigation of age-specific mate selection in adults. A comparison of the numbers of pairings among first-year birds and adults, however, showed that these age-classes mated selectively in some years but not in others (Table 28). The overall trend was for a greater number of adult x adult and first-year x first-year pairings, and fewer mixed pairings, than would have been expected by chance. This was true of the Scottish and the English studies, and similar to findings in Sparrowhawks (Newton *et al* 1981).

This does not necessarily mean that individuals were actively choosing to mate with partners of the same age class as themselves. In Scotland, some assortative mating arose because of the different arrival times of yearlings and adults, and Kestrels seemed to pair at random with the mates available at the time. Thus, when most adults paired, there were few first-year birds around, and the latter mated after most of the adults had already paired (Village 1985a).

One combination of pairing that was underrepresented, even allowing for the disparity of arrival dates, was first-year males with adult females. I have recorded this combination only ten times, compared with 60 pairings of adult males with first-year females. This is probably because much of the responsibility for the success of a breeding attempt falls on the male. He has to find enough food to allow his mate to lay and to incubate the eggs. Therefore, adult females might have avoided pairing with first-year males because the latter were less able to maintain a mate than were adult males. However, if this was the only reason, pairs where both partners were yearlings should be equally scarce, which was not true. This suggests that, given a choice, adult females may reject yearling males in favour of older birds.

In Scotland, there was a slight excess of males during the breeding season (Chapter 18), and this was greatest during the settling period. Females would thus have had several mates to choose from when they arrived, but males would only have a choice if several females arrived at once. First-year females thus experienced no more difficulty than adult females in finding a partner, and those present early in the season were quickly paired. This was not so for males, and the few yearlings present early in the season took longer than adults to find a partner (Village 1985a). Females may reject first-year males after pairing because they fail to provide enough food, or they may avoid them in the first place because their distinctive plumage reveals their age.

There has been little study of other factors that might affect mate choice in wild Kestrels. In the 319 pairings I observed between marked birds, I could find no correlation between male and female wing lengths, so there was no obvious assortative mating by size. One slightly esoteric aspect of mate choice has been examined in American Kestrels, where captive females were presented with a choice of two possible mates, one male being related to them, the other not (Duncan & Bird 1989). This sought to test the idea that females would avoid incestuous mating, presumably because of the assumed disadvantages of inbreeding. In the event, there was no evidence that females either avoided or preferred related mates.

If Kestrels really do select mates, rather than pairing with the first possible partner they encounter, some unsuited pairs formed early in the season should split, and the members remate with other individuals. Wing-tagging allowed me to note this on seven occasions, when pairs were seen together early in the season, but did not subsequently breed with each other. In all cases, it was the male that stayed on the territory and remated, and the female that disappeared. Some of these females may have died and been replaced, but three were known to have bred elsewhere, either in the same or in subsequent years. I could not tell if the females left of their own accord, or were displaced by another female, as happens in some circumstances (see p. 153). The difference between the sexes is consistent with the observation that males set up a territory and then try to attract a female.

BIGAMY

Kestrels are nearly always monogamous, but occasionally one male will pair with two females. Polygyny seems to be widespread but infrequent in Kestrels as it has been reported from a number of studies, but rarely in more than 1–2% of pairings (Village 1983b, Dijkstra et al 1982). I had one bigamous male at Eskdalemuir, in a good vole year, but none in the farmland areas. The bigamous male was an adult that had bred monogamously at the same site in at least two previous years, but in 1978 he fed (and presumably mated with) two females in nests about 150 m apart. The first female, his mate from the previous year, laid on 19 April and reared three young, while a 2-year old female laid in the second nest on 7 May and reared five young. I had no detailed records of how the male divided his time between the two females, but my impression was that the first female was left to feed the young once they were old enough not to need brooding.

Polygyny is possible only for males that have sufficient time to feed more than one female, and is probably confined to adult males during good vole years. Detailed information on what factors cause polygyny is lacking, however, because of its infrequency and the difficulty of detecting it in unmarked populations.

Polyandry (one female with two or more mates), is equally difficult to prove. The two reported cases in Kestrels I could find were each based on seeing two males at a nest (Glutz et al 1971, Packham 1985a). In one case both males fed the female, but even then it was not certain that both had mated with her prior to egg-laying, or whether one male started to help the pair after the young hatched. I have caught 'extra' males in traps on several nests during the nestling stage, but they were yearlings, and there was no evidence that they were feeding the young, so they may simply have been 'passing through'.

To have some flexibility in the mating system is advantageous for a species such as the Kestrel, that may have widely fluctuating food levels from year to year in some areas. Female Kestrels have a limited ability to increase their clutch size in response to high vole numbers, so the only response for males that have an over-capacity to feed a female is to find a second mate. This may not suit the first female, who would presumably do better with the male's undivided attention, but she may have little choice once she has eggs. Although females ought, on the same basis, to find two mates when food conditions are poor, this does not seem to happen as often, presumably because males defend their territory for most of the breeding season. Kestrels respond to poor vole densities either by moving elsewhere, laying fewer eggs or not breeding. Bigamy seems to involve a certain amount of deception by the bigamous partner, and it is hard to see how a female could deceive her mate as easily as he could deceive her.

COURTSHIP

At Eskdalemuir, where all pairs separated in winter, courtship could be said to be the period between pairing and egg-laying. To define the start of courtship in the farmland areas was more difficult, because many pairs stayed together between breeding seasons and courtship behaviour, such as food passes or mutual preening, occurred on some mild days during winter. Here, as at Eskdalemuir, however, the main period of courtship activity was from March to May, with displays reaching a peak near the mean laying date.

The duration of courtship
The duration of courtship at Eskdalemuir varied between years and between pairs. Annual differences depended on both the timing of arrivals in spring and the mean laying date. Thus courtships were protracted in 1976, when birds arrived early but laid at the usual time, and also in 1977, when birds arrived at the usual time but laying was delayed by poor vole numbers (Fig. 50). In 1978 and 1979, birds arrived at about the same time as in 1977, but laying was earlier, so courtships were correspondingly shorter.

The considerable variation in the duration of courtship between pairs was mainly because pairs settling later had shorter courtships (Fig. 52), a phenomenon also noticed by Tinbergen (1940) and (Meijer 1988) in Holland. Courtship, then, is not a fixed-duration stage of the breeding cycle, unlike the incubation and nestling stages, but can vary according to circumstances. At Eskdalemuir, adults usually paired early in the season, well before females were capable of laying eggs, and thus spent longer in courtship than did younger birds that paired late in the season. The early pairs still laid before the later ones, but the disparity in laying dates was less than that of pairing dates.

Prolonged courtship may enable pairs to respond as soon as environmental

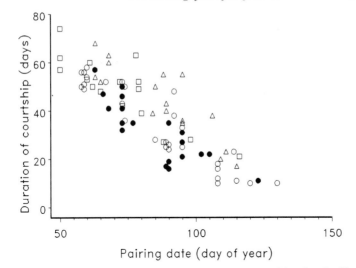

Fig. 52. *Duration of courtship (pairing to laying) in relation to pairing date for Kestrels in the Eskdalemuir area during 1976 (□), 1977 (△), 1978 (●) and 1979 (○). Pairs that formed late in the season had shorter courtship periods than those that formed early.*

conditions permit laying, and may lessen the chances of the pair failing once they have eggs. However, I know of no evidence that long courtship *per se* benefits pairs, and it may simply be that birds that arrive and pair early are also better breeders. Where I removed females from their mates late in the season (see Chapter 10), the widowed males were often able to acquire new mates that bred within two or three weeks. In these cases, the whole process of pair formation and courtship was reduced, but the new pairs often reared large broods, so long courtships are not obligatory for good breeding success.

BEHAVIOUR OF THE SEXES DURING COURTSHIP

During the early part of courtship, males and females have fairly similar behaviour patterns. Eventually, the male starts to feed his mate, and she decreases her hunting effort while he increases his. Tinbergen (1940) found that some males fed their mates almost as soon as they paired, whereas others began to do so only later. The date on which the male begins to feed the female has a major influence on when she lays and the clutch size. In a study in Holland, early laying pairs were those where the male began delivering prey early in the season, whereas late laying pairs were those where the male delayed courtship feeding (Meijer 1988). As courtship proceeds, the rate at which the male delivers prey increases and the female spends more and more time sitting near the nest. Tinbergen found an average increase from 3.5 to 6.5 feeds per day for three females during the three weeks before egg-laying. To cope with the extra demands, males have to increase their activity and may more than double the time they spend flight-hunting (Masman *et al* 1988b).

Courtship also involves an increase in the frequency of displays and territorial fights, which can take up a significant part of the male's day and require considerable energy. The need to defend the nest and the female from other Kestrels may restrict the distance males can go from the nest. In both my studies, males spent more time near the nest during courtship and early incubation than they did later in the season when feeding young (Chapter 7).

The food pass

The pattern of behaviour during prey deliveries to the nest is fairly fixed within a pair, and remains much the same until the young are well grown. In a typical food pass, the male arrives at the nest site with prey in his talons, perches near the nest and gives the '*heerre*' or '*tsick*' call. He often uses the same perch, usually a few metres from the nest, but will sometimes fly directly to the edge of the nest itself. The female flies to the male, collects the prey and takes it to a nearby spot where she will pluck and eat it. The male may stay preening on the perch or, during incubation, will cover the eggs until the female returns. In a study of three pairs of Kestrels in Germany, the male spent an average of 15 minutes covering the eggs at each prey delivery (Kochanek 1984), though females sometimes take nearly an hour to before returning to relieve their mates.

When the food pass goes smoothly, the male may have to give only a few *tsick* calls as he is flying in and the female will immediately come off the nest and take the food as he lands nearby. If the female is not present when the male arrives, he usually stays on the perch for several minutes giving increasingly energetic signal calls. If this fails to summon his mate, he may transfer the prey to his beak and fly to the nest and, if the prey is still not collected, he will eat it himself, or cache it.

Copulation

Copulation is the focus of courtship behaviour, and its early appearance in the breeding cycle, and high frequency, indicate that its function may be more than mere fertilisation. Copulation attempts occur even in winter between resident pairs, though only rarely, and may also continue after the clutch is completed. The main increase in frequency starts about three weeks before egg-laying and reaches a peak during the laying period.

Typically, the female solicits the male by signal calling, with the front of the body bent downwards, the wings lowered and the tail slightly raised. Kestrels are noisy when copulating, the male giving a rapid, alarm-like call and the female a typical signal call. The female moves her tail to one side while the the male balances with rapid wing beats and a fanned tail. The whole process lasts but a few seconds, and afterwards the pair may display onto the nest, or sit preeing nearby. In a single pair, watched for a whole day in early courtship, copulation was most frequent in the early morning, and throughout the day took place every 46 minutes on average (Mester 1980), the same frequency as Tinbergen (1940) reported for his pairs. These are probably close to maximum rates and estimates of 7–8 copulations per day have been reported elsewhere (Kochanek 1984, Masman *et al* 1988a).

SELECTION OF THE NESTING SITE

Another important aspect of early courtship is the selection and preparation of the nesting site. Although some pairs have little choice where they nest, others may have several suitable sites within their territory. At Eskdalemuir, for example, 60% of pairs had at least one other usable site within 500 m of where they nested. A pair may visit and scrape several sites during courtship, and may not finally choose one until just before the eggs are laid. There is some debate as to which sex chooses the nest. Some claim this is solely a male prerogative (Mester 1980, Piechocki 1982), but both sexes visit the nest prior to laying, and either may scrape a depression. Males certainly make a lot of noise on the nest and often seem to be trying to attract the female onto it. It may be that the male finds several sites and the female then chooses which she will lay in.

I have twice watched males that seemed to be prospecting for sites. The first was an adult male in Scotland that spent over half an hour hopping from branch to branch above the canopy of a thick spuce wood, stopping every now and then to peer downwards, apparently looking for old crow nests. The second was an unpaired juvenile male that visited several holes in succession in a clump of dead elms in the arable farmland area. His search was ended abruptly by a pair of Stock Doves that obviously had prior claim to one hole, and kept flying at him until he left!

As the female gets closer to laying she spends more time on the nest. One female spent 10–30% of the day in her nestbox in the week before she started laying (Kochanek 1984). I have flushed females from empty nests fairly often, especially in wet weather, when they seem to sit there in order to keep the scrape dry. They may also be trying out the nest to see if it is suitable, and may not lay eggs there if it is too exposed to rain or prone to disturbance (Zande & Verstrael 1985).

CHANGES IN BODY WEIGHT DURING COURTSHIP

As laying approaches, the female virtually stops flying and spends the whole day sitting on or near the nest. Coinciding with this decreased activity, females also start to gain weight (Fig. 53) and become reluctant to hunt, even from perches. This makes them difficult to catch with decoys, so I have few weights of females during late courtship and egg-laying. However, the data I do have show that the weight increase starts about 2–3 weeks before egg-laying, and results in an increase of at least 20 g per week. This dramatic increase is only partly due to the growth of the oviduct or eggs, and results mainly from the accumulation of body reserves necessary for incubation (Newton 1979). Much of the reserves are stored as fat in the abdomen, which becomes distended, but some may be laid down in the pectoral muscles, which are also enlarged at this time (Village 1983c). The extra weight leads to a laboured flight and, with experience, I have learnt to distinguish females that are near to laying from their appearance as they fly off during my visits to nests.

The reluctance of females to fly may be partly to lessen the likelihood of

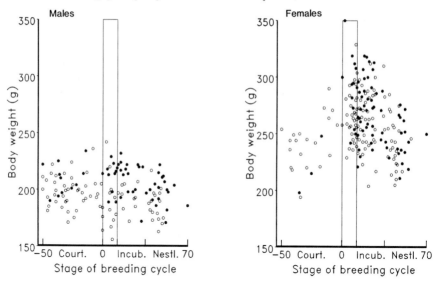

Fig. 53. Changes in the body weight of male and female Kestrels during the breeding season in the Eskdalemuir (●) and farmland (○) study areas. Numbers on the x-axes are days, taking 0 as the day that the first egg was laid. The bar shows the laying period. After Village (1983c), with additional data.

damage to the eggs during the laying period. This is unlikely to be the sole reason though, because the reduction in activity occurs well before the eggs are fully formed. Flight-hunting is energy-expensive, and females may be unable to accumulate reserves unless they reduce this expenditure as well as increasing food intake. Females that are not fed often enough by their mates, and therefore have to forage for themselves, will be unable to gain sufficient weight to breed. Males, in contrast to females, show little change in weight during courtship, and any increase in the time they spend hunting does not seem to be sufficient to reduce the levels of their body reserves.

SUMMARY

During the early part of the breeding season, Kestrels spend a considerable amount of time displaying in order to maintain the pair bond and fighting to defend their territory. Such behaviours were more frequent in the largely migratory Scottish population, where pairs formed afresh each spring, than in England, where many pairs were together in winter. In Scotland, migrants settled from February to May, with both sexes arriving at the same time, but adults before first-year birds. Pairs that formed late had shorter courtships, but nonetheless laid later than those that paired early. In most years, individuals were more likely to mate with a partner of the same age-class as themselves. In Scotland, this was at least partly due to the different arrival times of adults and yearlings.

As courtship proceeds, the male feeds his mate more frequently, and she spends less and less time hunting for herself. This results in a increase in her weight as reserves are laid down prior to egg-laying and incubation. Males spend more time flight-hunting in order to meet the extra demands of feeding their mates, but they maintain their body weight.

CHAPTER 12

The breeding cycle:
the egg stage

The eggs are normally laid on alternate days, so a clutch of six eggs takes eleven days to complete. I do not have the exact egg intervals for many clutches, as this would have involved too much disturbance, but it was evident that a few females laid at irregular intervals, with up to three or four days between some eggs. Piechocki (1982) and Hasenclever *et al* (1989) also report that some females laid the last egg of a clutch after a gap of up to five days. Further evidence of irregular laying intervals is the extreme asynchrony in the hatch of a few broods, with the last young hatching as much as a week after the first. These instances are unusual, however, and may occur only if females are short of food during the laying period.

Eggs develop in the ovary from follicles which form during the winter and which reach about 20% of the final yolk size some weeks or months before laying begins (Cavé 1968, Meijer 1988). The rapid stage of growth starts about a week before ovulation, and the formation of the albumen, shell membranes and shell in the oviduct takes a further two days. This means that during the laying period females may contain up to four or five eggs at various stages of development (Meijer 1988).

THE EGGS

Kestrel eggs are oval, measure about 34–44 mm by 28–34 mm and weigh about 20 g when first laid. Although there seems to be little regional variation in egg size in Europe, eggs from my Scottish grassland area were significantly longer, and broader, than those from the English farmland areas (Table 29). The difference in the means was slight (0.7 mm in length and 0.3 mm in breadth), but similar to that between Kestrel eggs from urban and rural environments in Czechoslovakia (Pikula *et al* 1984). In each case the larger eggs were from populations that laid earlier and had larger clutches, so the difference, although small, may reflect the influence of food supply on the size of eggs. There is clearly scope for more work to test the possibility of such a relationship.

Most eggs have a light brown background and are heavily speckled with dark red or brown. Colouration is highly variable, however, and ranges from pure white with a few brown spots, to a fairly uniform, deep chocolate brown. This makes Kestrel eggs similar to those of many other falcons, and it takes an experienced eye to distinguish them from the eggs of Hobbies or Merlins. The rich colouration and variability of falcon eggs has made them popular with collectors, though Kestrel eggs have never been as prized as those of the rarer Peregrine (Ratcliffe 1980). Nonetheless, Kestrel nests are often more accessible than Peregrine eyries, and egg collecting by children can be a problem at traditional sites near towns (Riddle 1987).

There is some variation between eggs within clutches, often because the last egg is paler than the rest. The red colour is due to the pigment protoporphyrin, and this may sometimes become depleted by the time the last egg is produced. As in Peregrines, I have found that particular females tend to lay eggs of a similar colouration in different years. This was most evident where I had marked females that laid unusual eggs. In one instance, egg pattern was useful in identifying a female that laid in one nest before deserting and repeating at another site. I caught her during incubation and she bred for several successive years at the second site, each time producing almost pure white eggs.

Eggs start with a matt texture, but acquire a shine as they are incubated, and this gives some indication of how recently they were laid. The original bright colours fade with age, and eventually bleach in any unhatched eggs that remain at the end of the season.

CLUTCH SIZE

The usual clutch size is four to six, though the range is from one to seven (Glutz *et al* 1971, Cramp & Simmons 1980). The largest clutch I have found was seven, and reports of bigger clutches are probably the result of two females laying in the same nest (Pikula *et al* 1984). Of the 351 clutches I have recorded,

Kestrel eggs from six complete five-egg clutches showing the variation in size, shape and colour within (across) and between (down) clutches. Photo: N. J. Westwood.

74% were either four or five, and 98% were between three and six, which agrees with the nest records of the British Trust for Ornithology (Table 30). Clutch size varies between years and with mean laying date (see Chapter 14), so meaningful comparisons between areas are difficult without additional information.

REPEAT CLUTCHES

Kestrels are single-brooded, but a small percentage of pairs lay a second clutch if the first fails or is not completed. Failures can occur if females are seriously disturbed during laying, if eggs are broken or removed by predators, or if the female deserts the clutch because she is suddenly short of food. Most repeat clutches are produced by the original pair, but a few are produced because one partner dies and is replaced by another bird of the same sex. In my studies, 60% of repeat clutches were laid in the same nest as the first, the remainder being at different sites up to 200 m away.

When the second clutch is laid in the same nest as the first, the original eggs may remain in the nest and be incubated with the new clutch. This can make the first clutch difficult to distinguish from the second, and gives the misleading impression of an unusually large clutch, unless the circumstances are understood. In my studies, as far as I could tell, the eggs of such first clutches never developed even though they were fully incubated with the second clutch. In most cases the first clutch was incomplete, so females were able to lay a normal-sized second clutch and still cover all the eggs. Females seemed unlikely to lay again in a nest that already had five or six eggs, probably because they were unable to incubate more than six or seven eggs and because the presence of so many eggs in the nest is the stimulus that normally inhibits further laying.

The frequency of repeat clutches was twice as high at Eskdalemuir as in the farmland areas (Table 31), possibly related to the earlier laying and better food supply in the grassland habitat of Eskdalemuir. Pairs that repeat are generally those that abandon the first clutch early in the season and early in their breeding cycle. If females are disturbed during laying, they sometimes move to another nest and continue producing eggs almost without a break. It is unusual for a female to start a second clutch if she deserts well into incubation, but this may be because such desertions are often associated with food shortage. When lack of food is not the cause of nesting failure, pairs may be able to breed again quickly, as happened to one pair in the arable area in 1986. They had bred together for at least three years, and were usually the first birds to lay, producing large clutches and always fledging young. Their nest was destroyed by boys in late May, when the female had almost finished incubation, but she began a second clutch of five eggs on 12 June, and fledged four young, the only young I have ever ringed in August.

INCUBATION

Incubation normally begins after the third egg is laid, though females laying

Clutch size in Kestrels is normally from four to six eggs, though clutches outside this range are sometimes reported. Photo: A. Village.

4–6 eggs can sometimes be flushed from single eggs, especially in wet weather. The onset of incubation, relative to the first-egg date, varies according to the final clutch size, with those females laying five or six eggs becoming broody later than those with only three or four (Beukeboom *et al* 1988). The increase in incubation behaviour seems to be associated with the cessation of laying, and nearly all females begin sitting in earnest on the fourth day before the clutch is completed.

The female starts to lose belly feathers before laying, and develops a typical avian brood patch by the time incubation starts. The brood patch is an area of bare skin, extending over the belly and chest, that is richly supplied with blood in order to transmit the female's body heat to the eggs. Males do not incubate as such, but merely cover the eggs for short periods while the female feeds, preens and bathes. None of the breeding males I caught had a brood patch and it is highly unlikely that males ever develop them, though this has been claimed for one male that seemed to spend an unusual amount of time covering the eggs (Packham 1985b).

Incubating females spend nearly all their time sitting on the eggs, and leave the nest for only about an hour a day during feeds by the male (Masman *et al* 1988b). Most females stay on the nest when producing pellets, and these gradually appear around the scrape, forming a soft cushion by the end of incubation. Females avoid defaecating on the nest, however, and droppings accumulate from the young only later in the nestling stage. Individuals vary in how easily they can be flushed from the nest and how quickly they return. Some leave as soon as anyone approaches, and may take over an hour to return, whereas others will leave only when the tree is being climbed, and return within minutes. A few refuse to leave the eggs even when the climber reaches the nest, and I have caught about 10% of my females by hand out of nestboxes or tree-holes.

Kestrels flushed suddenly from stick nests may sweep eggs or young chicks off the edge, so I normally try to alert birds before I climb, to give them time to sit up and leave the nest without panic. Females have a characteristic weaving and twisting flight when disturbed off the nest, as if they were trying to avoid being shot. I do not know if this behaviour is indeed an adaption to the persecution Kestrels used to suffer from gamekeepers, or whether it is a general anti-predator behaviour found even in populations where nesting females have never been shot.

The duration of incubation

There is some disparity in the lengths of incubation quoted in the literature, which may depend on how incubation is defined. Brown (1976) gives 27–29 days per egg, and Piechocki (1982) 28–31 days. I did not deliberately measure the duration of incubation, but occasionally my visits to check on hatching success would coincide with the day that hatch began. In 37 such instances I also knew the laying date, or could estimate it by assuming an laying interval of two days. If incubation started at the third egg (as seems likely in most females), the mean time to hatching of the first egg was 31 days, with a range of 26–34 days (Table 32). The disparity between my results and other published incubation periods may be because mine were based on larger samples, and because other workers used different criteria for the start and finish of incubation. There was no difference between study areas in my data, and no correlation with laying date or clutch size. Females will incubate addled clutches for days or even weeks beyond the normal hatching date, so the normal cue to end incubation must be the hatching of the young.

CHANGES IN BODY WEIGHT DURING LAYING AND INCUBATION

I tried to avoid catching females during egg-laying, for fear of disturbance, even though those I did trap on incomplete clutches seemed as untroubled by the experience as incubating females. The few weights I had of laying females were as high as 350 g in some cases, so it is likely that body weight peaks during the laying period, as it does in Sparrowhawks (Newton *et al* 1983). There is some weight loss after the clutch is complete, but this is only slight, and females remained heavier than normal throughout incubation (Fig. 53). There was considerable variation in incubating weights, the heaviest females being 320 g and the lightest 220 g. Only a fraction of this variation was related to the size of females, and it mainly reflected differences in the amount of stored fat. Lighter individuals were more likely to desert their clutches than heavy ones (Chapter 15), probably because they were less able to withstand food shortage. Heavier females, with their larger reserves, could presumably stay on the eggs for longer if the male was unable to deliver much food during wet weather.

Some females lose weight during incubation, but there was no significant decline in weight for the females I caught on the nest. There may have been a slight bias here, because light females were unlikely to reach the later stages of incubation and then to be trapped. Thus, only those birds that lasted until the hatch maintained their weight throughout incubation. Few males were caught during during the egg stage, but their weights were similar to those in the pre-lay period.

MALE PREY-DELIVERIES DURING INCUBATION

The role of the male during incubation is largely to provide food for the female. The female's inactivity, and the fact that she is sitting on a sheltered nest all day, mean that her food requirements are less than when she is laying, despite the added heat-drain from warming the eggs. Recent work in Holland measured female energy intake during incubation at about 309 kJ/day, slightly lower than during laying but higher than during courtship (Table 33), and equivalent to about 4–6 voles/day (Masman *et al* 1986). Male prey delivery rates increased during late courtship and laying, but levelled off during incubation (Meijer 1988). Tinbergen (1940) found a gradual increase in prey delivery rates from early courtship to late incubation in several pairs he studied. His estimates of prey consumed by females during incubation ranged from 5–13 items/day (mean = 9.3 n = 4). I am not sure why this figure is higher than the 4–6 voles/day given above, though the latter was based on the average size of vole prey. Males in Tinbergen's study might have delivered the same total energy per day but as smaller-sized prey.

Males spend about the same time flight-hunting during incubation as they do during courtship and egg-laying (Table 33), the main periods of increasing hunting effort being in early courtship and later in the nestling stage. Although there is less likelihood of cuckoldry after the female has finished laying, males remain aggressive around the nest and will attack intruders with undiminished vigour (C. G. Wiklund).

SUMMARY

Kestrels usually lay four to six eggs at two-day intervals, though clutches vary from one to seven, and laying intervals may be from one to five days. The reddish-brown eggs are about 40 x 30 mm and weigh around 20 g when laid. Egg colour is highly variable, and females tend to lay eggs of similar pattern from one year to the next. Incubation starts about four days before the last egg is laid, and lasts 26–34 days. The delivery of prey by the male increases during late courtship, and the resulting improvement in the female's body-condition seems to trigger the start of laying. Delivery rates peak during laying, levelling off during incubation to the equivalent of some 4–6 voles per day. Males show little change in body weight from courtship to the end of incubation, and continue to defend the nest area after the eggs have been laid.

CHAPTER 13

The breeding cycle:
the nestling stage

THE HATCH

Because the start of incubation is usually delayed until after the third egg has been laid, the first three or four eggs generally hatch on the same day, and the rest follow over the next few days. The asynchrony is less than in some other vole-eating birds of prey, such as owls, but it still means that the last hatched young of a large brood tends to be smaller than its siblings. It is widely assumed that this allows the brood to be reduced by sibling rivalry if food is short. Kestrel nestlings have been seen to kill and eat brood-mates (Piechocki 1982), but most deaths of Kestrel chicks are probably the result of failing to compete for food, rather than siblicide. I have found considerable variation in the degree of asynchrony; at some nests five or six young hatch within two days, whereas other broods take nearly a week to complete hatching. This difference may be due to variation either in egg-laying intervals or in the interval before incubation starts relative to the first-egg date.

The young can be heard calling from the egg a day or so before they hatch, though whether this serves to alert the female or synchronise the hatch is not known. Hatching takes about 24 hours, the chick gradually chipping away at the shell with the 'egg-tooth' on the upper beak. The egg-tooth is normally lost within 7–10 days of hatch, but in a few chicks it may be retained for up to two weeks or more (Piechocki 1982). The process of hatching is exhausting work for the young, and there is often some mortality during this stage.

After hatch, the female may remove the shells and drop them nearby, or eat them herself (Piechocki 1982). The newly hatched young are brooded by the female, and their fluffy white down soon dries. The chicks at this stage have relatively large heads and feet but tiny wings. The abdomen protrudes because the gut contains the last of the yolk, which becomes a source of food over the first crucial days of life.

GROWTH AND DEVELOPMENT OF THE YOUNG

Although their eyes are only partly open at first, the young are able to lift their heads and beg vociferously if the female leaves the nest to collect food. The begging call is a drawn out 'seep', that gradually becomes more like the adult signal call as the young grow. Small chicks have a startling ability to manipulate and swallow food, and will attempt to eat virtually any size of morsel that is offered. Although the female is careful to tear carcasses into small pieces, the young will occasionally grab a bird leg or vole haunch and try to eat it whole. This usually results in part of the prey sticking out of the chick's mouth, where it stays until it is swallowed, grabbed by a sibling or removed by the female.

With such voracious appetites, it is not surprising that the young grow quickly (Fig. 54a). Hatching weight is about 14–18 g, but this is doubled in two days and some chicks weigh over 100 g at the end of their first week. Weight increase during the 30 or so days in the nest shows a typical sigmoid pattern, weight gain being slow for the first few days, increasing suddenly then slackening off after the second week. Unlike Sparrowhawks, that can be sexed by size after only ten days (Moss 1979), there is considerable overlap in the size of male and female Kestrel nestlings, even at fledging. Brown's (1976) assertion that Kestrels could be sexed with certainty by nestling weights was presumably based on the erroneous assumption that they can also be sexed by plumage colour.

There have been several studies on the growth rates of wild Kestrels in Europe (Table 34), all of which give similar results. The maximum rate of weight gain is between the first and second week, and most broods reach 90% of maximum weight after about three weeks, some time before they leave the nest. There is a slight decline in weight in the last few days, but the young still leave the nest slightly heavier than normal adult weight. The extra weight is presumably fat reserves needed during the first few weeks out of the nest.

Coupled with the fast weight-gain is a rapid development of plumage and behaviour (Table 35). The original down is replaced by a grey coarser one, which in turn is lost as the juvenile body-plumage emerges in the third week. The first feathers to show are the primaries, the quills appearing on about the

Kestrel chicks just after hatching. At this stage the eyes are closed, the body is covered with a fine white down, and the 'egg-tooth' is still visible on the upper mandible. Photo: A. Kostrzewa.

At a week old, chicks are alert and can explore their surroundings. The second, coarser down is growing, but the juvenile plumage is yet to appear. Photo: A. Kostrzewa.

eighth day and the feathers erupting from the quills at about 2–3 weeks. The various parts of the body grow at different rates during the nestling stage, the legs and feet reaching near adult size before the flight feathers emerge (Fig. 54b). Feather growth continues after the young leave the nests, and full maturity, as measured by protein turnover, may not be reached until about 35 days of age (Kirkwood 1981c).

The rapid growth rate of Kestrel chicks is typical of atrical birds (those reared in nests), and has prompted a study by James Kirkwood (1981b) into their energetics and metabolism. Working with hand-reared Kestrels, he found that the metabolisable energy intake of chicks was as high as that recorded in any warm-blooded animal of a comparable size. This was combined with low production of heat and general inactivity, so that most of the food eaten was put directly into growth. The low heat production and slow plumage development makes young chicks vulnerable to cold, however, and they are unable to control their own body temperature until they are 7–10 days old.

The nest remains fairly tidy while the females feeds the young, but fur, feathers and bones soon accumulate in the scrape once the young are feeding themselves. Chicks produce pellets as soon as they start feeding themselves because they then ingest more fur and feathers with the meat. Kestrels occasionally hoard food in the nest, as do some owls, but any prey that is not eaten quickly is usually pushed to the edge of the nest where it rots. Even newly-hatched chicks show some regard for hygiene by directing their excreta outwards from the nest, though this behaviour does not develop fully until the second week and, even then, droppings do not always clear the nest. By the time the young are three or four weeks old, they are standing on a thick bed

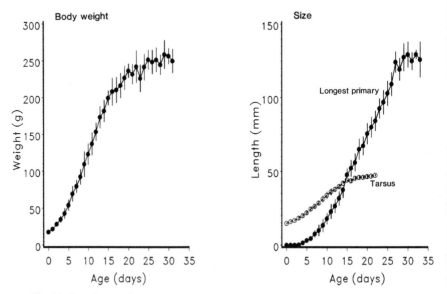

Fig. 54. Growth rates of 17 Kestrel chicks from five broods measured daily in the Eskdalemuir area, 1976. Vertical bars are ±2 SE.

The female broods the chicks for 10–14 days and will continue to feed them thereafter until they are old enough to tear prey themselves. This female had an unusually badly frayed wing-tag and she had to be re-trapped so that the tag could be replaced. Photo: N. J. Westwood.

of droppings, trampled feathers, pellets and, more often than not, maggots. This can give the inside of tree-holes and nestboxes a fairly piquant aroma, especially after several days of warm rain!

BEHAVIOUR OF THE ADULTS DURING THE NESTLING STAGE

For the first few days or so after hatch the female broods the young continuously, leaving them only when collecting food from the male. He continues to deliver prey to the female, but does not cover the young as he did the eggs. The young brood requires a considerable amount of food, and the male has to increase his hunting time and prey delivery rates to deal with the increasing demand (Table 33). The increase in hunting effort continues for much of the nestling stage and during early independence, though some males are helped by their mates after about ten days or so, when she has finshed brooding the young. The brooding behaviour of females gradually declines after a week, depending partly on the weather. During cold or wet spells, females continue to brood the young beyond ten days, whereas they may stop sooner if the weather is exceptionally warm.

The male plucks most of the feathers from bird carcasses for the young until the latter are several weeks old, though mammals are delivered with fur intact. Many of the prey items I have found on nests have been headless, and I assume the male eats the heads himself. This was also noticed in Czechoslovakia, where 52% of mammals (n = 59) and 75% of birds (n = 59) brought to nest had been decapitated (Pikula *et al* 1984). The skull must be difficult for chicks to deal with, and removing the heads of birds may also make them a neater bundle for the male to carry to the nest. These problems are common to many raptors, and decapitated prey is common at the nests of several species, including Sparrowhawks (Newton 1986).

Eventually, males deliver prey direct to the nest, though exactly when they start to do this seems to depend on the behaviour of the female. As long as she is there to collect prey, the male continues to land away from the nest and let her take it to the young. However, he soon changes to direct prey deliveries, with little or no calling, once the female begins to hunt. Males do not normally tear up food for the young, but Tinbergen (1940) found that one male eventually did so because his mate was injured in a severe hailstorm and unable to reach the nest for two days.

Tinbergen found that the rate of prey delivery to his four nests increased in the first three weeks after hatching (Fig. 55), but averaged about 13 items a day over the whole nestling period. This is similar to the rate during eleven whole-day watches of nests in Czechoslovakia during the late nestling stage (Pikula *et al* 1984). In the latter study, deliveries were evenly spaced on some

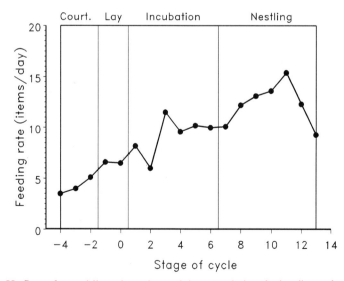

Fig. 55. Rate of prey delivery by males to their mates during the breeding cycle (from Tinbergen 1940). Each point is the mean of up to five nests over a five day period of the breeding cycle (0 = period in which the clutch was completed).

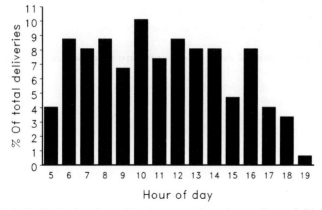

Fig. 56. Daily distribution of prey deliveries to nests in the late nestling period in Czechoslovakia. Based on 148 feeds observed during 11 whole-day watches at nests. From data in Pikula et al (1984).

days but clumped on others, with some prey delivered at intervals of less than five minutes. This was presumably because both parents were hunting, or because the female retrieved items that had previously been cached. Prey were brought throughout the day, but there was usually a decline during the late afternoon and early evening (Fig. 56), perhaps because the young were satiated. The weather can also produce day to day variations in prey deliveries, and Cavé (1968) found that deliveries were halved at six nests during a day of heavy rain, compared with the preceding dry day.

Tinbergen could detect no relationship between brood size and feeding rate, but recent work in Holland suggests that males can, in some circumstances, respond to an increase in the food requirements of their brood (Masman *et al* 1988b). Kestrels were induced to nest in boxes mounted on the side of caravans that served as combined hides and mobile laboratories. There was access to the boxes from within the caravans, so teams of students were able monitor both the nest and the male throughout the day. By borrowing young from another nest, and rotating them through the nestboxes, they ensured that the male (who could not tell his own young from others) always had a nest full of hungry chicks, even though the brood size remained constant. During experiments early in the nestling period, the males showed only a small increase in hunting behaviour, and delivered only slightly more food than they would normally. After the young were ten days old, however, there was a more marked increase in hunting behaviour and males greatly increased the deliveries of prey, from the usual 20 items a day to over 50 per day in some cases (Table 36). An increase of this proportion must be possible only if prey is easily caught, and males may be less able to respond in poor food conditions.

When the reverse was tried, and the young were given extra food, the male reduced his hunting effort and only 'topped' up with prey to fulfill the normal requirements of the brood. The two experiments showed that some males can respond to the hunger of the brood, and that, for a day or so, they were able to increase their prey delivery if the need arose. The difference in response to

By 3–4 weeks the down is rapidly being lost as the juvenile plumage develops. Chicks at this stage weigh almost as much as adults, but their flight and tail feathers are only half grown. Photo: N. J. Westwood.

young broods compared with older ones may have been due to a slight difference in the experimental design, but it also coincided with the point when males begin to deliver prey directly to the nest, and when they would be better able to judge the hunger of the chicks for themselves.

The extent to which the female feeds the young during the late nestling stage seems to vary between pairs. Tinbergen found that two of four females started bringing food after ten days or so, whereas the others brought no food at all. This accords with my own experience of visiting nests, when some females were invariably present, while others were hardly ever seen and were probably out hunting. In Sparrowhawks, well-fed females stay near the nest, but they will leave to hunt if food is scarce (Marquiss & Newton 1982a), and Kestrels seem similar in this respect. Males seem to continue to do most of the hunting in the late nesting stage, and the Dutch workers found that males spent twice as much time flight-hunting as females (Table 33).

WEIGHT CHANGES OF ADULTS IN THE NESTLING PERIOD

In the 10–14 days that she broods the young, the female rapidly loses weight (Fig. 53). Females that I caught during incubation and then later with young had invariably lost weight, and this seems to happen soon after hatch. Females become lighter because they give most of the delivered prey to the young, and eat only small amounts of skin and intestines themselves. This was noted by Tinbergen and more recently quantified by the Dutch study, where the energy intake of females dropped by 40% in the first ten days with young (Masman *et al* 1986).

Although the immediate cause of this loss of weight is the reduced food intake of the females, it is not clear if they choose to eat less, or are forced to do so in order to ensure that their young have sufficient food. Females might deliberately shed reserves in order to be more efficient at flight-hunting when they have to help feed the brood. Alternatively, those that lose weight because their partners cannot deliver sufficient food may also have to help their mates hunt later in the nestling stage. The latter idea seems most likely as it explains why some females hunt prey for the nestlings while others do not, and why providing food for brooding females reduces their loss of weight and the time they spend hunting (Masman 1986).

Males are also lighter during the nestling period, though the loss is less pronounced than in females because males accumulate smaller reserves to begin with. The decline is probably caused by the new demands of feeding the chicks, which require more flight-hunting and more energy expenditure. If males have to flight-hunt for more than about five hours a day, they cannot match their energy expenditure by catching more prey, and must therefore draw on body reserves to meet the short-fall (Chapter 5).

LEAVING THE NEST

The young start to leave the nest anytime from about 28 days of age, and can be seen on the branches of the nest tree, or perching near the nest ledge at cliff sites. Some chicks may wander from the nest well before flying, if it is in a suitable position. One three-week old chick was seen to wander around a staw stack for over an hour before it finally returned to its nest on top of a bale (N. Westwood). Even after fledging, the young frequently return to the nest, especially in the first few days while the parents are still bringing food there. This makes the time of leaving difficult to determine precisely, and it is probably quite variable, both between and within broods. The length of the nestling period is usually given as 27–32 days (Cramp & Simmons 1980). I have no data for fledging dates because I rarely visited broods late in the nestling stage. Kestrel chicks are prone to jump from the nest, and may attempt suicidal leaps even when still covered with down. For this reason, my last visit to broods was normally when they were 2–3 weeks old, by which time their tarsi were nearly full-grown and could easily take the correct size of ring.

Brown (1976) states that male nestlings are more active than females and leave the nest two or three days before them, though it is not clear how he came by this information, given the problems in sexing immatures. Nestling male Sparrowhawks certainly develop faster than their sisters (Newton 1986), so the same might be true for Kestrels, though the difference is probably less pronounced in Kestrels because the sexes are more similar in size.

When they leave the nest, chicks have lost almost all of their down and are soon able to fly (above and facing page). The flight feathers are still growing, however, givings the wings a shorter, more rounded appearance than in adults. Photos: N. J. Westwood.

THE POST-FLEDGING PERIOD

There has been little detailed study of the post-fledging period in Kestrels, and most of what is known comes from casual observations at a few nests. Young generally remain near the nest for at least two or three weeks, making longer and longer flights and gradually improving their co-ordination. Tinbergen found that the nest ceased to be used as a point of prey transfer once all the young had left. The adults then gave food to the young wherever they happened to be, often arriving with a signal call to which the young responded with excited wing-flapping and screaming. After about a week, the fledglings can fly up to meet their parents, but prey transfers are still on the ground or at a perch. Parents give food to the first fledgling that reaches them, so there is a strong incentive to get to the parents quickly. The young soon learn to take prey in mid-air, grabbing it from the parent's talons by rolling sideways.

Fledglings perch between feeds, sometimes preening the remnants of down from their feathers. They explore the surroundings by pulling at twigs and

turning over stones or similar objects. One bird was seen attacking a pine cone, apparently practicing for attacks at prey later in life (Tinbergen 1940). The ability to fly is instinctive in birds, but early attempts by young Kestrels are rather clumsy because the flight feathers are not fully developed. Landing seems to require considerable co-ordination and has to be learnt. Fledglings may make several abortive attempts to land on thin branches, grabbing wildly and hanging on until they either fall off or manage to haul themselves upright.

At some stage the young must start to hunt for themselves, though I know of no account describing in detail when and how this happens. First attempts seem to be attacks from perches at inanimate objects or slow-moving insect prey (Shrubb 1982), and it may be some weeks before juveniles become competent at hovering. Juveniles in autumn eat many insects (Chapter 3) and may not take much vertebrate prey until they are some months old. They can be seen flight-hunting in September but, although they make frequent strikes, they rarely seem to catch large prey.

SUMMARY

The hatch is partly synchronised within broods, the first three eggs usually hatching together, and the rest over the next few days. The young chicks are covered with down and have poor vision, but they grow most rapidly after the first few days, reaching adult size in under three weeks. They achieve this initial fast growth by assimilating relatively large amounts of energy for growth, rather than for maintenance of body temperature. This makes the young nestlings vulnerable to cold, and the female broods them until they are able to control their own body temperature at about 10–14 days.

Females give most of the prey delivered by the male to the young, and eat only the skin and entrails during the first week after hatch. They therefore lose weight rapidly if the male does not supply food in excess of the requirements of the brood. Some females, but not all, help the male to feed the brood after the first two weeks. Males still do most of the hunting while the young are in the nest, and may use body reserves to maintain high levels of flight-hunting.

Chicks leave the nest at around 30 days, but remain nearby for a further 2–4 weeks while they continue to be fed by their parents. Rather little is known of post-fledging behaviour, though the young gradually acquire the ability to hunt for themselves.

CHAPTER 14

The timing of breeding

Why Kestrels breed when they do is a question that requires two separate
responses: firstly to explain the gross regional differences in breeding seasons
between, say, Europe and Africa, and secondly to explain differences in laying
dates between pairs in any one population. At both these levels, food supply
is almost certainly the ultimate factor that determines when Kestrels breed.
However, the proximate controlling factors are different in each case, so it is
necessary to consider the timing of breeding seasons separately from the timing
of mean laying date.

BREEDING SEASONS

European Kestrels have a wide distribution, and it is not surprising that

189

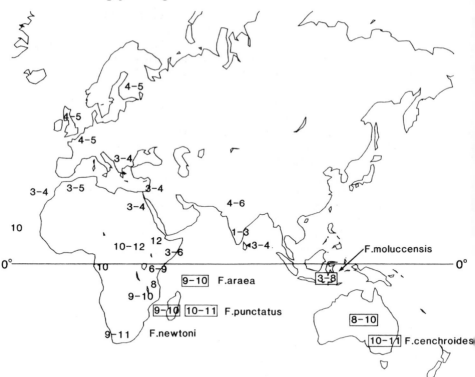

Fig. 57. *Approximate laying seasons of kestrels in the Old World. Numbers are the months in which most pairs start laying. All values refer to F. tinnunculus subspecies, apart from where indicated. Based on data in Cramp & Simmons (1980), Cade (1982), Brown et al (1982), Watson (1981) and Jones & Owadally (1985).*

they breed at different times within their geographic range (Fig. 57). In much of Europe, the first pairs start laying in mid to late April, and the last pairs in late May or early June. Laying is earlier in countries surrounding the Mediterranean, and clutches are sometimes started in mid March in places such as Greece, Israel and North Africa (Brown *et al* 1982).

In tropical Africa south of the Sahara, laying is usually in the latter half of the year, often in October or November. In most regions this coincides with the dry season, though an exception seems to be Somalia, where the local race apparently breeds in May or June, during the rainy season (Brown *et al* 1982). South of the tropics, the seasons revert to a more typically temperate pattern, so Kestrels in South Africa around the Cape breed during the southern spring, from September to November. This pattern is repeated with other kestrel species in the Old World, though there is little information for many parts of Asia.

Even within Europe there is a dearth of good data on laying dates for differing regions. In many studies, nests were found only after the clutch was completed, or when the young were well grown, so accurate laying dates could not be calculated. This is particularly so for national schemes, such as the BTO nest records, which tend to have much smaller samples of laying dates than of clutch sizes. In many instances, then, the only information available is the months in which laying occurs, with nothing on when most birds in the population start laying. This is unfortunate, because Kestrels in any one place have such a spread of laying dates that differences within Europe are largely due to shifts in the *mean* rather than the *range* of laying dates.

This latter point is well illustrated by the distribution of laying dates in my Scottish grassland and English farmland areas, which were separated by three degrees of latitude (Fig. 58). In both areas, the earliest pairs began laying in the third week of April and the latest in early June, but the mean laying date was some two weeks later in farmland. The shape of the distributions also differed between areas, being skewed towards later laying in Scotland but more or less symmetrical in England. In each area, the spread of laying in a particular year depended mainly on how early the first pairs started (Fig. 59). The duration of the laying season (difference between the first and last laying date) was more closely correlated with the laying date of the first pair

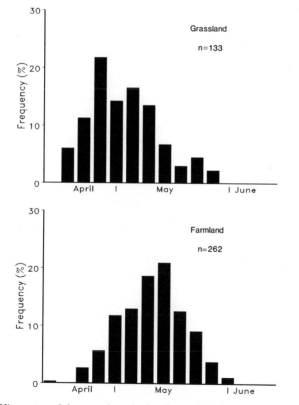

Fig. 58. Histograms of first-egg dates in five day periods for Kestrels in Eskdalemuir grassland (1976–79) and English farmland (1981–87). Mean laying date was earlier in Eskdalemuir than in farmland, though the latter area was over 300 km further south.

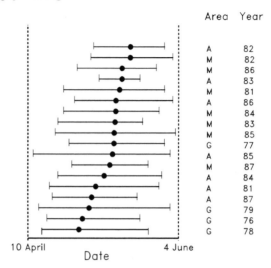

Fig. 59. *Start and finish of the laying season in relation to mean laying date in the Scottish grassland (G), mixed farmland (M) and arable farmland (A) study areas. The horizontal lines join the laying dates of the first and last pairs each year. The years are arranged in order of increasing mean laying date (●). The start, but not the finish, of the laying season varied with the mean laying date, so early seasons were generally longer than late ones.*

(r=0.83, df=16, P<0.001) than the last one (r=0.55, P<0.02). The mean laying date was also more closely correlated with the earliest laying date (r=0.76, P<0.001) than either the latest laying date(r=0.39, P<0.1) or the duration of the laying season (r=0.42, P<0.09). Thus the end of laying was about the same in all years, but the start of laying, and hence mean laying date, varied from year to year.

The range of laying dates in my studies probably encompass much of the variation found elsewhere in Northern Europe. Laying has been recorded as early as late March in some British pairs, but rarely later than early June. Over a very wide range, there is little evidence that mean laying date is correlated with latitude (Table 37). In my studies, laying was earlier in the north than in the south, the reverse of the trend suggested for Kestrels in Britain by Brown (1976). Over much of Europe, the exact limits of the breeding season are determined more by the habitat (and hence food supply) than by factors associated with latitude such as weather and the rate of daylength change in spring. Weather may delay the start of the breeding season in the most northerly parts of the range, but, even in Finland, Kestrels settle in March and April, before the snow fully melts (E. Korpimäki).

TIMING OF BREEDING SEASONS

A recent detailed analysis of the energy budgets of Kestrels in Holland showed that males could not complete the breeding cycle if they started

courtship between August and January because they would be unable to meet
the extra food demands during midwinter (Masman 1986). The yield per hour
of hunting in midwinter was half that in summer, and this meant that winter
days were too short to allow males to catch enough food to feed themselves
and their family. There was sufficient food to permit courtship to begin in
autumn, but breeding attempts started then could not succeed because hunting
yield would be too low by the time the young hatched. The breeding cycle
could theoretically be completed if it started any time between late January
and July, but the energy costs for the male were lowest if laying began between
late February and June (Fig. 60). This roughly coincides with the actual
breeding season of Kestrels in Europe, so the ultimate factor that determines
when Kestrels breed is the availability of food.

However, food supply cannot be the immediate trigger for breeding, otherwise Kestrels would start in autumn, when food is as abundant as in spring.
Instead, they begin to lay when food is scarce but increasing, so that the young
are raised and become independent when the food supply is near its annual
high. Kestrel breeding is therefore timed by two mechanisms; the first ensures
that Kestrels start breeding only within the 'window' when breeding is feasible,
the second determines exactly when pairs breed within that window.

Although hormone levels in European Kestrels have not been studied in
detail, it is likely that the proximate timing of laying is controlled phy-
siologically in relation to changes in daylength, as in many other birds. Con-
trary to previous ideas, it now seems that long days switch the breeding cycle
'off' and short days switch it 'on' (Dawson *et al* 1989). During the long days
of midsummer, birds become insensitive to increases in daylength (*photo-
refactory*) and can no longer come into breeding condition, whatever the food
supply. It is only after they have experienced short winter days that their

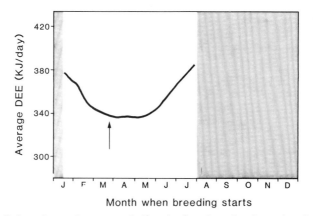

*Fig. 60. Estimated energetic costs to male Kestrels of starting to breed at various times during
the year, from Masman (1986). The line is the estimated average daily energy expenditure
(DEE) over the whole year if breeding started during that month. Males could not catch
enough food to complete the breeding cycle if they began between August and mid January
(stippled) because midwinter days were too short. Breeding could theoretically start any time
from January to July, but the costs for males were lowest between February and May, which
roughly coincided with the normal start of breeding in the area (arrow).*

hormonal system is 'reset', ready to respond to the lengthening days of the following spring. Captive American Kestrels that had just bred were induced to lay again in midwinter by exposure to artificially short daylengths earlier in October. After a month of these short days, ten pairs were given increasing daylength in November, and six of them bred in January, even though the ambient temperature was often below freezing (Bird *et al* 1980).

The use of increasing daylength as a cue to breeding ensures that Kestrels in temperate regions respond appropriately to the changing seasons. It initiates breeding well before the annual peak in prey abundance, and prevents breeding starting when food is plentiful but likely to decline by the time the young fledge. The control of breeding seasons in tropical regions may rely on quite different predictive factors, because daylength changes little during the year. Kestrels near the equator do show seasonality in breeding, but this may be related more to the cycle of rains, and hence the supply of food, than to annual changes in daylength. Black-shouldered Kites, which are ecologically similar to Kestrels, are able to breed throughout the year in southern Africa if rodent numbers are high, and there may be little synchrony between pairs breeding in the same area (Mendelsohn 1983). European Kestrels in Africa usually breed after the rains, but this seems to vary between races, and a more detailed investigation is needed to record breeding seasons accurately and identify the factors which time them.

TIMING OF LAYING

When daylength starts to increase in late winter, the hormonal system responds rapidly, resulting in growth and development of the gonads. The experiments on American Kestrels (Bird *et al* 1980) showed that birds can respond within a few weeks to an increase in daylength, but most wild pairs do not lay until some months after daylength has stimulated the reproductive system. Daylength may explain why Kestrels breed in spring and not autumn, but it sets only coarse limits to laying. Once Kestrels are photosensitive, the main factor determing when they lay is food supply. There are several lines of evidence to support this:

1. Differences between habitats. The earlier mean laying date found in the Scottish grassland area almost certainly reflected the much larger proportion of good vole habitat,there, than in the two English farmland areas. Although pairs had to form afresh every spring in Eskdalemuir, they were able to produce eggs within 2–7 weeks of arrival (Village 1985a). In the farmland areas, many pairs were resident all winter but were still unable to lay until well into May. Although northern birds experienced longer days than southern ones after the spring equinox, this was unlikely to explain why they laid earlier. Kestrels in Holland, occupying similar habitat to those in Scotland, also breed at about the same time, even though they are as far south as the English farmland pairs, and would experience similar daylength in late March and April.

2. Year to year differences in the same area. A second line of evidence that laying date is related to food supply comes from comparing annual fluctuations in mean laying date with fluctuations in vole numbers. As with breeding density (Chapter 10), this is most convincing where Kestrels eat mainly voles that show strong cycles of abundance. At Eskdalemuir, laying was two weeks later, on average, in the poor vole year of 1977 than in years when voles were more abundant (Table 38). In the farmland areas, however, there was no correlation between laying dates and vole or Woodmouse numbers, though laying was slightly earlier in the highest vole year of 1981. With so little vole habitat, the abundance of other prey, such as small birds, may have been equally important in affecting overall food supply.

Annual differences in rainfall and temperature may also affect laying dates, probably because weather indirectly affects the food supply. Heavy rain prevents Kestrels from hunting, and may also reduce the surface activity of voles. Cavé (1968) found that Kestrels laid earlier in warm, dry springs than in cold and wet ones. Low temperatures *per se* are unlikely to reduce food supply, but they may be associated with thick snow cover and hence reduced prey availability. Temperature may also effect the food demands of Kestrels because more energy is needed for thermoregulation in cold weather. The use of energy to maintain body temperature may slow the rate at which females can accumulate fat reserves, but whether by enough to delay breeding is unclear. The experiments on captive American Kestrels that induced them to lay at sub-zero temperatures demonstrate that temperature has little effect on laying date if breeding birds have ample food.

3. Feeding rates of early and late pairs. The Dutch raptor group was able to measure the food intake of females breeding at different dates in spring. It found that males started increasing their delivery of prey to females 2–3 weeks before laying, and that this increase started earlier in those pairs that laid earlier (Meijer 1988). Females started laying only when their food intake had been sufficiently high to allow them to accumulate body reserves.

4. Experimental manipulation of the food supply. This provides the most direct evidence that food supply affects laying date, and comes from work both on captive and wild birds. Cavé (1968) gave two groups of captive females either low or high food rations during late winter. Birds from each group were killed at regular intervals and their ovaries were examined to determine the state of development. Those females fed high rations had more advanced ovarian development in spring than the poorly fed females, suggesting they that would have laid earlier.

More recently, wild Kestrels breeding at the Lauwersmeer in Holland were given dead mice in their nestboxes from mid March until they started incubation (Dijkstra *et al* 1982). Supplementally fed birds laid earlier, and produced slightly larger clutches, than other birds breeding in the same year. The advance in laying dates exceeded three weeks during a poor vole year, but was less dramatic in good vole years, when many 'unfed' pairs were also able to lay early. There may be a limit to how early wild birds can be induced to lay, because it is difficult to feed them until they spend sufficient time near the nest site.

SUMMARY

In Europe, Kestrels start to lay between March and June, so that the brood is fed, and the young become independent, when food is becoming most abundant. This requires a proximate mechanism to ensure that breeding starts when food supply is low but increasing, rather than when it is high but decreasing. In temperate regions this mechanism works through changes in daylength which 'reset' the hormonal state of birds and enable them to respond to favourable conditions in spring. Whether this is true for Kestrels in the tropics is not clear and requires more study.

When the hormonal system is ready, laying is determined by the food supply to the female. Females cannot lay until their partners have increased the rate of courtship feeding to a sufficient level. When prey is abundant and hunting is easy, females are generally fed more often by their mates, and reach breeding condition sooner than in poor food years. The average laying date of a population seems to be delayed by roughly two weeks under poor food conditions, though there is always a range of around five or six weeks between the first and last pairs. Laying dates are also affected by rainfall and temperature, presumably because heavy rainfall reduces Kestrel hunting activity, and cold weather increases the amount of food necessary for females to maintain body temperature and therefore to accumulate reserves prior to laying.

CHAPTER 15

Breeding performance

From an evolutionary standpoint, the most important measure of an individual's breeding performance is the number of its offspring that survive to contribute to the next generation of breeders. This depends on how many times the individual breeds, how many young it produces at each attempt and what proportion of those young survive to breed. Gathering these data about long-lived birds such as raptors entails following a ringed population for many years. This has not yet been done for Kestrels, and the best measures of breeding performance currently available are the numbers of young produced in any one year. The date of laying (and hence fledging) is another important measure because early breeding is associated with larger clutches and more successful breeding, and because young from early nests have a better chance of survival than those from late ones (Chapter 19).

The largest clutches that Kestrels produce are six or seven eggs. In theory, all the birds present during the breeding season have the potential to fledge this number of young, but in practice very few achieve it. Some fledge no young at all, either because they fail to mate or because their breeding attempt fails at some stage between pairing and fledging. Others fledge some young, but less than the maximum possible, either because they lay small clutches, fail to hatch all their eggs or fail to fledge all their young.

SEASONAL TRENDS IN BREEDING PERFORMANCE

In both my studies, the date on which a pair produced their first egg was strongly correlated with the final clutch size, the chances of successfully fledging young, and the overall productivity (Fig. 61). In each case, earlier pairs fared better than later ones, so that those that began to lay in the first ten days of the laying period had clutches of 5–6 eggs and almost invariably fledged young, whereas those laying in the last ten days of the period produced only 3–4 eggs and less than 20% were successful. Partial losses were similar throughout the season, so the net effect of small clutches and high failure rate was that late pairs averaged one tenth the number of young of early pairs.

A seasonal decline in clutch size is widespread in many birds, and has been documented in Kestrels several times (Cavé 1968, Dijkstra *et al* 1982, O'Connor 1982, Riddle 1987). The slopes of the regression of clutch size on laying date are fairly similar in all these studies, and amount to an average decline of about one egg every three weeks of the laying period. The intercept shows more variation than the slope, however, suggesting there may be some slight regional variation in the mean clutch size for any given date. Mean clutch size was slightly larger for each ten-day period in my Scottish grassland area than in the farmland areas (Fig. 61a). Although the difference was not statistically significant in all periods, it was nonetheless significant in an analysis of variance that removed the effect of laying date on clutch size (area effect: $f = 4.68$; $df = 1,337$; $P < 0.03$). This suggests that the better food supply in the grassland area had some effect on clutch size other than through advancing laying date. The area effect was small, however, and averaged less than one egg, so the main reason for the large clutches in Eskdalemuir was the early laying.

The seasonal decline in nesting success was mainly due to an increasing probability that late nesting pairs would desert their clutch. If late nesters managed to hatch young, they were as likely to fledge them as early pairs, and the smaller brood sizes of later pairs were largely the result of their smaller clutches, rather than greater losses of young. This was also true for Sparrowhawks (Newton 1986), so it may be a widespread trend in small raptors.

EXPLANATION OF THE SEASONAL DECLINE IN CLUTCH SIZE

Several hypotheses have been proposed to explain the seasonal decline in performance in birds, and there is a continuing debate as to which is correct. The central conundrum arises because in Kestrels, as in many other species, food supply is apparently increasing during the laying period. Late pairs thus start breeding under better circumstances than early ones, yet they still produce

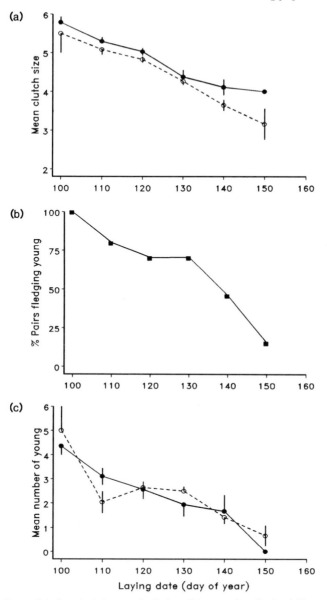

Fig. 61. Seasonal declines in (a) mean clutch size, (b) proportion of pairs failing and (c) young fledged per laying pair of Kestrels laying in 10-day periods. Data refer to Scottish grassland, 1976–79 (●) and English farmland, 1981–87 (○), or both areas (■). Vertical bars are ±1 SE.

fewer eggs and seem more prone to nesting failure due to lack of food. The two main hypotheses to explain this anomaly are either that natural selection has favoured restraint in the clutch size of late pairs, because this infers some selective advantage to parents or young (Lack 1966, Drent & Daan 1980); or that the clutch size of late nesting pairs is constrained by lack of food because they are poor hunters even under good food conditions (Newton & Marquiss 1984). Both explanations are consistent with the idea that food supply ultimately limits the clutch size of birds, but the restraint hypothesis implies that there is some sort of proximate mechanism, other than direct shortage of food, that inhibits late pairs from laying more eggs than they do.

An example of the first explanation is the 'Prudent Parent' hypothesis (Drent & Daan 1980), which was partly based on an analysis of Kestrel data collected in Holland. Ringing recoveries had shown that early fledged young survived better than late ones (Chapter 19), and these authors suggested that Kestrels may lay fewer eggs later in the season because the extra risk and investment required to rear a large brood would not be worthwhile if few of them will subsequently survive. Natural selection has thus favoured individuals that lay fewer eggs late in the season, either because fewer young survive from large, late clutches than from small, late ones, or because the rearing of large broods late in the season reduces the ability of the parents to survive to breed in subsequent years.

An alternative explanation is that the seasonal decline reflects the differing ability of pairs to produce eggs (Newton & Marquiss 1984). This idea assumes that pairs always try to produce a full-sized clutch, but poor hunters are unable to begin breeding until late in the season, are unable to produce many eggs and are prone to failure.

There is some evidence to support both these hypotheses, and it is possible that each may be involved in determining clutch size. Laying in early breeders is not terminated simply by lack of food. The immediate proximate factor that stops the further production of eggs seems to be the presence of the eggs already in the nest. Females normally produce more egg follicles than eggs, and surplus follicles are resorbed before the last egg is laid. If eggs are removed from the nest as they are laid, females will continue to lay, and this can force some individuals to produce over ten eggs, even in wild birds (Kirkwood 1980b, Beukeboom et al 1988). This is also the case with Sparrowhawks (Newton 1986), but only in the earliest-laying pairs.

A study of wild Kestrels in Holland found that late-laying females developed incubation behaviour sooner, relative to the first-egg date than those that laid early. This may have caused them to stop laying before a full clutch had been produced (Beukeboom et al 1988). In some bird species, the hormone prolactin is known to initiate brooding and prevent ovulation. Its production increases gradually during early summer, in response to increasing daylength, but levels rise dramatically once laying has begun (Dawson & Goldsmith 1982).

It has been suggested that prolactin increase may explain why late females produce fewer eggs. They start laying with high levels of prolactin because of the seasonal increase, and will reach levels that inhibit further egg formation sooner, and so at a smaller clutch size, than early females, which begin laying when their prolactin levels are lower. Such a hormonal mechanism has been suggested as the proximate control required by the 'restraint' hypothesis (Beukeboom et al 1988), and it may indeed explain how laying is terminated.

The main evidence that food supply does not directly limit clutch size in

Kestrels in Holland have been encouraged to breeding by erecting nestboxes on poles in recently reclaimed polders. Photo: A. Village.

Kestrels is based on experiments in which late pairs were artificially fed before laying (Meijer 1988). This was done in captive and wild pairs and, although this extra feeding advanced their laying dates somewhat, neither group laid clutches larger than those expected at that time of year. Females receiving extra food late in the season reached similar body weights to those laying large clutches early in the season, so large body reserves during laying did not guarantee a larger clutch.

The Dutch workers have proposed that females are enabled to lay because their mates increase the rate at which prey is delivered during courtship. Females lay when they reach their 'triggering weight', which is higher in early-laying females than in late ones. Early females therefore accumulate more reserves before laying than late ones, and so are better able to withstand food shortages during incubation. In all females the number of eggs produced depends solely on the date of laying, and is probably controlled hormonally by prolactin, as described above (Meijer 1988).

The above hypothesis is supported by experimental evidence and provides an attractive mechanism to explain the seasonal decline in clutch size. However, it does not wholly explain all the evidence, some of which implies that food supply may have a more direct effect on the number of eggs produced. The larger clutches of Kestrels in my Scottish grassland area at a given date, compared with those in the English farmland areas, are difficult to explain other than as a response to the better food supply in the good vole habitat. If photoperiod determines prolactin levels and clutch size in Kestrels, the northern population should have produced fewer eggs because days were longer than in England at any given date between the spring equinox and the summer solstice.

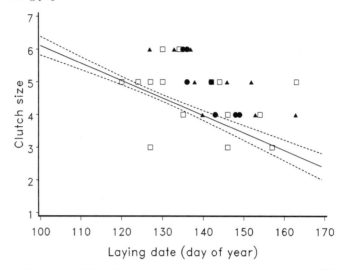

Fig. 62. Clutch size of Kestrel pairs laying after a natural breeding failure (□), after removal and replacement of one partner (●), or after occupying a nesting site late in the season (▲). The solid line is the regression of clutchsize on laying date for control pairs, with the 99% confidence limits for an individual mean value (broken lines). Most experimental or repeat-laying pairs had clutches larger than the average for that time of year.

A second line of evidence to suggest that clutch size is not always controlled solely by laying date, is the larger clutches of pairs that are obliged to lay late in the season, either because they fail and then repeat, or because they were part of my late-nest and removal experiments (described in Chapter 10). In most cases, such pairs produced larger than average clutches for that time of year (Fig. 62). The disparity was most obvious for experimentally manipulated pairs, but this was to be expected because some of the natural failures may have been caused by shortage of food. Experimental pairs were laying late because they lacked a nest site earlier, or had lost a partner, not because of any shortage of food. There was still a seasonal decline in clutch size among experimental pairs, suggesting that other factors may reduce clutch sizes late in the season.

Sparrowhawks also lay larger than expected clutches when repeating after nesting failure (Newton & Marquiss 1984); and American Kestrels nesting again after removal of the female, or removal of the first clutch, laid second clutches of a similar size to the first ones (Bowman & Bird 1985). It is hard to reconcile these results with a strictly date-determined clutch size, and they suggest that females that are well fed by their partners can lay large clutches early in the season and can also do so later in the year. My experiments were not designed specifically to test this point, however, so they could usefully be repeated with this in mind.

Further evidence that late pairs are normally short of food is the greater frequency of clutch desertion compared with early pairs. This is probably because late females have low body reserves and cannot withstand temporary food shortages during incubation. If they were not short of food, it is hard to understand why late females seem unable to accumulate more reserves before laying. The constraint hypothesis argues that insufficient food in the laying period would reduce both the number of eggs and the body reserves of the female.

There thus seems to be some evidence to support both the proximate, hormonal restraint of clutch size in Kestrels, and the more direct constraint by lack of food. A proximate mechanism which led to a seasonal decline in clutch size could evolve only if laying fewer eggs, and rearing fewer young, gave late pairs some selective advantage over late pairs that reared more young. So far, there is no evidence that young from large, late broods survive less well than those from small ones, though this has not been tested thoroughly in Kestrels. In Sparrowhawks, young in large broods survive better than those in small ones at all stages of the season (Newton 1986).

There is some indication that any advantage from reducing the size of late broods may accrue to the parents, rather than the offspring. Male Kestrels rearing reduced broods (ie those that suffered some partial loss of eggs or chicks) were more likely to breed the following year than those that reared complete, or artificially enlarged, broods (Dijkstra 1988). This was not so for females, so it may not necessarily be the reason why late clutches are smaller. If the detrimental effect of rearing a large brood late in the season falls on the male, females should still lay as many eggs as possible because the loss of the partner over winter is unlikely to affect their chance of breeding the next year. In my farmland data, I found no difference in survival for either sex between birds rearing naturally reduced broods and those rearing full ones.

BREEDING FAILURE AND LOSSES

At Eskdalemuir and in my English farmland areas, only a minority (20–30%) of pairs successfully hatched all their eggs and fledged all their young. Failure to do so arose because pairs either never laid at all, or because they laid and failed completely (Table 39), or because they lost some eggs or chicks before the young fledged. The frequencies of such failures and losses were roughly similar between the Scottish and English areas, with around 30% of pairs failing after producing eggs, and 32% of successful pairs losing some eggs or chicks (Fig. 63). The proportion of non-laying failures was significantly higher in English farmland (13% of 330 pair-years) than in the Scottish grassland area (6% of 154 pair-years), which presumably reflected the generally poorer food supply in farmland habitats.

Desertion of clutches
Complete nesting failure was much more frequent during incubation than after hatch, and the largest single cause of failure in all areas was clutch desertion. This accounted for over 70% of failures in the grassland area, and 50–60% of failures in the farmland areas (Table 39). Cavé (1968) also found that clutch desertion was the main cause of failure in his population, and it was most frequent in poor vole years or during cold, wet springs. Females

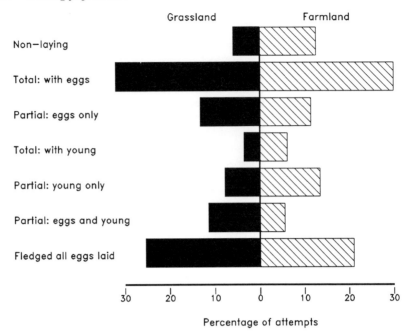

Fig. 63. Outcome of breeding attempts for 162 pairs in Eskdalemuir, 1976–79, and 342 pairs in farmland in England, 1981–87. Total failure and partial losses were most likely early in the breeding cycle, and most total failures were due to desertion of the clutch.

probably desert their clutches because they are not fed sufficiently by their mate and must hunt for themselves. Males have difficulty in supplying food in poor vole years or if prolonged rain prevents hunting. The highest frequency of failure at Eskdalemuir was during the wet May of 1976, when many pairs deserted clutches, or failed with small young, during several days of continuous rain (Table 40). In the farmland areas, however, there was no clear correlation between the proportion of clutches deserted each year and rainfall, temperature or the spring vole index.

Human-related failures

There were no failures due to humans at Eskdalemuir, doubtless because the area was so isolated. In the farmland areas, about 6% of pairs failed because of human activities (Table 39); sometimes deliberate interference because the nest was robbed or an adult shot, and sometimes accidental as a result of farming operations. The latter included the disturbance of straw bales for a pair nesting in a barn, and one pair that deserted after an irrigation pump was left running under the nest tree.

Pesticide-related losses

Work on other raptors, such as Sparrowhawks (Newton 1986), Peregrines (Ratcliffe 1980) and American Kestrels (Lincer 1975), has shown that egg-breakage and some addling is due to the effects of the organochlorine DDE, a metabolite of the pesticide DDT. In my studies, it was rare for Kestrels to fail totally because of egg-breakages, but they were important causes of partial failure in successful nests (Table 41). Of 263 eggs or chicks lost from successful nests, about 54% were eggs that failed to hatch, and most of these were addled. Not all such failures would have been directly caused by DDE because some addling occurred at low frequencies before organochlorines were introduced.

About 5% of eggs in my samples broke before hatch, possibly because they had thin shells due to the effects of DDE. Organochlorine pesticides were used more heavily in eastern England than in south-west Scotland during the 1960s and 1970s, so Kestrel prey at Eskdalemuir would be expected to have lower levels than those in the mixed or arable farmland areas. Eggs from farmland had higher levels of DDE and thinner shells (M. Blake), which presumably explained why they were more likely to break before hatching.

Predation

In both areas, predation of eggs or chicks was very infrequent, and accounted for less than 3% of failures. These were due to foxes or cats taking chicks from two ground nests (see Chapter 9), crows taking eggs in Eskdalemuir, and unknown predators (possibly crows or magpies) killing chicks in mixed farmland. Eggs often disappeared from failed nests and were probably taken by crows, jackdaws or squirrels. However, there was little evidence that this was the cause of failure, and in most instances the eggs were almost certainly removed after the Kestrels had deserted them.

Partial losses of chicks

Few breeding attempts failed completely during the nestling stage, but partial loss of broods was fairly common. The death of chicks from successful nests was probably due to starvation. However, this was difficult to prove in many cases because chicks often died just after hatch, or before they were a week old, and were eaten by their siblings or parents, leaving no trace. Losses at hatch could be difficult to separate from egg loss, but as most unhatched eggs remained in the nest for some weeks afterwards, I assumed that any eggs disappearing at hatch had produced young that subsequently died and were eaten.

The general pattern, then, was for a high proportion of failures among pairs during pre-lay and incubation, but few failures thereafter. About half the eggs laid failed to produce fledged young, and most were lost at the egg stage (Table 42). This is similar to the pattern in other small raptors, such as Sparrowhawks (Newton 1986), and seems to reflect the difficulties that most females have in achieving and maintaining sufficient body reserves to incubate successfully. Females require most food during egg-laying, and the need abates only slightly during incubation. Kestrels laying in April or early May are near the annual low of vole numbers, and may often experience spells of wet or cold weather. Some males are unable to provision their mates adequately, causing them to stop breeding, either before laying or during incubation.

The improved likelihood of success during the nestling stage may partly reflect the better supply of food by then, but nevertheless only the better pairs succeed in hatching young. In most years, late nesters lay at a time when early nesters are facing the much greater food demands of feeding the brood. Although males of both groups must experience similar conditions, the early breeders are much more likely to succeed that the late ones.

REGIONAL AND ANNUAL VARIATIONS IN BREEDING PERFORMANCE

As well as variations in the breeding productivity and success of pairs within seasons, there are also differences in the average performance of pairs between years and between areas. Breeding at Eskdalemuir in the poor vole year of 1977 was later, and mean clutch size smaller, than in years when voles were more plentiful. The late laying in the farmland areas in all years was associated with small clutches and low breeding success (Table 38). It seems likely that the annual differences in one area, and differences between areas, are both due to variations in Kestrel food supply, and breeding productivity shows the same response, irrespective of how the variation in food supply is caused.

Breeding productivity in raptors is usually expressed as young produced per territorial or laying pair. This is dependent on clutch size and subsequent losses, but excludes any effect due to variations in the density of pairs. Perhaps a better measure of the quality of a habitat for Kestrel breeding is the number of young fledged per unit area. This will depend on the density of pairs, how many of these pairs lay eggs, the number of eggs per pair and the frequency of failure and losses.

The density of fledged young in my study areas varied from 8–161/ 100km^2 in any one year, and was generally higher in the Scottish grassland area than in the farmland areas (Table 43). The area difference was largely because breeding density was higher in the grassland area, and, in most years, the density of pairs was the main factor determining how many young fledged in each area (Fig. 64). An exception was 1976, when productivity was lower than expected, partly because vole numbers were in decline and partly because many pairs failed during wet weather in May. The lower density of fledged young in farmland was due both to the higher frequency of non-laying pairs and to the smaller clutches of pairs that did lay, though these were comparatively minor influences compared with the low population density. The relationship of area productivity to Kestrel density was not linear, but increased logarithmically (Fig. 64). In high-density years, laying was early, clutches large and chick survival high. The net result was larger broods, which meant that productivity was greater than expected from the density of pairs.

The fact that the density of young fledged was positively correlated with the number of breeding pairs suggested that there was no density-dependent reduction in breeding productivity. Breeding density and performance were each largely determined by food supply, and if this was good early in the season, when density was determined, it was likely to be good later on, when breeding performance was determined. Reduced chick survival caused by competition between pairs is unlikely in Kestrels, which breed at relatively

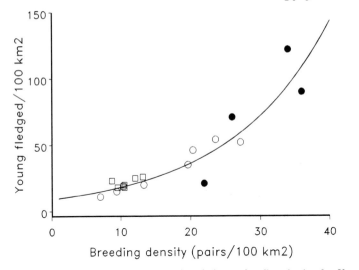

Fig. 64. *Production of young per unit area in relation to breeding density for Kestrel populations in Eskdalemuir (●), mixed farmland (○) and arable farmland (□). The relationship was not linear because more young were fledged per pair at high densities than at low ones.*

low densities, and any density-dependent effects are most likely to be found within broods, where there is direct competition for food between siblings. However, there was no evidence for any increase in percentage mortality in larger broods and, if anything, a higher proportion of chicks survived to fledging in large broods than in small ones (Table 44). Cavé (1968), during his study of Kestrels in Holland, also found no detrimental effect of brood size on survival in the nest.

VARIATIONS IN BREEDING PERFORMANCE WITHIN YEARS

The variations in performance between areas, or from year to year in the same area, were much smaller than the variation between pairs within the same year. The difference in mean laying date between the Scottish grassland and English farmland areas was about two weeks, but in most years there was as much as five or six weeks between the laying dates of the first and last pairs in each study area.

Laying date was a good index of breeding productivity because it was strongly correlated with clutch size and breeding success. Several factors may have influenced the date on which pairs laid. Some of these, such as vole numbers or habitat, were related to differences in the quality of the environment around nests, while others, such as pairing date, age or previous breeding experience, were related to the quality and behaviour of the pairs themselves. I shall consider these two variables separately, though they may be interrelated if better birds occupied the better quality habitats.

Environmental factors

At Eskdalemuir, I was able to measure the quality of the habitat around nests because they were usually in large, even-aged blocks of recently planted ground, with a known vole index for each block (Village 1986). This enabled some assessment of both the habitat and voles available to pairs within a 3 km radius of their nests, which was the maximum foraging range of most breeding males. Voles were the main prey and were much more abundant in the ungrazed grass of the young plantations than elsewhere, so Kestrels should have laid earliest if they had abundant voles and large areas of young plantation around their nest. However, there was no correlation between laying date and vole numbers in any of the four years, and no consistent correlation between laying date and the amount of young plantation around the nest (Table 45). Pairs often nested close together in the same block, and therefore had ranges of similar quality, but they sometimes had quite different laying dates.

The lack of a clear relationship between laying dates and the area of ungrazed grass around nests was surprising, given the much higher densities of voles there than in other habitats. The relationship may have depended on the relative abundance of voles and other prey between habitats. Thus laying was earlier at young plantation sites in 1979, which was the best vole year in that habitat, so the difference in vole abundance between young plantation and sheepwalk was greatest. In 1977, when voles were scarce in young plantation, pairs there laid later than those in sheepwalk, which may have had a better supply of alternative prey items (see Chapter 3). When voles were at intermediate densities, in 1976 and 1978, neither habitat offered any apparent advantage over the other, there being no correlation between habitat and laying date.

Factors related to individuals

Although there are many factors that may contribute to an individual's breeding ability, those that I could measure most easily were age, previous breeding experience and, in Scotland, pairing date. Although these may have been interrelated, because older birds were more likely to have bred than young ones, and adults arrived and paired sooner than first-year birds, it was possible to separate them to some extent by confining the analysis of breeding experience to adult pairs.

1. Pairing date and laying date . Birds that arrived early at Eskdalemuir also paired early and produced eggs sooner than those that paired late (see Chapter 11). The correlation between pairing and laying dates was statistically significant in all four years, even in 1976 and 1977 when most breeders were adults, so the relationship was not merely due to the earlier arrival and laying of adults compared to first-year birds. The reasons why some birds arrived earlier than others are discussed in Chapter 11. Laying dates may also be related to whether or not individuals are migratory. In a partially migrant population in Sweden, resident pairs laid earlier than pairs in which one or both partners were spring migrants (Wallin *et al* 1985).

2. Age and laying date. In both the Scottish grassland and English farmland areas, adult pairs laid earlier, on average, and were more likely to fledge young, than first-year pairs. Mixed aged pairs were intermediate between the two (Table 46). The relative difference between the different age groups was similar in each area, even though laying was generally later in farmland than at Eskdalemuir. Mixed pairs in which the female was adult, laid earlier than those where she was a first-year bird, suggesting that female-age may have had more influence on laying date than male age. However, it was hard to be sure of this because pairings between first-year males and adult females were infrequent. Laying date may be related to adult ages, but I had too few known-age adults to test this fully. Adults known to be at least three years old generally laid earlier than two-year olds, though this could not easily be separated from breeding experience.

3. Breeding experience and laying date. By the time my studies were established, adult breeders present in the study areas in spring consisted of previously tagged birds that were known to have bred before and others, mostly untagged, that probably had not. Some marked birds were breeding with the partner of the previous year, whereas others were breeding with a new partner that might or might not have bred before. Pairs in which both birds had bred in the area before laid earlier, on average, than those where one or both partners had previously been unmarked. This was true in both Eskdalemuir and the farmland areas, but the difference was statistically significant only in the former area (Table 47). Where birds changed to an experienced partner, they showed no significant difference in laying dates from those that kept the same partner, so experience of breeding may be more important than experience with a particular partner.

INDIVIDUAL VARIATION IN BREEDING PERFORMANCE

In general, factors related to individuals, such as age, seemed to have more influence on within-year variations in laying dates than environmental factors, such as habitat quality or local variations in prey density. Within the size range of my study areas (100–200 km^2), variations in food supply between nesting territories in the same area were probably small compared to the annual fluctuations caused by vole cycles and weather, or gross differences in habitat between Scottish grassland and English farmland. There was no evidence of any segregation of early and late nesters within each area, so the large variation in performance between adjacent pairs must have related to the ability of the pairs themselves.

Because food supply seems to be the major factor affecting laying dates in Kestrels, the age and experience of individuals were probably a reflection of hunting ability. Older birds may have been able to catch more food from a given area than younger ones, and thus reach breeding condition sooner. In theory, hunting ability should be more important in males than in females, because the male has to feed the female and bring her into breeding condition. However, in most years, laying date was most closely related to female age. This may have been because older females tended to pair with older males (I could not test this in adults), or because adult females were in better condition at the start of the breeding season than first-year females and therefore required less time to reach laying condition.

BREEDING PERFORMANCE AND FEMALE BODY WEIGHT

If food supply is important in determining the breeding performance of Kestrels, then it ought to achieve its effect through the body condition of the female. Because there is little decline in weight between laying and hatching, weight during incubation is probably strongly correlated with that during laying, and provides a useful way of comparing females. Within each of my studies, both clutch size and incubation weight were correlated with laying date, so that females that laid early were heavier and produced larger clutches than those that laid late (Table 48). This meant that, in the farmland areas at least, clutch size was correlated with female body weight, a result also found for Kestrels in Holland (Drent and Daan 1980). Although this implies that heavier weight (equivalent to more fat reserves) *caused* larger clutches, this may not necessarily be so. In Holland, late-breeding females had lower weights during laying than did early ones, but were unable to produce more eggs even if their body weights were increased by artificial feeding (Meijer 1988). Partial correlation analysis of my data showed that weight was weakly, but significantly, correlated with clutch size even after allowing for laying date. This is in line with the small but significant effect of habitat on clutch size in Fig. 61a, and suggests that body weight does have some direct influence on clutch size.

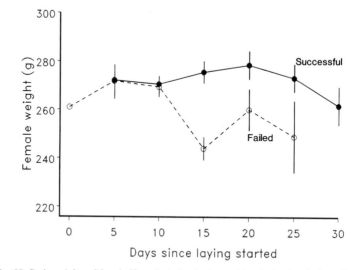

Fig. 65. Body weights of female Kestrels during laying and incubation in relation to hatching success (combined data for the Eskdalemuir and farmland study areas). Females that failed to hatch eggs started at similar weights to successful females, but became lighter as incubation progressed. Vertical bars are ± 1SE.

Female body weight during incubation was also related to clutch desertion. Females that failed to hatch their eggs began incubation at about the same average weight as successful ones, but those weighed in the second half of incubation were significantly lighter than successful females (Fig. 65). This supports the idea that females deserted their eggs because they received insufficient food to maintain adequate body weight. When the reserves were gone, females could continue incubating only if they were regularly fed by their mates.

SUMMARY

Kestrels are capable of laying up to seven eggs, but few pairs ever fledge this number of young in one year. Inability to achieve full potential can be caused by failure to produce eggs, by laying less than the maximum clutch, by losing eggs or chicks from successful nests, or by total nesting failure. In any year, pairs may start laying at any time in a six week period, but those laying early have larger clutches and are more likely to fledge young than those that lay late. The seasonal decline in clutch size seems to be due both to a proximate hormonal mechanism that links the number of eggs laid to the daylength when laying starts, and to the nutritional state of the female.

Most breeding failures are due to failure to lay or because females desert their clutches during incubation. Lighter females are more likely to desert, suggesting that they leave the eggs because they are short of food. Failures tend to be at an early stage of the breeding cycle, and most pairs that hatch their eggs also fledge some young. The breeding performance of pairs is related to their age and previous breeding experience, while environmental factors, such as the food supply or habitat around the nest, are poor predictors of the variation in performance between pairs in the same year. The ability of males to supply food to their mates may be the main factor influencing the timing and success of breeding.

CHAPTER 16

Movements and migrations

The two main types of movement dealt with in this chapter are the dispersal of recently fledged Kestrels away from their natal area, and the seasonal migrations of adults and juveniles. Dispersal and migration are linked to some extent, but not entirely so because juveniles in all populations disperse, yet not all populations migrate. Kestrels are almost entirely migratory in north-east Europe, and the northern limit of their winter distribution roughly follows the line of permanent winter snow cover (Fig. 66). South of this line, Kestrels are partially migrant, in that some individuals remain in all but the severest winters, while others migrate each autumn. In lowland and coastal areas of north-west Europe, and in southern Europe, most of the breeding population is resident, and winter numbers may be augmented by an influx of northern migrants.

Before migration begins, the recently independent young disperse from their natal territories and settle in surrounding areas. In migrant populations this may be a prelude to the true migration, but in more sedentary populations the young birds may become resident on their new-found territories.

SOURCES OF INFORMATION

Although the general patterns of Kestrel migration could be deduced from the differences between summer and winter population densities across Europe, most of our detailed knowledge comes from the recovery of birds ringed under various national ringing schemes. Ringing in Britain is co-ordinated by the British Trust for Ornithology, and just over 10% of the 23,000 Kestrels ringed

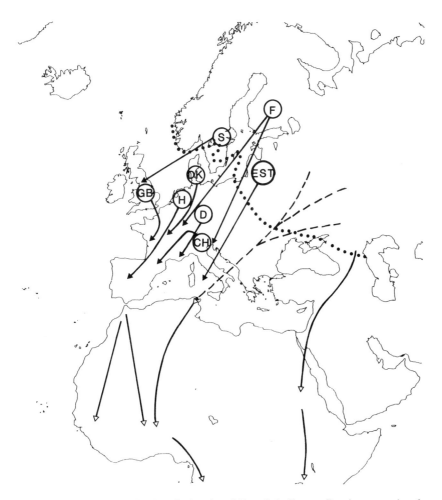

Fig. 66. Approximate direction of migration of Kestrels in Europe. Based on recoveries of birds ringed as nestlings in the countries indicated (solid lines), or on spring migration at Cape Bon, Tunisia (broken line). Open arrows show the presumed movements of Kestrels that migrate to Africa. The dotted line shows the northern limit of the wintering range, and roughly corresponds to the southern limit of permanent winter snow-cover.

before 1985 have been recovered, the majority being birds ringed as nestlings. Although this means most recoveries are of known-aged birds, few of these were sexed when ringed, and the BTO data I analysed gave no indication of the sex of any recovered birds. The Kestrels I trapped when full-grown could be sexed and aged (first-year or older). They yielded a much smaller sample of recoveries, but many of these were birds with a known breeding history.

With any recoveries there are certain unavoidable biases that may hinder interpretation. Dead Kestrels are more likely to be found where people are numerous, so the absence of ring recoveries from sparsely populated regions is not necessarily because these regions are less favoured by Kestrels. As it happens, the highest concentrations of people in Europe tend to be in lowlands or other areas without permanent winter snow-cover, and lowlands are where Kestrels are likely to spend the winter. However, the scarcity of ring recoveries from Africa may underestimate its importance for wintering European Kestrels, which are seen there in considerable numbers. In poorer parts of the world, lack of education or adequate communications may mean that any ringed birds found are unlikely to be reported. Misleading results can also arise within Europe because persecution is heavier in some countries than in others. For example, most recoveries of Dutch-ringed Kestrels from Belgium in the 1960s were shot birds, and this may have over-emphasised the south-westerly direction of movements compared with other directions, where shooting was less likely (Cavé 1968).

Despite these drawbacks, ringing has given tremendous insight into the movements of Kestrels, and the species' abundance and its popularity with ringers have ensured good samples of recoveries from Britain and elsewhere in Europe. I have used the recoveries of Kestrels from my study areas in Scotland and England to illustrate the differences between largely migrant and largely sedentary populations, but have included all the recoveries from the National Ringing Scheme (up to 1984) where my samples were too small.

Another source of information on the migration of Kestrels is counts made at places where raptors concentrate while on passage. Such concentrations are usually at short sea-crossings, such as the Strait of Gibraltar or the Bosporus, but they may occur wherever the topography 'funnels' birds from a wide area through one place. However, Kestrels migrate on a fairly 'broad-front' and do not concentrate to the same extent as do broad-winged hawks. This, coupled with their small size, means that Kestrels are not recorded as often or as accurately as larger raptors during migration, so that counts of visible migration seriously underestimate the true scale of Kestrel movements. Nonetheless, such data as there are give a rough idea of the timing of migration in different places, and have in one case shown that adult males migrate later in autumn than the rest of the population (Gatter 1972).

POST-FLEDGING DISPERSAL

Young Kestrels disperse from their nesting areas from July onwards, during the first few weeks of independent life, and are recovered at increasing distances from where they were ringed. The dispersal occurs fairly quickly and, even in

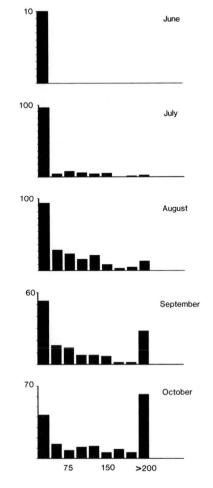

Fig. 67. Histograms of the distances travelled by ringed Kestrels recovered in their first few months after fledging. Initially, most recoveries were within 25 km of the nest, but some individuals had already dispersed considerable distances by July. The increase in recoveries over 200 km from the birth place after August indicates the gradual onset of migration in Kestrels from northern Britain.

July, recoveries typically show an exponential decline with distance from the nest (Fig. 67). This means that while most juveniles are found within a few kilometres of the nest, a few are reported much further afield. For example, one nestling ringed on 17 June in Dumfriesshire, was recovered 24 days later over 300 km away, near Aberdeen. Most dispersal is over a shorter distance, however, and more than 70% of recoveries at this stage are within 75 km of the ringing site (Table 49). The dispersal phase seems to last for much of July and August, and true migratory movements are uncommon in British Kestrels before September. In southern Britain there is no evidence of any preferred direction to movements before October, and even in the north there is only a slight south-easterly bias in August and September. The latter is probably indicative of early migration, though it may arise because Kestrels dispersing to the north and west are less likely to be recovered because of the lower human population density.

This pattern of a random post-fledging dispersal up to about 150 km, was first noticed by Thomson (1958) and Snow (1968) in earlier analyses of British ring recoveries, and seems to happen elsewhere in Europe (Cavé 1968, Nielsen 1983). In Switzerland, there is a tendency for a north-westward movement of juveniles during July and August, and most are recovered in France or Belgium (Schifferli 1965). This may again be an artifact, due to human population density, or levels of persecution, though it could arise if young birds, ringed in the Northern Alps, moved away from the mountains towards the nearest expanse of lowlands.

I do not know if young birds are forced out of their natal territory by aggressive parents, or if they leave because they are no longer being fed, though I suspect the latter. In either case, establishing a new territory evidently involves competition with adults and other juveniles, and there is a marked increase in aggressive encounters during early autumn (Chapter 7). Juveniles may simply move away from the nest until they are able to establish a territory where they can hunt without being driven away by other Kestrels. They may then stay all winter if the food supply holds, but move away if it declines.

Brood-mates leaving the nest must experience the same local conditions and, having a similar genetic make-up, might be expected to respond in similar ways. Among 18 siblings I ringed that were subsequently recovered, there was no correlation in the distance they moved, but a significant correlation of direction ($r = 0.62$, $P < 0.01$). However, the latter may have reflected the general direction of migration within populations, because a similar correlation held between unrelated birds reared at the same nest site in different years. In Sparrowhawks, the opposite seems to be true, as siblings travel about the same distance, but not necessarily in the same direction (Newton 1986). In some cases, Kestrel brood-mates may travel together, at least judged from some of my local retraps. I caught two females on adjacent territories at Eskdalemuir, in October 1977, that had been ringed at the same nest 20 km away; likewise male and female brood-mates that moved 5 km in the arable farmland area in 1984. These instances may have arisen if one bird followed the other, or by chance if siblings encountered the same conditions and then responded in the same way.

Distance dispersed in relation to fledging date
Because of the variable laying dates of Kestrels, young leave their nests over a six week period, from early June to late July. This may allow early-fledged young to establish their winter territories sooner, and nearer their birthplace, than late-fledged ones. In the national ringing recoveries, the mean date for ringing nestlings was 23 June, so I used this as the dividing date between early and late fledging. Young that fledged early moved sooner than those that

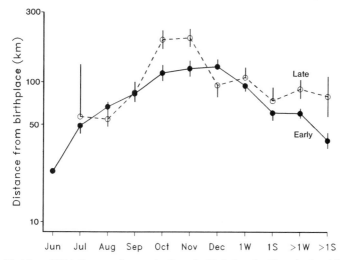

Fig. 68. Mean (SE) distance of recoveries from the birthplace for Kestrels ringed in early broods (●) and late ones (○) in the National Ringing Scheme. Late-fledged birds moved further away from their birthplace than early fledged ones during their first autumn, and this difference was also apparent later in life. 1W = first winter, 1S = first summer, > 1W = all subsequent winters, > 1S = all subsequent summers. Notice the logarithmic scale for distance.

fledged late, and were found further away from the nest, on average, during July and August (Fig. 68). By September, however, late-fledged young had caught up, and during October and November they had dispersed further than the early young, which seemed to settle where they were. The difference was not apparent in late winter, but seemed to hold in later life, both in summer and winter. The greater dispersal of late- than early-fledged young in early winter was statistically significant, even though most early young were from the north of Britain, and might have been expected to move further than southern ones (see below). The pattern in Fig. 68 is what might be expected if early fledged young occupied the locally available territories, and then prevented later ones from settling there. In sedentary populations this initial dispersal probably determines where individuals will eventually breed. In both my studies, but particularly in farmland, I noticed that juveniles would often breed near to where they settled in their first autumn, albeit two years later in some cases.

The differences in dispersal between early- and late-fledged young may have affected their chances of being recruited into the local breeding population at an early age. About 5% of the nestlings I ringed subsequently bred in the study areas, but the earliest fledged young were twice as likely to do so. If recruitment at any age was considered, the difference was not statistically significant, but it was when comparing the chances of breeding in the first year of life (Table 50). Early young were five times more likely to breed locally when yearlings than were those fledged in mid to late season, a result that has also been found in Holland (Dijkstra 1988). The delayed local recruitment of late young may have partly reflected their greater dispersal, so that they were as likely as early young to breed in their first year, but less likely to do so near their natal site. The difference in dispersal distances of the two groups was not sufficient to fully explain the disparity in age of local recruitment, however, and there was almost certainly a genuine difference in the age of first breeding. Being able to establish a territory early in the autumn seems to be important, both for enhancing survival in winter and for enabling juveniles to breed the following spring.

POST-BREEDING MIGRATIONS

Movements within Europe and Africa

In Britain, the main period of autumn migration is during September and October, and this seems similar to other European countries such as Switzerland (Schifferli 1965), Germany (Gatter 1972), Denmark (Nielsen 1983) and Sweden (Wallin et al 1987). The onset of migration in Britain results in an increase in the proportion of long distance (over 150 km) ring recoveries, and these have a marked south-easterly orientation (Fig. 66). This is in contrast to the mainly south-westerly direction of migration on the Continent, and most British Kestrels tend to move to the south or west if they cross the Channel (Snow 1968). Some long-distance migrants from Europe reach North and Central Africa, going as far as Nigeria and Ghana in the west, and to the equator in the east (Mead 1973, Brown et al 1982). Most recoveries in Africa are of Continental birds, and the extreme southerly recoveries of British Kestrels to date are two nestlings ringed in Northumberland and the Grampians that were found in Morocco.

Although they migrate over a fairly broad front, Kestrels do concentrate to some extent at either end of the Mediterranean and, in spring, at Cape Bon in Tunisia. Kestrels ringed at this latter site have been recovered in summer as far east as the river Volga (Glutz et al 1971). This, together with the recovery of a Czech bird in Ghana (Mead 1973), suggests that most European birds that winter in Africa do so in the north or west, rather than the east. There is a considerable passage of Kestrels at the eastern end of the Mediterranean, but few ring recoveries to show their origin or destination. Presumably, many of them breed in the largely uninhabited areas of Kazakstan and winter in the East African savannahs.

That Kestrels regularly make fairly long sea crossings is shown by the recoveries of Scandinavian birds in Britain. There are about nine such recoveries of nestlings ringed in Norway, Sweden or Finland, mostly from the east of England, though one reached south-west Ireland. Britain may be a more important wintering ground for Scandiavian birds than these few recoveries suggest, and there are regular sightings of Kestrels at oil platforms in the North Sea during autumn and spring (Riddle 1985).

Migration of British Kestrels

The winter recoveries of my Scottish and English Kestrels illustrate the more migratory habits of Kestrels in northern Britain (Fig. 69). Most of the recoveries

Fig. 69. Location of recoveries during winter (October-March) for Kestrels ringed in (a) the Scottish grassland area and (b) the English farmland areas. ● = ringed as adults, otherwise ringed as juveniles and recovered in first winter (○) or subsequent winters (◑). In England, 32 ringed as juveniles and 9 ringed as adults were subsequently recovered less than 80 km from the ringing site (ie within the large circle shown).

from Scotland were of birds in their first winter, but a few were adults that were known to have bred in the area at least once, but migrated away in the intervening winter (Table 51). I could not tell if their final recovery was typical of where they would normally have spent the winter, but the distances they moved were highly variable: one was found in low-ground some 40 km away, while another was recovered in western France. I also had reports of a known migrant that was regularly seen in winter lower down the Esk Valley. This bird, and the one found 40 km away, were both early arrivals in previous springs, and I suspect some migrants may have moved to the nearest low-ground and returned to Eskdalemuir as soon as the weather improved in spring. Others must have gone further south, and may, indeed, have wintered in my subsequent farmland study areas in England. In one of those hard-to-believe coincidences, a breeding Kestrel I wing-tagged at Eskdalemuir in 1979 was caught during the following winter by a colleague within the grounds of Monks Wood Experimental Station, near Huntingdon! Unfortunately, I did not see this bird in Scotland in 1980, so I could not be certain that it had returned to breed again.

The winter recoveries of breeding birds from the farmland areas in England have nearly all been within a few kilometres of where they last bred (Table 51), and even juveniles showed little tendency to move long distances (Fig. 69). Although there was a slight preference for south-easterly movements, this was much less marked than in Scotland (Fig. 70), so most of the English recoveries were probably birds that had dispersed, rather than migrated.

The trends in my study areas were confirmed in the larger samples of the National Ringing Scheme. I compared the finding locations of all birds ringed in the north or south of Britain, using 53° N as a dividing line between the two populations. This runs from North Wales to The Wash and, though it may seem rather arbitrary, it is based on David Snow's (1968) finding that Kestrels from northern England seem to be as migratory as those from Scotland. Kestrels ringed in the north moved further, on average, during their first winter than did those from the south (Fig. 71). The average movement from ringing to finding place was about 150 km in the north (or 1.3 degrees in latitude), compared with 66 km (0.3 degrees) in the south. This difference was lost in the first and subsequent summers, as birds from both areas moved nearer to their birthplace, but was maintained to a lesser exent in subsequent winters.

In both north and south, juveniles seem to migrate further in winter than

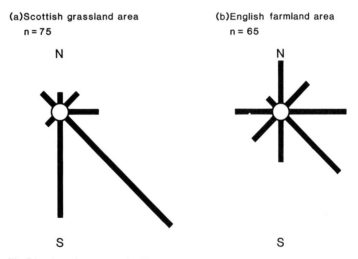

Fig. 70. *Direction of movement for Kestrels ringed in (a) the Scottish grassland area and (b) the English farmland areas, based on recoveries at least 10 km from the ringing site. Length of lines is proportional to the numbers of recoveries. Scottish birds showed a much stronger preference for south or south-easterly directions than English ones, reflecting their greater migratory tendency.*

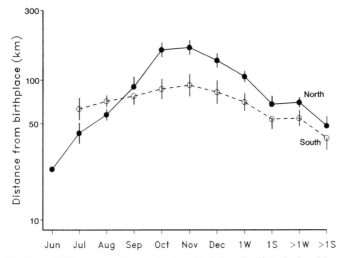

Fig. 71. Mean (SE) distance of recoveries from birthplace for Kestrels ringed in northern (●) and southern (○) Britain, using 53° N as the dividing line for the two groups. Northern birds were significantly further away in winter, but returned to their natal area in summer. Legend for axes as in Fig. 68.

adults, though this may not necessarily reflect what individual birds actually do. The decrease in the average distance moved from the first to subsequent years may have arisen if first-year mortality was higher among long-distance migrants than short-distance ones. Individuals may therefore have returned to the same wintering grounds each year, but only those that made shorter migrations survived to be recovered after the first year. There is little evidence to test this, though some to suggest that birds may show fidelity to winter territories. In the farmland areas I caught three birds in winter that were seen on the same territory the next year, but were absent during the intervening summer. One of these, a female caught in autumn 1981, returned to the same territory for three successive winters, but was never seen between March and August.

If a bird survives its first winter on a particular territory, its best option may be to return there the next year, as it is one place that it knows can support it over winter. The same could be true for birds returning to their natal area: inexperienced birds may not be able to recognise a good breeding area, but returning to where they were born will put them in an area where successful breeding is possible in at least some years. This may seem a rather inefficient way of choosing a breeding or wintering area, especially if food supply varies from year to year. Nonetheless, it provides a relatively simple, instinctive mechanism that will almost certainly give a better outcome than choosing areas at random. Not all birds return to their natal area, and very few will actually breed on their natal territory, so any homing instinct in migrants is clearly capable of being overridden if suitable conditions are encountered en route.

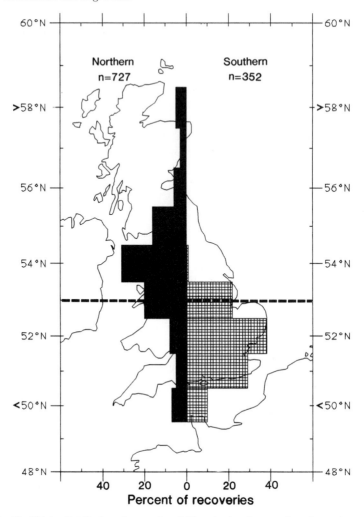

Fig. 72. Winter distribution of recoveries of Kestrels ringed as nestlings in northern and southern Britain as part of the National Ringing Scheme. Histograms show the percentage of Kestrels ringed north (shaded) or south (cross-hatched) of latitiude 53° N (broken line) that were recovered at each latitude. Northern Kestrels moved further than southern ones, but most still wintered in northern Britain.

DISTRIBUTION OF WINTER POPULATIONS

Despite the longer movements of northern Kestrels compared with southern ones, British Kestrels do not show a true 'leap-frog' migration, in which most northern birds winter further south than southern ones. The majority of winter recoveries of northern birds are north of the Wash, and their mean recovery latitude is about two degrees north of southern birds. Some northern birds spread into the southern zone, though the reverse is less common, and there is considerable overlap around 52° N, which includes much of the east Midlands and East Anglia (Fig. 72). Despite their proximity to the Continent, southern Kestrels were less likely to be recovered there than were northern ones (Table 52), though this is not so for those ringed in the counties bordering the English Channel (Snow 1968).

The totally migrant populations elsewhere in Europe may show a more definite leap-frog migration, and this seems to be so in Sweden, where northern birds winter further south-west, on average, than southern ones (Wallin *et al* 1987). Northern birds start to move south before the rest, and are in the same areas as southern Kestrels in September, but subsequently overtake them. Similarly in spring, the northern birds move earlier, and are in the same areas as southern birds when the main spring migrations begin.

Although the migration routes of Kestrels in Europe are roughly parallel, there must be a considerable mixing of birds from different areas in winter. Most long-distance migrants from countries bordering the North Sea are funnelled through central France en route to the Iberian peninsular. Spanish recoveries of foreign-ringed Kestrels include individuals from Britain, Belgium, Holland, Denmark, Germany, Switzerland, Sweden and Holland (Mead 1973). It is possible that some wintering birds remain where they are and subsequently breed, while others may migrate in spring to countries other than those where they were born. Foreign birds have been recovered in Britain during the breeding season (one from Sweden, two from Belgium), and British ringed nestlings have been recovered in subsequent summers in several countries from Norway to Spain. Most of these were first-year birds, though a few were older and may have been breeding. Such genetic exchange between distant regions, although apparently rare, seems sufficient to prevent the formation of subspecies within Europe. This is not true of the highly sedentary and isolated races of *tinnunculus* on the Canary and Cape Verde Islands (Chapter 2), which are much less likely to mix with the nominate race.

SPRING MIGRATIONS

The peak migration of Kestrels in spring is during March and April, but some birds start earlier, especially long-distance migrants. In West Africa, migrants begin to leave in early March and most have gone by April (Brown *et al* 1982). A few remain until May, which might explain the Moroccan recovery of a British Kestrel at that time of year (Mead 1973). The peak passage around the Mediterranean is mid March to May (Evans & Lathbury 1973), and at extreme northern sites late April to May (Dementiev & Gladkov 1954). At Eskdalemuir, the first migrants usually arrived in late February, and the last in early May, with a peak from mid March to mid April (Village 1985a). Kestrels wintering close to their breeding grounds may return as soon as the weather becomes mild, and arrivals at Eskdalemuir were earlier in 1976 following a mild winter, than after harsher ones (Chapter 11). In general, there seems to be a considerable spread in the timing of migration within populations, so that some northern breeders may have returned and begun courtship while others are still crossing the Mediterranean. Late arrivals can make up some lost time by shortening their courtship (Chapter 11), but are still likely to breed late, if at all.

The return routes are not necessarily identical to the outward ones, and points of concentration in spring are not always the same as those in autumn, probably for reasons of topography and wind direction. For example, birds migrating south out of Sweden in autumn are channelled along the coast, and tend to depart from Falsterbo, the most south-westerly point. Returning birds cross the coast over a much wider area, and the spring concentration is much less marked (Ulfstrand *et al* 1974). Snow (1968) suggested that British Kestrels may cross the Channel in spring further to the east than in autumn, because most spring recoveries abroad are from north-east France and Belgium.

AGE AND SEX DIFFERENCES IN MIGRATION

The longer migration of first-winter birds has already been mentioned, but differences may also exist between the sexes in the timing of movements. Migrating adult males can be distinguished from females or juvenile males by careful observers, and formed a higher proportion of the late autumn-migrants in the Schwabian Alps in south Germany (Gatter 1972). This may have been because all the early migrants were juveniles or because females left earlier than males. Later settling of adult males than females on winter territories has been recorded in American Kestrels wintering in Florida (Smallwood 1988). The age-difference is reversed in spring and, at Eskdalemuir, adults of both sexes arrived before first-year birds (Chapter 11). The trend for adults to leave breeding areas later, and arrive sooner, than young birds seems to be typical of other partially-migrant raptors (Newton 1979). It may reflect both the better ability of adults to remain in breeding areas under poor food conditions, and the greater pressure on them to get breeding territories.

At Eskdalemuir, the winter sex ratio was often biased towards males, and if one partner migrated it was usually the female rather than the male. Despite this, males that did migrate apparently went further, on average, than females, at least judged by recoveries of birds I ringed when full grown (Table 51). The samples were too small to test this adequately, and the trend appeared to be reversed in the recoveries of Kestrels from the farmland areas, where both sexes were fairly sedentary once they had reached breeding age.

MIGRATION AND SUBSEQUENT BREEDING SUCCESS

At Eskdalemuir, the summer population consisted of both migrants and residents. I had no cases of migrants becoming resident once they had migrated, nor did residents migrate after they had remained a whole winter. This implies that Kestrels may keep the same migratory habits through life. Leaving the area in winter must have had both advantages and disadvantages: staying increased the chance of keeping the same territory and mate (Village 1985b), and may have helped in securing a suitable nest site the following year. However, in some years residents had to endure periods of prolonged snow cover which were unpredictable in duration, and which must have greatly reduced the availability of voles. Migrants avoided these problems, but faced a possibly hazardous journey and the necessity of finding a winter territory and then a nest site the next spring.

It would be interesting to know if migrants had different survival or breeding success to residents, but collecting enough suitable information is not easy. In Scotland, wintering birds nearly always paired with incomers in spring, and I had only one pairing between birds that had wintered in the area. Pairs where one member had wintered generally laid earlier than those where both were incomers, but this did not distinguish incomers that were new to the area, and bred only once, from true migrants that were returning after previous breeding attempts. Pairs where neither partner was a resident laid slightly later, and fledged fewer young, than resident-migrant pairs, but the difference was slight and not statistically significant (Table 53). Resident males had to wait for a migrant partner to arrive before they could pair, and in many cases the early migrants paired at the same time as resident males, and seemed not to have been seriously disadvantaged.

Resident pairs in Sweden have been shown to breed earlier than migrants (Wallin *et al* 1987), but this analysis apparently grouped adults and first-year birds, and treated all non-residents as migrants. Whether the differences in breeding success observed were solely due to the benefits of residence is not clear. More work needs to be done on this topic, and ideally the life-time reproductive success of residents and migrants should be compared. This may show if higher reproductive output in residents is paid for by reduced survival. Both behaviours persist in the same population, possibly because residents do better in some years and migrants in others. If the net benefits are closely balanced, the behaviour adopted by an individual might depend on chance factors operating in the first few months of its life.

SUMMARY

Juvenile Kestrels disperse in random directions after fledging and recoveries fall away exponentially from the birthplace up to about 150 km (extreme 300 km). The true autumn migration begins in September and lasts until November. Kestrels that breed in areas of permanent winter snow-cover are all migratory, and travel further south than more southern breeders, reaching as far as Central Africa. In Britain, Kestrels are partially migrant in Scotland and Northern England, but largely resident in Southern and Central England. There is not a true 'leap-frog' migration, because many northern birds winter in the Midlands and East Anglia, but a higher proportion of then reach the Continent than those ringed in southern Britain.

Juveniles migrate further than adults during winter, and late-fledged juveniles further than early-fledged ones, the latter difference possibly persisting throughout life. Late fledging is associated with a lower likelihood of breeding locally in the first year of life, though the difference is less marked when recruitment in later years is included. There is some evidence that residents in partially migrant populations may breed earlier, and more successfully, than migrants, though this requires more investigation.

CHAPTER 17

Population turnover

Population turnover is the recruitment and loss of individuals over time due to birth or immigration and death or emigration. Turnover may be a measure of changes within a given area, changes at particular territories or nest sites, or changes of mate. In populations with low turnover, individuals tend to stay in one place for most of their lives and, if they survive long enough, often breed at the same nest site with the same partner in successive years. Turnover will be high if individuals are short-lived, or if they frequently change territory or partners. Turnover is not necessarily related to the level or stability of population density, because stable numbers can result either from no change in the individuals present, or because high losses are matched by equally high recruitment.

The only satisfactory way of measuring turnover is to follow the fate of individually marked birds. Wing-tagging of Kestrels has enabled me to monitor particular birds, sometimes over several years, from when they first arrived in the area until eventually they left or died. Individuals not seen for two years were unlikely to be recorded again, so their wing-tag colour combination was used on another bird. In most years I was able to trap, or identify from wing-tags, the majority of the breeding population of both sexes, so untagged Kestrels caught after the first year of study were assumed to be new to the area. The loss of both tags was so unusual (twice in over 200 retraps), that untagged birds were almost invariably new to the area and, even if I failed to catch them, they indicated a change of partner if the previous one had been tagged.

Turnover in a given area tends to be a rather arbitrary measure, as the chance of an individual remaining there when it changes territory depends on the size and shape of the study area. Mine were roughly the same size, and each contained 30–40 breeding sites at maximum densities. Although varied in shape, they were at least 10 km wide and 10–20 km long, so movements of up to 15 km could be recorded within areas, and up to 40 km between the two farmland areas. It was sometimes difficult to decide if a bird had changed nesting territory if there were changes in nest spacing from year to year. Nesting territories occupied by one pair in one year might contain two or more separate pairs the next. I assumed that a bird had changed territory between years if its new nest was more than 750 m from the last, as this was the maximum likely radius of nest defence. I measured turnover at given nesting sites by using instances when Kestrels bred in the same crow nest or tree hole in successive years.

DURATION IN THE STUDY AREA

An important component of turnover is the persistence of birds in an area. If individuals stay only a short while, there must be a high turnover if a steady population density is to be maintained. When a bird disappears from an area, it may have died or moved elsewhere, and it is difficult to tell which has happened. The proportion of individuals remaining from year to year can be used as an estimate of 'local survival', though it will underestimate true survival rates if some losses are due to emigration. I measured persistence in the study area in several ways, using tagged birds to indicate trends in the population as a whole.

Proportion of year-round residents

Most tagged birds could be classed either as a *year-round resident* (present for at least a successive summer and winter), a *migrant* (present for two or more summers, but absent in winter), or a *single-season resident* (present for either one winter or one summer only).

At Eskdalemuir, I tagged 96 males and 111 females from October 1975 to July 1979, and recorded their presence or absence in the summers of 1976–80 and the winters of 1975–77. Combining the sexes, the majority (66%) was present for only a single season, and a mere 11% were year-round residents (Table 54). Slightly more (17%) were summer migrants, but there were no winter migrants and the area did not seem to be a regular wintering ground for birds that bred elsewhere. The proportion of single-season residents was slightly higher among females than males (72% versus 61%), but this was due to the short residence of first-year females, and there were no marked differences between the sexes in adults.

In England I could classify 115 males and 116 females, and the proportion

Changes of occupants at nesting sites between years could be easily detected if the population was wing-tagged. Photo: N. J. Westwood.

of year-round residents was about 52%, much higher than in Scotland (Table 54). There were no summer migrants, but a few were apparently winter migrants as they were seen in successive winters but not in the intervening summer. Overall, single-season residents were less frequent, accounting for 46% of tagged birds compared with 76% in Scotland. Most single-season residents in Scotland were there in summer, rather than winter, but the opposite was true in England, which agreed with the pattern of migration in the two areas (Chapter 16).

Number of breeding attempts

The different proportions of year-round residents in the Scottish and English studies was also reflected in the number of breeding attempts per bird. The

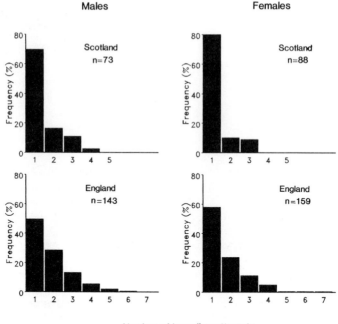

Fig. 73. *Number of breeding attempts recorded for individually marked Kestrels in the Scottish grassland area (1976–80) and English farmland areas (1981–87). The maximum possible number of attempts that could have been recorded was five in Scotland and seven in England.*

pattern obtained was influenced to some extent by the duration of each study, and only birds caught in the first year of study could achieve the maximum number of attempts. Nonetheless, all birds had the chance of being recorded breeding at least twice, but a large number in both studies bred only once (Fig. 73). The proportion breeding more than once was similar between the sexes, but significantly higher in England than in Scotland. In the latter area, females that bred as yearlings were less likely to breed again than either first-year males or adults, but this trend was not apparent in England. The high numbers breeding once only meant that the average number of attempts per tagged bird was less than two, even among those that bred at least once.

First and last sighting dates

The most direct way of measuring a bird's duration in the area was to use the interval between first-catching and last-sighting. The difficulty with this method was that birds already present when the study began, or those caught near its end, were not recorded for their full duration. Only those that stayed a comparatively short time were likely to start and finish their residence during the study. In Scotland, the mean stay of year-round residents was 35 months (n = 10) for all males, but only 23 months (n = 4) for birds whose residence began and ended during the study. A similar difference was apparent in females (Table 55) but, even allowing for these discrepancies, the duration of either sex was short of the maximum possible, and would be even smaller if single-season residents were included. In England, there were many more year-round residents, but their average duration in the area was roughly similar to Scotland, being 21 months for all birds, and 19 months for birds whose complete residence period was known (Table 55).

These three measures were obviously interrelated, and it was not surprising that they all led to similar conclusions about the persistence of Kestrels in a given area. There were no marked differences between the sexes and, apart from first-year females in Scotland, males and females had similar rates of loss. The main difference between the study areas was the absence of summer migrants in England, and the greater likelihood that individuals would stay throughout one or more years. The few year-round residents in Scotland seemed to stay as long as those in England, which may have been because their loss reflected mortality, rather than movement. The results were in line with the greater migratory habits of northern Kestrels (Chapter 16), which seemed less likely than southern birds to breed in the same area twice. The similarity in residence periods of males and females suggests they had fairly similar survival rates.

TURNOVER IN THE STUDY AREAS

Once I had begun marking Kestrels in each area, I could detect the arrival or loss of individuals in any month, provided I was regularly trapping incomers. In Scotland, I monitored most of the area fairly closely during October to July from 1975 to 1978, and could estimate the turnover by the proportion of the marked birds present that either arrived, or were last seen, during each month (Village 1985b). In England, the trapping effort was less even, and the apparent influx of birds in April was mainly because I caught birds at the start of the breeding season that could have arrived in the preceding months. When these seasonal irregularities were averaged, the mean level of turnover was 26% per month at Eskdalemuir, but 13% in the English farmland areas (Table 56). In Scotland, there was some seasonality, and turnover was higher in autumn and spring than in mid winter or summer, but unrelated to population size or vole density (Village 1985b). These estimates were only approximate, but they were in line with the short residence of most individuals, and indicate a high level of turnover in Kestrel populations. Even in the relatively stable farmland population, at least 10% of the birds present at one time would have either arrived within the last month or would disappear in the next.

The greater turnover in the Scottish grassland area was also apparent in the breeding population. After the first year of each study, most unmarked birds in the area were new recruits, so I used the ratio of unmarked to previously tagged Kestrels as an indication of the turnover of breeding birds. Overall, about one third of the breeding population had bred the previous year, and about two-thirds was unmarked. The proportion of new breeders was significantly higher in the Scottish grassland than in the English farmland (Table 57). This was partly because the increase in the Eskdalemuir breeding population in 1978, after the previously poor vole year, drew in many yearlings. However, this was not the sole cause for the high turnover in the Scottish grassland area, because the proportion of newcomers was also high in 1979, when the population density was similar to that of the previous year. In farmland, the populations were either stable, or declining, and recruits made up a smaller proportion of breeding birds in most years. Nonetheless, less than half the breeding birds present were known to have been breeding in the area the previous year, so turnover was still high.

Persistence in the area was associated with breeding performance in the previous year, and successful breeders were more likely to breed in the area again than unsuccessful ones. In Scotland, this trend was true for both sexes, but in England breeding performance was more strongly associated with subsequent return of males than of females (Table 58).

TURNOVER AT BREEDING SITES

The rate of turnover in an area can also be estimated by recording the changes of occupants at particular nest sites. Changes of occupant from one year to the next may occur if individuals frequently change nest sites within the study area, or if there is a high turnover due to high losses from the area. Turnover at particular nesting sites in Scotland was high in both sexes, and 71% of successive male occupants were different individuals and 82% of successive females (Fig. 74). The higher figure of females was due to the low return of first-year birds, and there was no sex difference when the first occupants were adults.

In England, there was again no difference between the sexes, but turnover was significantly lower than in Scotland, with occupants changing at only about half the sites each year. The lower figure was as expected from the greater number of birds breeding more than once, and it shows that many of them did so at the same nest site in successive years. However, even the lower turnover in England represented a considerable rate of change at nesting sites, and few sites would be used by the same pair for several successive years.

FIDELITY TO NEST SITES AND NESTING TERRITORIES

A slightly different way of estimating turnover within study areas was to record the movements of particular individuals that bred in successive years. If turnover at a site is high, but few individuals change sites, a large proportion of the breeding population must either die or move outside the study area between breeding attempts. Fidelity to nest sites was likely to be related in some degree to fidelity to the study area, because Kestrels that moved a long

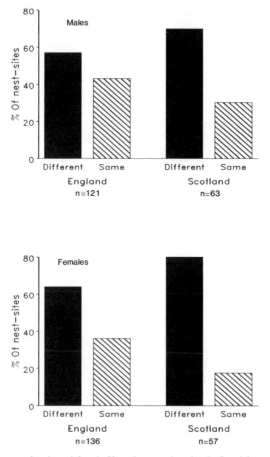

Fig. 74. Turnover of male and female Kestrels at nesting sites in Scottish grassland (1976–79) and English farmland (1981–87). Based on nest sites that were occupied in successive years and where the identity of one or other sex could be established in both years. Bars show the percentage of sites at which the second occupant was the same or a different individual.

distance between successive breeding attempts were likely to move out of the area as well. The distinction was worthwhile making, however, because some birds that did not return to the area would have died, whereas confining analysis to birds that moved within the study area would at least distinguish movements from mortality, even if extreme movements could not be recorded.

The average distance moved between breeding attempts was similar in Scotland and England, being about 0.7 km in males (n = 163) and 1.0 km in females (n = 153). These figures were influenced by the large number of birds that used the same nest twice, and the mean distances for birds that changed nest were 1.1 km for males (n = 99) and 1.6 km for females (n = 95) (Fig. 75). The difference between the sexes was statistically significant, suggesting a

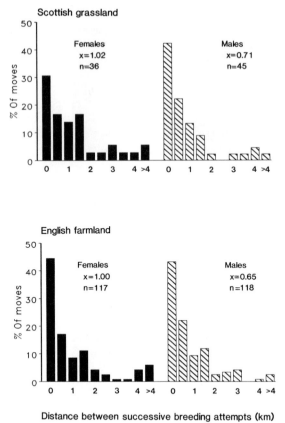

Fig. 75. Histograms of distances moved between successive breeding attempts for males and female Kestrels in Scottish grassland (1976–79) and English farmland (1981–87). The distances moved were similar in each area, but females generally moved further than males.

greater site fidelity by males, similar to that found in many bird species, including other raptors (Newton 1979).

Among females, fidelity to the nesting territory was related to mate fidelity, and those that remated with the same partner were more often on their original territory than those that changed partner (Table 59). This was also true for males, but the trend was less obvious and not statistically significant.

Kestrels in both studies also became more sedentary as they grew older, and were less likely to change nest site or nesting territory on their third or subsequent breeding attempts. Some 40% of individuals changed nesting territory between their first and second breeding attempts, whereas the figure was only 26% for later moves (Table 60). This trend was most obvious in females because males tended to remain on their first territory whatever the outcome of their breeding attempt. The number using exactly the same nesting site in successive years increased with the number of attempts, so fidelity seemed to be to a particular cavity or stick nest, as well as to a particular nesting territory. In some pairs this may have been because there were few alternative sites, but many would have had several to choose from each year.

Movements between nesting territories within study areas were also influenced by breeding performance, and birds that fledged young in a particular territory were more likely to breed there the following year than those that failed. The trends were similar in both studies, so I was able to combine their data to examine the influences of age and breeding performance separately (Table 60). In moves made after first breeding attempts, females were more strongly influenced by success than were males, but the sex difference was reversed in later moves.

FIDELITY TO MATE

Among birds that bred for more than one year, some remained faithful to their partner and others did not. Those that changed partner may have done so because their previous mate was no longer present (*'widowhood'*), or because he or she was mated with another partner (*'divorce'*).

At Eskdalemuir, pairs separated over winter, so all birds had to re-select a mate in spring. Most changes in mate were because the previous partner was absent and, if both partners were present in spring, they usually remated (14 of 20 cases). The chances of remating were related to which partner, if any, had stayed in the area over the intervening winter (Table 61). It seemed that males, but not females, would increase their chance of mating with the same individual the following year if they remained on their breeding territory in winter. A common situation was that the male remained on the breeding area, and the female left in winter. These migrant females usually returned early in the following spring, and would mate with the same male if he was still on his territory.

If both partners left in winter (which happened in 72% of 92 pairings), there was less chance that both would return the following year and, if they did, that they would mate with each other again. This possibly because there was less likelihood of finding each other before they found another, unmated, bird. In England, pairs often remained together in winter, but the frequency of mate fidelity was only slightly higher than in Scotland (Table 62), so the frequent changes of partner among Kestrels were not strongly influenced by migratory behaviour.

Fidelity to mate was, however, influenced by previous breeding success, and in the English areas, both sexes were more likely to breed with the same partner the following year if they succeeded in their current breeding attempt than if they failed (Table 62). The same was true for males in Scotland, but too few failed females bred in consecutive years to tell if they changed partner more often than successful females.

About 17% of females changed mate while their previous partner was still alive, but this was less frequent in males, and only 6% with a new partner were divorced rather than widowed (Table 63). Thus, although both sexes that changed mate the following year usually did so because their previous partner was absent, females were more likely to abandon partners and find a mate elsewhere. This may have been because mate choice was largely by the female and she would go to another male if the first was unsuitable. The difference between the sexes could also have arisen if females were more likely to die or move away after breeding, as this would result in more widowed males than females present in the spring population.

CONCLUSIONS ON TURNOVER

In both areas, there was a high population turnover of Kestrels and frequent changes of nest site and mate. Such a high turnover is typical of other small raptors such as Sparrowhawks (Newton 1986) and Black-shouldered Kites (Mendelsohn 1983), and was partly due to the high mortality rates both of adults and juveniles (Chapter 19). Even in totally sedentary populations, estimated adult mortality implied that about 30% of breeding birds had to be replaced each year to maintain stable numbers. In practice, about half the birds were lost from the study areas between years, so some birds that failed to return probably bred elsewhere. The high turnover means that, where numbers are stable, they are maintained by a 'dynamic equilibrium' between losses and gains. Population density will decline rapidly if recruitment is curtailed, unless there is a matching reduction in losses. Conversely, the fluidity of the population may allow Kestrels to colonise suitable habitat quickly, an important asset in a species that is subject to fluctuating food supplies. An extreme example of this is the Black-shouldered Kite, which feeds almost exclusively on rodents, and is virtually nomadic, with very high population turnover in some areas (Mendelsohn 1983). Kestrels are less dependent on a single prey species, and this may buffer them somewhat from fluctuations in food supply, so turnover is intermediate between nomadic and entirely sedentary species.

The differences between the Scottish and English areas were due to the more sedentary behaviour of the latter population, which in turn was due to the greater stability of the food supply both within and between years. More Kestrels were able to winter in the English farmland areas, and this resulted in more residents and fewer migrants. The lower return to the study area in spring in Scotland may have been due to a higher mortality in migrants, or because they were less likely to breed in the same place than those that wintered on their breeding grounds. The trend was most marked in first-year birds, and there was no difference in successful adults in the two areas, so once northern birds found a suitable breeding site they were as likely to breed there again as were resident southern birds. Thus the greater turnover at nest sites in Scotland was due mainly to the lower fidelity to the area, and movements within the study area were similar to those in England. The rate of return in Scotland was possibly influenced by the low vole year early in the study, which meant that few birds present in the first year were likely to persist. However, this had only a minor effect on the overall results because few birds were marked in my first year of study.

Changes of territory were most likely early in life and after breeding failure, which suggests individuals moved in order to better their chances of breeding successfully. This is also true of Sparrowhawks, which tend to move from low to high-grade territories, especially when their first breeding attempt fails (Newton 1986). There was some evidence that male Kestrels were less inclined to move than females, but the difference was only slight. Greater site-fidelity by males may have explained some of the biased sex ratios in wintering Kestrels (Chapter 18). Because the male is responsible for much of the food provision during breeding, those males that are competent enough to breed can probably do so with virtually any female, but females must be much more choosey because they depend heavily on the ability of their mates. Kestrels can be prevented from breeding by lack of nest sites under some circumstances (Chapter 10), so it is likely that the male's priority is to find a suitable nest site, whereas the choice of a male with a site may be more important for females.

SUMMARY

Kestrels in the Scottish and English study areas had a fairly high turnover, with a substantial proportion of individuals present for only a single season and breeding only once. There were more year-round residents and fewer summer migrants in England than Scotland, and Kestrels in the English areas were more likely to breed in the same place in successive years. This caused greater turnover at nest sites in the Scottish area, but movement of individuals between sites were similar in both populations. Males were slightly less likely than females to change nesting territories between years and they seemed to be the most site-tenacious sex. Changes of nesting territory and mate were most likely early in life or after breeding failure, and Kestrels may have changed site or mate in order to improve their chances of breeding successfully.

CHAPTER 18

Age and sex ratios

The ratio of males to females or adults to first-year birds in the Kestrel population varies over time and between areas. Variations in the age ratio are inevitable, because the output of young per adult differs from year to year, and because juveniles have a lower survival rate than adults. The proportion of juveniles in the population will thus be highest immediately after a productive breeding season, and will decline in the course of the winter. The sex ratio in the breeding population is virtually equal because bigamy is so rare, but it may be distorted in the population as a whole if the ratio among nestlings is uneven, or if the survival of the sexes differs later in life.

Such variations could occur irrespective of how birds settle across the landscape, but differential movements, or segregation by habitat, can create local variations both in age and sex ratios that may distort, or even reverse, those in the whole population. Estimates of these ratios are therefore influenced by problems of scale. Habitat preference may change ratios within parts of the

238

same study area, so the ratio observed will depend on how much of each habitat is sampled. Similarly, the ratio in a particular area may be unequal because of a genuine bias in the whole population, or because differential movements have created regional variation in the distribution of the sexes or age classes.

ESTIMATING AGE AND SEX RATIOS

These problems make it virtually impossible to measure 'global' age or sex ratios in Kestrels, and this chapter is confined to comparisons of the ratios prevailing in my three study areas. The ratios of interest during the breeding season are the age ratio of breeding birds and the age and sex ratios among non-breeders. In winter, Kestrels do not always remain in pairs, so variations in age and sex ratios are possible.

Although Kestrels are fairly easy to see in winter, it is difficult to estimate the proportion of males to females without trapping them, because juveniles of both sexes resemble adult females. This is not so in American Kestrels, which are unusual in having a distinct and sexually dimorphic juvenile plumage, so they can be aged and sexed by sight alone. Jim Koplin (1973) first noticed that males and females were segregated by habitat in winter when he did some roadside counts of Kestrels in California. This was confirmed elsewhere, and there has been a lively debate as to the cause of this segregation (Mills 1976, Stinson *et al* 1981, Meyer & Balgooyen 1987, Smallwood 1988).

In European Kestrels, roadside counts could indicate the proportion of adult males in an area, but this value would be affected by changes in either the number of females, the number of juvenile males, or both. If one takes the proportions among trapped and tagged birds these problems are avoided because full-grown birds can be accurately sexed and aged (as first-year or older) in the hand. Trapping may be biased toward juvenile birds if they are more easily caught than adults, but in my case I could follow birds after release and would know if there were many unmarked birds still in the area. My trapping thus avoided adults that were already tagged, and it was better to use the age and sex ratios among tagged birds known to be present in a given area than the ratios among newly trapped birds.

In the Scottish area, the proportion of adult males seen at large was similar to that among tagged birds, so I used the tagged population to indicate the age and sex ratios in the whole population from October 1975 to July 1978 (Village 1985b). In England, my trapping effort was split between two areas, and this meant that tagged birds were not always representative of the composition of the overall population. For example, if I did no trapping in one area in autumn the influx of recently arrived juveniles would not be tagged, and the age ratio among tagged birds would be biased towards adult birds that were still present after the previous breeding season. For this reason, Table 64 includes only data for those periods when I was trapping in a particular study area, and only for those parts of the study area where most of the Kestrels were tagged.

SEX RATIOS AMONG NESTLINGS

If there is an inequality in the sex ratio of the total Kestrel population, it must arise because more of one sex are born than the other, or because one sex has a better survival rate. Both these possibilities may be true, but the available data are not sufficient to test either, thoroughly. Estimating the sex ratio among nestlings presents problems because their plumage is not always sexually dimorphic. Although a degree of separation is possible using size or plumage, some uncertainty remains, and for that reason I have not attempted to sex nestlings. Cavé (1968) found a biased sex ratio in favour of females, which he claimed must have existed in the eggs at laying. The result almost certainly arose because he counted all brown-tailed nestlings as males, but correcting his results from the known frequency of brown juvenile males suggested the true ratio was probably 1:1 (Village *et al* 1980).

Recent work by the Raptor Group at Groningen, suggests that it may, in fact, be possible to sex nestlings on the basis of the colour and markings of the upper tail-coverts (Dijkstra 1988). Males have grey feathers or narrow bars, whereas in females these feathers are brown and heavily barred. They correctly identified 99% of 191 nestlings sexed in this way that were caught later in life and sexed on their adult plumage. However, I have been unable to confirm this method of sexing nestlings, and 16% of the juvenile males I trapped had upper tail-coverts that were totally brown and barred.

If their method does prove to be correct, they have uncovered some surprising findings on the seasonal changes in the sex ratios of Kestrel broods. The overall ratio was unity, but early broods had more males than females, whereas the reverse was true for late broods. The reason for this seemed to be that the first eggs of early clutches were usually males, and later eggs of the same clutch were females, but the opposite was true for late clutches. This startling result implies that female physiology may influence the sex of eggs, or at least the laying sequence of eggs of a particular sex. The Dutch workers also found that late-fledged males, unlike their sisters, stood little chance of being recruited into the breeding population in the year following their birth. Parents laying late in the season would therefore leave more viable offspring if they produced mainly female eggs. If this is indeed true for Kestrels, it must also hold for many other bird species where yearlings of one sex are less likely to reach breeding age. It will be interesting to see if these results can be confirmed in Kestrels elsewhere, or in other species where the sexing of nestlings is easier than in Kestrels.

SEX RATIOS IN WINTER

In the Scottish grassland area, there was a slightly higher proportion of males than females present in most winter months (Fig. 76). This was largely due to a bias among adults, and the sex ratio in juveniles was, if anything, slightly in favour of females. The proportion of males in the tagged population was normally about 60–70%, but this rose as females left in greater numbers during the poor vole winter of 1976–77, and there were no tagged females

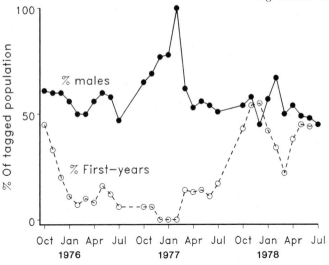

Fig. 76. Age and sex ratio among wing-tagged Kestrels in the Scottish grassland area, 1976–78. From Village (1985b).

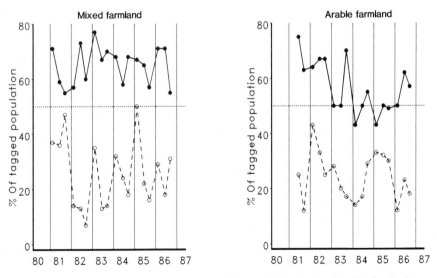

Fig. 77. Age and sex ratio among wing-tagged Kestrels in the mixed and arable farmland areas in England, 1981–86. Yearlings were assumed to become adults on 1 August (vertical lines). Legend as in Fig. 76.

present by February. The ratio approached unity during the breeding season, as males and females both arrived in the area, but in most summer months there was still a slight preponderance of males.

The winter sex ratios in the English farmland areas were different, both from each other and from those in Eskdalemuir (Fig. 77, Table 64). In the mixed farmland, males predominated in most years, comprising about 60–70% of the population from 1980 to 1984. Most of the adult females present were paired with adult males, and the majority of unpaired birds were males. Unlike Eskdalemuir, males were also the most frequent sex among first-year birds, and there were few wintering first-year females in most years. In the arable farmland, I trapped intensively mainly in later years, and the sex ratio there was more even, though there was still a slight majority of males when all years were combined (Table 64). There was less year-to-year variation in the sex ratio in the farmland areas than in Eskdalemuir, and the proportion of males in the total population never rose above 80%, even in mixed farmland. The farmland results suggested that females may have preferred open fenland to the more wooded environment in mixed farmland, but, even so, they were outnumbered by males in both farmland habitats.

REASONS FOR THE SKEWED SEX RATIO IN WINTER

Differential mortality

The combined trend for all areas was thus for an excess of males in the wintering population. This may have been because males were over-represented among tagged birds, though I had no reason to think that this was so. If my areas were typical of all wintering areas, it would suggest a greater frequency of males in the 'global' population, which must presumably be due to a higher mortality rate among females at some stage of the life cycle. Alternatively, there may be some areas to the south of my study areas where females comprise the majority of the wintering population. If, as suggested above, males are fledged earlier on average than females, they ought to stand a better chance of survival in the first crucial months of independent life (Chapter 19). Males would thus be more abundant in the yearling population than females, and there is indeed some evidence for a higher winter mortality among females (Chapter 19). The sex difference in survival was probably not large enough by itself to explain all the uneven sex ratios I observed, and other factors must also have been involved.

Differential migration

Some of the variation in the winter sex ratios of Kestrels between my study areas probably resulted from differential migration. The unequal sex ratio among adults in Eskdalemuir seemed to be due to more females leaving than males, which may have been because adult males were more tied to their nest sites than females or juveniles. Remaining on the breeding territory over winter may have improved the chances of getting a nest site the following year. Most wintering adults had several potential sites in their territories, but this was not so for the juveniles present in 1977–78. Males were largely responsible for finding and retaining the nest site, so those likely to breed the next year may have been under greater pressure than females to hold a winter territory on the breeding grounds. Eskdalemuir was a fairly harsh environment in winter, and males staying there risked the possibility of a severe decline in food supply if snow fell, or in poor vole years. If they had more to gain than females by enduring these conditions, it would explain why only adult males persisted through the late winter of 1976–77, when voles were extremely scarce.

Habitat segregation

Differential migration may have explained the higher number of females wintering in arable farmland than in the Scottish grassland area, but the difference between the two farmland areas was presumably due to habitat segregation, as they were only a short distance apart. As in American Kestrels, males predominated in the more wooded, mixed farmland habitat. The sex ratio was not strongly skewed the other way in the more open fen areas, though females made up more of the population there than in mixed farmland. The distribution of nest sites could again have influenced this segregation if males tended to select territories that had the highest densities of potential nest sites. Breeding density was low in the fens, so there were large open areas in autumn only sparsely populated by post-breeding adults. Kestrels may have been able to establish winter territories more easily in such areas than where they had to find space between densely-packed adult territories. Females may have been content to settle where there were no suitable nest sites, whereas males may have tried harder to find a range containing a potential nest site. This idea could presumably be tested experimentally by manipulating the availability of nest sites outside the breeding season.

Several other raptors have unequal sex ratios in some habitats in winter. As in American Kestrels, male Sparrowhawks are found mainly in areas of woodland, whereas females are found in more open areas (Marquiss & Newton 1982b). In South Scotland, male Hen Harriers winter mainly in low ground, or near the coast, but females spend more time in the hills (Marquiss 1980). In Sparrowhawks and Hen Harriers, the separation may occur because the sexes have differing food requirements, and each goes to where its preferred prey is most abundant. Kestrels are less sexually dimorphic than many other raptors, and any habitat separation is unlikely to be due solely to differences in the diet of males and females. This is supported by the almost equal sex ratios of juveniles wintering in the Scottish grassland area, where the preponderance of males was mainly among adults.

There have been several attempts to explain the winter habitat separation in American Kestrels. Some hypotheses favour competition for food between the sexes, and suggest that males are ousted from preferred habitats by the larger females (Mills 1976), or that the sexes separate by choice and thereby reduce competition (Koplin 1973). Other theories evoke different reasons, such as a reduced risk of predation for smaller males where there is more cover (Meyer & Balgooyen 1987). The territories of female Kestrels in California were larger, with higher rodent and bird densities, than those of males (Meyer & Balgooyen 1987). Females also ate more vertebrate prey than did males, but whether this was due to, or caused, the habitat separation was not clear.

A study of the settling patterns of autumn migrants in Florida showed that females arrived before males, and occupied the best foraging areas (Smallwood 1988). Males that did arrive early were as likely as females to get a good territory, so it seemed that the habitat segregation was largely the result of differences in the timing of migration by the sexes, rather than the superior competitive ability of females. However, this begs the question of why males should delay their migration if this resulted in low-grade winter territories.

The habitat segregation of American Kestrels is most noticeable in areas where the winter population consists largely of migrants. If a similar segregation exists in European Kestrels, it is likely to be most evident in areas such as Iberia, where there is a major influx of winter visitors. In areas where most of the population is sedentary, or departs in autumn, there may be a genuine bias in the sex ratio, rather than a separation by habitat.

SEX RATIOS AMONG NON-BREEDERS IN THE BREEDING SEASON

The slight excess of tagged males during the summer in the Scottish grassland area implied that they were more frequent among the non-breeding population. However, non-breeders comprised only 7% of the tagged summer population, on average, and numbers were too low to properly assess the ratio of the sexes. In the farmland areas, I had sufficient non-breeding Kestrels marked during summer to compare the sex ratio in adults and first-years. Among 115 adults present in summer which did not pair, 57% were males and 43% females, which was the same as the ratio in tagged breeders. In 79 first-year birds, however, 67% were males and 33% females, which was the reverse of the ratio in breeders (Table 65). This meant that the greater number of yearlings among breeding females was not because yearling females were more abundant than yearling males, but because they were better able to breed. The fact that I had more adult non-breeders than first-years did not necessarily mean that they were more frequent in the population as a whole, because the age ratio depended mainly on my trapping effort the previous winter. However, the sexes were equally likely to be trapped, so the differences in the sex ratios were probably genuine.

AGE RATIOS IN WINTER

The mortality rate of juvenile Kestrels is about twice that of adults, and most deaths occur in the first six months of independence (Chapter 19). The proportion of juveniles in the population will therefore decline from August onwards, and this was the pattern at Eskdalemuir in all three winters (Fig. 76). The ratio of first-years to adults in midwinter depended on both the rate of this decline and the number of juveniles settling after the previous breeding season. In 1976 the local breeding productivity was very low, and this was probably true for much of northern Britain. Vole numbers were in decline after high densities in 1975, and were to reach a trough in spring 1977 (Fig. 2). There were few juvenile Kestrels at Eskdalemuir in October 1976, and all had moved away or died by midwinter. Breeding productivity was much better in 1977, and there were many more juveniles present in October than in the preceding year. Although first-year birds disappeared more rapidly than adults over the next few months, they still made up a much higher proportion of the marked population than they had in 1976–77. The age ratio of the Eskdalemuir

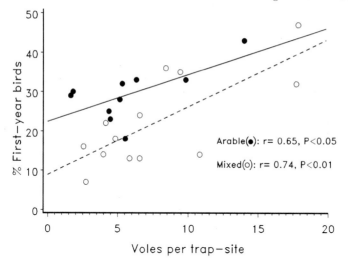

Fig. 78. Age ratio among marked Kestrels during winter in the English farmland areas in relation to vole abundance. Each point is the proportion of first-year birds present in October, January or April in mixed (○) or arable (●) farmland. Sample sizes given in Table 64.

wintering population was thus related both to vole abundance and Kestrel numbers. When voles were scarce, there were few Kestrels present, and nearly all were adults. As voles increased, more Kestrels settled in the area, and most of these were first-year birds.

The changes in age ratios during the year were not solely due to differences in the mortality rates of adults and first-year birds. This was evident from the increase in the ratio of first-year birds to adults in spring, which must have been due to a higher proportion of first-year birds among incoming migrants than among the wintering population. This agrees with the greater tendency for juveniles to migrate (Chapter 16), and some of the decline in the proportion of first-year birds in autumn was probably due to higher emigration than adults. The suitability of the area was clearly related to the vole density, and if juveniles were poorer hunters than adults they would be able to remain in winter only if voles were easy to catch. There was little alternative prey for them in winter, especially easily caught invertebrate prey, which was more abundant in the south.

The proportion of first-year birds in the winter population also varied from year to year in the farmland areas, but not to the same extent as in the Scottish area (Fig. 77). The ratio was highest in the winter of 1980–81, which also coincided with the highest winter vole numbers, and in both areas the proportion of first-year birds present in winter was correlated with the prevailing vole index (Fig. 78). The relationship was closer in mixed farmland, where voles were the main mammal prey, than in arable farmland, where Woodmice featured heavily in the diet. Local productivity seemed to have little influence on the numbers of juveniles settling in autumn, which were as high in arable

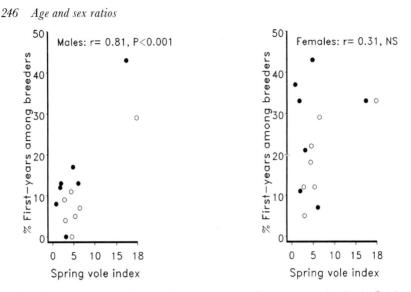

Fig. 79. Age ratio among breeding Kestrels in mixed (○) and arable farmland (●) in relation to spring vole numbers. First-year males formed a higher proportion of the breeding population in good vole years in both areas, but there was no significant correlation in females.

as in mixed farmland, despite the lower overall productivity in the arable fenlands. In mixed farmland there was always a decline in the proportion of first-year birds from autumn to winter, but in arable farmland there was sometimes a slight increase, partly because of continuing immigration.

AGE RATIOS IN SUMMER

Kestrels are capable of breeding in their first summer, but most do not. In all three study areas, yearling females made up a higher proportion of the breeding population than yearling males (Table 66). This meant adult males were more likely to pair with first-year females than *vice versa*, and possible reasons for this have been discussed more fully in Chapter 11. Yearlings made up about 20–30% of the breeding females, on average, compared with about 10–15% in males. In England there were sufficient tagged non-breeders present in summer to show if yearlings bred according to their frequency in the tagged population. Combining all years, the proportion of non-breeders was higher among yearlings than adults, in both sexes, but the difference was more extreme in males (Table 67). In most years, yearling females were as likely to breed as adults, but this was never so for yearling males.

The proportion of first-year birds in the breeding population varied significantly between years in both the Scottish and English study areas. In Scotland, this was only partly related to vole numbers, because there were few first-year birds present in 1976, when voles were abundant in spring but declined thereafter, and few in 1979, even though the voles were more plentiful than in the previous year. The proportion of first-year birds was highest in both sexes in 1978, when the population was expanding from the previous low density in 1977. This suggests that individuals will breed in their first-year if food is abundant and there are vacant breeding territories. If food supply is constantly high, adults may persist for longer on their breeding territories, and there will be few 'gaps' appearing each year. Yearlings will have to compete with older birds for these and, in males especially, they are unlikely to succeed.

In both farmland areas, the overall age ratio of breeders was roughly the same as in Scotland and showed similar degrees of annual variation. The proportion of yearlings among breeders was significantly correlated with the vole index for males, but not for females (Fig. 79). The correlation in males arose largely because of the high proportion of first-year males breeding in both farmland areas in 1981, when voles were also high. The lack of correlation in females was because some yearling females could breed in low vole years by pairing with adult males.

CONCLUSIONS ON AGE AND SEX RATIOS

The variations in age and sex ratios in my study populations indicate how Kestrel density might be adjusted to fluctuations in the food supply, brought about by vole cycles or seasonal patterns of prey availability. Adults and first-year birds left Eskdalemuir in winter as the food supply fell, but the latter left sooner than the adults, and adult females before adult males. These movements were presumably to places that offered a better chance of survival over winter, which implies that adult males may have compromised their chances of survival by remaining on northern breeding territories in winter.

In summer, first-year males bred mainly when the food supply was high and there were suitable nest sites available. First-year females could sometimes breed in poorer circumstances by pairing witrh an adult male. Increasing populations usually had a high proportion of breeding yearlings, so changes in the age of breeding may be one way in which breeding density can increase rapidly from year to year. There was no evidence to suggest that breeding early in life jeopardised subsequent survival. Tagged breeders were more likely to breed the following year than tagged non-breeders, at least in farmland (Table 68), so breeding early in life was probably associated with greater lifetime reproductive output, as it is in Sparrowhawks (Newton 1986).

The chances of a particular individual being able to breed in its first year may depend largely on the state of the vole cycle when it is born. Although more young are fledged in peak vole years, they are likely to encounter lower vole numbers the following year as the cycle goes into decline. Fewer Kestrels are fledged in low vole years, but they may be more likely to breed in their first year of life because voles often increase rapidly following a trough. These comments would apply only to areas with strong vole cyles that are synchronised over wide areas, but this seems to be the case for much of Northern Europe.

SUMMARY

Age and sex ratios could be estimated in each study area from the ratios among wing-tagged Kestrels known to be present, provided trapping was done regularly. Males were in the majority in all three study areas in winter, but the proportion was highest for adult males during the poor vole winter in the Scottish grassland area. Females were more abundant in the open arable area, possibly because they were less tied to nest sites during winter than were males. The proportion of first-year birds present in winter was related mainly to the food supply in autumn, rather than the local breeding production. High vole numbers were associated with high proportions of first-year birds in both the winter and the breeding populations. The overall sex ratio in the population may have been biased toward males because females had lower survival rates, but the evidence for this was not conclusive, and local variations in sex ratios were probably also the result of differential migration or habitat segregation.

CHAPTER 19

Mortality

All Kestrels die, but some die younger than others. Ornithologists studying mortality have mainly been interested in estimating what proportion of birds of a given age die (*Age-specific mortality*) and why they die. These apparently simple questions are much easier to ask than to answer. Most of the methods currently available are based on recoveries of ringed birds of known age, but they rely on assumptions which may not always hold. Ringed birds should be representative of the population as a whole, should not lose their rings as they get older and, when they die, should stand the same chance of recovery from year to year. For some analyses, the probability of survival at a given age in the first few years of life can be estimated only if it is assumed to become constant in later life; an assumption that may lead to unreliable results if it is violated even slightly (Lakhani & Newton 1983).

The cause of death of recovered birds could be used to indicate what kills birds in the population as a whole, but this will almost certainly give misleading results. Recovered birds are mainly those that die through human agency, or near human habitation. Birds that succumb from starvation, predation or disease are much less likely to be found than those that are hit by cars, fall into rain barrels or fly into windows. The data available for Kestrels are more extensive than for most other raptors but, even so, it is difficult to draw many reliable conclusions from them. This is particularly evident when trying to see how mortality varies within populations over time or between populations in different areas.

AGE-SPECIFIC SURVIVAL RATES

Analysts of ringing data have usually expressed their results as the probability of survival (S), rather than of mortality (M), from one year to the next. There is no particular reason for this, and the two are inversely related (ie M = 1-S). Survival rates are normally calculated from *dynamic life tables*, produced by recording the recovery dates, and hence age at death, of nestlings ringed over a number of years. To accrue a large enough sample, all birds are treated as if they were ringed in the same year. The average annual mortality among birds that survive to a given age is then estimated from the proportion that subsequently died within a year (Lack 1951).

The other method, based on *static life tables*, uses the ratio of the number of birds of different ages in the population at any one time. Adult Kestrels cannot be aged exactly unless they were ringed in their first year, so it takes some years of constant ringing to get a large population of known-aged birds. I have used a modified static life table to estimate adult survival from the ratio of known-aged Kestrels in my farmland areas, but the study has not lasted long enough to be confident of the results, and most of this chapter is based on dynamic life tables produced from the national ringing recoveries.

Estimates from national ringing recoveries

There have been several estimates of Kestrel survival rates in Europe made from ringing recoveries. Most have used 'complete' data, where enough time was allowed after ringing for all the likely recoveries to come in, so that birds dying in old age were not under-represented. The longest-lived British recovery was a bird of 15 years old, but this was exceptional, and leaving a 12 year interval after the last year of ringing ensured that over 95% of recoveries were already reported.

Using all the national ring recoveries of nestlings ringed to 1972 and reported by 1984, I estimated survival rates of 66% per annum for adults and 32% for birds in their first-year (Table 69). This was similar to an earlier analysis of the same data up to 1956 by David Snow (1968), though he defined age classes from April to March, while I used August to July. This had a noticeable effect on estimates for the first and second years, because his method measured first-year mortality over only 9–10 months, while mine used a full year for every age class. Snow's estimate of first-year survival was therefore higher, and second-year survival lower, than mine because some yearlings were included with two-year old birds. So while Snow found a trend for an increasing probability of survival from two to three-year olds, I did not. Allowing for these sorts of discrepancies between studies, the British ringing data give roughly similar estimates of Kestrel survival rates to those of the Continent (Table 69).

Estimates from wing-tagged Kestrels

The general ringing recoveries did not distinguish the sexes, but I could make an approximate estimate of adult survival in males and females by using the ratio of known-age birds in my breeding populations (Newton *et al* 1983a). The results for the farmland studies, 67% annual survival for females and 74% for males, were similar to adult survival in the general ringing recoveries, though they were not amenable to statistical analysis, so I could not tell if the lower survival of females was genuine, or a chance effect.

The above analysis was based on the persistence of known-age birds in the breeding population from one year to the next, and did not include any estimate of the survival of birds during their first winter. In the farmland study areas, I had sufficient data to measure 'local survival' during winter by recording which of the wing-tagged Kestrels present in autumn were also present the following spring. The results were not true annual survival rates because some losses from the area may have been due to movements, rather than mortality, and because they did not cover the whole year. Movements out of the area would reduce the the survival estimates, whereas including only the winter months would inflate them. This was particularly so for juveniles, which were wing-tagged in autumn only if they survived to be caught between October and December. Nonetheless, the estimates covered survival in midwinter, when first-year mortality was highest, and enabled a comparison of adults with juveniles, and males with females.

Local winter survival of adults was relatively high and stable between years, but in juveniles it was lower and more variable (Table 70). There were fewer data for juveniles because their survival in a given year could be estimated only if sufficient were trapped in that autumn. In adults there was nearly always a large sample of tagged breeding birds present from the previous summer, and trapping effort in autumn was less critical. To examine age-specific survival rates, I used those cases where I had known-age birds present in autumn, combining data for both farmland areas and all years, 1980–86 (Table 71). The results confirmed the poor survival of first-winter birds, and also indicated that survival in the second winter was slightly lower than later in life. Females of all ages were less likely than males to persist over winter, which confirmed the earlier trend from breeding birds.

The survival of first-year Kestrels was thus about half that of adults, and this is true of many birds, including other similar-sized raptors such as American Kestrels and Sparrowhawks (Henny 1972, Newton *et al* 1983a). The lower survival in juveniles probably results from their inexperience in hunting and the difficulties they have in competing with adults for good territories. The national ringing recoveries suggest little consistent variation in adult survival with age, though, as mentioned, my local winter survival estimates point to a slightly lower survival for second-year birds. Presumably birds must eventually suffer from the effects of old age, but the sample sizes among old birds were too low to detect it.

Females seemed to have lower survival than males in terms both of persistence in the breeding population and local winter survival. I could not tell if this was because females were more likely to die than males or more likely to leave the area, and both may have been true. The difference is consistent with the surplus of males present in winter and during the breeding season in both the Scottish and English study areas (Chapter 18).

SEASONAL TRENDS IN MORTALITY

In the National Ringing Scheme the number of recoveries of ringed Kestrels varied during the year, but the pattern was different in the first year from later in life. The number of recoveries of juveniles was highest in autumn and declined steadily during the first year of life. This would be expected even if mortality was constant, because the number of ringed first-year birds at risk declines as the year proceeds. Allowing for this, the main period of risk for juveniles seems to be November to February (Fig. 80). Among adults, the recoveries were more evenly spaced during the year, though second-year birds were recovered more frequently during autumn and winter than in summer.

The seasonal patterns of ring recoveries roughly match those in the number of Kestrel carcasses sent in by members of the public to Monks Wood Experimental Station from 1963–79, as part of the Pesticide Monitoring Scheme (Newton *et al* 1982). The latter study found that starvation was the main cause of death among first-year birds and was particularly frequent during autumn and winter (Table 72). This is further evidence that inexperienced immatures have difficulty in finding food, and many die as a result.

The low recovery rate of adults during the breeding season may reflect a genuine decrease in mortality, or may result from a reduced likelihood of dead birds being found. Many northern migrants return to breeding grounds where

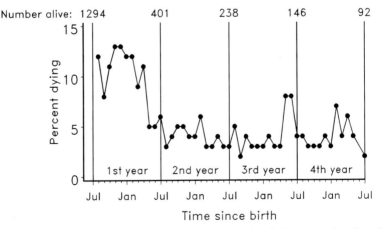

Fig. 80. Seasonal patterns of mortality in Kestrels in relation to age. Based on the ring recoveries of 1,294 nestlings from the National Ringing Scheme. Most recoveries of first-year birds were during winter, whereas recoveries during subsequent years were more evenly distributed through the year.

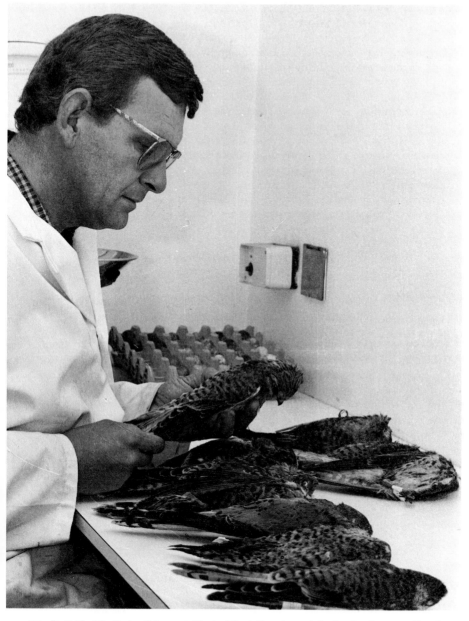

The Pesticide Monitoring Scheme at Monks Wood Experimental Station has been recording the levels of pollutants in Kestrel carcasses since the early 1960s when the detrimental effects of pesticides on birds of prey were first noticed. Photo: I. Wyllie.

there are fewer people than in the lowlands where they had wintered. Birds dying in summer also decay faster than in winter, and this may make them less liable to be recovered. Unlike Sparrowhawks (Newton 1986), there was no increase in recoveries in early spring, even though this is when vole numbers are at their lowest, and food supply should be poorest. Changes in vole behaviour later in spring may make them more vulnerable to predation (Masman *et al* 1988b), thus maintaining the food supply. Kestrels may also have alternative food sources in spring, particularly if the weather is mild and earthworms and beetles are active on the surface. These may not be sufficient to enable birds to breed, but could keep some individuals alive if vertebrate prey were scarce. Kestrels seem to suffer food shortages during thick snow cover, and this is so unpredictable in Britain that there is unlikely to be any clear pattern if recoveries from many years are combined. Prolonged snow cover usually results in an increase in Kestrel carcasses sent to Monks Wood (I. Newton), and similar observations were made in this country and abroad during the severe winters of 1962/63 (Brogmus 1966).

CAUSES OF MORTALITY

The main sources of information on what kills Kestrels are the reports sent in with ring recoveries and the post-mortems of carcasses sent by the public to the Pesticide Monitoring Scheme or similar schemes elsewhere (Keymer *et al* 1981, Newton *et al* 1982). These give an unrepresentative picture of the causes of death in the general Kestrel population, for reasons already outlined. Nonetheless, they are the best information we have, and at least give some insight as to how some Kestrels die, and how this varies with age and over time. The following account is drawn both from the national ringing recoveries up to 1984, and on the carcass collection schemes mentioned above.

A glance through the ringing recoveries shows that Kestrels exit this world in an ingenious variety of ways. Reporting circumstances include the unhelpful 'found dead' (the most frequent), the succinct 'shot', 'drowned' or 'killed', as well as detailed descriptions of the bird's last moments. Autopsies of carcasses can often give better clues as to what finally killed a bird, though confining diagnosis to a single cause can be misleading. A bird that is heavily infested with parasites may have died because of them, or may have become heavily infested because it was injured or starved.

The most frequently recorded causes of death among Kestrels are:

1. Starvation. This is rarely reported as such in ringing recoveries (less than 5% of the total), possibly because few people can diagnose it and therefore report the bird as 'found dead'. About 30% of the Kestrels sent to Monks Wood were thought to have starved to death, but this rose to over 50% for juveniles in autumn (Newton *et al* 1982). In the ring recoveries, some 6% of 1,729 first-year recoveries were of birds in 'poor condition', compared with about 3% of 880 adults, a statistically significant difference. Even the highest figure (50%) may underestimate the true impact of food shortage on the survival of young Kestrels. Individuals that become weak and emaciated through lack of food may be prone to disease or predation, which might often be only a secondary cause of death. The same may be true for accidental collisions if hungry birds become desperate and take risks near traffic, or are weakened and unable to get out of the way. Finally, there is evidence from Sparrowhawks that using fat reserves during starvation can release accumulated pesticides into the blood stream, which may then reach lethal levels (Newton 1986).

2. Collisions and accidents. These include collisions with stationary objects, entanglement in wires or netting, and traffic accidents. Road deaths have

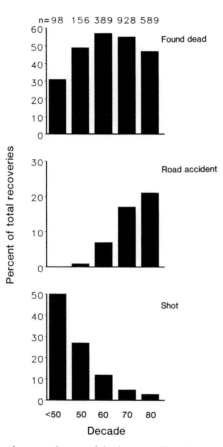

Fig. 81. Changes in the reported cause of death among Kestrels recovered in the National Ringing Scheme, 1912–1984. Over the last 30 years, the proportion killed by cars has increased, while the proportion reported as shot has decreased. The peak in the proportion reported as 'found dead' in the 1960s may reflect an increase in poisoning due to organochlorine pesticides, which were most heavily used at that time. Similar patterns have been found in owls (Glue 1971) and Sparrowhawks (Newton 1986).

increased in frequency during the past thirty years, and are now the most commonly reported cause of death in ring recoveries (Fig. 81). The same trend is evident for owls and Sparrowhawks (Glue 1971, Newton 1986), and presumably results from the greater volume and speed of modern traffic. Among the Monks Wood autopsies, 23% died from collisions or accidents, though this included other traumatic deaths, and only half were road accidents. Drowning is a surprisingly frequent accident, usually because Kestrels fall into water troughs and rain barrels when attempting to drink or bathe.

3. Shooting. Kestrels have never posed a serious threat to game rearing, but they have been shot and trapped nonetheless. It became illegal to do so in 1954 and this, coupled with a decline in gamekeeping, probably explains why the proportion of shot birds reported in ring recoveries declined during the 1950s and 1960s (Fig. 81). Kestrels are still killed in this way, though, and about 4% of the Monks Wood post-mortems revealed gunshot wounds or shotgun pellets. The decline in shot birds could also have been due to them being less often reported by their killers, for fear of prosecution. Illegally killed birds are likely to be hidden, and I located one radio-tagged female that had been shot and stuffed down a rabbit burrow. The person responsible obviously had no idea what a radio transmitter meant! Shooting has probably never been sufficient to reduce the overall Kestrel population level but, even so, it remains an unnecessary and inexcusable practice.

4. Poisoning. Kestrels rarely take carrion, so they are less vulnerable to poison baits than are other raptors such as buzzards or eagles. Few Kestrels in the national ringing scheme are reported as poisoned, but indirect poisoning, by accumulation of organochlorine pesticides, may be a more significant cause of death than this suggests. Autopsies at Monks Wood found 13% of 616 Kestrels had signs of internal haemorrhages which were not obviously due to impacts of any kind and which were symptomatic of organochlorine poisoning. Over half these birds had more than 10 ppm of HEOD (the active ingredient of the organochlorine pesticides dieldrin and aldrin) in the liver (Table 73). Dieldrin was used to control outbreaks of wheat bulb-fly in parts of eastern Britain, and has been stongly implicated in the deaths of Peregrines and Sparrowhawks (Ratcliffe 1980, Newton 1986). About 20% of Kestrels found dead in high pesticide areas had haemorrhages, compared with only 9% from elsewhere (Newton *et al* 1982).

Poisoning in this way seemed more frequent in spring than in autumn, and more frequent among adults than juveniles. Dieldrin was first used as a seed dressing for autumn and spring-sown cereals. Poisoning in spring may have been more prevalent because there was less alternative food for the small birds and rodents that fed on treated seed. The low frequency of poisoning in juveniles may have been because they were likely to die of starvation in autumn, before they were exposed to the poison in spring (Newton *et al* 1982).

Rather less is known of the lethal effects of other pollutants on Kestrels. Mercury compounds have been used as seed dressings, and can accumulate in small mammals that feed heavily on treated seed (Jefferies & French 1976). A decline in Kestrel numbers in Sweden has been linked to the use of mercury-based pesticides (Wallin *et al* 1983), but there is little direct evidence for this. Organochlorines have been largely replaced by organophosphorous pesticides, which are less persistent, but more toxic. They are widely used in my arable farmland area to kill nematodes by injection into the soil during the planting of potatoes. No work has been done to investigate the effects of organophosphorous compounds on Kestrels, but I have had several reports of Kestrels found dead on potato fields in spring, and I suspect that they may have been eating contaminated earthworms that were at the surface in wet weather.

5. *Disease.* This is bound to be under-represented in ringing recoveries because diseased birds are unlikely to be found and, if they are, to be diagnosed. About 6% were reported as 'diseased' or 'sick', which was about half the percentage thus diagnosed in the Monks Wood scheme. In nearly all cases, disease can only be identified by a post-mortem, and even then it is difficult to tell if it was chronic or fatal. Diseases identified in Kestrels include infections (such as tuberculosis, aspergillosis, enteritis and nephritis), lesions of the kidney or gut, and internal nematode parasites. Most diseased carcasses sent to Monks Wood were also emaciated, but whether this resulted from, or caused, the disease could not be told.

6. *Predation.* Almost by definition, Kestrels taken by predators are going to be hard to find, so this is another cause of death that may be underestimated from ring recoveries. Kestrel remains have been found at raptor nests and in pellets, so they obviously suffer some mortality by predation. In some cases, the Kestrels may have been eaten by scavengers after they had already died from some other cause. The most likely killers are Goshawks and Eagle Owls, though in Britain the main species are probably Peregrines, Tawny Owls and Sparrowhawks (Newton 1979). The usual indications of such predation are Kestrel feathers that have been plucked (rather than chewed as by foxes), or finding Kestrel remains in raptor pellets. In one instance, a ring I put on a nestling at Eskdalemuir was recovered from a Golden Eagle pellet. Kestrels can presumably out-manoeuvre most larger raptors, and may only fall victim if they are caught by surprise or if they become weakened or diseased. At the nest, incubating females and young seem to be at most risk from predation by owls.

Kestrels occasionally get caught on the ground by carnivores such as cats or foxes. At Eskdalemuir, foxes shot by forest rangers were routinely gutted to examine the stomach contents, and one was found to have just eaten a Kestrel. No ring was found, but the tiny bits of chewed wing-tag enabled me to identify it as an adult male that had been breeding at a nearby site.

The above list covers most of the finding circumstances of dead Kestrels, but gives little clue as to the importance of each in limiting or regulating Kestrel numbers. It is worth bearing in mind that 90% of ringed Kestrels are never found, and only half of those reported died of known causes. The possibilities for misjudging the main reasons for mortality are very real, and the currently available data need to be augmented by a more detailed study, perhaps using radio-tracking.

VARIATIONS IN SURVIVAL WITHIN POPULATIONS

Although a generalised estimate of the survival rate of Kestrels is a useful figure in itself, it would be interesting to see if the chance of survival varies, either between sub-groups within a population or in a whole population over time. I have already shown that juveniles have a poorer chance of surviving than adults, and that, on limited data, there is a slight difference in survival rates of males and females.

Survival of early versus late fledged young
One factor that seems to influence the survival of juveniles is the date on which they fledge. Cavé (1968) first showed this for Dutch Kestrels, where 53% of 303 young that fledged before 30 June died in their first year of life, compared with 65% of 118 young fledged after that date. This difference, although small, was statistically significant, and was even more marked when deaths before 1 September were considered. I found the same trend among the British ring recoveries and, again, the disparity was most noticeable from October to December (Table 74). This fits with the dispersal patterns of early

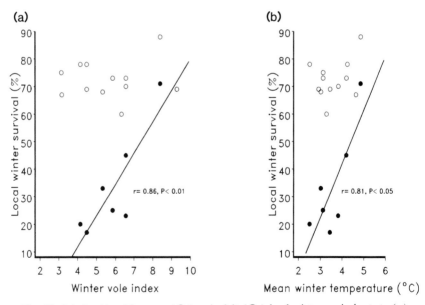

Fig. 82. Relationship of first year (●) and adult (○) local winter survival rate to (a) the January vole index and (b) mean temperature December–March. Lines are linear regressions fitted to first-year values only; there was no significant correlation in adults in either case.

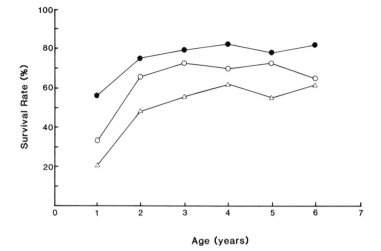

Fig. 83. *Annual survival rates of Kestrels of various ages in years of high (●), medium (○) or low (△) vole density. Based on data from the Dutch Ringing Scheme, after Dijkstra (1988). Survival was better for all ages groups in good vole years than in poor ones, but the difference was most noticeable among first-year birds.*

and late fledged young, as the two groups mix together in September, but late young then move further away from their natal area in the ensuing two months (Chapter 16). A recent, more detailed, analysis of the Dutch ringing data has also come to the same conclusions (Dijkstra 1988). It seems that early young have a distinct advantage at this time of year, both in terms of survival and age of first breeding (Chapter 16), and this may be an important selective pressure shaping the timing of egg laying. Kestrels seem to lay eggs as early as they can in spring (Chapter 14), and this may have evolved because early young have a better chance of surviving to breeding age.

Survival and winter food supply

The annual estimates of winter local-survival in the farmland areas (Table 70) were significantly correlated with both the winter vole index and mean winter temperature in first-year birds, but not in adults (Fig. 82). In the years for which I had estimates of first-year survival, vole numbers were strongly correlated with temperature, so it was difficult to isolate the effect of each on juvenile survival. Low temperatures were associated with an increased likelihood of snow cover, which would make voles more difficult to catch. Both factors may have influenced survival through variations in prey density or availability. In thick snow, Kestrels in farmland relied heavily on small birds as they were the only food available. Birds were difficult to catch, especially for juveniles, which normally ate fewer birds and more invertebrates than did adults (Chapter 3). Low vole numbers, or cold weather, would thus affect juveniles more seriously than adults, and this seems to have been reflected in their winter survival.

Survival rates during vole cycles

If poor food supply is a major cause of mortality in Kestrels, survival should be better in vole peak years than during troughs. Snow (1968) looked for variations in the first-year survival of nestlings, and in the mortality of adults, between vole peak and decline years. The results were rather inconclusive and, if anything, suggested better survival of adults in decline than in peak vole years. Analysis of the more extensive Dutch ringing data has shown that survival of all age groups is markedly better when voles are plentiful than when they are scarce (Dijkstra 1988, Fig. 83). The effect was again most obvious for first-year birds in early autumn, which agrees with the winter local-survival in my farmland areas. The more noticeable effect in the Dutch than in the British ringing data may be because vole numbers were better monitored in Holland, or because vole cycles were more pronounced and synchronous across Holland than throughout Britain. In Britain, vole numbers fluctuate mainly in the north, but many northern-bred Kestrels move south in autumn (Chapter 16), where they may experience quite different food levels and eat other prey besides voles.

Survival in relation to pesticides and protection

Two changes which may have affected the survival rates of Kestrels were the legal protection of the species and the use of harmful pesticides. Both must have altered the pattern of Kestrel mortality, but whether any effects on overall survival rates can be detected is another matter. The widespread killing of Kestrels by pesticides might increase the numbers of recoveries, but this would not have an immediate effect on survival, as estimated by complete ring-recovery data, if it increased mortality in all aged birds equally. It may, on the other hand, kill birds that would die of other causes anyway, and so go undetected because of a compensatory decrease in 'natural' mortality. In the opposite case, of legal protection from shooting, survival rates may improve for a while, but must eventually decrease again unless there is either a reduction in productivity, or an ever expanding population, neither of which seems to happen. As if these complications were not enough, the introduction of protection and pesticides happened at about the same time in Britain, where the 1954 Protection of Birds Act was followed, two years later, by the first use of dieldrin as a seed dressing.

In Britain, there has been a steady rise in the number of Kestrels ringed each year, and this means a growing volume of recoveries. Sufficient time has elapsed to compare survival before and during the pesticide era, using complete life-tables, and a few more years will allow an estimate of survival in the post-pesticide period. Until then, we have to rely on methods using incomplete data, which are less than satisfactory and may give misleading answers.

There was no change in the proportion of British-ringed Kestrels recovered dead as adults during the years when dieldrin was in heaviest use (Table 75). An increase in the proportion might be expected if the accumulation of pesticides over several years was required before birds were killed, or if the first-years, but not the adults, that were poisoned would have died anyway. I used the ratio method (Newton *et al* 1983a) to compare the mortality of adults and first-years, as this enabled me to include recoveries after 1976, when the main uses of dieldrin were finally banned. I divided recoveries into those found in high or low pesticide usage areas, based on the incidence of wheat bulb fly, the main pest treated with dieldrin (Newton 1986). Dieldrin was introduced in 1956 and withdrawn in 1976, so I compared survival during this period with that before and after (Table 76). Adult survival in the low pesticide areas was always higher, even when dieldrin was not being used, but the difference was most marked during the pesticide period, when survival declined in the high use area. First-year survival showed no similar trend, and juveniles seem to have been less affected than adults. These figures are only indications, and could not be tested for statistical significance, so they may have arisen by chance.

Analysis of Swedish ring recoveries has also suggested adult, but not first-year, survival was reduced after 1955 (Wallin *et al* 1983), but the method used maximum likelihood estimates that can give unreliable results. In Denmark, increases in survival in 1926 and 1967 were attributed to protective legislation introduced in those years (Noer & Secher 1983). Although these trends may be real, it is hard to believe that both effects could work independently in adjacent populations that must share much of their winter range.

Perhaps the most obvious conclusion to this section is that, despite the massive effort that has gone into ringing Kestrels, and the undoubted decline in their numbers in some areas of high pesticide use, the data we have from ringing recoveries are unable to give us a firm picture of how pesticide poisoning or protective legislation affected Kestrel survival rates.

SUMMARY

On average, about 30–40% of ringed Kestrels survive their first year of life; adult survival is higher, at about 60–70%. Starvation appears to be a major cause of death, especially among juveniles in autumn and midwinter. Deaths due to road accidents have increased over the past decades, and pesticide poisoning was implicated in the cause of death in about 13% of Kestrels examined from 1961–79.

Mortality during the first year of life is higher among late-fledged young than early ones, and the difference is most noticeable in recoveries during autumn and early winter. Survival of juveniles seems to be best in good vole years and mild winters, suggesting that food shortage may be the primary cause of much Kestrel mortality. There is some indication that survival rates in Kestrels have changed as a result of pesticide usage and protective legislation, but the evidence may not be reliable and requires more support.

CHAPTER 20

Population regulation

My main interest in studying Kestrels has been their population ecology, and particularly the way in which numbers are adjusted to match the availability of resources. The picture that has emerged is of a complex process, which may vary over time or from one area to another. This chapter draws upon the various lines of evidence already presented and tries to suggest possible mechanisms that control Kestrel population density. The evidence is incomplete, and some of the ideas that follow are necessarily speculative. They may, nonetheless, provide hypotheses that can be tested by further research on Kestrels or other raptors.

CONCEPTS AND TERMINOLOGY

Before dealing with details, it is necessary to clarify some of the terms used, and to outline some basic ideas of raptor population regulation. Many of these ideas were first suggested by Ian Newton (1979) after a comprehensive review of raptor population ecology, and I have modified or added to them in the light of my experience with Kestrels.

The numbers of any species in a given area must ultimately be determined by the effects of gains through births or immigration, and losses through deaths or emigration. The relative importance of births and deaths versus movements will partly depend on the size of the area: movements will have more influence on density over small areas than over large ones. If the study area is much larger than the distances over which individuals disperse, movements will be significant only near the boundaries. Ultimately, the size of the global population of a species depends solely on the levels of natality and mortality, and any imbalance in the two that has acted in the past. Raptor biologists nearly always work in areas that are much smaller than the dispersal distances of the species they study, so movements will often be important in the regulation of numbers. At this scale, population regulation depends largely on how individuals disperse over the landscape, and how and why they concentrate in some areas but not in others.

Raptor densities may be controlled either by the level of resources, or by excessive mortality which holds density below the level that resources would permit (Newton 1979). In populations not interfered with by man, densities are normally limited by the availability of resources such as food or nesting sites. Excessive mortality results in a lack of individuals to use these resources, and in raptors this is usually because of human persecution or pesticide poisoning. Numbers may be temporarily held below resource levels for other reasons, such as predation, disease or slow dispersal of birds into vacant areas. Although Kestrel breeding density may have been limited by pesticide-induced mortality in some parts of Britain in the past (Chapter 10), there was little evidence of this in my study areas. The populations I observed had been profoundly influenced by human activity, but this was largely through alteration of the habitat, and hence resource levels, rather than by direct mortality.

An important concept in population ecology is the idea of *limiting factors* which prevent a population from further increase. Numbers at any given time are usually held in check by a single 'key' limiting factor, and if this is removed the population increases until it reaches a new level set by a different factor. Limiting factors may be the availability of particular resources, or mortality due to predation, disease, or other causes. Some factors may be 'proximate', in that they merely mediate the effects of other 'ultimate' factors. An example might be deaths from disease among individuals that are in poor condition because they are starved. Disease could be said to be limiting the population density, but the ultimate cause is lack of food.

The terms 'regulation' and 'limitation' require some clarification, because they refer to slightly different processes. If numbers are regulated, it implies that there is a particular optimum density toward which the population will always tend. If density departs from this optimum level, individuals will tend to be lost if the density is higher, and gained if it is lower. Such regulation is termed *density-dependent* if the direction and extent of change depends on the population density. Populations might be limited, rather than regulated, so that density is prevented from increasing beyond a certain level, but may fall below it.

In practice, it is difficult to distinguish a regulated population from a limited one. Regulation may only be apparent if the population is studied long enough for it to adjust to the equilibrium density. Density-dependence is difficult to detect unless the equilibrium density is constant, so that even closely regulated populations may fluctuate widely from year to year if the resource level is unstable. An analogy might be the dial of an oven thermostat that is frequently moved: the temperature is always regulated, but varies according to the setting. Fluctuating resource levels may mask density-dependence in Kestrel populations because vole cycles can produce marked changes in food supply from year to year.

In my study areas, the population density of Kestrels in winter depended on the numbers settling there in autumn and the numbers that were subsequently lost. Both processes seemed to be related to the supply of food, and specifically to the abundance of rodents. The correlations between Kestrel and vole (or Woodmouse) numbers were statistically significant in all three areas, but only when autumn and winter values were treated together (see Figs 42 & 43). Correlations based solely on autumn values were not significant, possibly because year to year variations in small-mammal numbers were slight or because there were insufficient data. The evidence linking annual variations in autumn density to small-mammal abundance was thus rather weak, and other factors may have influenced the number of individuals settling during the post-fledging dispersal of juveniles. Autumn densities were poorly correlated with the local production of young in the previous breeding season, and most juveniles settling were from outside the study areas. Invertebrates and small birds were important in the diet of Kestrels in autumn, and this may have enabled some Kestrels to survive locally even when the vole density was low. Furthermore, Kestrels may take some weeks to succumb to a shortage of food, so autumn numbers may remain above the resource levels until mortality or emigration has acted to bring them in line. This could explain why Kestrel density in mixed farmland was better related to vole numbers in winter than in autumn.

Population density in midwinter
When the autumn settling period was over, the Kestrel density depended mainly on the rate of loss through mortality or emigration. Density declined in midwinter, and this coincided with the decrease in vole densities in the grassland and mixed farmland areas, and with decreasing Woodmouse densities in arable farmland, where mice were more important prey. The lower Kestrel densities at Eskdalemuir than in the farmland areas in midwinter (Table 14) must have been due mainly to the reduced availability of voles, rather than their lower density. The high probability of snow cover, and lack of an alternative prey, resulted in a poor winter food supply for Kestrels at Eskdalemuir, despite better vole habitat than in farmland. In farmland, local survival of juveniles in winter was related to the food supply (Fig. 82), and their greater vulnerability than adults to starvation caused a reduction in the proportion of juveniles in the population as winter progressed (Fig. 77). Variations in winter densities between years were therefore due mainly to variations in the number of juveniles settling in autumn and how many survived thereafter.

The lack of replacement of Kestrels that died or were experimentally removed from their winter territories (Table 15) suggested that density was not regulated after October. The fact that removed birds could re-establish on their previous territory when released later in the same winter showed that, while they were absent, numbers remained below the carrying capacity of the area. This raises the possibility that temporary food shortages, such as might be caused by heavy snowfall, could deplete the winter population and leave it below resource levels when the availability of food increased as the snow melts.

REGULATION OF BREEDING DENSITY

The Kestrel population in spring and summer consists of pairs and unpaired individuals. I have defined 'breeding density' as the number of pairs per unit area, including pairs that defend a nesting site but do not lay eggs. In my study areas, the proportion of such pairs was usually less than 10% (Table 21), so breeding density depended mainly on the size of the total spring population and the proportion of that population which formed territorial pairs. Both these factors were ultimately determined by the food supply, but their relative importance differed between the study areas.

Total spring population density
In the Scottish grassland area, most of the breeding population arrived from elsewhere in spring, and the extent of this influx determined the total population density. For the three years in which I did roadside counts, total Kestrel density and the spring vole index were positively correlated, though there were too few years to test for statistical significance (Fig. 42).

In the farmland areas, most of the breeding birds had been present in winter, and there was little influx of Kestrels in spring. Kestrel density showed little relationship to spring vole numbers, and was probably determined mainly by the effects of winter food supply on the survival of juveniles (see above). Most Kestrels return to breed in the region where they were born, so northern birds on spring passage may have stayed in the farmland areas only if the food supply was exceptionally good. This could have happened in mixed farmland in 1981, when voles were at least three times more numerous than in other years, and Kestrel numbers increased from winter to spring (Fig. 41).

In the arable area, there were fewer Kestrels present in summer than in winter, and the size of the spring population may have depended on how many birds left the area at the end of winter. The main winter food in this area was Woodmice, and these invariably reached low densities by April. Spring Kestrel densities were likewise uniformly low, so there was insufficient variation to show if the two were closely correlated. The high vole numbers in the arable area 1981 were not associated with higher Kestrel numbers, so spring densities may have depended largely on the extent of the seasonal decline in Woodmice.

Density of territorial pairs
The spring population density sets an upper limit on the breeding density, but the number of pairs will depend on the ease with which individuals are able at least to start the breeding cycle. Kestrels do not normally pair unless

they have a nesting site, and new pairs are unlikely to remain together for long if the male is unable to provision his partner adequately. The number of pairs present in spring is likely, therefore, to depend on the availability of nesting sites and the food supply. Both these resources limit Kestrel breeding density under some circumstances, but their exact role varies from place to place. To understand what limits the density of territorial pairs in an area, it is helpful to know if there are unpaired birds present and, if so, why they do not breed.

In all three study areas there were unpaired Kestrels present in spring and summer. In the Scottish grassland area, these mainly lived in the open, away from the nesting territories of breeding pairs, and I had little idea of what proportion of the total population they formed. In the farmland areas, I had larger samples of tagged birds in spring, and about a quarter of the adults and half the yearlings were unpaired (Table 67). These were minimum estimates, but they were roughly in line with estimates for the similar-sized Sparrowhawk, based on survival rates and age of first breeding (Newton 1985). The high proportion of singletons in the spring population implied that there was no shortage of birds to occupy vacant nesting territories, and that breeding density was likely to be controlled by resource availability.

In the Scottish grassland area, some birds remained unpaired because they lacked a suitable nesting site. Shortage of sites was most obvious in the large open areas, where there were few crags or trees with old crow nests. Kestrels do occasionally nest on the ground, but this is rare where there are mammalian predators such as foxes or stoats. It could be argued, then, that the risk of predation ultimately limits breeding density in open habitats, because ground-nesting would presumably be more frequent if it was likely to succeed.

Overall, there was always a surplus of nesting sites at Eskdalemuir (Table 19), but some Kestrels were unable to find somewhere to breed because of the territorial behaviour of established pairs. Most of the potential sites were old crow-nests in woods in the valleys. Many of these woods had several stick nests that were not occupied by Kestrels or owls, but some Kestrels were denied access to such sites by pairs already breeding at different sites in the same woods. The limiting resource was not, therefore, the actual number of nesting sites, but the number that were outside Kestrel territories.

In good vole years, pairs had smaller territories around their nest, allowing more pairs access to nearby nesting sites and thereby increasing the breeding density. Food supply thus seemed to be the ultimate factor controlling breeding density in the Scottish grassland area, but it acted through territorial behaviour, which restricted access to nesting sites.

In the English farmland areas, there was no evidence that lack of nesting sites prevented Kestrels from breeding. Nesting sites were more evenly spaced than in the grassland area, and few Kestrels defended territories large enough to exclude other pairs from many potential sites. Breeding males were aggressive in spring, but mainly within a few hundred metres of their nest (C. G. Wiklund), so nesting sites further than that from occupied sites should have been available to other Kestrels.

The reason why some farmland Kestrels were not breeding seemed to differ between the sexes. Females were able to mate successfully with 'widowed' males in removal experiments, suggesting they had not bred sooner because

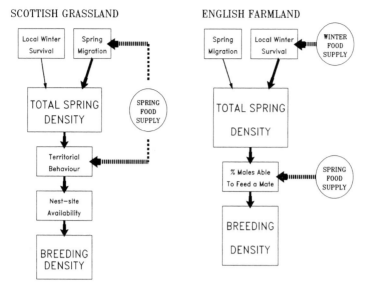

SCOTTISH GRASSLAND   ENGLISH FARMLAND

Fig. 84. Summary of the main factors regulating Kestrel breeding density in the Scottish grassland and English farmland areas. Spring food supply was the most important factor in the migratory Scottish population, but winter food supply was also important for the more sedentary English population.

they lacked a mate. There were unpaired males in the vicinity, however, and males seemed to form the majority of the non-breeding population (Table 65). These non-breeding males were probably poor hunters, unable to catch sufficient food to feed a female adequately. The few males that did occupy a vacated territory during removal experiments, presumably had the same food supply as the previous occupant. That they still did not breed successfully suggests that they were unable to contend with the low vole densities in farmland habitats. The idea that food supply directly limited breeding numbers was consistent with the late laying and poor breeding productivity of Kestrels in farmland areas compared with those in the better vole habitats of the Scottish grassland area (Table 38).

If sufficient individuals survived the winter in farmland, years when voles were numerous in spring would result in high Kestrel breeding densities because a greater proportion of males would be able to feed a mate. This was especially critical for first-year males, whose survival was related to winter food supply, and whose ability to breed depended on spring food supply (Figs 82 & 79). The large proportion of first-year males in the 1981 breeding population arose because high survival of juveniles in winter was followed by unusually high vole abundance in spring.

The main differences in the regulation of breeding numbers in the Scottish grassland and English farmland areas are summarised in Fig. 84. The Scottish population was largely migratory, so spring food supply was the main factor affecting both the number of migrants settling and the proportion of the spring population that formed pairs. In the more sedentary farmland populations, winter food supply was important in affecting the total spring population, and spring food supply more directly controlled the number of males able to pair.

THE ROLE OF TERRITORIAL BEHAVIOUR IN LIMITING DENSITY

Kestrels defend territories at most times of year, and territorial fighting was most obvious when population density was being determined in autumn or spring (Fig. 37). This implies that aggression was involved in some way in the process of population regulation. In autumn and winter, Kestrels defended all of their home range, whereas in summer they defended mainly an area around the nest. Despite this seasonal difference in the nature of territories, aggression probably had a similar underlying influence on population density in summer and winter.

The role of territorial behaviour in autumn

There was a sharp increase in the frequency of fights between Kestrels during September, when they were attempting to establish winter territories. Kestrel decoys presented to resident Kestrels in arable farmland were rarely attacked in August, but invariably so after September (C. G. Wiklund). It seemed that the increase in fights in September was partly because birds were more likely to encounter one another as more incomers arrived, and partly because of an increase in aggression. Despite this heightend aggression, territory size declined as more birds arrived, and appeared to be determined by the number of individuals that settled, rather than *vice versa*.

Aggressive encounters between juveniles were often inconclusive, with neither combatant appearing to succeed in expelling the other. The need to fend off rivals may, however, have increased the difficulties which confronted individuals trying to settle in an area. Incomers might persist if food was easily caught, leaving them with time and energy to fight established territory-holders. If food was scarce, the depletion of reserves by fighting may have led to mortality or forced poor hunters to move elsewhere.

The above idea does not require the level of aggression in resident territorial birds to be related to the food supply. When adults became aggressive in September they attacked all decoys with maximum vigour, and the response seemed all-or-nothing, rather than graduated. Even if the average level of aggression was constant from year to year, territory size (and hence density) would still be related to the food supply if the persistence of settlers depended on how well they were fed. If food was plentiful, persistent settlers would compress residents into smaller territories; when food was scarce there would be less pressure on residents and their territories would remain large.

The role of territorial behaviour in spring

The fact that some Kestrels in the Scottish grassland area were unable to breed because territorial pairs excluded them from nearby, vacant nesting sites, suggests that the food supply could have supported more breeding pairs if the nesting sites had been more evenly spaced. The need to fight for a nesting place seems to have prevented some birds from breeding, but others were able to gain possession of unused crow nests close to existing pairs. Presumably more of the Kestrels that arrived in spring would have been able to breed if pairs were not aggressive around the nest. Pairs would then have formed until all the usable sites were occupied, or no more birds arrived in the area.

Territorial behaviour thus seemed to hold breeding density at a lower level than might have been possible had the only competition between pairs been in hunting or the depletion of the food supply. This in itself might explain why breeding pairs invest a considerable amount of time and energy in defending a territory, because fewer neighbours in the vicinity of the nest would increase the available food supply. However, males also had to defend their females against mating attempts by surplus males (see Chapter 7), and the exclusion of other males from nearby potential nesting sites could have been a secondary result of mate guarding.

Throughout the year, then, aggressive behaviour seemed to hold the population density at a lower level than might otherwise have been possible. The need to defend against attack imposes an additional burden that prevents some individuals from settling in autumn or, in some areas, from pairing in spring. Aggressive individuals presumably gain from this because the available food resources are then divided among fewer individuals.

SUMMARY

The Scottish grassland area had a migratory population, a potentially high but variable food supply, and unevenly distributed nesting sites. The movements of dispersing juveniles in autumn, and returning migrants in spring, allowed population density to be adjusted to the food supply in both seasons. Density in winter was limited by the decreasing food supply, but could fall below the level set by vole density if snow cover reduced prey availability. There were few Kestrels passing through the area in midwinter, so improvements in food availability when the snow melted would not be matched by increased Kestrel density until migrants arrived in spring.

The same was true in the farmland areas, though the lack of spring migrants meant that spring population density depended mainly on the survival of individuals over winter. In juveniles, survival was determined by the abundance of voles and their availability as affected by snow cover. If sufficient males survived the winter, the proportion that was able to feed a mate seemed to depend on the spring food supply.

Territorial fighting was most evident when new arrivals were settling in autumn or spring. At both times of year it seemed to hold the total population, or the density of territorial pairs, at lower levels than food supplies would otherwise permit.

CHAPTER 21

Conclusions

European Kestrels have sometimes been thought of as 'generalised' predators showing little specialisation compared to other raptors. In fact, Kestrels have many complex adaptations that allow them to live in a wide range of open habitats under varying conditions, and they are better regarded of as being highly specialised to fill a wide predatory niche.

Kestrels in Europe occur in the same habitats as other birds of prey of about the same size, such as Sparrowhawks, Hobbies, Merlins and some owls, or

270

larger species such as Hen Harriers, Common Buzzards and larger owls that also feed on small mammals. The biology of Kestrels is similar to many of these other species, either because of their common size or because they share the same food supply. The life span, age of first breeding, population density and breeding productivity of Kestrels are similar to other small raptors, which are said to be '*r-selected*' (MacArthur & Wilson 1967, Newton 1979). This means that individuals are short-lived, start breeding early in life and produce a relatively large number of young per breeding attempt, enabling populations to increase rapidly under suitable conditions. Large raptors, in contrast, are more '*K-selected*', being long-lived, having delayed maturity and producing few young per breeding attempt (Newton 1979).

Kestrels are well adapted to fluctuating food supplies, and the important influence of vole numbers on their behaviour has emerged repeatedly in chapters of this book. Few raptors are likely to have a completely stable supply of food, but those feeding on rodents face the likelihood of larger, more regular annual fluctuations than those that mainly eat birds, insects or carrion. Vole feeders need to be able both to survive during vole troughs and to exploit vole peaks. Different species do this in slightly different ways, but many show similar responses to vole cycles (Table 77):

1. Variable diets. Most vole-feeding raptors that have been studied show some ability to take alternative prey when voles are scarce. Such prey are either other mammals (such as shrews, mice or rabbits), birds or invertebrates. Kestrels can do this more readily than many species, which probably explains why they can occupy poor vole habitats, and can also maintain reasonable densities during vole troughs. In my Scottish area, for example, Kestrels occupied grazed sheepwalk (where voles were relatively scarce) thoughout the study, even in the poorest vole year. Short-eared Owls, in contrast, were barely able to persist in the study area during the vole trough, and were seen in sheepwalk only at the higher vole densities (Village 1987a). A change to other prey does not completely compensate for a decline in voles and, even in Kestrels, population density and breeding productivity are invariably lower when the diet is varied than when it consists entirely of voles (Korpimäki 1986b).

The degree to which a species can switch from small mammals to small birds or invertebrates depends partly on its repertoire of hunting methods. The two most effective ways of catching small mammals are by hovering (commonly used by Kestrels, Black-shouldered Kites, Rough-legged Buzzards and Hawk Owls) and by low-level slow flight (used by harriers, *Asio* owls and Barn Owls). Other prey can be taken by these methods (hovering Kestrels sometimes take insects, and harriers may take small birds), but less efficiently. Either hunting method requires considerable energy, but whereas hovering species have long tails and hunt by sight, those using low-level flight have a light wing-loading (ie a large wing area for their body weight) and hunt mainly by sound, using their facial disc to focus prey noises on their ears. Such physical adaptations make it difficult for these species to change from one hunting method to another, and it happens rarely, if at all.

In Kestrels, and many other raptors, perched-hunting is an important foraging technique, and can be used against a wider variety of prey than when hunting by hovering or low-level flight. Species that can most successfully switch to non-mammal prey when voles are scarce are largely those that can hunt from perches, or by other methods such as soaring. Species such as Short-eared Owls, that hunt almost exclusively on the wing, are more obligate vole feeders that may sometimes take birds but virtually never feed on invertebrates.

Black-shouldered Kites are hovering raptors of a similar size to European Kestrels. They feed almost exclusively on rodents and are adapted to fluctuating food supplies. Photo: M. Van Rsiet.

2. Movement away from poor food areas to good ones. An alternative way of responding to spatially varying vole numbers is to move from places of scarcity to where voles are more plentiful. Migrations are an example of movements in response to a seasonally varying food supply, and they are common in many bird species that breed in temperate regions. Vole feeders, however, can experience large year-to-year changes in food availability, and breeding sites that are suitable one year may be unsatisfactory the next. When voles become scarce, some species move large distances between breeding attempts, or erupt out of their normal range. Such 'nomadic' behaviour is common in northern species of owls that feed largely on voles or lemmings. At Eskdalemuir, breeding

Owls often compete with Kestrels for food or nest sites. Short-eared owls (above) are specialist vole-feeders that nest on the ground. Long-eared Owls (below) also feed on voles, and further compete with Kestrels for nest sites such as disused crow nests. Photos: K. Taylor.

Short-eared Owls that I wing-tagged in 1976 were reported as far apart as Shetland and Spain during the following year when vole numbers crashed (Village 1987a). Species requiring particular nest sites may be less inclined to move long distances between breeding attempts. Male Tengmalm's Owls, which defend scarce nesting-holes, are largely sedentary, but females do not defend sites and some are nomadic (Korpimäki 1987).

The number of Kestrels fluctuates widely from year to year in some areas, and such changes must be due to movements as well as to changes in mortality rates. I know of no reports of marked individuals moving large distances between breeding attempts, so there is no evidence that Kestrels are a truly nomadic species. Such evidence is hard to come by, however, so the possibility cannot be ruled out for Kestrels breeding in the most northern parts of their range. In most places, however, concentrations where voles are numerous are most likely when juveniles are dispersing in autumn, or during spring in migrant populations. So in terms of movements and population turnover, Kestrels lie somewhere between highly sedentary species such as Tawny Owls, that remain in the same territory all their adult life, and highly mobile ones such as Short-eared Owls, that sometimes breed hundreds of kilometres apart from one year to the next.

3. Non-breeding and age of first breeding. Some sedentary species respond to small-mammal cycles by not breeding in years of extreme scarcity. A classic example is the Tawny Owl, where most pairs do not produce eggs when there is a crash in small-mammal numbers (Southern 1970). A missed breeding attempt may be of little consequence to long-lived individuals that are likely to survive until another vole peak, but it is less advantageous to Kestrels, about a third of which die each year, even as adults. In my studies, non-laying among pairs was more frequent in the poor-vole farmland areas than in the Scottish grassland area, but rarely in more than 20% of the territorial pairs (Table 21). The proportion not laying was little affected by annual changes in vole abundance, and fluctuations in breeding density were caused mainly by variations in the numbers of territorial pairs.

In my study areas, the main response of Kestrel populations to varying vole numbers seemed to be changes in the age at which individuals started to breed, with more first-year males breeding in good vole years than poor ones. Changes in the age of first breeding by males are probably a major cause of fluctuations in Kestrel breeding density from year to year, especially in sedentary populations. In many areas there are probably excess nesting sites and a reservoir of Kestrels that can breed when one or two years old if food is plentiful.

4. Variable mating systems. During vole peak years, male Kestrels may be capable of feeding more young than they do, but are unable to exploit this largesse because females rarely lay more than six eggs. One way of overcoming this is to have more than one mate (polygyny), which will enable males, but not necessarily females, to produce more offspring. This practice seems unusual in most vole-feeding raptors, though it occurs with a few Kestrels and some owls in good vole years. Harriers more commonly mate polygynously, especially if voles are abundant (Hamerstrom 1969, Simmons *et al* 1986). Polyandry (in

Sparrowhawks are of a similar size to Kestrels but they are specialised bird-feeders. Their ecology thus shows both similarities and differences from that of vole-feeding Kestrels. Photo: N.J. Westwood.

which females have more than one mate) might be expected in years when prey is scarce, but it seems even less frequent than polygyny. Both forms of polygamous mating are difficult to detect, however, and may be more common than the present evidence suggests. In Africa, female Black-shouldered Kites sometimes show 'serial' polyandry by abandoning the brood to their first mate and going off in search of another (Mendelsohn 1983). This behaviour, which also occurs in Tengmalm's Owls (Korpimäki 1987), enables some females to exploit high rodent densities effectively by breeding twice in one year.

5. Adjusting breeding output to vole numbers. Individuals breeding in good vole years can also take advantage of the abundant food by fledging more young. They can do this by laying more eggs, increasing nestling survival or by producing a second brood. Kestrels have slightly larger clutches in good vole years, but nestling survival is little affected, and there are no certain cases of pairs having second broods. This is in contrast to species such as Short-eared Owls or Barn Owls, which produce much larger clutches, and sometimes second broods, in good vole years. The marked asynchrony in hatching of owl chicks not only spreads the food demands of the brood, but also allows brood size to be reduced by the sacrifice of small chicks if there is insufficient food. In Kestrels, breeding productivity is adjusted to food supply mainly by small alterations in clutch size and by increased desertion of clutches when food is scarce. The relatively small variations possible in clutch size mean that Kestrels are unable to exploit the full potential of exceptionally good vole years. This may be the price they pay for being able to exist in a wide variety of habitats and breed under low vole conditions.

Kestrels can thus adapt to both a fluctuating and a fairly stable food supply. In parts of their range where there are large areas of vole habitat, marked vole cycles and severe winter weather, Kestrels show similarities to more obligate vole-feeders such as Short-eared Owls or Rough-legged Buzzards. Kestrels are able to respond to sudden increases in food supply, though perhaps not to the same extent as vole specialists. Kestrels can survive and breed in areas where voles are less abundant, or where food fluctuates less from year to year, and in these circumstances their biology is more akin to raptors with a stable food supply. Density and productivity in such areas never achieve the levels seen in good vole areas during peak years, and Kestrels cannot fully escape their dependence on voles as the main source of food.

This flexibility has enabled Kestrels to survive, and sometimes to thrive, during major changes in habitat caused by man's agriculture and urbanisation. Kestrels will hopefully always be a familiar sight, whatever changes we inflict on our landscape in the future. That they are common-place makes them no less fascinating to study, and I hope that this book has shown both the complexity of their lives and how much more we still have to learn.

Measuring Kestrel diet

This appendix is intended to review the various methods used to estimate Kestrel diets and to provide a detailed description of pellet analysis for those unfamiliar with the technique. There are four main ways of measuring the frequency of the different types of prey eaten by Kestrels:

DIRECT OBSERVATION

In theory, this is the easiest and least biased method, as it simply involves watching birds and recording what they eat. Alas, life is rarely so simple, as anyone who has tried to follow a Kestrel for more than a few minutes knows. Kestrels are often lost from sight when they dive at prey and this makes it hard to know if a kill is made and, if so, what it was. Those prey that can be identified tend to be the larger items, such as mammals or birds, which are usually carried to a prominent perch before eating. Small invertebrates are picked up directly with the beak and are often eaten immediately, before they can be identified.

Direct observation can be useful in determining the ratio of mammals to birds or invertebrates, because strikes at these different types of prey are fairly distinct. Strikes at mammals usually follow hovering bouts and are almost vertical, ending with a sudden plunge to the ground. Those at invertebrates are slow and shallow, while attacks on small birds are usually fast, shallow glides. Provided the frequency of successful strikes is known for each prey, this method may give a less biased estimate of invertebrates than pellet analysis. However, direct observation is very time consuming and is normally used to estimate hunting success, rather than diet. An exception is to count items brought to the nest. Although this may not reflect the prey eaten by adults, it is the most accurate way of recording the diet of nestlings, particularly if the hide is close enough to allow mammals and birds to be identified to the species level.

RECORDING PREY REMAINS AT NESTING SITES

During the breeding season, the male brings prey to the female at the nest and she plucks and eats it nearby. Females often have a favourite location for eating, such as a fence post, grass bank or farm track, and prey remains gradually accumulate at these places. Provided that only recent kills are counted, they can be used to estimate diet because fur and feathers seem roughly similar in their detectability and persistence. This method gave useful results at Eskdalemuir, where the trees were conifers and most females ate on the ground. Where there are large deciduous trees, kills are sometimes eaten on horizontal branches, scattering the remains over a wide area and making them impossible to count.

Kills are often found on the nest after the young hatch, either intact, or as a pile of recently plucked fur or feathers. I normally record only fresh kills because trampled feathers remain intact longer than fur, thereby overstating the importance of birds. However, recent work in Finland has shown that prey remains and pellets collected from a single visit to the nest at the end of the nesting period gave similar results to collections made at the nest throughout the breeding cycle (Korpimäki 1985a). Identification of bird feathers is also the best way of measuring the range of avian species in the diet.

PELLET ANALYSIS

This is the method most frequently used to assess the diet of Kestrels. It can be applied throughout the year and is the quickest way of sampling a large number of individuals. The food of most birds contains some indigestible matter; for Kestrels this includes the larger bones of mammals and birds, teeth, some fur or feathers and the chitinous parts of invertebrates. Kestrels avoid eating some of these by plucking fur or feathers from the carcass and by picking flesh away from large bones. Nonetheless, some fur and bones are eaten, and those that are not digested sufficiently to pass through the gut are formed into an elongated pellet and regurgitated. Kestrel pellets are usually about 20–30 mm long by 12–17 mm wide, and often have a tapered end, which helps to distinguish them from those produced by owls. They are normally regurgitated just after dawn while the bird is roosting (Duke *et al* 1976), and are scattered under roosts or nests.

Counting items versus presence or absence in pellets
Pellets analysis involves a careful sifting of the matrix of fur and identifying the fragments found. This sounds simple enough, but there are a number of problems which have to be considered when interpreting the findings. Firstly, the types of prey vary in their digestibility. Whereas vole remains may include fur, bones or teeth, earthworms leave behind only a few microscopic parts such a chaetea (the tiny bristles used for gripping the soil). Small, soft-bodied prey may leave no trace, and will be under-represented in pellets.

Even when prey do leave remains, it is not always easy to tell how many items the remains represent. Kestrels digest their prey much more thoroughly than do owls, and frequently the only skeletal parts are a few teeth and bone fragments. The small bones of shrews are often lost entirely, and fur may be the only indication that any were eaten. This makes counting difficult because bones or jaws have to be matched in order to estimate the minimum number of individuals represented in the sample. Counting insects poses particular problems because of the number and variety of remains some-times found. Earthworms cannot be counted at all, though Yalden and Warburton (1979) digested five samples of worms in trypsin, weighed the remains and used this to estimate the number of worms represented by a given weight of soil in a pellet. Needless to say, the results were only approximate, and the analysis of each pellet took anything from 30–70 minutes. Despite the problems, most studies of Kestrel diet have tried to count the number of items in each pellet, though the accuracy must vary from one person to another.

One way around the difficulty of counting items is to record instead the presence or absence of items in pellets. This also involves careful dissection of the pellet, but it is much quicker because the hard parts have only to be identified and not matched or counted. The importance of items is then expressed as the proportion of pellets containing the item. Although this method does not quantify items in pellets, it does allow a comparison of diets over time or from different places.

Evaluation of pellet analysis

There has been little detailed assessment of the accuracy of pellet analysis, and the two studies of which I am aware dealt solely with vertebrate prey (Crichton 1976, Yalden and Yalden 1985). In each case, the number of laboratory mice or birds fed to captive Kestrels was compared with the number subsequently counted in the pellets. Recovery rates were around 25%, and it seems likely that the number of items counted may seriously underestimate the number eaten. This would not matter if the errors were the same for each type of prey, because the relative frequency in pellets would still be the same as in the diet. However, recovery rates for small items must be very poor compared to mammals, though this has not been measured directly.

Given the sources of error, recording the presence or absence of items seems as accurate as counting them, and is certainly much quicker. I have used this technique in my work as it was necessary to sample large numbers of pellets collected over many years, and I would recommend it to anyone contemplating a large-scale analysis of Kestrel diets. The number of pellets containing a particular type of prey probably reflects the number of days on which such prey were eaten, which may be a more ecologically meaningful measure than the actual number of each prey type that survives digestion sufficiently to be counted in pellets.

Collecting and analysing pellets

Although the methods of recording prey in pellets vary, the process of collecting and examining them is fairly standard. Pellets are found at roosts or nests, the quantity varying seasonally and from site to site. In the farmland studies, regular winter roosts were not usually occupied until October or November. In early autumn Kestrels seemed to use a variety of roosts, often in trees, and it was only when the trees lost their leaves that the more easily found roosts on buildings or straw stacks were common.

Even well-used roosts, with abundant droppings, may yield few pellets. This may be because the roost is so high and exposed that pellets are widely scattered, or because the occupant produces pellets away from the roost. I have seen several Kestrels regurgitate pellets during the day, including one female that regularly used a roost where I found few pellets. How often Kestrels produce day-time pellets is not known, though Long-eared Owls fed radio-tagged mice were found to produce pellets frequently when hunting during winter (Wijnandts 1984). Pellets may also disintegrate before or after they are collected, and this can be another source of error because those with many invertebrate remains are more friable than those consisting mainly of fur.

Pellet samples can be stored for long periods if they are dried thoroughly and protected from moths. Drying to constant weight in a consistent manner allows pellet weights to be compared (Village 1982a). Pellets are usually measured (length and breadth) and weighed before being teased apart dry. Wetting pellets to separate fur and bones, as used sometimes on owl pellets, is not a useful method for Kestrels because it makes the fur matrix difficult to examine for invertebrate remains. Prey items can be identified by reference to keys that outline the diagnostic features of bones, fur or invertebrate exoskeleton (Day 1966, Yalden 1977, Yalden and Warburton 1979).

ANALYSIS OF STOMACH CONTENTS

This has been used to measure Kestrel diets in a few studies that had access to large samples of dead birds. Such samples were readily available when Kestrels were considered vermin and could be legally shot, but fortunately they are now better protected in most countries. This is not always so, however, and the activities of Italian 'sportsmen' have provided material for several more recent studies (Lovari 1974, Silvano 1981). The Pesticide Monitoring Scheme at Monks Wood, which autopsies birds of prey found dead by the public, has provided some stomach contents that are fairly fresh and only partly digested. These have shown that Kestrels may frequently eat soft-bodied arthropods, such as spiders, that rarely leave traces in pellets (N. J. Westwood).

SUMMARY

Pellet analysis is the most useful and widely applied method of assessing Kestrel diet. It suffers from some bias because Kestrel pellets are well digested and contain few remains of small or soft-bodied prey. Counting the number of items in pellets is more time consuming, and no more accurate, than recording the proportion of pellets in which various prey items occur.

Measuring the size of home ranges and territories

Although the concepts of home range and territory are easy enough to understand, it is necessary to be clear about their definition when trying to quantify them. The places visited by an animal will vary during the day, from day to day and over a whole season. The animal's total home range covered during the year will generally be larger than that used in a particular season, which in turn will be larger than that used in one day. When an individual suddenly moves into a new area, it is often difficult to tell if it has actually enlarged, or moved, its home range, or if it is simply visiting an infrequently used part of it. Errors arising from this can be reduced by measuring home ranges over standardised time-periods that are long enough for the occupant to have visited most of its current range. Kestrels can usually fly from one end of their home-range to the other in a few minutes, so they clearly have the capacity to cover much more ground than they do. Individuals usually visit most of their range in the course of a few days, and following them for a few weeks is normally long enough to discover all the areas they frequently use.

Territory can also be difficult to define. Strictly, it is the area defended against members of the same species, either by ritualised display, or by physical combat. However, such behaviour may be infrequent, especially when a population is stable, and the absence of overt defence does not necessarily mean that an individual is not territorial. Some workers have tried to measure Kestrel territories by using stuffed dummies, or live decoys, to elicit defensive attacks from wild birds (Cade 1955, Cavé

1968, C. G. Wiklund). Kestrels will sometimes attack dummies, but if they don't it may be because the latter are a poor substitute for the real thing. Live decoys are much more likely to evoke a response than stuffed ones, but measuring territory size in this way is too time consuming to use on more than a few pairs at a time.

An alternative approach is to define territory as that part of the home range that is used exclusively by one bird, or pair of birds (Pitelka 1959). The assumption here is that such exclusive areas exist because they are defended, even if such defence is rarely seen. This is probably true for Kestrels at all but very low population densities, and I found that the exclusive area of the home range was the best index of territory size for my purposes.

MARKING KESTRELS

One of the first problems I had to tackle when I started work on Kestrels was to find some way of marking them, so that they could be individually recognised in the field. A number of workers have tried to estimate the range-size of unmarked Kestrels (Craighead & Craighead 1956, Pettifor 1983b), but this has drawbacks that can bias the results. To make sense of the plotted locations of unmarked birds, it is usually necessary to assume that clusters of sightings are of the same bird. This may, or may not, be true. The problem is even greater for outlying points between clusters, especially if neighbouring birds are of the same age and sex and therefore look alike. The chance of misidentifying unmarked birds increases if ranges are large and overlap. It then becomes impossible to distinguish birds using the same place at different times, and the tendency is to assume there are non-overlapping ranges, irrespective of how the birds are actually behaving. Intensive observation of unmarked birds can give reasonable results where the ranges are small and birds are territorial (Pettifor 1983b), but only for small samples of individuals.

Most of the various methods for individual marking of birds have been used on Kestrels at one time or another. Numbered leg-rings are the best means of permanently marking large samples, and are normally used whatever additional methods are chosen. Obviously, they are of little use for range studies because the birds have to be retrapped to be identified. Coloured leg-rings or jesses are an improvement, but they are not entirely satisfactory on Kestrels because the ring is often hidden from sight, and can rarely be seen from close enough to distinguish colours. Researchers in America have used triangular-shaped jesses to mark American Kestrels (Meyer & Balgooyen 1987), and these are more easily seen. Dyes or notches cut into feathers (Enderson 1960) can also be used to make individual marks, but their life is limited to that of the feathers, and it is difficult to devise patterns for a large sample of birds. The best ways of marking Kestrels are wing-tags or radio transmitters.

Wing-tags of various shapes and sizes have been widely used on many bird species, and I was lucky to be able to draw on the experience of others when I started. I used soft tags made of the woven nylon cloth that is normally used to make waterproof sheets or sails. This is available in a variety of colours, which allows about 100 Kestrels of each sex to be marked individually using a single-colour tag on each wing. The tags were 20 x 50 mm, which was large enough to be easily seen with binoculars, but not so large as to interfere with flight in any way. Most Kestrels soon adjusted to these pliable tags, which they could preen into the wing-coverts. The tags were attached by passing a small nylon rod through the patagium (the thin flap of skin at the leading edge of the wing) and sealing it over nylon washers with a naked flame (Plate *). A soft washer under the wing prevented birds pulling the tag off, and virtually eliminated tag loss. Some tags became so badly frayed after a few years that they had to be replaced, though this seldom prevented me from identifying a bird in the field. Although some of the brighter colours bleach in hot sun, this was not a serious problem in my areas, given the typical British climate!

Another way of marking birds is to use radio transmitters. These are small electronic packages, weighing 2–4 g, which emit a pulsed signal at constant frequency. The signal is picked up by a directional aerial and a special receiver that can be tuned to the frequencies of several different transmitters. Radio-tagged individuals are then located by finding the direction of the strongest signal. Transmitters can be attached to birds by a body-harness or by sewing them into the tail feathers. I prefer the latter method, because it is less likely to interfere with flight. Sewing the transmitter onto the barb of a feather doesn't hurt the bird, and the transmitter sits comfortably on the base of the tail, with the short anntena lying along the central feathers. The transmitter is shed when the tail feathers are moulted in late summer and transmitters that are still functioning can sometimes be recovered.

Radio-tracking has advantages and disadvantages compared to wing-tagging. The most obvious benefit is that birds can be found whenever necessary and followed for long periods, even if they cannot be seen. Ranges can then be measured quickly and accurately, with less bias arising from differences in visibility across the terrain. Unfortunately, transmitters and receivers are expensive, and the cost per bird radio-tagged is several hundred times more than wing-tagging. Although transmitters can be recovered and reused after changing the battery, my recovery rates were usually less than 50%, and transmitters were likely to fail after being recycled several times. A second major disadvantage is the limited battery life, which is normally 3–4 months for the transmitters used on Kestrels.

Radio-tags are thus short-term marks compared with wing-tags, and can only be used on comparatively small samples. They are indispensable where birds are difficult to see, or where ranges have to be measured quickly and accurately. At Eskdalemuir, where the terrain was open, I used transmitters mainly to check the accuracy of ranges based solely on wing-tagging. In mixed farmland, however, Kestrels were more elusive, and I often used transmitters, particularly during winter removal-experiments (Chapter 8). In all cases, radio-tagged birds were also wing-tagged, so they could be identified even after the transmitter stopped working.

COLLECTING RANGE DATA

I collected range data either by spot observations, that is noting the location of each individual whenever I found it, or by following individuals continuously and recording each new place they visited. Sightings of unmarked birds were used only if I could reliably assign them to an individual that was tagged at a later date. This was fairly easy if most birds were marked already, because any unmarked arrivals could be distinguished from their neighbours. All observations were numerically coded by date, time, ring number, map reference and behaviour. I was fortunate to be able to do the analysis by computer, because in ten years I amassed over 15,000 records.

I also used spot observations when radio tracking, either moving from bird to bird after each was located, or taking radio-fixes 'at random' whenever I happened to be near the bird's range. At Eskdalemuir, I usually tried to find the bird by sight alone, and used the radio receiver only as a last resort. This gave two sets of locations for each radio-tagged bird: one based on sightings alone, and a longer list of radio locations which comprised all the sightings plus those locations when I could not find the bird by sight. Comparing these two lists enabled me to judge the accuracy of sightings, and so adjust the range estimates of birds that were wing-tagged only.

ESTIMATING RANGE SIZE FROM LOCATIONS

To compare ranges between years, I grouped sightings in to three seasons: autumn (October-November), winter (December-March) and summer (April-July). In Scot-

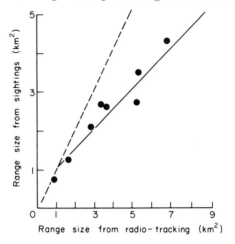

Fig. 85. Comparison of Kestrel home-range size as estimated from sightings of wing-tagged individuals with that obtained using radio-tracking (from Village 1982b). Each point represents a single Kestrel that was followed by sight and by radio telemetry over the same period. The broken line is the fit expected if sightings were as accurate as radio-telemetry. Sightings underestimated the 'true' range size when ranges were larger than about 2 km².

land, March locations had to be excluded because the sudden influx of birds made range boundaries unstable. Ranges in the breeding season were based on males, because females spent most of the time near their nest until the young were well grown. For each range I calculated the *Maximum Polygon Area* (MPA), which was the area enclosed when all the outer locations were joined to form a convex polygon. Although not all the area enclosed by the polygon may have been used by the bird, the MPA was easy to calculate and made no assumptions about the distribution of points in the range. This gave it an advantage over other indices of range size, which assume the range is either circular or elliptical and that the data points follow a particular statistical distribution.

Unfortunately, the MPA gave artificially low estimates of range size when there were only a few observations of a particular individual. I overcame this problem by correcting the range size of birds with less than 20 observations, using a correction factor based on the correlation of range size and number of sightings for birds with large numbers of sightings (Village 1982b). I excluded any bird seen less than ten times in any one season, as there was no way of accurately estimating ranges based on such limited data.

Even after correcting for lack of data points, some range sizes based on sightings were still underestimated because of the difficulty of finding birds not fitted with radios. A comparison of the estimated range size with the 'true' value, based on radio-locations, showed that the accuracy of the sightings estimate depended on range size. When ranges were less than 1 km², wing-tagging alone gave the correct result, but ranges of 7–8 km² were under-estimated by as much as 50% (Fig. 85). I was able to use the relationship of sightings to radio-location range size to correct the estimates of sightings ranges that were larger than 1 km².

Thus two corrections were sometimes needed to estimate the true range size: one for ranges based on less than 20 observations and another if the range was large and based solely on sightings. This highlights the difficulty of accurately measuring the range size of even such, apparently, easily seen birds as Kestrels. Fortunately, the corrections made little difference to the results given in Chapter 7, and the conclusions were not affected by applying these correction factors. They did, however, make the range sizes more realistic and allowed me to compare ranges from the different studies, even though the farmland estimates were based on more radio-tracking than those for Eskdalemuir.

Scientific names of vertebrates in the text

BIRDS

American Kestrel *Falco sparverius*
Australian Kestrel *Falco cenchroides*
Avocet *Recurvirostra avosetta*
Banded Kestrel *Falco zoniventris*
Barn Owl *Tyto alba*
Blackbird *Turdus merula*
Black-shouldered Kite *Elanus caeruleus*
Carrion Crow *Corvus corone*
Collared Dove *Streptopelia decaocto*
Common Buzzard *Buteo buteo*
Dickinson's Kestrel *Falco dickinsoni*
Eagle Owl *Bubo bubo*
European Kestrel *Falco tinnunculus*
Fox Kestrel *Falco alopex*
Goshawk *Accipiter gentilis*
Greater Kestrel *Falco rupicoloides*
Great Grey Owl *Strix nebulosa*
Great Tit *Parus major*
Green Woodpecker *Picus viridis*
Grey Kestrel *Falco ardioacius*
Hawk Owl *Surnia ulula*
Hen Harrier *Circus cyaneus*
Heron *Ardea cinerea*
Hobby *Falco subbuteo*
House Sparrow *Passer domesticus*
Jackdaw *Corvus monedula*
Lesser Kestrel *Falco naumanni*
Long-eared Owl *Asio otus*
Madagascan Kestrel *Falco newtoni*
Magpie *Pica pica*
Mauritius Kestrel *Falco punctatus*
Meadow Pipit *Anthus pratensis*
Merlin *Falco columbarius*
Moluccan Kestrel *Falco moluccensis*
Peregrine Falcon *Falco peregrinus*
Pheasant *Phasianus colchicus*
Pygmy Owl *Glaucidium passerinum*
Red-headed Falcon *Falco chicquera*
Red-footed Falcon *Falco vesperinus*
Rook *Corvus frugilegus*
Rough-legged Buzzard *Buteo lagopus*
Seychelles Kestrel *Falco araea*
Short-eared Owl *Asio flammeus*
Skylark *Alauda arvensis*
Snowy Owl *Nyctea scandiaca*
Song Thrush *Turdus philomelos*
Sparrowhawk *Accipiter nisus*
Starling *Sturnus vulgaris*

Stock Dove *Columba livia*
Tawny Owl *Strix aluco*
Tengmalm's Owl *Aegolius funereus*
Turtle Dove *Streptopelia turtur*
Ural Owl *Strix uralensis*
Woodpigeon *Columba palumbus*

MAMMALS

Bank Vole *Clethrionomys glareolus*
Common Shrew *Sorex araneus*
Common Vole *Microtus arvalis*
Grey Squirrel *Sciurus carloinensis*
Fox *Vulpes vulpes*
Hare *Lepus europaeus*
Harvest Mouse *Micromys minutus*
House Mouse *Mus musculus*
Mole *Talpa europaea*
Pygmy Shrew *Sorex minutus*
Short-tailed Vole *Microtus agrestis*
Stoat *Mustela erminea*
Rabbit *Oryctolagus cuniculus*
Water Shrew *Neomys fodiens*
Water Vole *Arvicola amphibius*
Weasel *Mustela nivalis*
White-toothed Shrew *Crocidura russula*
Woodmouse *Apodemus sylvaticus*

REPTILES

Slow Worm *Anguis fragilis*

AMPHIBIANS

Common Toad *Bufo bufo*

Bibliography

ADAIR, P. 1891 & 1893. The Short-eared Owl and the Kestrel in the vole plague districts. *Ann. Scot. Nat. Hist. Soc.* 6: 219–231 & 8:193–202.

ARAUJO, J. 1974. Falconiformes del Guadarrama. *Ardeola* 19: 250–277.

BALFOUR, E. 1955. Kestrels nesting on the ground in Orkney. *Bird Notes* 26: 245–253.

BALGOOYEN, T. G. 1976. Behaviour and ecology of the American Kestrel (*Falco sparverius*) in the Sierra Nevada of California. *Univ. Calif. Publ. Zool.* 103: 1–83.

BANG, J. 1986. (Results of erecting nest-boxes for Kestrels *Falco tinnunculus*). *Dansk. Orn. Foren. Tidsskr.* 80: 23–28.

BATTEN, L. A. 1959. Kestrel catching a fish. *Br. Birds* 52: 314.

BEICHLE, U. 1980. Siedlungsdichte, Jagdreviere und Jagdweise des Turmfalken (*Falco tinnunculus*) im Stadtgebiet von Kiel. *Corax* 8: 3–12.

BERNDT, R. 1970. Zur Bestandsentwicklung der Greifvögel (Falconiformes) in Drömling. *Beitr. Vogelkunde* 16: 3–12.

BEUKEBOOM, L., DIJKSTRA, C., DAAN, S. & MEIJER, T. 1988. Seasonality of clutch size determination in the kestrel *Falco tinnunculus*: an experimental approach. *Ornis Scand.* 19: 41–48.

BIRD, D. M. & LAGUE, P. C. 1982. The influence of forced re-nesting, seasonal date of laying and female characteristics on clutch size and egg traits in captive American Kestrels. *Canad. J. Zool.* 60: 71–79.

BIRD, D. M., WEIL, P. G. & LAGUE, P. C. 1980. Photoperiodic induction of multiple breeding seasons in captive American Kestrels. *Canad. J. Zool.* 58: 1022–1026.

BLAKE, E. R. 1977. *Manual of neotropical birds*. Vol. 1. Chicago: University Press.

BONIN, B. & STRENNA, L. 1986. Sur la biologie du Faucon Crécerelle *Falco tinnunculus* en Auxois. *Alauda* 54: 241- 262.

BOWMAN, R. & BIRD, D. M. 1985. Reproductive performance of wild American Kestrels laying replacement clutches. *Canad. J. Zool.* 63: 71–79.

BOYCE, D. A. & WHITE, C. W. 1987. Evolutionary aspects of Kestrel systematics: A scenario. Pp. 1–21 in '*The Ancestral Kestrel*', ed. D. M. Bird & R. Bowman. Quebec: Raptor Res. Found., Inc.

BROGMUS, H. 1966. Kältewinter und Greifvögel. *Tier und Umwelt* 3: 1–36.

BROWN, L. H. 1976. *British birds of prey*. London: Collins.

BROWN, L. H. & AMADON, D. 1968. *Eagles, hawks and falcons of the world*. London: Country Life Books.

BROWN, L. H., URBAN, E. K. & NEWMAN, K. 1982. *The Birds of Africa*. Vol. 1. London: Academic Press.

BURTON, P. J. K. 1986. Raptor and owl nestbox scheme and survey, 1986. (*unpublished manuscript*).

CADE, T. J. 1955. Experiments on winter territoriality of the American Kestrel (*Falco sparverius*). *Wilson Bull.* 67: 5–17.

CADE, T. J. 1982. *The falcons of the world.* London: Collins.

CAVÉ, A. J. 1968. The breeding of the kestrel, *Falco tinnunculus* L., in the reclaimed area Oostelijk Flevoland. *Netherlands J. Zool.* 18: 313–407.

CLEGG, J. 1971. Kestrel hoarding food. *Scott. Birds* 6: 276- 277.

COLLOPY, M. W. 1977. Food caching by female American Kestrels in winter. *Condor* 79: 63–68.

COOKE, A. S., BELL, A. A. & HAAS, M. B. 1982. *Predatory birds, pesticides and pollution.* Cambridge: Institute of Terrestrial Ecology.

CRAIGHEAD, J. J. & CRAIGHEAD, F. C. 1956. *Hawks, owls and wildlife.* Pennsylvania: Stackpole Co.

CRAMP, S. 1985. *The birds of the Western Palearctic.* Vol. 4. Oxford: University Press.

CRAMP, S. & SIMMONS, K. E. L. 1980. *The birds of the Western Palearctic.* Vol. 2. Oxford: University Press.

CRICHTON, J. 1977. *The pellet analysis technique as a method of investigating the food habits of the kestrel.* University of Edinburgh: Honours thesis.

DAAN, S. & SLOPSEMA, S. 1978. Short-term rhythms in foraging behaviour of the Common Vole, *Microtus arvalis. J. comp. Physiol.* 127: 215–227.

DARLINGTON, P. J. 1957. *Zoogeography: The geographical distributions of animals.* New York: John Wiley & Sons Inc.

DAVIS, T. A. W. 1975. Food of the Kestrel in winter and early spring. *Bird Study* 22: 85–91.

DAWSON, A. & GOLDSMITH, A. R. 1982. Prolactin and gonadotrophin secretion in wild starlings (*Sturnus vulgaris*) during the annual cycle and in relation to nesting, incubation and rearing young. *Gen. comp. Endocrinol.* 48: 213–221.

DAWSON, A, NICHOLLS, T. J., GOLDSMITH, A. R. & FOLLET, B. K. 1989. Comparative endocrinology of photorefractoriness. *Proc. Int. Orn. Congr.*, Ottawa, 1986.

DAY, M. G. 1966. Identification of hair and feather remains in the gut and faeces of Stoats and Weasels. *J. Zool., Lond.* 148: 210–217.

DEMENTIEV, G. P. & GLADKOV, N. A. 1954. (*Birds of the Soviet Union.* Vol. 1). Moscow: State Publishing House.

DIJKSTRA, C. 1988. *Reproductive tactics in the Kestrel* Falco tinnunculus. University of Groningen: PhD thesis.

DIJKSTRA, C., VUURSTEEN, L., DAAN, S. & MASMAN, D. 1982. Clutch size and laying date in the kestrel *Falco tinnunculus*: effect of supplementary food. *Ibis* 124: 210- 213.

DOBBS, A. 1982. Kestrels breeding in Nottinghamshire, 1979- 81. *Birds of Nottinghamshire Ann. Rept. 1981* 32–35.

DRENT, R. H. & DAAN, S. 1980. The prudent parent: energetic adjustments in avian breeding. *Ardea* 68: 225–252.

DUKE, G. E., EVANSON, O. A. & JEGERS, A. 1976. Meal to pellet interval in 14 species of captive raptor. *Comp. Biochem. Physiol.* 53A: 1–6.

DUNCAN, J. R. & BIRD, D. M. 1989. The influence of relatedness and display effort on the mate choice of captive female American Kestrels. *Anim. Behav.* 37: 112–117.

ENDERSON, J. H. 1960. A population study of the Sparrowhawk in east-central Illinois. *Wilson Bull.* 72: 222–231.

EVANS, P. R. & LATHBURY, G. W. 1973. Raptor migration across the Strait of Gibraltar. *Ibis* 105: 572–587.

FAIRLEY, J. S. 1973. Kestrel pellets from a winter roost. *Irish Nat. J.* 17: 407–409.

FAIRLEY, J. S. & McLEAN, A. 1965. Notes on the summer food of the kestrel in Northern Ireland. *Br. Birds* 58: 145- 148.

FENNEL, C. M. 1954. Notes on the nesting of the kestrel in Japan. *Condor* 56: 106–107.

FRERE, H. T. 1886. Changes in the plumage of the kestrel. *Zoologist* 1886: 180.

FUCHS, E. 1980. Greifvogelbestandsaufnahmen im aargauischen Reusstal. *Orn. Beob.* 77: 73–78.

GARŻON, J. 1974. Las Falconiformes en Espana Central. *Ardeola* 19: 278–329.

GATTER, W. 1972. (Systematic observations of autumnal migration of birds of prey across the Randecker Maar, Suabian Alb.) *Anz. orn. Ges. Bayern* 11: 194–209.

GLUE, D. E. 1971. Ringing circumstances of small birds of prey. *Bird Study* 18: 137–146.

GLUTZ von BLOTZHEIM, U. N., BAUER, K. & BEZZEL, E. 1971. *Handbuch der Vögel Mitteleuropas.* Vol. 4. Frankfurt am Main: Akademische Verlagsgesellschaft.

GRIFFITHS, M. E. 1967. The population density of Kestrels in Leicestershire. *Bird Study* 14: 184–190.

HAGEN, Y. 1952. *Rovfuglene og Viltpleien.* Oslo: Gyldendal Norsk Forlag.

HAGEN, Y. 1969. (Norwegian studies on the reproduction of birds of prey and owls in relation to micro-rodent population fluctuations.) *Fauna* 22: 73–76.

HAMERSTROM, F. 1969. A harrier population study. Pp. 367–385 in *'Peregrine Falcon populations: their biology and decline.'* ed. J. J. Hickey. Madison, Milwaukee & London: Univ. Wisconsin Press.

HAMERSTROM, F., HAMERSTROM, F. N. & HART, J. 1973. Nestboxes: an effective management tool for kestrels. *J. Wildl. Manage.* 37: 400–403.

HARTLEY, P. H. T. 1946. The food of the kestrel in Palestine. *Ibis* 88: 241–242.

HASENCLEVER, H., KOSTRZEWA, A. & KOSTRZEWA, R. 1989. (The breeding biology of the kestrel *Falco tinnunculus* in eastern Westfalia, 1972–87.) *J. Orn.* 129: 229–237.

HASS, G. 1961. Federsee-Jahresbericht, 1960. *Anz. Orn. Ges. Bayern* 6: 157–161.

HAURI, R. 1960. Siedlungsdichte beim Turmfalken *Falco tinnunculus*. *Orn. Beob.* 57: 69–73.

HENNY, C. J. 1972. An analysis of the population dynamics of selected avian species. *Bureau of Sport, Fisheries & Wildlife Res. Rep. 1* Washington DC: Govt. Printer.

HILL, D. 1988. Population dynamics of the avocet (*Recurvirostra avosetta*) breeding in Britain. *J. Anim. Ecol.* 57: 669–683.

HYUGA, I. 1956. (Breeding colonies of Japanese Kestrels.) *Tori* 14: 17–24.

ITÄMIES, J. & KORPIMÄKI, E. 1987. Insect food of the kestrel, *Falco tinnunculus*, during breeding in western Finland. *Aquilo Ser. Zool.* 25: 21–31.

JEFFERIES, D. J. & FRENCH, M. C. 1976. Mercury, cadmium, zinc, copper and organochlorine insecticide levels in small mammals trapped in a wheat field. *Environ. Pollut.* 10: 175–182.

JONES, C. G. 1986. *The biology of the critically endangered birds of Mauritius.* University College Swansea: M.Sc. Thesis.

JONES, C. G. & OWADALLY, A. W. 1985. The status, ecology and conservation of the Mauritius Kestrel. *ICBP Technical Publication No 5:* 211–222.

KEMP, A. C. 1978. Territory maintenance and use by breeding Greater Kestrels. Pp. 71–76 in *Proc. Symp. African Predatory Birds.* Pretoria: Northern Transvaal Ornithol. Soc.

KEYMER, I. F., FLETCHER, M. R. & STANLEY, P. I. 1981. Cause of mortality in British Kestrels (*Falco tinnunculus*). Pp. 143–151 in *'Recent advances in the study of raptor diseases.'* eds. J. E. Cooper & A. G. Greenwood. Keighley: Chiron Publications.

KIRKWOOD, J. K. 1980a. Energy and prey requirements of the young free-flying kestrel. *Hawk Trust Ann. Rep.* 10: 12–14.

KIRKWOOD, J. K. 1980b. Management of a colony of Common Kestrels (*Falco tinnunculus*) in captivity. *Laboratory Animals* 14: 313–316.

KIRKWOOD, J. K. 1981a. Maintenance energy requirements and rate of weight loss during starvation in birds of prey. Pp. 153- 157 in *'Recent advances in the study of raptor diseases.'* eds. J. E. Cooper & A. G. Greenwood. Keighley: Chiron Publications.

KIRKWOOD, J. K. 1981b. *Bioenergetics and growth in the kestrel* (Falco tinnunculus). University of Bristol: PhD thesis.

KIRKWOOD, J. K. 1981c. Energy and nitrogen exchanges during growth in the kestrel (*Falco tinnunculus*). *Proc. Nutr. Soc.* 40: 6.

KOCHANEK, H-M. 1984. (Notices to the breeding biology of the kestrel *Falco tinnunculus*). *Die Vogelwelt* 105: 201–219.

KOPLIN, J. 1973. Differential habitat use by sexes of American Kestrels wintering in Northern California. *Raptor Res.* 7: 39–42.

KORPIMÄKI, E. 1983. (Results of the experimentation in nestboxes of the kestrel *Falco tinnunculus*). *Lintumies* 18: 132–137.

KORPIMÄKI, E. 1984. Food piracy between European Kestrel and Short-eared Owl. *Raptor Res.* 18: 113–115.

KORPIMÄKI, E. 1985a. Diet of the Kestrel *Falco tinnunculus* during the breeding season. *Ornis Fenn.* 62: 130–137.

KORPIMÄKI, E. 1985b. Rapid tracking of microtine populations by their avain predators: possible evidence for stabilizing predation. *Oikos* 45: 281–284.

KORPIMÄKI, E. 1986a. Reversed size dimorphism in birds of prey, especially Tengmalm's Owl *Aegolius funereus*: a test of the "starvation hypothesis". *Ornis Scand.* 17: 326–332.

KORPIMÄKI, E. 1986b. Diet variation, hunting habitat and reproductive output of the kestrel *Falco tinnunculus* in the light of optimal diet theory. *Ornis Fenn.* 63: 84–90.

KORPIMÄKI, E. 1986c. Niche relationships and life-history tactics of three sympatric *Strix* owl species in Finland. *Ornis Scand.* 17: 126–132.

KORPIMÄKI, E. 1987. Selection for nest-hole shift and tactics of breeding dispersal in Teng-malm's owl *Aegolius funereus. J. Anim. Ecol.* 56: 185–196.

KORPIMÄKI, E., IKOLA, S., & HAAPOJA, R. 1979. (Food requirements and weight develop-ment of nestling kestrels). *Lintumies* 14: 49–53.

KOSTRZEWA, R. 1988. (Density of kestrels (*Falco tinnunculus*) in Europe: a review and some critical comments.) *Die Vogelwarte* 34: 216–224.

KOSTRZEWA, R. & KOSTRZEWA, A. 1987. (Biometic measurements of juvenile kestrels *Falco tinnunculus* – a key for ageing). *Ökol. Vögel (Ecol. Birds)* 9: 119–125.

KULGAWCZUK, I. 1962. (The faculty of colour-discrimination in the kestrel). *Zeszytynaukowe uniwersttetu Jagiellonskiego 1962:* 217–233.

KURTH, D. 1970. Der Turmfalke (*Falco tinnunculus*) im Münchener Stadtgebiet. *Anz. orn. Ges. Bayern* 9: 2–12.

KUUSELA, S. 1979. Tuulihaukka lekuttelee sinnikkäästi. *Suomen Luonto* 38: 162–165.

KUUSELA, S. & SOLONEN, T. 1984. The growth of kestrel nestlings in Southern Finland. *Ann. Zool. Fennici* 21: 309- 312.

LACK, D. 1951. Population ecology of birds. *Proc. Int. Orn. Congr.* 10: 409–448.

LACK, D. 1966. *Population studies of birds.* Oxford: University Press.

LAKHANI, K. H. & NEWTON, I. 1983. Estimating age-specific bird survival rates from ring recoveries- can it be done? *J. Anim. Ecol.* 52: 83–91.

LESHEM, Y. 1984. Kestrels on your windowsill. *Israel- Land and Nature* 10: 16–23.

LINCER, J. L. 1975. DDE-induced eggshell-thinning in the American kestrel: a comparison of the field situation and laboratory results. *J. Appl. Ecol.* 12: 781–793.

LOVARI, S. 1974. The feeding habits of four raptors in central Italy. *Raptor Res.* 8: 45–47.

MACARTHUR, R. H. & WILSON, E. O. 1967. *The theory of island biogeography.* Princeton: University Press.

MACMILLAN, A. T. 1969. Scottish bird report for 1968. *Scott. Birds* 5: 319.

MAKATSCH, W. 1974. *Die Eier der Vögel Europas.* Melsungen: Neumann-Neudamm.

MARQUISS, M. 1980. Habitat and diet of male and female Hen Harriers in Scotland in winter. *Br. Birds* 73: 555–560.

MARQUISS, M. & NEWTON, I. 1982a. A radio-tracking study of the ranging behaviour and dispersion of European Sparrowhawks *Accipiter nisus. J. Anim. Ecol.* 51: 111–133.

MARQUISS, M. & NEWTON, I. 1982b. Habitat preference in male and female Sparrowhawks. *Ibis* 124: 324–328.

MÄRZ, B. 1949. Der Raubvögel und Eulenbestand einer Kontrollfläche des Elbsandsteingebirges in den Jahren 1932–1940. *Beitr. Vogelkunde* 1: 116–146.

MASMAN, D. 1986. *The annual cycle of the kestrel,* Falco tinnunculus, *a study in behavioural energetics.* University of Groningen: PhD thesis.

MASMAN, D. & DAAN, S. 1987. The allocation of energy in the annual cycle of the kestrel, *Falco tinnunculus.* Pp. 124- 136 in '*The Ancestral Kestrel*', ed. D. M. Bird & R. Bowman. Quebec: Raptor Res. Found., Inc.

MASMAN, D., DAAN, S. & BELDHUIS, J. A. 1988a. Ecological energetics of the kestrel: daily energy expenditure throughout the year based on the time-budget, food intake and doubly labelled water methods. *Ardea* 76: 64–81.

MASMAN, D., DAAN, S. & DIJKSTRA, C. 1988b. Time allocation in the kestrel (*Falco tinnunculus*), and the principle of energy minimization. *J. Anim. Ecol.* 57: 411–432.

MASMAN, D., GORDIJN, M., DAAN, S. & DIJKSTRA, C. 1986. Bioenergetics of the kestrel, *Falco tinnunculus:* the variability of natural intake rates. *Ardea* 74: 24–38.

MASMAN, D. & KLAASSEN, M. 1987. Energy expenditure during free flight in trained and free-living Eurasian Kestrels (*Falco tinnunculus*). *Auk* 104: 603–616.

MEAD, C. J. 1973. Movements of British Raptors. *Bird Study* 20: 259–286.

MEIJER, T. 1988. *Reproductive decisions in the kestrel* Falco tinnunculus. University of Groningen: PhD thesis.

MENDELSOHN, J. M. 1983. Social behaviour and dispersion of the Blackshouldered Kite. *Ostrich* 54: 1–18.

MESTER, H. 1980. Uber die Paarbildung und das Sexualverhalten des Turmfalken (*Falco tinnunculus*). *Orn. Mitt.* 32: 150–152.

MEYER, R. L. & BALGOOYEN, T. G. 1987. A study and implications of habitat separation by sex of wintering American Kestrels (*Falco sparverius* L.). Pp. 107–123 in '*The Ancestral Kestrel*', ed. D. M. Bird & R. Bowman. Quebec: Raptor Res. Found., Inc.

MILLS, G. S. 1976. American kestrel sex ratios and habitat selection. *Auk* 93: 740–748.

MONTIER, D. 1968. Breeding distribution of the Kestrel, Barn Owl and Tawny Owl in the London area in 1967. *London Bird Rep.* 32: 81–92.

MORBACH, J. 1963. *Vögel der Heimat*, Vol. 5.

MOSS, D. 1979. Growth of nestling Sparrowhawks (*Accipiter nisus*). *J. Zool., Lond.* 187: 297–314.

NEWTON, I. 1979. *Population ecology of raptors*. Berkhamsted: Poyser.

NEWTON, I. 1985. Lifetime reproductive output of female Sparrowhawks. *J. Anim. Ecol.* 54: 241–253.

NEWTON, I. 1986. *The Sparrowhawk*. Carlton: Poyser.

NEWTON, I., BELL, A. & WYLLIE, I. 1982. Mortality of Sparrowhawks and Kestrels. *Br. Birds* 75: 195–204.

NEWTON, I. & MARQUISS, M. 1982a. Food, predation and breeding season in Sparrowhawks (*Accipiter nisus*). *J. Zool., Lond.* 197: 221–240.

NEWTON, I. & MARQUISS, M. 1982b. Moult in the Sparrowhawk. *Ardea* 70: 163–172.

NEWTON, I. & MARQUISS, M. 1984. Seasonal trend in the breeding performance of sparrowhawks. *J. Anim. Ecol.* 53: 809–829.

NEWTON, I., MARQUISS, M. & MOSS, D. 1981. Age and breeding in sparrowhawks. *J. Anim. Ecol.* 50: 839–853.

NEWTON, I., MARQUISS, M. & ROTHERY, P. 1983a. Age structure and survival in a sparrowhawk population. *J. Anim. Ecol.* 52: 591–602.

NEWTON, I., MARQUISS, M. & VILLAGE, A. 1983b. Weights, breeding and survival in European Sparrowhawks. *Auk* 100: 344–354.

NIELSEN, B. P. 1983. (Migratory behaviour and dispersal of Danish kestrels *Falco tinnunculus*). *Dansk. Orn. Foren. Tidsskr.* 77: 1–12.

NOER, H. & SECHER, H. 1983. Survival of Danish Kestrels *Falco tinnunculus* in relation to protection of birds of prey. *Ornis Scand.* 14: 104–114.

NORÉ, T. 1979. Rapaces diurnes communs en Limousin pendant la periode de nidification. *Alauda* 47: 259–269.

O'CONNOR, R. 1982. Habitat occupancy and regulation of clutch size in the European Kestrel *Falco tinnunculus*. *Bird Study* 29: 17–26.

OSBORNE, P. 1982. Some effects of Dutch elm disease on nesting farmland birds. *Bird Study* 29: 2–16.

OSBORNE, T. O. & COLEBROOK-ROBJENT, J. F. R. I. 1982. Nesting of the Greater Kestrel *Falco rupicoloides* in Zambia. *Raptor Res.* 16: 71–76.

PACKHAM, C. 1985a. Bigamy by the kestrel. *Br. Birds* 78: 194.

PACKHAM, C. 1985b. Role of male kestrel during incubation. *Br. Birds* 78: 144.

PARR, D. 1969. A review of the status of the Kestrel, Tawny Owl and Barn Owl in Surrey. *Surrey Bird Rep. (1967)* 15: 35–42.

PETER, H-U. 1983. Turmfalke- *Falco tinnunculus* L. Pp. 29–36 in 'Berichte zur Avifauna des Bezirkes Gera'. Herausgeber: Kulturbund der DDR, BFA Ornithologie Gera.

PETER, H-U., & ZAUMSEIL, J. 1982. (Population ecology of the Kestrel (*Falco tinnunculus*) in a colony near Jena). *Ber. Vogelwarte Hiddensee* 3: 5–17.

PETTERSSON, J. 1977. (Owls and raptors at Kvismaren, 1956-76). *Vår Fågelvärld* 36: 129–133.

PETTIFOR, R. A. 1983a. Seasonal variation, and associated energetic implications, in the hunting behaviour of the Kestrel. *Bird Study* 30: 201–206.

PETTIFOR, R. A. 1983b. Territorial behaviour of Kestrels in arable fenland. *Br. Birds* 76: 206–214.

PETTY, S. J. 1985. A negative response of Kestrels *Falco tinnunculus* to nestboxes in upland forests. *Bird Study* 32: 194–195.

PHELAN, F. J. S. & ROBERTSON, R. J. 1978. Predatory responses of a raptor guild to changes in prey density. *Canad. J. Zool.* 56: 2565–2572.

PICOZZI, N. 1984. Sex ratio, survival and territorial behaviour of polygynous Hen Harriers *Circus c. cyaneus* in Orkney. *Ibis* 126: 356–365.

PICOZZI, N. & HEWSON, R. 1970. Kestrels, Short-eared Owls and Field Voles in Eskdalemuir in 1970. *Scott. Birds* 6: 185–191.

PIECHOCKI, R. 1982. *Der Turmfalke*. Wittenberg: Lutherstadt Ziemsen Verlag.

PIKE, G. V. 1979. Kestrels in the Birmingham area. *West Midland Bird Rep. (1978)* 45: 23–25.

PIKE, G. V. 1981. Nesting kestrels tolerating excessive disturbance. *Br. Birds* 74: 520.

PIKULA, J., BEKLOVÁ, M. & KUBÍK, V. 1984. The nidobiology of *Falco tinnunculus*. *Acta Sc. Nat. Brno* 18: 1–55.

PITELKA, F. A. 1959. Numbers, breeding schedule and territoriality in pectoral sandpipers in Northern Alaska. *Condor* 61: 233–264.

PIZZEY, G. 1980. *A Field Guide to the Birds of Australia*. Sydney: Collins.

PORTER, R. D. & WIEMEYER, S. N. 1972. Reproductive patterns in captive American Kestrels (Sparrow Hawks). *Condor* 74: 46–53.

PRESTT, I. 1965. An enquiry into the recent breeding status of some of the smaller birds of prey and crows in Britain. *Bird Study* 12: 196–221.

RAPTOR GROUP RUG/RIJP. 1982. Timing of vole hunting in aerial predators. *Mammal Rev.* 12: 169–181.

RATCLIFFE, D. 1980. *The Peregrine Falcon.* Calton: Poyser.

REICHHOLF, J. 1977. (Long-term and seasonal changes in the abundance of the kestrel). *Anz. orn. Ges. Bayern* 16: 191–196.

RICHARDS, B. A. 1947. Crustacean remains in pellets of kestrel. *Br. Birds* 40: 152.

RICKLEFS, R. E. 1967. A graphical method of fitting equations to growth curves. *Ecology* 48: 978–983.

RIDDLE, G. S. 1979. The Kestrel in Ayrshire 1970–78. *Scott. Birds* 10: 201–215.

RIDDLE, G. S. 1985. Kestrels attending oil instalations in the North Sea. *North Sea Bird Club Rep. (1985)*: 63–70.

RIDDLE, G. S. 1987. Variation in the breeding output of kestrel pairs in Ayrshire 1978–85. *Scott. Birds* 14: 138- 145.

RIJNSDORP, A., DAAN, S. & DIJKSTRA, C. 1981. Hunting in the kestrel, *Falco tinnunculus*, and the adaptive significance of daily habits. *Oecologia* 50: 391–406.

ROCKENBAUCH, D. 1968. Zur Brutbiologie des Turmfalken (*Falco tinnunculus* L.). *Anz. orn. Ges. Bayern* 8: 267–276.

RUDOLF, S. G. 1982. Foraging strategies of American Kestrels during breeding. *Ecology* 63: 1268–1276.

SCHIFFERLI, A. 1964. Lebensdauer, Sterblichkeit und Todesursachen beim Turmfalken, *Falco tinnunculus*. *Orn. Beob.* 61: 81–89.

SCHIFFERLI, A. 1965. Vom Zugverhalten der in der Schweiz brütenden Turmfalken, *Falco tinnunculus*, nach den Ringfunden. *Orn Beob.* 62: 1–13.

SCHUSTER, S. & WERNER, H. 1977. Der Greifvogelbestand des Bodanrücks. *Anz. orn. Ges. Bayern* 16: 10–17.

SEAGO, M. J. 1967. *The Birds of Norfolk.* Norwich: Jarrold.

SHRUBB, M. 1970. The present status of the Kestrel in Sussex. *Bird Study* 17: 1–15.

SHRUBB, M. 1980. Farming influences on the food and hunting of the Kestrel. *Bird Study* 30: 201–206.

SHRUBB, M. 1982. The hunting behaviour of some farmland Kestrels. *Bird Study* 29: 121–128.

SHUTT, L. & BIRD, D. M. 1985. Influence of nestling experience on nest-type selection in captive kestrels. *Anim. Behav.* 33: 1028–1031.

SILVANO, F. 1981. Note sull'alimentazione del Gheppio nell'Italia Nord-occidentale. *Riv. Piem. St. Nat.* 2: 231- 235.

SIMMONS, R. BARNARD, P. MACWHIRTER, B. & HANSEN, G. L. 1986. The influence of microtines on polygyny, productivity, age and provisioning of breeding Northern Harriers: a 5-year study. *Canad. J. Zool.* 64: 2447–2456.

SIMMS, C. 1961. Indications of the food of the Kestrel in the upland districts of Yorkshire. *Bird Study* 8: 148–151.

SMALLWOOD, J. A. 1988. A mechanism for sexual segregation by habitat in American Kestrels (*Falco sparverius*) wintering in south-central Florida. *Auk* 105: 36–46.

SMITH, D. G., WILSON, C. R. & FROST, H. H. 1972. The biology of the American Kestrel in central Utah. *Southwest Nat.* 17: 73–83.

SMYTHIES, B. E. 1960. *The Birds of Borneo.* Edinburgh: Oliver & Boyd.

SNOW, D. W. 1968. Movements and mortality of British Kestrels. *Bird Study* 15: 65–83.

SNOW, D. W. 1978. *An atlas of speciation in African non-passerine birds.* London: British Museum of Natural History.

SOUTHERN, H. N. 1970. The natural control of a population of Tawny Owls (*Strix aluco*). *J. Zool., Lond.* 162: 197–285.

STINSON, C. H., CRAWFORD, D. L. & LANTHNER, J. 1981. Sex differences in winter habitat of American Kestrels in Georgia. *J. Field Ornithol.* 52: 29–35.

TARBOTON, W. R. 1978. Hunting and the energy budget of the Black-shouldered Kite. *Condor* 80: 88–111.

TAYLOR, S. M. 1967. Breeding status of the kestrel. *Proc. Bristol Nat. Soc.* 31–33: 293–296.

THIOLLAY, J. M. 1963. Notes sur le régime alimentaire du Faucon Crécerelle *Falco tinnunculus* en hiver. *Nos Oiseaux* 27: 71–73.

THIOLLAY, J. M. 1968a. Le régime alimentaire de nos rapaces: quelques analyses Françaises. *Nos Oiseaux* 29: 251–269.

THIOLLAY, J. M. 1968b. Notes sur les rapaces diurnes de Corse. *L'Oiseau* 38: 187–208.

THOMSON, A. L. 1958. The migrations of British falcons (Falconidae) as shown by ringing results. *Br. Birds* 51: 179–188.

TINBERGEN, L. 1940. Beobachtungen über die Arbeitsteilung des Turmfalken (*Falco tinnunculus*) während der Fortpflanzungszeit. *Ardea* 29: 63–98.

ULFSTRAND, S., ROOS, G., ALERSTAM, T. & ÖSTERDAHL, L. 1974. Visible bird migration at Falsterbo, Sweden. *Vår Fågelvärld suppl.* 8.

VIDELER, J. J., WEIHS, D. & DAAN, S. 1983. Intermittent gliding in the hunting flight of the kestrel *Falco tinnunculus* L. *J. exp. Biol.* 102: 1–12.

VILLAGE, A. 1980. *The ecology of the kestrel* (Falco tinnunculus) *in relation to vole abundance at Eskdalemuir, south Scotland*. Edinburgh University: Ph.D. thesis.

VILLAGE, A. 1981. The diet and breeding of Long-eared Owls in relation to vole abundance. *Bird Study* 28: 129–138.

VILLAGE, A. 1982a. The diet of kestrels in relation to vole abundance. *Bird Study* 29: 129–138.

VILLAGE, A. 1982b. The home range and density of kestrels in relation to vole abundance. *J. Anim. Ecol.* 51: 413–428.

VILLAGE, A. 1983a. Seasonal changes in the hunting behaviour of kestrels. *Ardea* 71: 117–124.

VILLAGE, A. 1983b. The role of nest-site availability and territorial behaviour in limiting the breeding density of kestrels. *J. Anim. Ecol.* 52: 635–645.

VILLAGE, A. 1983c. Body weights of kestrels during the breeding cycle. *Ringing and Migration* 4: 167–174.

VILLAGE, A. 1984. Problems in estimating kestrel breeding density. *Bird Study* 31: 121–125.

VILLAGE, A. 1985a. Spring arrival times and assortative mating of kestrels in south Scotland. *J. Anim. Ecol.* 54: 857–868.

VILLAGE, A. 1985b. Turnover, age and sex ratios of kestrels in south Scotland. *J. Zool., Lond.* 206: 175–189.

VILLAGE, A. 1986. Breeding performance of kestrels at Eskdalemuir, south Scotland. *J. Zool., Lond.* 208: 367–378.

VILLAGE, A. 1987a. Numbers, territory-size and turnover of Short-eared Owls *Asio flammeus* in relation to vole abundance. *Ornis. Scand.* 18: 198–204.

VILLAGE, 1987b. Population regulation in kestrels. Pp. 28–42 in '*The Ancestral Kestrel*', ed. D. M. Bird & R. Bowman. Quebec: Raptor Res. Found., Inc.

VILLAGE, A., MARQUISS, M. & COOK, D. C. 1980. Moult, ageing and sexing of kestrels. *Ringing and Migration* 3: 53–59.

WALLIN, K., JÄRÅS, T., LEVIN, M., STRANDVIK, P. & WALLIN, M. 1983. Reduced adult survival and increased reproduction in Swedish Kestrels. *Oecologia* 60: 302–305.

WALLIN, K., WALLIN, M. L., JÄRÅS, T. & STRANDVIK, P. 1987. Leap-frog migration in the Swedish Kestrel *Falco tinnunculus* population. Pp. 213–222 in '*Proceedings of the Fifth Nordic Ornithological Congress, 1985.*' ed. M. O. G. Eriksson. Goteborg: Kungl. Vetenskaps- och Vitterhets-Samhallet.

WASSENICH, V. 1965. Der Bestand von Mausebussard und Turmfalke in Luxemburg. *Regulus* 8: 24–35.

WATSON, A. 1957. The behaviour, breeding and food-ecology of the Snowy Owl *Nyctea Scandiaca*. *Ibis* 99: 419–462.

WATSON, J. 1981. *Population ecology, food and conservation of the Seychelles Kestrel* (Falco araea) *on Mahé*. University of Aberdeen: PhD thesis.

WENDLAND, V. 1953. Populationsstudien an Raubvögeln II. *J. Orn.* 94: 103–113.

WIJNANDTS, H. 1984. Ecological energetics of the Long-eared Owl (*Asio otus*). *Ardea* 72: 1–92.

WILLE, H. 1965. Brutnachweise von Greifvögeln 1965. *Charadrius* 1: 41–42.

YALDEN, D. W. 1977. *The identification of remains in owl pellets*. Reading: Mammal Society.

YALDEN, D. W. 1980. Notes on the diet of urban Kestrels. *Bird Study* 27: 235–238.

YALDEN, D. W. & WARBURTON, A. B. 1979. The diet of the Kestrel in the Lake District. *Bird Study* 26: 163–170.

YALDEN, D. W. & YALDEN, D. W. 1985. An experimental investigation of examining Kestrel diet by pellet analysis. *Bird Study* 32: 50–55.

ZANDE, A. N. & VERSTRAEL, T. J. 1985. Impact of outdoor recreation upon nest-site choice and breeding success of the kestrel. *Ardea* 73: 90–98.

ZIESEMER, F. 1973. Siedlungsdichte und Brutbiologie von Waldohreule, *Asio otus*, und Turmfalke, *Falco tinnunculus*, nach Probeflächenuntersuchungen. *Corax* 4: 79–92.

TABLE 1: *Description of the study areas. Meterological data were from the summaries of the monthly weather reports (Meterological Office) for Eskdalemuir (grassland), Caldecott (mixed farmland) and Mepal (arable farmland). Raindays were those with >0.1 mm of precipitation and snowdays were those with snow lying at 09.00 GMT.*

	Latitude (N°)	Size (km²)	Elevation (m)	Years of study	Mean annual rain (mm)	Mean annual raindays	Mean annual snowdays	Habitat
Scottish upland grassland	55.3	100	200–540	1976–79	1519	182	39	Ungrazed grass in young conifer plantations and grazed sheepwalk. Mature conifer shelterbelts
English mixed farmland	52.6	120	30–100	1981–87	633	117	16	Cereals and pasture with small woods and hedgerows
English arable farmland	52.4	80 250	0–19	1981–83 1984–87	562	109	13	Intensive cereals and root crops, few trees

TABLE 2: Geographic range, size and plumage-scores of kestrel species and subspecies. Species numbers refer to those used on the distribution maps (Figs 6 & 7). Latitude of the range is given as northern (N) and southern (S) limits in degrees, negative values being south of the equator. Values for species wing length used in Fig. 8a were simple means of the two sexes. Tar = tarsus length, Toe = middle toe length (excluding claw), M = male, F = female, B = both sexes. The plumage/size index (PSI) was calculated for rufous kestrels by ranking the head, back, undersides and tail according colour and feather markings on a scale of 1 to 5, and adding a score for general colour (1–5) and wing chord (1–6). Low scores indicated grey on the head or tail, pink on the back, white undersides, light colouration, lack of feather marking and small size (ie 'male' characteristics). High scores resulted from brown on the head, back and tail, dark colouration, heavy marks on the feathers and large size (ie 'female' characteristics).

The dimorphism index (DI) was the absolute difference of the male and female PSI. Data mainly from skins in the British Museum (Natural History), Tring, with additional information from: Cramp & Simmons (1980), Brown & Amadon (1968), Cade (1982), Blake (1977) (F. sparverius), Watson (1981) (F. araea) and Jones (1986) (F. punctatus).

Kestrel group	Species	Subspecies	Species number	Breeding distribution	Geographic range N	S	Area km² (000)	Size (mm) Wing M	Wing F	Tail B	Tar B	Toe B	PSI M	PSI F	DI	Hovers?
Rufous	tinnunculus	tinnunculus	1.0	Europe	70	30	42000.0	244	254	165	39	27	23	42	19	Yes
		canariensis	1.1	Canary Is.	33	27	91.1	222	235	156	.	.	27	41	14	
		dacotiae	1.2	Canary Is.	29	27	14.4	221	233	149	.	.	22	38	16	
		neglectus	1.3	Cape Verde Is.	17	17	5.0	210	217	137	.	.	30	42	12	
		alexandrei	1.4	Cape Verde Is.	16	15	4.0	218	228	148	.	.	30	43	13	
		rupicolaeformis	1.5	N. Africa	32	20	3000.0	239	244	160	.	.	25	40	15	
		archeri	1.6	Somalia	12	-2	1000.0	227	231	151	.	.	20	34	14	
		rufescens	1.7	Central Africa	15	-10	8000.0	230	242	156	.	.	28	43	15	
		rupicolus	1.8	S. Africa	-10	-33	4000.0	237	249	150	.	.	23	28	5	
		interstinctus	1.9	Asia	50	28	11500.0	244	252	169	.	.	26	42	16	
		objurgatus	1.10	S. India	13	8	180.0	232	244	157	.	.	33	46	13	
	newtoni	newtoni	2.0	Madagascar	-12	-26	600.0	189	196	128	37	24	28	30	2	Yes
		aldabramus	2.1	Aldabra Is.	-10	-10	3.4	175	190	.	.	.	28	25	3	
	araea	araea	3.0	Seychelles	-5	-5	0.4	149	157	107	31	22	20	20	0	No(?)
	moluccensis	moluccensis	4.0	East Indies	-2	-4	190.0	221	229	153	39	29	42	40	2	Yes
		bernsteini	4.1	" "	2	-2	130.0	229	244	153	42	29	34	40	6	

Group	No.	Taxon	Locality												Mig.
	4.2	*timorensis*	„	−7	−11	250.0	.	.	.	.	.	30	35	5	
	4.3	*microbalia*	„	2	−9	910.0	.	.	.	.	.	29	37	8	
	4.4	*renschii*	„	−9	−10	31.0	.	.	.	.	.	30	38	8	
	4.5	*jarvensis*	„	−6	−9	280.0	.	.	.	.	.	35	42	7	
cenchroides	5.0	*cenchroides*	Australia	−11	−43	7500.0	248	260	158	41	24	17	30	13	Yes
	5.1	*baru*	New Guinea	−3	−5	12.0	.	.	.	.	.	16	41	25	
punctatus	6.0	*punctatus*	Mauritius Is.	−21	−21	2.0	175	184	131	40	27	34	38	4	No(?)
naumanni	7.0	*naumanni*	Europe/Asia	52	30	25000.0	236	238	145	31	22	17	37	20	Yes
rupicoloides	8.0	*rupicoloides*	S. Africa	−19	−34	500.0	278	281	159	48	29	42	42	0	Yes
	8.1	*arthuri*	E. Africa	4	−4	165.0	246	252	.	.	.	36	37	1	
	8.2	*fieldi*	Somalia	13	10	25.0	242	249	.	.	.	34	36	2	
alopex	9.0	*alopex*	N. Africa	15	5	4600.0	279	287	191	44	30	39	38	1	No
Grey *ardosiaceus*	10.0	*ardosiaceus*	N. Africa	20	−15	1960.0	225	244	150	42	32	.	.	.	Yes
dickinsoni	11.0	*dickinsoni*	SE Africa	−2	−25	4300.0	223	219	133	37	27	.	.	.	Rarely
zoniventris	12.0	*zoniventris*	Madagascar	−12	−24	740.0	217	226	145	38	30	.	.	.	Rarely
New-world *sparverius*	13.0	*sparverius*	N. America	62	30	13500.0	183	195	130	36	23	.	.	.	Yes
	13.1	*paulus*	Florida	33	25	650.0	.	.	.	.	.	.	.	.	
	13.2	*peninsularis*	NW Mexico	30	23	380.0	173	182	121	.	.	.	.	.	
	13.3	*tropicalis*	C. America	30	15	2100.0	.	.	.	.	.	.	.	.	
	13.4	*sparvoides*	Carribean	24	19	690.0	.	.	.	.	.	.	.	.	
	13.5	*dominicensis*	„	20	18	290.0	.	.	.	.	.	.	.	.	
	13.6	*caribearum*	„	18	12	300.0	171	177	121	.	.	.	.	.	
	13.7	*brevipennis*	„	12	12	11.0	176	185	121	.	.	.	.	.	
	13.8	*isabellinus*	S. America	12	0	1400.0	185	192	125	.	.	.	.	.	
	13.9	*ochraceus*	„	11	0	780.0	167	177	.	.	.	.	.	.	
	13.10	*nicaraguensis*	C. America	16	8	500.0	194	201	136	.	.	.	.	.	
	13.11	*aequatorialus*	S. America	−2	−2	65.0	185	196	130	.	.	.	.	.	
	13.12	*peruvianus*	„	−16	−15	860.0	195	198	131	.	.	.	.	.	
	13.13	*cinnamomninus*	„	−34	−55	4300.0	.	.	.	.	.	.	.	.	
	13.14	*fernadensis*	Fernaden Is.	−5	−34	43.0	.	.	.	.	.	.	.	.	
	13.15	*cearea*	S. America	−5	−33	3500.0	180	195	125	.	.	.	.	.	

TABLE 3: *Diet of Kestrels in the Scottish grassland area during two-monthly periods from April 1976 to July 1979 (from Village 1982a). Periods are numbered by the first month.*

Habitat	Year	2-month period	No. of pellets	Vole	Shrew	Bird	Beetle	Worm	Other	Vole-only
Sheepwalk	1976	4	42	93	36	38	19	0	0	40
	1976	6	35	80	14	74	20	0	0	23
	1977	2	52	90	19	6	33	75	10	8
	1977	4	50	86	38	8	72	18	16	16
	1977	6	53	89	51	74	36	0	8	8
	1977	10	18	94	56	0	67	8	6	6
	1977	12	50	90	40	10	66	46	2	14
	1978	2	50	96	34	8	24	54	0	20
	1978	4	55	100	29	13	24	22	6	33
	1978	6	55	96	9	47	20	0	6	40
	1978	12	50	96	0	4	54	50	8	30
	1979	2	50	96	28	10	12	30	8	36
	1979	4	50	100	14	14	38	14	14	34
	1979	6	50	96	18	56	22	0	18	30
Young plantation	1976	4	40	100	35	25	5	0	3	45
	1976	6	50	88	26	40	10	0	2	36
	1976	10	50	88	32	12	64	2	8	20
	1977	2	52	100	6	10	31	12	25	40
	1977	4	50	96	22	14	46	4	14	36
	1977	6	53	83	59	40	40	0	9	21
	1977	10	50	90	40	6	64	2	18	22
	1977	12	50	94	36	4	36	10	4	38
	1978	2	50	94	18	6	14	8	2	48
	1978	4	55	98	29	4	20	15	2	49
	1978	6	54	98	20	28	4	2	2	57
	1978	12	50	98	8	2	8	10	16	68
	1979	2	50	98	44	6	8	6	8	34
	1979	4	50	100	6	2	14	4	4	82
	1979	6	50	98	6	36	36	0	6	38

TABLE 4: *Diet of Kestrels in the English farmland areas, 1981–85. Explanation as in Table 3.*

	Year	Month	No. of pellets	Vole	Shrew	Mouse	Bird	Insect	Beetle	Grass-hopper	Worm	Vole-only
rable	1981	2	30	77	10	50	43	57	53	0	40	3
	1981	4	28	93	21	21	25	82	79	0	86	4
	1981	10	37	100	8	16	38	86	65	47	43	5
	1981	12	15	73	0	13	53	27	27	0	40	13
	1982	2	30	83	0	17	33	33	33	0	47	17
	1982	4	52	67	8	13	38	62	62	0	37	25
	1982	6	28	75	7	0	86	57	57	0	0	7
	1982	8	29	93	10	3	31	83	83	25	28	10
	1982	10	46	52	7	35	26	33	33	0	22	17
	1982	12	55	60	13	36	64	51	49	0	49	4
	1983	2	55	73	22	31	73	84	78	0	55	2
	1983	4	49	78	20	33	33	100	100	4	69	0
	1983	6	40	67	20	10	97	88	88	0	27	0
	1983	8	20	70	30	10	80	80	55	25	10	0
	1983	10	65	74	35	51	32	75	48	73	12	8
	1983	12	105	49	24	53	56	45	40	4	25	1
	1984	2	55	71	18	25	51	44	44	0	45	9
	1984	4	65	86	42	12	49	60	57	0	45	9
	1984	6	60	82	17	2	80	65	65	0	10	10
	1984	8	52	96	17	10	73	75	58	31	6	4
	1984	10	62	69	13	45	71	87	58	39	45	0
	1984	12	70	49	10	41	66	24	14	24	19	6
	1985	2	95	82	16	29	44	43	37	10	46	7
	1985	4	125	87	31	9	54	65	63	1	71	4
	1985	6	108	86	27	4	83	74	71	0	10	3
Mixed	1980	10	30	97	50	23	40	93	87	4	43	3
	1980	12	35	89	20	9	43	63	63	0	54	9
	1981	2	55	95	24	5	55	36	35	0	73	5
	1981	4	60	97	23	2	43	65	62	0	70	5
	1981	6	63	95	11	5	83	59	59	0	51	3
	1981	10	89	90	9	8	45	76	73	16	46	8
	1981	12	63	73	13	13	60	46	44	0	37	8
	1982	2	30	93	3	0	33	50	50	0	77	10
	1982	4	78	76	15	1	27	58	55	0	67	13
	1982	6	44	73	14	2	77	59	59	0	9	11
	1982	8	40	85	22	5	40	88	85	11	40	2
	1982	10	50	76	4	12	32	70	70	0	58	8
	1982	12	89	87	12	6	48	67	67	0	53	11
	1983	2	55	87	22	7	64	71	69	0	76	2
	1983	4	55	95	29	5	45	73	71	0	64	9
	1983	6	50	82	34	6	72	62	62	0	4	8
	1983	8	40	90	22	10	77	67	65	7	27	7
	1983	10	60	87	25	20	63	88	68	25	40	0
	1983	12	83	81	16	7	71	75	67	5	41	6

TABLE 4 (*continued*)

			No. of							Grass-		Vole-
										Percentage of pellets containing:		
	Year	Month	pellets	Vole	Shrew	Mouse	Bird	Insect	Beetle	hopper	Worm	only
Mixed	1984	2	82	91	29	5	35	46	45	0	70	11
	1984	4	65	92	43	2	28	77	75	0	78	2
	1984	6	63	87	29	5	71	65	65	0	13	11
	1984	8	50	88	6	8	52	80	74	10	54	6
	1984	10	85	82	7	18	55	94	92	14	79	1
	1984	12	72	75	11	14	72	71	65	4	53	1
	1985	2	94	88	12	9	56	56	51	0	64	5
	1985	4	111	87	42	4	33	67	63	1	68	8
	1985	6	57	96	32	2	70	67	67	0	18	11

TABLE 5: *Regional variation in Kestrel diets. Based on studies that counted prey items in pellets, stomachs or at nests from March to September. Insects expressed as a percentage of all items, lizards as a percentage of vertebrate items, and grasshoppers (Orthoptera) as a percentage of insects.*

	Lat. (deg)	No. of items	Percentage of items:			Source
			Insects	Lizards	Grass-hoppers	
Finland	63	2613	25	1	1	Itämies & Korpimäki (1987)
Scotland	55	890	.	1	.	Village (1982a)
England						
– North	54	999	84	7	20	Yalden & Warburton (1979)
– Central	52	625	88	1	20	N. J. Westwood
France						
– Paris	49	108	2	0	0	Thiollay (1968a)
– Vendée	47	4104	11	0	6	Thiollay (1968a)
– Camargue	43	5929	76	8	83	Thiollay (1968a)
– Côte-d'Or	47	?	.	2	.	Bonin & Strenna (1986)
Czechoslovakia	49	322	.	10	.	Pikula et al (1984)
Italy						
– Genoa	45	47	55	24	48	Silvano (1981)
– Tuscany	43	161	85	54	68	Lovari (1974)
Corsica	42	1559	83	31	61	Thiollay (1968b)
Spain						
– Central	40	108	.	.	35	Garzon (1974)
– Central	41	17	.	29	.	Araujo (1974)
Israel						
– Haifa	33	.	57	62	.	Leshem (1984)
– Tel-Aviv	32	.	.	73	.	Leshem (1984)
– Gaza	31	67	.	77	.	Hartley (1946)

TABLE 6: Hunting performance of Kestrels and other hovering raptors in relation to hunting method and prey type. Performance is recorded in terms of the percentage of strikes that were successful (%S), the strike rate per hour (SR) and the hunting yield (HY) in kills per hour. Total time is the number of hours birds were observed either flight-hunting (FH), soaring (SOAR) or perched-hunting (PH).

Season	Method	Invertebrates %S	SR	HY	Mammals %S	SR	HY	Birds %S	SR	HY	All vertebrates %S	SR	HY	Total time	Country/habitat	Source
(a) European Kestrel																
Autumn	FH	49	16.1	7.90	24	9.8	2.40	—	—	—	24	9.8	2.4	7.4	Scotland/grassland	Village (1983a)
	PH	59	7.6	4.60	33	1.9	0.70	—	—	—	33	1.9	0.7	7.5		
All	FH	—	—	—	39	10.0	3.90	28	0.20	0.06	36	10.2	3.7	884.9	Holland/grassland	Masman et al (1988b)
	SOAR	—	—	—	56	0.1	0.06	9	0.30	0.02	14	0.4	0.1	122.7		
	PH	—	—	—	32	0.4	0.13	24	0.08	0.02	29	0.5	0.1	2283.0		
Winter	FH	17	4.9	0.80	32	4.5	1.50	—	—	—	32	4.5	1.5	5.1	England/mixed farmland	This study
	PH	60	3.7	2.20	32	0.6	0.20	5	2.00	0.10	11	3.1	0.4	68.3		
Summer	FH	—	—	—	18	1.9	0.40	25	0.70	0.20	24	3.6	0.9	11.5		
	SOAR	—	—	—	—	—	—	—	0.50	0.00	—	0.5	0.0	2.1		
	PH	60	3.7	2.20	25	0.2	0.04	10	1.20	0.10	11	1.4	0.2	26.9		
Winter	FH	—	—	—	21	5.9	0.90	—	—	—	—	—	—	13.5	England/arable fenland	Pettifor (1983a)
	PH	—	—	—	21	3.0	0.50	—	—	—	—	—	—	76.3		
Summer	FH	—	—	—	16	9.2	1.10	—	—	—	—	—	—	46.5		
	PH	—	—	—	9	3.3	0.20	—	—	—	—	—	—	46.2		
(b) Black-shouldered Kite																
All	FH	—	—	—	19	6.1	1.20	—	—	—	—	—	—	20.8	S. Africa/grassland	Tarboton (1978)
	PH	—	—	—	17	2.4	0.20	—	—	—	—	—	—	51.3		

TABLE 7: *Cache sites of European and American Kestrels. Data for European Kestrels refer to the farmland study areas, those for American Kestrels are for pastureland in California (from Collopy 1977). Both species cache mainly on the ground, especially in clumps of grass.*

	European Kestrel	American Kestrel
Number of caches	45	64
Percentage on the ground:		
– at base of post, pole or tree stump	22	5
– tuft of grass or straw	33	87
– clod of earth	16	0
– stone	2	0
Total % on ground	73	92
Percentage above ground:		
– on buildings	5	0
– on fence posts	5	5
– on straw stacks	11	0
– in trees or shrubs	6	3
Total % above ground	27	8

TABLE 8: *Mean (SE) body weight of male and female Kestrels during the breeding cycle, in Eskdalemuir grassland and English farmland. Non-breeding weights were for birds caught March–July that were not paired. The early nestling period was before the chicks were 11 days old, the late nestling period any time thereafter until the chicks left the nest. Differences between the means for each area were tested using 't'-tests:* $* = P < 0.05$, $** = P < 0.01$, *otherwise not significant.*

	Stage of cycle	Grassland Mean (SE) weight (g)	N	Farmland Mean (SE) weight (g)	N
Females	Non-breeding	255 (11)	8	227 (3)	33*
	Courtship	220 (15)	3	239 (4)	31
	Laying	284 (12)	9	264 (5)	15
	Incubation	276 (3)	78	266 (2)	96**
	Early nestling	246 (7)	7	251 (5)	24
	Late nestling	246 (4)	19	233 (6)	11
Males	Non-breeding	213 (5)	10	200 (2)	45**
	Courtship	208 (3)	17	197 (2)	55**
	Laying	208 (5)	7	193 (8)	10
	Incubation	209 (2)	31	192 (2)	22**
	Early nestling	198 (3)	7	192 (2)	17
	Late nestling	201 (3)	16	180 (4)	10**

TABLE 9: *Proportion of male and female Kestrels showing signs of arrested moult during the nestling stage. Individuals were assumed to have stopped moulting if they had one or more new primary feathers, but no growing feathers in the wing or tail. Arrested moult was apparent only during the nestling stage, and there was no indication of it in 165 females and 52 males examined during incubation. The proportion with arrested moult was significantly higher in males than in females: $\chi^2 = 6.64$, $P < 0.01$.*

	Number examined in the nestling stage	Percentage with signs of arrested moult
Males	28	36%
Females	46	11%
Both sexes	74	20%

TABLE 10: *Start of primary moult in Kestrels in relation to age and sex, in Eskdalemuir grassland (1977–79) and farmland in England (1981–87). Date is the day of the year, and differences between the two areas were tested using a 't'-test: $** = P < 0.01$, $*** = P < 0.001$, otherwise not significant. Males generally started moulting later than females, and both sexes started later in the farmland areas than in grassland. Adults and first-year birds moulted at about the same time, even though adults were usually the first to lay.*

		Grassland			Farmland		
		Mean start of moult	SE (days)	N	Mean start of moult	SE (days)	N
(a)	Females						
	Adult	131	4	8	147	2	21**
	First-year	132	2	17	143	4	14**
	Both	132	2	25	146	2	35***
(b)	Males						
	Adult	151	5	11	154	8	3
	First-year	148	10	3	157	3	5
	Both	151	4	14	156	3	8

TABLE 11: *Proportion of Kestrels examined during incubation that had started to moult their primary feathers. Data from the Scottish grassland area 1978–79 and the English farmland areas 1981–87. Moult was more likely to have started during the incubation stage in females than in males, and in first-year females than in adults. Incubation started earlier, on average, in the grassland area, but Kestrels of both sexes were, nonetheless, more likely to have started moult than those in farmland. Differences between the two areas were tested using the Chi-squared or Fisher Exact Test: NS = not significant, * = P<0.05, ** = P<0.01, *** = P<0.001.*

		Males		Females	
		Number examined	% that had started moult	Number examined	% that had started moult
Adults	Grassland	13	54 *	23	35 NS
	Farmland	17	12	56	20
First-years	Grassland	11	27 NS	32	91 **
	Farmland	4	25	32	66
Both	Grassland	24	42 *	55	67 ***
	Farmland	21	14	88	36

TABLE 12: *Size and overlap of Kestrel ranges in the Scottish grassland and English farmland areas. For calculation of range size, see Appendix II. Data for grassland are from Village (1982b). Overlap was the percentage of the range that was shared with other Kestrels. Values for the grassland area in autumn and winter 1977 refer to the north (N) or south (S) of the study area.*

		Year	Season	Range size (km²): Mean	SE	% range overlap	number of ranges
Grassland		1975	Autumn	1.14	0.35	10	6
			Winter	2.06	0.69	12	7
		1976	Summer	3.11	0.38	43	9
			Autumn	2.12	0.53	9	10
			Winter	4.87	0.82	13	5
		1977	Summer	5.69	0.95	35	19
	N		Autumn	0.74	0.19	6	10
	S			2.29	0.97	6	5
	N			1.37	0.68	30	5
	S			3.74	0.81	12	5
		1978	Summer	4.08	0.47	49	20
Arable		1981	Autumn	2.48	0.61	14	18
			Winter	2.25	0.38	15	3
		1982	Summer	9.09	1.42	9	3
			Autumn	4.00	0.68	14	9
		1983	Summer	12.86	1.13	—	2
			Autumn	2.87	0.17	—	2
		1984	Summer	7.88	1.42	17	7
			Autumn	2.40	0.29	12	24
		1985	Autumn	4.03	0.59	9	15
Mixed		1980	Autumn	2.61	0.19	5	27
			Winter	2.25	0.27	6	11
		1981	Summer	4.36	0.84	9	15
			Autumn	2.53	0.28	10	16
			Winter	2.21	0.26	13	8
		1982	Summer	5.81	1.90	4	4
			Autumn	3.56	0.36	13	40
			Winter	3.38	0.34	10	11
		1983	Summer	4.81	1.23	10	6
			Autumn	3.08	0.51	20	30
			Winter	4.55	1.58	25	6
		1984	Summer	6.50	0.97	28	7
			Autumn	2.33	0.42	9	5

TABLE 13: *Extension of winter territories by wing-tagged Kestrels following the disappearance of a neighbour in the Scottish grassland area 1977–78 (from Village 1982b). The extension of ranges seemed to happen soon after the loss of a neighbour, sometimes in less than 24 hours. A = adult; J = juvenile; M = male; F = female.*

Individual extending its range:			Individual disappearing from its range:		
Age/ sex	Date extension first seen	Age/ sex	Date bird last seen		Fate
AM	9/11/76	AF	5/11/76		Not seen again
AM	13/1/77	AM	13/1/77		Not seen again
JM	24/1/78	JF	15/12/77		Found long dead 7/3/78
JF	24/1/78	JF	30/12/77		Found freshly dead 26/1/78
JM	30/12/77	AM	19/12/77		Not seen again
AM	8/11/77	J?	7/11/77		Not seen again

TABLE 14: *Average density of Kestrels in each study area during the winter months. Density was estimated from roadside counts, using calibrations to convert to absolute densities. Based on three winters in Eskdalemuir grassland (1975/6 to 1977/8) and seven in English farmland (1980/1 to 1986/7).*

Density was higher in the farmland areas than in grassland in midwinter but, unlike grassland, there was no increase in early spring.

	Mean (SE) density (Kestrels/100 km^2)		
Month	Grassland	Mixed farmland	Arable farmland
September	— (—)	49 (11)	58 (4)
October	64 (15)	55 (4)	55 (2)
November	40 (9)	60 (5)	54 (1)
December	25 (8)	56 (5)	52 (2)
January	14 (5)	44 (4)	52 (1)
February	29 (7)	49 (5)	51 (1)
March	46 (10)	56 (5)	51 (1)
April	67 (14)	41 (5)	47 (1)
May	72 (13)	46 (37)	43 (1)

TABLE 15: *Results of removing Kestrels from their winter territories in the mixed farmland study area, 1982–83. Intruders were tagged neighbours that were recorded in the vacated territory at least once after the owner was removed. Removed birds were released as shown, with radio-transmitters attached, and their persistence on their original territory for the rest of the winter was monitored. FY = first-year, A = adult, M = male, F = female, NR = not replaced.*

Age/sex of removed bird	Date of removal	Date of replacement	Age/sex of replacement	Duration on territory	Number of intruders	Date of release	Remained on territory?
FY M	25.10.82	28.10.82	FY?	3 days	3	—	—
FY M	10.11.82	NR	—	—	1	29.11.82	Yes
A F*	10.11.82	NR	—	—	1	—	—
FY M	19.1.83	26.1.83	A M	12 days	1	14.3.83	Yes
FY M	19.1.83	NR	—	—	0	24.2.83	Yes
A M	21.1.83	NR	—	—	0	1.3.83	Yes
FY M	21.1.83	NR	—	—	1	18.2.83	Yes
FY M	17.10.83	10.11.83	A M	5 days	4	31.10.83	No
A F	15.11.83	NR	—	—	0	14.12.83	Yes
FY M†	31.10.83	NR	—	—	1	—	—

* This female was radio-tagged and found freshly shot on the same day as its neighbour (the previous male) was removed.
† This male was killed by a car, two days before I was due to trap and remove it anyway.

TABLE 16: *Regional variation in the type of nest sites used by Kestrels (excluding nestboxes and baskets). Sample size given either as number of sites (S), with each counted only once, or number of breeding attempts (A), with some sites recorded more than once over several years.*

	Habitat	Sample size	Frequency of site type (%)						Source
			Tree Stick-nest	Tree-hole	Rock-ledge	Building	Pylon	Ground	
Scotland	Upland	61(S)	89	3	7	0	0	1	Grassland study area
	Upland	222(S)	47	1	49	1	0	2	Riddle (1979)
	Lowland	123(S)	42	7	28	23	0	0	Riddle (1979)
England	Lowland	287(S)	7	81	0	11	0	1	Farmland study areas
Britain									
– North	Upland	351(A)	22	18	44	17	0	0	Brown (1976) BTO nest record
– South	Lowland	287(A)	20	62	9	9	0	0	cards
Finland	Lowland	73(S)	100	0	0	0	0	0	Korpimäki (1983)
Germany									
– South	Upland	122(A)	30	0	21	48	1	0	Rockenbauch (1968)
– South	Urban	61(A)	31	⎰	0	69	0	0	Kurth (1970)
– North	Lowland	74(A)	89	3	0	8	0	0	Zeisemer (1973)
France	Upland	91(A)	27	13	0	59	0	0	Nore (1979)
Czechoslovakia	Urban	44(A)	2	45	2	50	0	0	Pikula et al (1984)
	Lowland?	281(A)	35	51*	4	11	0	0	Pikula et al (1984)

*Tree sites were assumed to be stick-nests if coniferous and holes if deciduous.

TABLE 17: *Dispersion of Kestrel home ranges and nests during the breeding season (from Village 1987b).*

Species	Dispersion of individuals	Dispersion of nests	Sources
F. araea	Exclusive territories	Regularly spaced	Watson (1981)
F. naumanni	Shared hunting range, some defence of nest	Mainly colonial	Cramp & Simmons (1980)
F. rupicoloides	Exclusive territories	Regularly spaced?	Kemp (1978) Osborne & Colebrook-Robjent (1982)
F. sparverius	Exclusive territories	Irregularly spaced?	Craighead & Craighead (1956) Phelan & Robertson (1978) Balgooyen (1976)
	Shared hunting range, territory around nest	Irregularly spaced and clumped	Cade (1955) Smith et al (1972)
F. tinnunculus	Shared hunting range, territory around nest	Irregularly spaced and clumped	Cavé[1] (1968) Village (1982b)
	Shared hunting range, defence of nest	Colonial	Peter & Zaumseil (1982)
	Some overlap of hunting range, large territory around nest	Irregularly spaced	Farmland study areas
	Exclusive territories	?	Pettifor (1983b)

TABLE 18: *Instances of colonial nesting in European Kestrels.*

	Habitat	Nest-site	No. pairs	Source
Norway	Upland	Birch woods & crags	20+	Hagen (1952)
Germany	Rural	Rookery	15	Piechocki (1982)
– Leipzig	Urban	Gasometer	7–9	Piechocki (1982)
– Cologne	Urban	Cathedral	7	C. Saar
– Jena	Rural	Motorway bridge	10–28	Peter & Zaumseil (1982)
USSR	Steppe	Stick-nests in small woods	10+	Johansen (1957) (quoted in Piechocki 1982)
Japan	?	Cliffs	17	Hyuga (1956)

TABLE 19: *Density and percentage occupation of potential Kestrel nesting sites in the Eskdalemuir grassland and English farmland study areas. Based on all usable sites available early in the breeding season, both natural and artificial. In every year, in each study area, there was a surplus of potentially usable nesting sites.*

	Year	Study area km²	No. usable sites	Density of sites 100 km²	% occupied by Kestrels
Grassland	1976	100	69	69	43
	1977	100	79	79	34
	1978	100	74	74	57
	1979	100	59	59	63
	Mean			70	49
Arable	1981	76	20	26	45
	1982	76	31	41	26
	1983	91	37	40	41
	1984	240	62	26	50
	1985	241	80	33	38
	1986	241	80	34	35
	1987	241	85	35	26
	Mean			34	36
Mixed	1981	103	70	68	43
	1982	103	83	80	28
	1983	127	88	70	39
	1984	127	83	65	33
	1985	127	100	78	22
	1986	127	100	78	12
	1987	127	108	85	10
	Mean			75	25

TABLE 20: *Estimates of Kestrel breeding density in relation to the size of study area (from Village 1984). Habitats were the major type in each study area, F = farmland, Ur = urban, Up = upland, P = parkland, W = woodland.*

	Habitat	Decade	Density of pairs /100 km²	Area km²	Source
England					
– Cambridgeshire	F	80	12	80	Arable farmland area
– Hampshire	F	70	25	67	C. Packham
– Leicestershire	F	60	7	58	Griffiths (1967)
– London	Ur	60	4	3255	Montier (1968)
– Nottinghamshire	F	80	10	2164	Dobbs (1982)
– Richmond	P	60	203	10	Parr (1967)
– Rutland	F	80	27	120	Mixed farmland area
– Somerset	F	60	4	1168	Taylor (1967)
– Surrey	F	60	1797	7	Parr (1967)
– Sussex	F	60	16	73	Shrubb (1970)
Scotland					
– Ayrshire	Up	70	31	42	G. Riddle
– Dumfries	Up	70	42	17	Picozzi & Hewson (1970)
– Dumfries	Up	70	32	100	Grassland area
– Speyside	Up	60	7	518	Macmillan (1969)
Germany (W & E)					
– Bodanrucks	Up	70	20	135	Schuster & Werner (1977)
– North Berlin	W	50	8	135	Welland (1953)
– Upper Elbe	Up	30	200	6	Marz (1949)
– Dromling	F	60	14	80	Berndt (1970)
– Federsee	?	60	150	20	Hass (1961)
– Kiel	Ur	70	21	56	Beichele (1980)
– Munich	Ur	60	20	311	Kurth (1970)
– Nordwurttemberg	F	60	40	400	Rockenbauch (1968)
– Schleswig-Holstein	F	70	10	200	Ziesemer (1973)
Luxembourg					
– Bettembourg	F	60	108	12	Wassenich (1964)
– Frisingen	?	40	47	17	Morbach (1963)
– ?	?	60	18	78	Wille (1965)
Finland					
– Hammen	F	70	3	14000	Kuusela (1979)
Sweden					
– Kvismaren	F	50	30	40	Pettersson (1977)
Switzerland					
– Reuss Valley	Up	70	34	21	Fuchs (1980)
– Fribourg	F	50	54	12	Hauri (1960)

TABLE 21: *Density of territorial and laying kestrel pairs in the Eskdalemuir grassland and English farmland study areas.*

	Year	Area searched km^2	Density ($/100 km^2$) of: Territorial pairs	Laying pairs	% of pairs not laying
Grassland	1976	100	30	22	27
	1977	100	27	26	4
	1978	100	35	34	3
	1979	100	36	36	0
		Mean(SE):	32 (2.1)	30 (3.3)	6
Arable	1981	76	12	11	8
	1982	76	11	11	0
	1983	91	16	13	19
	1984	240	13	12	8
	1985	241	12	10	17
	1986	241	12	10	17
	1987	241	9	9	0
		Mean(SE):	12 (0.9)	11 (0.6)	8
Mixed	1981	103	29	27	7
	1982	103	22	20	9
	1983	127	27	24	11
	1984	127	21	20	5
	1985	127	17	13	24
	1986	127	9	9	0
	1987	127	9	7	22
		Mean(SE):	19 (3.0)	17 (2.8)	11

TABLE 22: *Results of erecting nestboxes early in the season in the farmland study areas. In each area, 25 boxes were erected in a 7 × 7 km plot during January and February 1985. Results expressed as density of sites per 100 km². Providing nestboxes made no appreciable difference to the breeding density of Kestrels in either area.*

| | | | Arable | | Mixed | |
			All usable sites	Occupied sites	All usable sites	Occupied sites
Before experiment:						
1984	Control		25	12	73	24
	Experimental		28	16	53	16
After nestboxes erected:						
1985	Control		26	13	74	15
	Experimental		63	12	85	20
1986	Control		26	11	71	12
	Experimental		61	12	92	6
1987	Control		29	9	80	12
	Experimental		57	8	94	4
1985–87	Control	Mean(SE)	27 (1.0)	11 (1.2)	75 (2.6)	13 (1.0)
	Experimental	Mean(SE)	60 (1.8)	10 (1.3)	90 (2.7)	10 (5.0)

TABLE 23: *Changes in the breeding status of Kestrels as mentioned in county bird reports, 1955–74. No symbol = status not reported, '·' = status reported as unchanged or no indication of any change, 'D' = decline, '+' = increase. Counties are arranged from east to west and south to north, so those in south-east, where pesticides were heavily used, are near the top of the table, and those in the north and west, with lower pesticide usage, are near the bottom. Declines were noticed before the hard winters of 1961/62, but few counties continued to report on Kestrel numbers after an initial recovery in the mid 1960s.*

Year	55	56	57	58	59	60	61	62	63	64	65	66	67	68	69	70	71	72	73	74
Suffolk						D	D	D	·	·	·	+	+		+	+				
Norfolk							D	D	·	+										
Kent	+	+	+	D	D	D	D	·	+	+	+	·	·							
Essex	·			D		·	·	+	+	+	+	·	+	+		·	·		·	·
Sussex											·	+	·							
Surrey							·	D	D	+	+	+	+							
Lincolnshire			D	·	D	·	D	+	+	+	+	·								
Cambridgeshire							D	D	·	·	+	·	·	·	·					
Leicestershire						D	·	·	·	·	·									
Hampshire							D	D	D	+	·	+	+	·	·	·				
Oxfordshire											·	·	·							
Yorkshire	·	·	·	·		D	·		+	+	·	·	·							
Derbyshire						·	·	·	·	·	+	·	D							
Northumberland								D	+	·	·	·								
Dorset						·	·	·	·	+	·									
Gloucestershire						·	·	·	·	·	·									
Somerset							D	D	+	·	·	·								
Herefordshire						·	·	·	·	·	·									
Cornwall						·				·	·									

TABLE 24: *Details of removal experiments, and natural losses of Kestrels, during the breeding season in grassland and farmland study areas. Age/sex: AM = adult male, FM = first-year male, AF = adult female, FF = first-year female, N = not replaced. Stage: PL = pre-lay, LY = laying, IN = incubation. NYF = number of young fledged.*

		Bird removed or lost:				Bird that replaced it:				Fate of removed birds:
Year	Age/sex	Stage	Date	Reason	Age/sex	Laid	NYF	Released	Fate
Grassland									
1977	AF	PL	16 May	Injured	FF	26 May	4		
1978	AM	IN	3 May	Expt.	FM	16 May	6		
1978	AF	LY	3 May	Expt.	N				
1979	FF	IN	4 May	Expt.	AF	1 June	0		
1979	FM & AF	PL	4 May	Expt.	N				
Arable									
1981	AF	LY	1 May	?	FF	16 May	4		
1982	AF	PL	1 May	?	FF	28 May	0	28 May	Not seen again
1983	AM	PL	22 Apr	Expt.	N			29 April	Bred with original female
1983	AM	PL	23 Apr	Killed	AM	non-laying	0		
1984	AM	PL	19 Apr	Expt.	N				
1984	AF	IN	10 May	Expt.	JF*	27 May	3	11 June	Re-paired with male in winter
1984	AF	IN	10 May	Expt.	JF*	28 May	(0)	11 June	Re-paired with male next year
1985	AF	IN	3 May	Expt.	AF*	15 May		4 June	Took over clutch of replacement
1985	AF	IN	8 May	Expt.	N			4 June	Not seen again
1985	AM	PL	19 Apr	Expt.	JM	23 May	0	4 June	Remained in area
1986	AF	IN	13 May	Expt.	AF	22 May	5	16 July	Remated with male next year
1986	AF	LY	23 May	Died	FF	29 May	1	16 July	Not seen again
1986	AM	IN	13 May	Expt.	N				
1987	AF	LY	15 May	Expt.	N				
1987	AM	IN	26 May	Died?	N				
1987	AM	LY	4 May	Expt.	N				
Mixed									
1983	AM	PL	27 Apr	Expt.	N			9 May	Remated with female next year
1983	AM	PL	28 Apr	Expt.	N			7 May	Remated with female same year
1984	AF	IN	23 May	Expt.	N			14 June	Not seen again
1984	AM	LY	6 May	Expt.	FM	non-laying		14 June	Remained until winter
1985	AF	LY	15 May	Expt.	FF	13 June	0	6 June	Bred elsewhere next year
1985	AM	LY	15 May	Expt.	N			6 June	Not seen again
1985	AM	LY	9 May	Expt.	N			7 June	Bred same site next year
1986	AF	LY	20 May	Expt.	N			9 June	Not seen again
1986	AM	IN	9 May	Expt.	N			9 June	Not seen again

* The replacement female was the same bird at this site in both years.

TABLE 25: *Details of late-nest experiments in the Scottish grassland and English farmland study areas. All sites were made available outside existing Kestrel territories after 1 May.*

	Year	Number of nest sites: Made available	Occupied	Laid in
Grassland	1978	11	9	9
	1979	8	3	1
	All	17	12	10
Arable farmland	1983	15	0	0
	1984	13	0	0
	1985	12	0	0
	1986	14	0	0
	All	54	0	0
Mixed farmland	1983	17	0	0
	1984	15	0	0
	1985	10	0	0
	1986	15	0	0
	All	57	0	0

TABLE 26: *Intervals between nest availability, or removal of bird, and laying by second pair in late-nests and removal experiments.*

	Interval between start of experiment and laying of first egg of the new clutch (days): Mean	SE	N
Grassland	14.1	1.9	12
Farmland	15.2	2.8	7
Both	14.5	1.5	19

TABLE 27: *Age ratios among incomers in late-nest and removal experiments. AD = adult, FY = first-year.*

In each area, the proportion of first-year birds of each sex was significantly higher than in the rest of the breeding population.

	Males FY	AD	Females FY	AD
Grassland	5	3	5	1
Farmland	3	1	6	2
Both	8 (67%)	4	11 (79%)	3

TABLE 28: *Assortative mating by age among first-year and adult Kestrels. P = probability of random mating with respect to age-class. FM = first-year male, FF = first-year female, AM = adult male, AF = adult female.*
Overall, there were more even-aged pairs, and fewer mixed-aged pairs than expected by chance.

	Year	FM–FF	FM–AF	AM–FF	AM–AF	Total number of pairs	P
		Number of pairings between:					
Grassland	1977	1	0	4	17	22	0.2
	1978	12	1	7	18	37	0.001
	1979	4	2	11	18	35	0.2
	All years	17	3	22	53	95	0.0001
Farmland	1981	6	1	3	20	30	0.001
	1982	1	0	2	22	25	0.1
	1983	3	0	4	29	36	0.005
	1984	3	1	12	36	52	0.07
	1985	2	1	5	39	47	0.05
	1986	1	4	5	31	41	0.6
	1987	0	0	7	25	32	—
	All years	16	7	38	202	263	0.0001
Both areas		33	10	60	255	358	0.0001

TABLE 29: *Mean size and weight of Kestrel eggs in Europe. Ranges, where available, are given in parentheses.*

	No. eggs	Length mm	Breadth mm	Weight g	Source
Europe					
– central	306	39(34–43)	31(29–34)	—	Makatsch (1974)
– western	51	39(36–43)	32(30–33)	—	Makatsch (1974)
– southern	40	40(37–42)	32(30–34)	—	Makatsch (1974)
E. Germany	258	39	31	—	Peter (1983)
Poland/Germany	239	39(36–47)	31(27–39)	—	Glutz et al (1971)
Poland/Germany	82	—	—	21	Glutz et al (1971)
Belgium	184	39	32	20	Glutz et al (1971)
Czechoslovakia					
– urban**	197	40(36–45)	32(29–35)	21	Pikula et al (1984)
– rural	369	39(35–44)	32(29–35)		
Britain	100	40(35–44)	32(30–34)	—	Makatsch (19774)
– England**	133	40(35–43)	32(29–34)	—	Farmland study
– Scotland	73	41(37–44)	32(29–34)	—	Grassland study

** Differences in egg length between areas within these countries were significant at the 1% level.

TABLE 30: *Percentage frequency of different clutch sizes of Kestrels in Britain. Data from Brown (1976) refer to BTO nest records.*

| | Number of clutches | % of clutches with this number of eggs: | | | | | | | Mean clutch size | Source |
		1	2	3	4	5	6	7		
Southern Britain	234	0	2	6	30	46	15	1	4.7	Brown (1976)
Northern Britain	300	1	1	7	24	46	19	1	4.8	Brown (1976)
English farmland	233	1	2	14	30	47	6	<1	4.4	This study
Scottish grassland	118	0	0	4	16	53	26	1	5.0	This study

TABLE 31: *Frequency of repeat clutches after natural failure for Kestrels in the Eskdalemuir grassland and English farmland study areas.*

| | Pairs laying eggs | No. (%) failing with eggs | Number repeating | Frequency of repeats as a % of: | |
				Laying pairs	Failing pairs
Grassland	133	44(33)	11	8	25
Farmland	280	97(35)	11	4	11
χ^2 for difference between areas:		0.10		3.37	4.29
Significance of difference		Not significant		$P<0.06$	$P<0.04$

TABLE 32: *Frequency of the duration of incubation in the Eskdalemuir grassland and English farmland areas. Based on nests for with known laying and hatching dates and assuming incubation started on the fifth day after laying.*

					Number with duration (days):						
	N	26	27	28	29	30	31	32	33	34	*Mean*
Grassland	12	0	0	0	1	4	1	6	0	0	30.8
Farmland	25	1	2	1	2	5	3	5	4	2	30.8
Both areas	37	1	2	1	3	9	4	11	4	2	30.8

TABLE 33: *Changes in weight, energy balance and hunting behaviour during breeding for male and female Kestrels. Weights are combined values for the Eskdalemuir grassland and English farmland areas, energy and flight-hunting from Masman et al (1986 & 1988a). M = males, F = females.*

Stage of breeding cycle	Mean (sample-size) body weight g		Energy balance: Intake KJ/d		Expenditure KJ/d		Flight-hunting hours/d	
	M	*F*	*M*	*F*	*M*	*F*	*M*	*F*
Courtship	200(72)	238(34)	220	251	290	300	3.8	0.2
Laying	199(17)	272(24)	267	371	360	220	3.5	0.1
Incubation	202(53)	270(174)	279	309	360	225	3.9	0.1
Early nestling	194(24)	250(31)	416	182	355	260	4.4	0.8
Late nestling (> 10d)	191(26)	241(30)	391	265	395	270	4.9	2.6

TABLE 34: *Growth of nestling Kestrels from various European studies. Growth rates were calculated using graphical method (Ricklefs 1967), fitting a logistic model to mean weight (g) against age (days).*
The growth rate constant, K, is proportional to the overall rate of growth. The duration of growth is the time taken to grow from 10 to 90% of the asymptote.

	Asymptote (g)	Age at maximum rate of growth (days)	Growth rate K	Duration of most growth (days)	Number of: Nestlings	Broods	Source
Scotland	258	10	0.221	20	17	5	This study
Holland	266	9	0.249	18	17	4	Cavé[1] (1968)
Germany							
– East	225	13	0.236	19	4	1	Piechocki (1982)
– West	230	10	0.275	16	4	1	Kostrzewa & Kostrzewa (1987)
Finland							
– West	220	7	0.226	19	17	4	Korpimäki et al (1979)
– South	224	8	0.312	14	15	4	Kuusela & Solonen (1984)
Czechoslovakia	250	10	0.166	26	?	6	Pikula et al (1984)

TABLE 35: *Normal physical and behavioural development of Kestrel chicks in the nest. Data from Cramp & Simmons (1980), Kochanek (1984), Kostrzewa & Kostrzewa (1987) and unpublished observations.*

Age (days)	Behaviour	Physical development
1	Food begging not directed at adult	Eyes partly closed. Fine white down. Sit on legs and belly
3	Excrete by resting on chest and wings and raising anus. Preen sides and belly	Eyes fully open
6	Begging directed at female	
8	Grab at prey in adult's beak. Move backwards to edge of nest to excrete	Second down starts to grow. Primary quills emerge
11	No longer brooded. Preen tail stump. Interact with siblings	Tail quills emerge. Egg tooth lost. Stand on feet
13	Grab at prey in adult's claws. Eat food by themselves	Primary feathers erupt from quills
14	Clean and pull at claws	
17	Tear at prey in claws	
19	Excrete away from nest from a standing position	
20	Mantle over prey. React to call of adults before they arrive with food	Achieve adult weight. Wings half adult size
26	Preen as adults. May wander from nest cup	Down starts to shed as juvenile body feathers emerge
35	Start to leave nest	Down mostly gone. Primary and tail feathers almost full-grown

TABLE 36: *Results of experimental manipulation of the food demands on male Kestrels during the nestling stage, from Masman et al (1988b). FH = flight-hunting (hours/d), Yield = hunting yield (prey/hour of FH), TD = total delivery of prey to nest (prey/d), n = number of nests. All measurements were made over two days before the experiment started and for the two days of the experiment. For details of how the demand was increased, see page 183.*

	Early nestling n=3			Late nestling n=6		
	FH	Yield	TD	FH	Yield	TD
Normal demand	2.88	6.75	19.4	3.46	6.39	22.1
Increased demand	4.47	6.96	31.1	6.61	7.21	47.7

TABLE 37: *Mean laying dates of Kestrel populations in various parts of Europe.*

	Latitude °N	Good vole year	Laying dates: Poor vole year	All years	No. nests	Source
Finland	61	—	—	13 May*	136	Korpimäki (1986a)
	63	—	—	7 May*	131	Korpimäki (1986a)
Sweden	57	—	—	1 May†	37	Wallin et al (1987)
Scotland	55	28 April	11 May	3 May	127	Grassland area
	55	18 April	8 May	29 April*	142	Riddle (1987)
England	53	4 May	17 May	12 May	263	Farmland area
Holland	53	16 April	24 May	27 April	705	Meijer (1988)
West Germany	52	—	—	29 April	68	Hasenclever et al (1989)
Czechoslovakia						
– urban	49	—	—	26 April	44	Pikula et al (1984)
– rural	49	—	—	2 May	252	Pikula et al (1984)
France	47	22 April	11 May	3 May	82	Bonin & Strenna (1986)

* These values are median laying dates, ie the date on which half the breeding females had started laying.
† Calculated from the mean hatching dates given, assuming laying started 36 days prior to hatching.

TABLE 38: *Mean laying date, clutch size and brood size of Kestrels in the Eskdalemuir grassland and English farmland areas. Sample sizes (N) vary within years because some values were missing and because some pairs failed as the season progressed. SE = standard error of mean. The small-mammal indices were the numbers caught per trap-site in April, and were not comparable between the grassland and farmland areas.*

	Year	Laying date			Clutch size			Brood size at hatch			Brood size at fledge			Vole index	Mouse index
		Mean	SE	N	Mean	SE	N	Mean	SE	N	Mean	SE	N		
Grassland	1976	28 Apr	1.9	22	5.1	0.2	19	3.7	0.4	10	2.6	0.4	8	13.6	.
	1977	11 May	1.9	26	4.6	0.2	27	4.2	0.2	21	3.6	0.3	21	5.8	.
	1978	28 Apr	1.6	40	5.1	0.1	48	4.8	0.2	37	4.4	0.2	37	16.1	.
	1979	2 May	1.7	45	5.0	0.1	45	4.5	0.2	29	4.3	0.2	26	20.0	.
	All	3 May	1.0	127	5.0	0.1	139	4.5	0.1	97	4.0	0.1	81		
Arable	1981	4 May	8.4	5	4.7	0.4	6	4.0	1.0	3	2.8	0.5	4	15.7	0.0
	1982	17 May	2.7	8	4.0	0.3	8	4.0	0.4	5	3.8	0.3	4	4.4	0.4
	1983	14 May	1.7	10	4.5	0.2	11	4.1	0.5	7	3.4	0.5	7	0.8	0.4
	1984	6 May	1.9	29	4.7	0.2	30	4.1	0.3	20	3.5	0.3	18	1.7	0.0
	1985	11 May	3.0	21	4.3	0.2	21	3.6	0.3	16	3.1	0.3	14	1.8	0.0
	1986	12 May	1.8	30	4.5	0.2	26	3.9	0.3	17	3.5	0.3	19	5.6	0.7
	1987	4 May	1.8	24	4.6	0.2	24	4.2	0.3	17	4.0	0.3	15	2.9	0.3
	All	10 May	1.0	127	4.5	0.1	126	4.0	0.1	85	3.5	0.1	81		
Mixed	1981	13 May	1.9	25	4.4	0.2	25	3.8	0.3	17	3.6	0.2	16	17.8	0.0
	1982	17 May	1.8	18	4.2	0.2	16	3.8	0.2	14	3.4	0.2	14	2.8	0.0
	1983	12 May	1.3	28	4.4	0.1	27	4.0	0.2	21	3.6	0.3	19	4.0	0.3
	1984	11 May	1.9	23	4.1	0.2	21	4.2	0.3	13	3.4	0.4	12	4.9	0.0
	1985	11 May	2.3	20	4.5	0.2	13	4.3	0.4	9	3.7	0.4	9	2.6	0.1
	1986	14 May	2.6	14	3.8	0.2	12	3.7	0.3	9	2.3	0.4	9	5.9	0.1
	1987	11 May	3.4	8	4.3	0.3	7	4.1	0.3	7	2.8	0.4	5	4.1	0.0
	All	13 May	1.0	136	4.3	0.1	121	4.0	0.1	90	3.4	0.1	84		
All areas		09 May	0.6	396	4.6	0.05	386	4.2	0.07	272	3.6	0.08	257		

TABLE 39: *Causes of total nesting failure among Kestrel pairs in the Eskdalemuir grassland and English farmland study areas. Frequency of each cause is expressed as a percentage of all failures at that stage.*

	Grassland	Arable	Mixed	All areas
Number of laying pairs that failed to fledge young:	47	50	61	158
Number (%) failing with eggs:	41 (87)	40 (80)	50 (82)	131 (83)
– % deserted	78	58	54	63
– % deserted (eggs lost)*	12	8	20	14
– % due to predators	2	3	2	2
– % due to humans:				
– robbed	0	0	0	0
– accidental	2	5	6	4
– % nest flooded/collapsed	0	5	0	2
– % parent died	2	3	4	3
– % clutch failed to hatch	2	5	0	2
– % all eggs broken	0	5	6	4
– % cause unknown	0	10	8	6
Number (%) failing with young:	6 (13)	10 (20)	11 (18)	27 (17)
– % deserted	0	0	0	0
– % due to predators	0	0	18	7
– % due to humans:				
– robbed	0	20	9	11
– accidental	0	0	9	4
– % nest flooded/collapsed	0	0	9	4
– % parent died	0	10	0	4
– % all young died (starvation?)	83	50	18	44
– % cause unknown	17	20	36	26

* Nests where eggs disappeared after the pair had already deserted.

TABLE 40: *Frequency of clutch desertion in the Eskdalemuir grassland and English farmland study areas in relation to spring vole abundance and weather during May. The proportion of clutches deserted was positively correlated with rainfall in the grassland area* $(r = 0.998, df = 3, P < 0.002)$ *and for all areas combined* $(r = 0.62, df = 16, P < 0.006)$, *but all other relationships within areas were not statistically significant.*
The vole index was not directly comparable between the grassland and farmland areas.

	Year	Number of clutches	% deserted	Spring vole index	Rainfall in May mm	Temperature in May C°
Grassland	76	22	45	13.6	165	8.8
	77	27	26	5.8	59	7.9
	78	49	16	16.1	16	9.9
	79	46	31	20.0	88	6.5
	All	144	27			
Arable	81	7	14	15.7	42	11.8
	82	8	38	4.4	63	11.9
	83	12	33	0.8	102	10.6
	84	32	22	1.7	63	9.4
	85	25	8	1.8	70	11.0
	86	29	24	5.6	68	11.7
	87	23	13	2.9	50	10.5
	All	136	20			
Mixed	81	33	30	17.8	73	11.3
	82	25	20	2.8	34	10.9
	83	30	20	4.0	98	10.1
	84	26	35	4.9	56	9.3
	85	17	24	2.6	68	10.5
	86	12	25	5.6	64	11.3
	87	8	0	4.1	43	9.8
	All	151	25			
All areas	All	431	24			

TABLE 41: *Causes of partial loss of eggs or young from Kestrel nests that fledged at least one young in the Eskdalemuir grassland and English farmland study areas. Expressed as percentages of the number lost during the egg or nestling stage.*

	Grassland	Arable farmland	Mixed farmland	All areas
Total eggs or young lost from successful nests:	95	80	84	259
Number (%) lost before hatch:	50 (53)	43 (54)	32 (38)	125 (48)
– % broken in nest	6	9	13	9
– % fell from nest	4	7	0	5
– % not hatching	72	82	72	76
– % cause unknown	16	2	16	10
Number (%) lost after hatch:	45 (47)	37 (46)	52 (62)	134 (52)
– % fell from nest	9	0	6	5
– % lost at hatch	31	32	21	28
– % starved (?)	54	52	58	55
– % cause unknown	7	16	15	13

TABLE 42: *Total mortality of eggs and young in Kestrel nests in the Eskdalemuir grassland and English farmland areas.*

	Grassland	Arable	Mixed	All areas
Total eggs laid:	696	534	515	1745
% lost as				
– total failure with eggs	29	28	23	27
– partial egg loss	9	10	8	9
– total failure with young	3	5	6	5
– partial young loss	6	7	10	8
% fledging:	52	51	53	52

TABLE 43: *Production of young by Kestrel populations in relation to the total density of pairs, the spring vole index and rainfall during April–May. The total number of young fledged per 100 km² depended more on the total density of pairs settling than on either vole abundance or rainfall. The vole index was not directly comparable between the Eskdalemuir grassland and English farmland areas.*

	Year	Density of pairs (/100 km²): All	Successful	Number of young fledged: /successful pair	/territorial pair	/100 km²	Vole index	Rainfall (mm)
Grassland	1976	30	8	2.6	0.7	21	13.6	111
	1977	27	20	3.6	2.7	71	5.8	90
	1978	35	28	4.4	3.5	122	16.1	25
	1979	36	21	4.3	2.6	90	20.0	95
Arable	1981	12	7	2.8	1.6	18	15.7	52
	1982	11	5	3.8	1.9	20	4.4	37
	1983	16	8	3.4	1.6	26	0.8	93
	1984	13	7	3.5	1.9	25	1.7	36
	1985	12	6	3.1	1.4	18	1.8	55
	1986	12	5	3.5	1.8	19	5.6	64
	1987	9	6	4.0	2.6	23	2.9	38
Mixed	1981	29	15	3.6	1.6	52	17.8	76
	1982	22	14	3.4	1.7	46	2.8	23
	1983	27	15	3.6	2.0	54	4.0	92
	1984	21	10	3.4	1.6	35	4.9	32
	1985	17	6	3.7	1.6	20	2.6	58
	1986	9	6	2.3	1.8	15	5.9	65
	1987	9	4	2.8	1.4	11	4.1	53

TABLE 44: *Mortality of Kestrel chicks in relation to the initial brood size for the Eskdalemuir grassland and English farmland study areas. Expected values are the number of young fledged if broods of all sizes were equally likely to suffer some mortality. There was no significant difference in mortality between broods of different sizes ($\chi^2 = 4.26$, $df = 5$, $P > 0.1$).*

Size of brood	No. broods	Hatched total	Fledged total	Fledged per brood	Fledged expected	Chi-squared value
1	5	5	5	1.0	4	0.25
2	16	32	22	1.4	26	0.62
3	52	156	111	2.1	125	1.57
4	83	332	264	3.2	267	0.03
5	92	460	376	4.1	370	0.10
6	24	144	130	5.4	116	1.69
						$\chi^2 = 4.26$

TABLE 45: *Details of annual regressions of laying date* (*y*) *on* (*a*) *the percentage of young plantation and* (*b*) *the mean vole index within 3 km of the nest in the Eskdalemuir study area* (*from Village 1986*). *Figures in parentheses are 1 SE of the slope. P = probability of the slope being different from zero:* * = *P < 0.05,* ** = *P < 0.01, NS = Not Significant.*

X-variable	Year	Regression equation	df	P
% young	1976	$y = 119.3 \; +0.01(0.06)x$	20	NS
plantation	1977	$y = 122.2 \; +0.17(0.05)x$	24	**
	1978	$y = 119.3 \; -0.02(0.05)x$	36	NS
	1979	$y = 127.1 \; -0.09(0.04)x$	40	*
Vole index	1976	$y = 126.4 \; -0.53(0.34)x$	17	NS
	1977	$y = 131.3 \; +0.04(0.74)x$	20	NS
	1978	$y = 117.0 \; +0.27(0.28)x$	33	NS
	1979	$y = 125.4 \; -0.33(0.21)x$	33	NS

TABLE 46: *Mean laying dates of Kestrels in relation to male and female age. FY = first-year, AD = adult, SE = standard error of the mean* (*days*), *N = number of pairs. Data for grassland exclude 1977, when there were no first-year pairs, and laying was unusually late. All-adult pairs generally laid sooner than mixed or first-year pairs.*

Age of:		Grassland			Laying date: Farmland			Both		
Male	Female	Mean	SE	N	Mean	SE	N	Mean	SE	N
FY	FY	8 May	2.5	11	17 May	2.0	13	13 May	1.8	24
AD	FY	2 May	1.1	17	15 May	1.7	32	10 May	1.4	49
FY	AD	28 Apr	4.3	3	6 May	3.1	4	2 May	3.0	7
AD	AD	26 Apr	1.7	33	10 May	0.7	175	8 May	0.8	208

TABLE 47: *Laying date of pairs in relation to previous breeding experience in the study area. Data exclude first-year birds, and all pairs during 1976–77 (grassland) and 1981 (farmland). SE = Standard error of mean, N = number of pairs. Pairs where both partners were new to the area generally laid later than others, but experience with the same partner seemed to have little effect.*

Previous experience of pair	Grassland Mean	SE	N	Laying date: Farmland Mean	SE	N	Both Mean	SE	N
Both new to area	3 May	4.1	4	14 May	1.7	31	11 May	2.0	35
One partner new to area	27 Apr	2.3	13	11 May	1.7	45	8 May	1.4	58
Both partners bred before, but not with each other	25 Apr	2.5	8	7 May	1.7	8	1 May	1.5	16
Breeding together for at least the second time	21 Apr	1.4	7	11 May	1.7	40	8 May	1.8	47

TABLE 48: *Correlation of laying date (LD), clutch-size (CS) and body weight (WT) for female Kestrels caught during incubation. (a) Pearson correlation coefficients, (b) partial correlation coefficients for the relationship of clutch size to weight or laying date after removing the correlation of weight on laying date. Most of the correlation of clutch size on body weight could be explained by the heavier weights of early laying females, but there was a small residual correlation even after allowing for laying date.* $* = P < 0.05$, $** = P < 0.01$, $NS =$ not significant.

			Grassland $N = 78$	Farmland $N = 95$	Both areas $N = 173$
(a)	Correlation:				
	CS	LD	-0.52 **	-0.55 **	-0.57 **
	CS	WT	0.20 NS	0.37 **	0.34 **
	WT	LD	-0.33 **	-0.34 **	-0.37 **
(b)	Partial correlation:				
	CS	LD	-0.28 **	-0.31 **	-0.26 **
	CS	WT	0.01 NS	0.06 *	0.15 *

TABLE 49: *Frequency of recoveries at various distances from birthplace for Kestrels ringed as nestlings in the National Ringing Scheme, 1912–1984. Winter recoveries more than 150 km from the birthplace were mainly of migrants.*

	Number recovered	% found at following distance (km) from birthplace:						
		0–25	26–50	51–75	76–100	101–125	126–150	>150
1st-year:								
June	10	100	0	0	0	0	0	0
July	143	74	4	6	5	4	4	4
Aug	238	43	13	11	8	10	4	11
Sept	138	38	12	10	6	6	5	23
Oct	170	25	8	5	6	7	4	45
Nov	170	19	10	9	8	8	4	42
Dec	155	27	10	7	8	3	5	41
Jan–Mar	302	33	12	8	6	4	4	33
Apr–Jul	174	44	17	8	5	3	4	19
Adults:								
Winter (Oct–Mar)	441	48	14	8	5	3	3	21
Summer (Apr–Sept)	146	63	10	5	5	3	2	12

TABLE 50: *Frequency with which Kestrels ringed as nestlings subsequently bred in the study area, in relation to fledgling date. Combined totals for the grassland (1976–78) and farmland (1981–85) areas. Fledgling periods were based on the mean laying date for the year in which young were born, and the intervals were chosen to give roughly equal numbers in each period. The earliest fledged young were more likely to be recruited into the local breeding population, but the difference was statistically significant only for recruitment in the first year of life.*

Fledging period	Number ringed	Percentage (number) that:	
		Bred in study area	Did not breed in study area
(a) Recruitment at any age:			
Early	186	7.0 (13)	93.0 (173)
Mid	196	3.6 (7)	96.4 (189)
Late	199	3.5 (7)	96.5 (192)
		$\chi^2 = 3.39$, $P < 0.2$	
(b) Recruitment as yearlings:			
Early	186	4.8 (9)	95.2 (177)
Mid	196	0.5 (1)	99.5 (195)
Late	199	1.0 (2)	99.0 (197)
		$\chi^2 = 10.5$, $P < 0.01$	

TABLE 51: *Distance moved in winter by post-breeding adult Kestrels from the Scottish grassland and English farmland areas. Based on birds recovered by the public during October–March that were known to have bred in the study area at least once. Differences between males and females were tested by the non-parametic Wilcoxon's 'Z' test, NS = Not significant. In Scotland, males moved further away from the breeding grounds in winter than females, but this was not so in the English farmland areas, where both sexes were more sedentary.*

	Number recovered at this distance from ringing place (km):					*Mean*	*(Range) (km)*
	< 10	*10–50*	*51–100*	*101–200*	*> 200*		
Scottish grassland:							
Males	0	0	0	1	4	394.4	(182–856)
Females	1	1	1	4	3	158.7	(0–398)
				Wilcoxon's 'Z' = 2.02, P < 0.05			
English farmland:							
Males	8	0	0	0	0	3.0	(0 8)
Females	13	3	0	0	0	5.2	(0–24)
				Wilcoxon's 'Z' = 0.26, NS			

TABLE 52: *Recoveries outside Britain of Kestrels ringed in north or south Britain from 1912–1984. The dividing line was taken as 53°N, and recoveries from Ireland were excluded. The proportion of northern-ringed birds found outside Britain was significantly higher than in those from the south ($\chi^2 = 3.98$, df = 1, P < 0.05).*

Birth-place	Total nestlings ringed	Number (%) recovered Great Britain	Elsewhere
North	1366	1264 (92.5)	102 (7.5)
South	699	663 (94.8)	36 (5.2)

TABLE 53: *Breeding performance of resident and migrant Kestrels in the Eskdalemuir grassland study area, 1977–79. Resident pairs were those where at least one partner had spent the previous winter in the study area, whereas migrant pairs had at least one partner that was known to have bred in the area before, but migrated away in the intervening winter. Any pairs with first-year birds were excluded, as were pairs of adults where both partners were recorded in the area for only one breeding season. Laying date is day of the year.* t = *Student's 't' for difference in the means.* NS = *not significant.*

	N	Mean (SE) laying date	Mean (SE) number fledged
Resident pairs	18	120.7 (2.6)	4.1 (0.4)
Migrant pairs	13	123.0 (3.1)	2.9 (0.5)
		t = 0.55, NS	t = 1.83, P < 0.08

TABLE 54: *Percentages of residents and migrants among wing-tagged Kestrels in the Scottish grassland and English farmland areas. Year-round residents were present for at least one adjacent summer and winter, while migrants were present for at least two summers or winters, but not in the intervening season.*

	Number tagged	% Single-season residents: Winter	Summer	% Year-round resident	% Migrants: Winter	Summer
Grassland						
Males	96	17	44	13	0	21
Females	111	13	59	9	0	14
Both sexes	207	14	52	11	0	17
Farmland						
Males	115	25	17	57	1	0
Females	116	28	22	47	3	0
Both sexes	231	26	20	52	2	0

TABLE 55: *Mean duration in the study area for year-round residents in Scottish grassland (1975–78) and English farmland (1980–86). Duration is given separately for all wing-tagged Kestrels and for those whose residence in the area both began and ended during the study ('Complete stays'). Although grassland Kestrels were more likely to migrate, those that were resident stayed as long in the area as Kestrels in the more sedentary farmland population.*

| | | Duration in the study area (months): | | | |
| | | All residents | | Complete stays only | |
		Mean (SE)	N	Mean (SE)	N
Scottish	Males	35	10	23	4
grassland	Females	24	10	15	4
English	Males	22 (1.2)	140	19 (1.7)	65
farmland	Females	21 (1.3)	117	19 (1.5)	55

TABLE 56: *Monthly estimates of gains and losses of Kestrels in the Scottish grassland (October 1975 to July 1978) and English farmland (October 1980 to July 1986) study areas. The table shows the mean proportion of marked birds present during the month that were either first seen (% gained) or last seen (% lost) in that month. The April peak in England was largely due to an uneven trapping effort, and many birds caught then would have arrived during the preceding winter.*
Both = %gained + %lost.

| | | Grassland | | | | Farmland | | |
| | Mean number present | Mean percentage: | | | Mean number present | Mean percentage: | | |
		Gained	Lost	Both		Gained	Lost	Both
Aug	—	—	—	—	67.4	4.4	3.6	8.0
Sept	43.5*	29.0	29.5	58.5	76.6	14.2	3.0	17.2
Oct	24.0	0.0	18.7	18.7	76.8	7.7	4.3	12.0
Nov	19.0	0.0	23.3	23.3	75.8	3.3	5.2	8.5
Dec	14.7	0.0	26.3	26.3	74.7	4.2	5.2	9.4
Jan	10.7	0.0	11.0	11.0	76.6	3.6	4.2	7.8
Feb	13.0	24.0	0.0	24.0	74.6	2.8	5.2	8.0
Mar	38.0	61.3	1.7	63.0	79.2	11.2	4.6	15.8
Apr	49.3	23.0	4.7	27.7	101.2	27.8	8.8	36.6
May	51.7	9.0	7.0	16.0	93.2	1.4	14.8	16.2
June	48.7	0.3	14.7	15.0	79.6	0.6	12.4	13.0
July	45.3	2.7	4.3	7.0	70.2	0.6	9.2	9.8
All months	32.5	13.6	12.8	26.4	78.7	6.7	6.6	13.3

*Estimate for August and September based on birds gained or lost between July and October.

TABLE 57: *Annual turnover among the Kestrel breeding population in the Scottish grassland (1977–79) and English farmland (1982–87) areas. The table gives the proportion of the breeding population that were known to have been breeding the previous year. Unmarked birds were assumed to be new to the breeding population, which may have slightly overestimated the rate of turnover as not all breeding birds were marked in every year. Values of individual years were summed, so birds breeding for several years would appear more than once. In both sexes, a higher proportion of the breeding population was breeding again in the study area in farmland than in grassland.*

	Number (%) of males:		Number (%) of females:	
	Breeding again	New to area	Breeding again	New to area
Grassland	34 (26)	98 (74)	25 (19)	108 (81)
Farmland	111 (41)	157 (59)	111 (41)	157 (59)
	$\chi^2 = 9.4$, $P < 0.002$		$\chi^2 = 20.3$, $P < 0.0001$	

TABLE 58: *Persistence in the breeding population of wing-tagged Kestrels in successive years in relation to age and breeding performance. Data are for the Scottish grassland area (1976-79) and the English farmland areas (1981-86), excluding birds in removal or late-nest experiments. Successful birds were those that fledged at least one young.*

P = probability of a significant difference between successful and failed birds, tested using a Chi-squared test with 1 df.

* = P < 0.05, ** = P < 0.01, NS = not significant.

There were no significant differences between males and females in any category. Differences between the study areas were significant only in failed females:† = P < 0.05, †† = P < 0.01, ††† = P < 0.001.

	Number of successful breeders	% Present following year	Number of failed breeders	% Present following year	P
Scottish grassland					
Males					
First-year	10	50	6	33	NS
Adult	63	51	18	22	*
All	73	51	24	25	*
Females					
First-year	26	19	13	8	NS
Adult	54	54	10	10	**
All	80	43	23	9	**
English farmland					
Males					
First-year	8	63	17	47	NS
Adult	115	58	75	44	*
All	123	58	92	45	*
Females					
First-year	21	43	23	39†	NS
Adult	115	54	60	45††	NS
All	136	52	83	43†††	NS

TABLE 59: *Fidelity to mate in relation to fidelity to nesting territory for Kestrels in Scottish grassland 1977–79 and English farmland 1981–87. Individuals were assumed to have changed territory if they moved more than 0.75 km between breeding sites in successive years. Females that changed territory were more likely to change partner than those that stayed put, but there was no such difference in males. Tested using Chi-squared test with 1 df: * = P < 0.05, *** = P < 0.001, NS = Not significant.*

	Territory change	Number breeding in successive years	Number (%) with the same partner
Grassland:			
Males	Same	29	12 (41)
	Different	11	3 (27) NS
Females	Same	17	13 (76)
	Different	15	3 (24) ***
Farmland:			
Males	Same	72	36 (50)
	Different	35	13 (37) NS
Females	Same	62	37 (60)
	Different	35	13 (40) *

TABLE 60: *Fidelity to nesting territory for wing-tagged Kestrels in relation to breeding success and number of breeding attempts. Combined data for Scottish grassland area (1977–79) and English farmland areas (1981–87). First-attempts included both adults and yearlings recorded as breeding in the study area for the first time. Successful birds were those that fledged at least one young. Differences between failed and successful birds were tested with a Chi-squared test with 1 df: NS = Not Significant, * = P < 0.05, ** = P < 0.01. Combining breeding performance, females were less likely to change territory in subsequent than in first moves ($\chi^2 = 4.7$, P < 0.02), but the trend was not significant for males.*

	Attempt	Outcome of breeding attempt	Number present next year	Number (%) breeding at: same territory	different territory	
Males						
	First	Failed	35	20 (57)	15 (43)	
		Successful	60	43 (72)	17 (28)	NS
		Both	95	63 (66)	32 (34)	
	Subsequent	Failed	17	9 (53)	8 (47)	
		Successful	51	43 (84)	8 (16)	**
		Both	68	52 (76)	16 (24)	
Females						
	First	Failed	29	9 (31)	20 (69)	
		Successful	59	38 (64)	21 (36)	**
		Both	88	47 (53)	41 (47)	
	Subsequent	Failed	17	10 (59)	7 (41)	
		Successful	48	36 (75)	12 (25)	NS
		Both	65	46 (71)	19 (29)	

TABLE 61: *Fidelity to mate among summer migrants and year-round residents in Scottish grassland, 1977–79 (from Village 1985b). The difference between the sexes was significant in migrants ($\chi^2 = 7.4$, $P < 0.01$), but not in the small sample of residents ($\chi^2 = 0.9$, NS). The difference between migrants and residents was significant in males ($\chi^2 = 4.2$, $P < 0.05$), but not females.*

		Number breeding in successive years	Number (%) mated with previous partner
Summer migrants:			
	Males	23	5 (22)
	Females	23	13 (57)
Year-round residents:			
	Males	17	9 (53)
	Females	9	3 (33)

TABLE 62: *Fidelity to mate among Kestrels breeding in successive years in the Scottish grassland area (1977–79) and English farmland areas (1982–1987), in relation to breeding performance. There were no significant differences in mate fidelity between males and females, or between grassland and farmland, but successful birds were more faithful than unsuccessful ones. Differences tested using a Chi-squared test with 1 df. $* = P < 0.05$, $** = P < 0.01$, $*** = P < 0.001$.*

	Outcome of breeding attempt	Number present next year	Percentage with: same partner	Percentage with: different partner
Grassland				
Males	Failed	6	0	100
	Successful	34	44	56*
	Both	40	38	62
Females	Failed	1	—	—
	Successful	31	52	48
	Both	32	50	50
Farmland				
Males	Failed	38	24	76
	Successful	69	58	42***
	Both	107	46	54
Females	Failed	33	30	70
	Successful	64	63	37**
	Both	97	52	48

TABLE 63: *Frequency of 'divorced' and 'widowed' Kestrels among males and females breeding with a different partner from the previous year. Individuals were classed as divorced if their previous partner was breeding elsewhere, and widowed if he or she was not present in the area. Most birds that changed partner were widowed, but the proportion was higher among males than females. Differences between the sexes were tested using a Chi-squared test with 1 df. * = P < 0.05, NS = Not significant.*

		Number breeding with a different partner from previous year	Number (%) divorced	Number (%) widowed	
Grassland					
(1977–79)	Males	25	2 (8)	23 (92)	
	Females	16	4 (25)	12 (75)	NS
Farmland					
(1982–87)	Males	58	3 (5)	55 (95)	
	Females	47	7 (15)	40 (85)	NS
Both areas					
	Males	83	5 (6)	78 (94)	
	Females	63	11 (17)	52 (83)	*

TABLE 64: *Age and sex ratios during winter in the farmland study areas, based on proportions among wing-tagged Kestrels known to be present in the study area. Time periods spanned three months (labelled by middle month), and were included only when trapping was intense enough to give a reasonable estimate of the proportion of first-year birds present. Both = all first-year birds (used in Fig. 78).*

| | | | | % that were: | | | |
	Number tagged	Adult Males	Adult Females	First-year Males	First-year Females	Both	Vole index
Mixed farmland							
Jan 1981	39	33	31	26	10	36	8.4
Apr 1981	60	28	25	27	20	47	17.8
Oct 1981	14	57	29	0	14	14	10.8
Jan 1982	15	67	20	7	7	14	5.9
Apr 1982	30	53	40	7	0	7	2.8
Oct 1982	31	52	13	26	9	35	9.4
Jan 1983	30	53	33	13	0	13	6.6
Apr 1983	44	59	27	11	2	13	4.0
Oct 1983	25	40	28	28	4	32	17.7
Jan 1984	33	37	39	21	3	24	6.6
Apr 1984	22	55	27	14	5	19	4.9
Jan 1985	23	43	35	22	0	22	4.2
Apr 1985	37	46	38	16	0	16	2.5

TABLE 64 (*continued*)

	Number tagged	% that were: Adult Males	Adult Females	First-year Males	First-year Females	Both	Vole index
Arable farmland							
Oct 1981	14	29	29	36	7	43	14.0
Apr 1982	12	42	33	25	0	25	4.4
Oct 1982	18	33	39	17	11	28	5.2
Apr 1984	42	45	26	10	19	29	1.7
Oct 1984	27	27	41	17	16	33	9.8
Jan 1985	34	26	41	24	9	33	5.3
Apr 1985	71	31	40	18	11	29	1.8
Jan 1986	13	46	31	15	8	23	4.5
Apr 1986	67	48	34	9	9	18	5.6

TABLE 65: *Sex ratios among breeders and non-breeders in the tagged Kestrel population present during the breeding season in the farmland study areas, 1981–86. Data for these years were combined, so some individuals were recorded more than once. The sex ratio among the total breeding population was 1:1, but males formed a slightly higher proportion of the tagged population because they were easier to trap than females. In first-years, the breeding population had a higher proportion of females, and lower proportion of males, than the non-breeding population.*

		Number (%) of: Males	*Females*	*Total tagged*
Adults:				
	Breeding	200 (51)	189 (49)	389
	Not breeding	66 (57)	49 (43)	115
				$\chi^2 = 1.3$, NS
First-years:				
	Breeding	26 (34)	51 (66)	77
	Not breeding	53 (67)	26 (33)	79
				$\chi^2 = 17.3$ $P < 0.001$

TABLE 66: *Age ratio among breeding Kestrels in the Eskdalemuir grassland and English farmland areas. There was a higher proportion of first-year birds among females than among males in all areas, though the age ratio in each sex varied considerably from year to year.*

	Number of males	% First-years	Number of females	% First-years
Grassland				
1976	18	0	6	0
1977	25	4	22	23
1978	37	27	33	45
1979	35	17	40	45
All years	115	12	101	28
Mixed farmland				
1981	34	29	27	33
1982	27	4	22	5
1983	35	11	28	18
1984	24	5	25	12
1985	23	9	17	12
1986	14	7	14	29
1987	10	0	9	22
All years	167	9	142	20
Arable farmland				
1981	7	43	4	25
1982	6	17	7	43
1983	13	8	9	33
1984	33	12	30	37
1985	31	13	28	11
1986	31	13	28	7
1987	25	0	24	21
All years	146	15	130	25

TABLE 67: *Proportion of unpaired Kestrels among the tagged population present in the farmland areas in summer. Differences between adults and first-years birds in each sex were tested by chi-squared test, with 1 df:* $* = P < 0.05$, $** = P < 0.01$, $*** = P < 0.001$, $NS = $ not significant.

In both sexes, there was a higher proportion of unpaired birds in first-years than in adults, but the difference was most marked in males.

	Percentage (N) of each age/sex class not paired:						
	Males			Females			
	Adult		First-year		Adult		First-year
1981	6% (18)		50% (20)**		5% (22)		25% (16) NS
1982	26 (38)		67 (6)*		8 (26)		33 (6) NS
1983	27 (52)		55 (11)*		20 (35)		11 (9) NS
1984	19 (52)		79 (14)***		28 (58)		29 (17) NS
1985	26 (53)		78 (18)***		30 (54)		33 (12) NS
1986	32 (53)		80 (13)**		16 (43)		59 (17) ***
All	25 (266)		67 (79)***		21 (238)		34 (77) **

TABLE 68: *Probability of being present in the next breeding season for tagged breeders and non-breeders in the farmland study areas, 1981–86. Data include a few individuals that were experimentally removed from their territories and released a few weeks later. P = probability that difference between breeding and non-breeding birds was due to chance. NS = not significant. Breeding birds were slightly more likely to be present the next year than non-breeders, though the effect was most obvious in first-year birds.*

	Males			Females		
	Number present in year n	Number (%) present in year (n + 1)	P	Number present in year n	Number (%) present in year (n + 1)	P
(a) Adults						
Breeding	200	119 (60%)		189	103 (55%)	
Non-breeding	66	33 (50%)	NS	49	23 (47%)	NS
(b) First-years						
Breeding	26	17 (65%)		51	26 (51%)	
Non-breeding	53	23 (43%)	0.07	26	8 (31%)	0.1
(c) All ages						
Breeding	226	136 (60%)		240	129 (54%)	
Non-breeding	119	56 (47%)	0.02	75	31 (41%)	0.06

TABLE 69: *Estimates of juvenile and adult survival rates from recoveries of Kestrels ringed as nestlings in Europe. In each case, enough time was allowed for all the recoveries of birds ringed in the last year to be reported. Survival was calculated from the proportion of ringed birds that survived to a given age, ie the percentage of those 'at risk'.*

	Years of ringing	Number of recoveries	Age-change date*	Est. survival (%) at age: 1	2	3+	Source
Britain	1912–55	189	1 April	40	53	66	Snow (1968)
	1912–72	665	1 August	32	66	69	This study
Switzerland		301	31 December	61	65†		Schifferli (1964)
Finland		115	31 December	53	56†		,, ,,
Holland	1911–55	527	20 June	49	59	58	Cavé[1] (1968)
	1911–76	2721	1 June	51	58	63	Dijkstra (1988)

*Date on which birds were assumed to become one year older. †Combined estimate for all adults.

TABLE 70: *Annual variations in the local winter survival of Kestrels in mixed and arable farmland, 1980–86. Survival is expressed as the percentage of wing-tagged Kestrels, present in the study areas between October and December, that were still present the following April. First-year survival is thus based on those juveniles that survived to be trapped and marked between September and December. Individuals surviving several years would be counted more than once. There were insufficient first-year birds marked in any one year to make separate estimates for each sex.*

| | | Percentage (n) that survived the winter: | | | |
		Adult males	*Adult females*	*All Adults**	*First-years**
Arable	1980	— (0)	— (0)	— (0)	— (0)
	1981	75 (4)	56 (6)	60 (10)	— (4)
	1982	91 (11)	40 (10)	67 (21)	— (3)
	1983	85 (13)	67 (12)	76 (25)	— (3)
	1984	75 (24)	62 (34)	67 (58)	33 (18)
	1985	68 (28)	67 (30)	67 (58)	17 (6)
	1986	94 (16)	93 (14)	93 (30)	— (0)
	All years	79 (96)	65 (106)	72 (202)	21 (34)
Mixed	1980	89 (9)	83 (6)	87 (15)	71 (7)
	1981	77 (30)	67 (18)	73 (48)	25 (6)
	1982	79 (33)	65 (23)	73 (56)	45 (11)
	1983	65 (37)	77 (26)	70 (63)	23 (13)
	1984	79 (19)	75 (16)	77 (35)	20 (6)
	1985	63 (16)	82 (11)	70 (27)	— (2)
	1986	— (4)	63 (8)	75 (12)	— (2)
	All years	74 (148)	72 (108)	73 (256)	38 (40)
Both areas					
	All years	76 (244)	69 (214)	73 (458)	30 (74)

* Values in these columns were used in Fig. 82.

TABLE 71: *Age-specific local winter survival of Kestrels in the English farmland areas, 1980–86. For calculation of survival rates, see Table 70. Data are combined values for all known-aged birds in both study areas in all years. Survival was lower in first-year birds than in adults, and in females than in males. In both sexes, second winter birds had a slightly lower survival than older ones.*

| | Percentage (n) surviving at age: | | | |
	1	*2*	*3*	*>3*
Males	36 (50)	76 (45)	86 (28)	77 (22)
Females	17 (24)	63 (38)	68 (25)	67 (9)

TABLE 72: *Seasonal variations in the cause of death of Kestrels received by the Pesticide Monitoring Scheme at Monks Wood Experimental Station, 1963–79. From Newton et al 1982. Starvation was the main cause of death diagnosed, especially for juveniles in autumn. Haemorrhages were more frequent in adults than juveniles, and were probably due mainly to pesticide poisoning (see following table).*

	Jan	Feb	Mar	Apr	May	Jun	Jul	Aug	Sep	Oct	Nov	Dec	Total
No. received:	58	49	62	45	23	16	44	97	41	71	57	53	616
% Caused by:													
Collision	5	2	5	0	4	6	2	0	0	0	0	6	2
Vehicles	12	4	6	7	0	25	14	19	15	17	14	7	12
Other trauma	9	6	5	13	9	19	9	7	15	10	7	6	9
Shooting	3	4	3	7	9	0	2	3	5	4	4	2	4
Haemorrhages	31	33	27	22	30	19	2	1	5	7	2	4	13
Disease	0	16	15	13	4	6	14	3	17	11	19	15	11
Starvation	17	12	11	9	9	13	50	51	22	34	40	34	29
Unknown	22	23	27	29	35	13	7	16	22	17	14	25	20

TABLE 73: *Relationship of DDE and HEOD levels in the liver to the cause of death in Kestrels received in the Pesticide Monitoring Scheme, from Newton et al 1982. DDE is from DDT and HEOD is from aldrin and dieldrin. Haemorrhaging was associated with higher levels of HEOD than in other known causes of death. ppm = parts per million in the liver.*

| | | Percent of Kestrels with: | |
Cause of death	Number	> 100 ppm DDE	> 10 ppm HEOD
Collision	119	3	4
Shooting	21	5	0
Haemorrhaging	75	8	55
Disease	57	4	2
Starvation	150	0	2
Unknown	98	3	30

TABLE 74: *Frequency of recovery of ringed Kestrels in relation to ringing date, based on the National Ringing Scheme data. Ringing periods were chosen to give roughly equal sample sizes in each. The difference in frequencies between the four periods was highly significant ($\chi^2 = 21.3$, df = 9, P < 0.011).*

Ringing period	Number ringed	Before 1 Oct	Percentage recovered: 1 Oct–31 Dec	1 Jan–31 Jul	As adults
Before 15 June	473	22	18	27	33
15 June–21 June	434	23	24	23	30
22 June–30 June	527	25	22	21	32
After 30 June	500	25	28	21	26

TABLE 75: *Proportion of adults among ring recoveries of Kestrels in the high and low pesticide areas before, during and after the period when dieldrin was in heaviest use (1956–75). The high pesticide-use areas were the wheat-bulb fly areas (Newton et al 1982), mainly in south-east England, the East Midlands, East Anglia and east Scotland. In both areas, there was no significant change between periods in the proportion of ringed nestlings that were recovered as adults.*

| Recovered during: | Dieldrin use | High pesticide areas | | Low pesticide areas | |
		Number of recoveries	% adults	Number of recoveries	% adults
1912–55	None	71	23	94	29
1956–75	Heavy	213	27	395	28
1976–82	Reduced	186	24	340	30

TABLE 76: *Estimated survival rates of first-year and adult Kestrels in high and low pesticide areas. For explanation of periods and areas, see the previous table. The estimates were made using the ratio of recoveries from one year class to the next and pooling for all birds recovered in the relevant period and area. For further details of the method, see Newton et al (1983a). The ratios used to calculate the estimates were not amenable to statistical testing.*

| Recovered during | Dieldrin use | Estimated survival rates % of: | | | |
| | | First-years | | Adults | |
		High-use area	Low-use area	High-use area	Low-use area
1912–55	None	28	37	62	68
1956–75	Heavy	29	34	55	73
1976–82	Reduced	30	39	61	72

TABLE 77: *Responses of various vole-eating raptors and owls to variations in prey abundance during vole cycles. Each response has been rated according to the following approximate scale: 0= none, * = slight or occasional response, ** = moderate response, *** = strong response. ? = no information. M = male response, F = female response. For hunting techniques: L = low-level flight, H = hovering, P = perched-hunting, S = soaring. Data from Cramp & Simmons (1980) and Cramp (1985), with additional information from: (a) Hamerstrom (1969), Picozzi (1984), Simmons et al (1986); (b) Mendelsohn (1983), Brown et al (1982); (c) Watson (1957); (d) Korpimaki (1986c); (e) Korpimaki (1987)*

	Hen Harrier	Short-eared Owl	Long-eared Owl	Barn Owl	Rough-legged Buzzard	Black-shouldered Kite	Kestrel	Hawk Owl	Common Buzzard	Snowy Owl	Eagle Owl	Tawny Owl	Ural Owl	Great grey Owl	Teng-malms Owl	Pygmy Owl
Additional sources:	a					b				c		d	d	d	e	
Main hunting method	L	L	L	LP	HL	H	HPS	PH	PS	PL	P	P	P	P	P	P
Change to alternative prey when voles are scarce	***	*	**	**	*	*	**	*	***	*	****	**	**	**	**	**
Resident, non-breeding when voles are scarce	0	0	*	**	**	0	*	0	***	0	**	***	***	0	**M 0F	**
Nomadic, move to good vole areas	**	***	*	*	**	***	*	***	0	***	0	0	0	***	0M **F	*
Breed as yearlings when voles are abundant	*	**	**	**	0	?	***	**	0	?	0	*	**	***	**	**
Some polygynous matings when voles are abundant	***	*	*	*	?	?	*	0	*	0	0	*	0	*	**	0

TABLE 77 (continued)

	Hen Harrier	Short-eared Owl	Long-eared Owl	Barn Owl	Rough-legged Buzzard	Black-shouldered Kite	Kestrel	Hawk Owl	Common Buzzard	Snowy Owl	Eagle Owl	Tawny Owl	Ural Owl	Great grey Owl	Teng-malms Owl	Pygmy Owl
Some polyandrous matings when voles are scarce	0	0	0	*	?	0	0?	0	0	0	0	0	0	0	*	0
Females abandon brood to male and remate	0	0	0	0	0	**	0	0	0	0	0	0	0	0	**	0
Clutches larger when voles are abundant	*	***	**	***	**	*	*	***	**	***	*	*	**	**	***	**
Asynchronous hatch: brood reduction when voles are scarce	**	***	***	***	**	*	*	**	**	***	***	**	*	***	**	0
Double-brooded when voles are abundant	0	*	*	*	0	0M ***F	0	0	0	0	0	0	0	0	0M *F	0

Index

Accidents, causing deaths, 120, 255–6
Age
    and breeding performance, 208–9
    and diet, 57
    and fidelity, 234–5, 236–7
    and hunting performance, 71
    and migration, 159–61, 220–1, 224
    and moult, 89
    and plumage, 31, 239
    and survival rate, 250–4, 256, 259
    and weight, 84
    at first breeding, 247, 259, 271, 274
    methods of ageing juveniles, 31, 239
    of non-breeders/replacements, 153
Age-ratios, 238–40, 244–7
Aggression, see Behaviour, aggressive
Anatomy, 29–31
    adaptions for hunting, 30, 63
    size, 18, 83–4, 270–1
Arable farmland study area, 21–3
Assortative mating
    by age, 162, 209
    by size, 163
Asynchronous hatch, 177, 275
Autopsies, 254

Behaviour
    adjusting daily patterns, 74–5
    aggressive, 102, 104–5, 107, 122, 131, 137, 156,
        176, 216, 266, 268–9, 281–2, see also Ter-
        ritorial fighting
    breeding displays, 137, 157–9
    calls, 156, 166, 177
    courtship, 109, 165–7
    division of labour in the sexes, 165–7, 173–6,
        181–4
    feeding, 75–6, see also Eating prey and Hunting
    incubation, 166, 174–5
    of nestlings, 177–80
    pair-formation, 159–63, see also Mate selection
    parental, 181–88
    territorial, 86, 158–9
Birds, as prey, 50–1, 54, 55, 61, 68, 109, 195, 254,
    259, 277–8
Black-shouldered Kite, 45, 69–70, 194, 236, 271,
    275
Body temperature, 96–7, 180
Body weight, 18
    and age, 84
    and breeding success, 175, 210–11
    and clutch size, 210
    and energy budgets, 83–6
    and sex, 83–4, 168
    and size, 83
    during the breeding cycle, 84, 167–8, 175–6,
        184–5, 210

of nestlings, 178–80
seasonal variation of, 83–4
Breeding attempts, number of, 229–30
Breeding cycle
    calls and displays during, 156–9
    courtship, 164–9
    egg stage and incubation, 170–6
    nestling stage, 177–88
    pair formation, 159–163
Breeding density
    and breeding productivity, 206–7
    and food supply, 143–6, 265–8
    and habitat, 144
    and mortality, 143, 148
    and nest-site availability, 143, 146–8, 151, 263,
        268–9
    and pesticides, 148–50
    and weather, 145–6
    errors in estimating, 141–2
    regulation of, 265–8
Breeding experience, and performance, 209
Breeding failure, 142, 150, 203–7
    and site fidelity, 235, 236–7
    causes of, 198, 203–7
    frequency of, 198–9, 204
    partial losses, 204–5
Breeding performance/success
    and body weight, 175, 210–11
    and mate/nest fidelity, 235, 236–7
    and turnover, 232
    and type of nest site, 135–6
    annual variation of, 204, 206–7
    causes of failure, see Breeding failure
    individual variation in, 207–10
    of migrants, 224–5
    regional variation of, 203, 206–7
    seasonal trends in, 198–203
Breeding seasons, 18, 155, 189–92
    timing of, 72, 192–4
Brood
    depletion, 177, 203
    mates, dispersal of, 216
    patch, 174
Brooding of young, 181
Buzzard, 156, 271, 276

Cacheing, 76–8
Calls, see Behaviour, calls
Cat, as predator, 132, 257
Clutch desertion, 198, 203–4
    and female weight, 210–11
    and food supply, 173, 202–3, 204, 276
Clutch size
    and body weight, 210
    and laying date, 197–203
    in Britain, 171–3